“一带一路”语言攻略

汉英对照

刘友法　张力军◎著

LANGUAGE STRATEGY ALONG THE BELT AND ROAD

中共中央党校出版社

图书在版编目（CIP）数据

“一带一路”语言攻略：汉英对照 / 刘友法，张力军著 .-- 北京：中共中央党校出版社，2022.1

ISBN 978-7-5035-7189-3

Ⅰ . ①一… Ⅱ . ①刘… ②张… Ⅲ . ①英语 – 干部教育 – 学习参考资料 Ⅳ . ① H31

中国版本图书馆 CIP 数据核字（2021）第 227589 号

“一带一路”语言攻略 汉英对照

责任编辑 刘海燕
责任印制 陈梦楠
责任校对 王明明
出版发行 中共中央党校出版社
地　　址 北京市海淀区长春桥路 6 号
电　　话 （010）68922815（总编室）　（010）68922233（发行部）
传　　真 （010）68922814
经　　销 全国新华书店
印　　刷 北京盛通印刷股份有限公司
开　　本 710 毫米 ×1000 毫米 1/16
字　　数 547 千字
印　　张 37
版　　次 2022 年 1 月第 1 版　2022 年 1 月第 1 次印刷
定　　价 78.00 元

微 信 ID：中共中央党校出版社　　**邮　　箱：**zydxcbs2018@163.com

前　言

21 世纪是中华民族全面振兴的世纪。在实现第二个百年目标的历史进程中，中国在政治、经济、科学、技术和文化领域将全面融入世界民族之林，并将为国际和平、发展与合作作出应有的贡献。随着“一带一路”建设进程不断推进，我国许多公司正向丝路沿线伙伴国家延伸生产链、价值链和供应链，各界人士有大量机会出国旅行、生活、学习、工作、经商。在东道国，他们需要主办或参加国际会议、商业谈判、学术研讨和跨文化交流活动，因而需要补齐英语交际能力的“短板”。

笔者谨依据国际交往与语言交流一般规律，以及40余年的留学、教学、外交和学术研究工作实践，以中英对照方式，系统地介绍新时期各界人士在国外旅行、生活、求学、学术交流、工作或经商期间各项须知，分专题介绍英文思维逻辑、习惯表达法和口头交流技巧，助力读者提升英语思维、交谈、演讲、论述、理论和抗辩能力，有效适应国外居家生活新环境，有效主持和参与跨文化社交和文化娱乐活动，有效实现职业理想，有效彰显当代中国公民的文化形象。

本书50余万字，分三十章论述。由于写作时间有限，笔者语言功底有限，若书中出现任何错漏之处，敬请批评指正。

刘友法

2021 年 3 月 16 日

于中国北京

Preface

The 21st century is a century of all-round rejuvenation of the Chinese nation. During the historical period of realizing the second centennial goal, China is to fully join the family of nations of the world, in terms of politics, economy, science, technology and culture, and render its due contribution to the international peace, development and cooperation. While the joint construction of the Belt and Road has been moving forward in full steam, many Chinese companies have been extending their production chains, value chains and supply chains in the partner countries along the silk road, and people from all walks of life are having more opportunities to travel, live, work, study and do business in the host countries. They are to host or participate in international conferences, business negotiations, academic research and cross-cultural communication. In view of this, many of them need to mend their "short boards" of language communication abilities, especially English.

Based on the above analysis, this author has ventured to seek references from the general rules of international English communication, and take stock from his personal experience of more than 40 years in overseas study, teaching, diplomatic service as well as academic research, systematically illustrates, both in English and Chinese, the things to be aware of for those who are traveling, living, studying, carrying out academic exchanges, working or doing business in the host countries, especially in the countries along the Belt and Road, and systematically introduces the English logic of thinking, idiomatic expressions and oral communication skills, in order to enhance their capability in handling cross-cultural conversations, speeches, presentations, reasoning and debates, to effectively adapt to the life in the new environment, effectively host or participate in cross-cultural social and recreational activities, realizing their career aspirations, demonstrating the contemporary cultural images of the Chinese citizens.

Language Strategy along the Belt and Road covers more than four hundred thousand words and thirty chapters. Due to the time availability and the limitation of the language constraints of the author, it is natural that there are mistakes and mis-presentations here and there across the book. Therefore, the author is appreciative for any constructive comments and suggestions.

Dr. LiuYoufa

March 16, 2021

Beijing, China

目　录

第一章

社会交谈

*

我们经常认为，交谈的艺术是上天赐给少数幸运者的专有技能，而大多数人拥有笨拙的舌头。事实上，有些人天生拥有能言善谈的魅力，但这也是我们每个人都能获得的一种技能。通过反复实践，我们都能掌握交谈技巧，从而在宴会上受人尊敬，在私人聚会或社交活动中脱颖而出，赢得更多的朋友。

Chapter One

Social Conversations

*

It's easy to think the art of conversation is the skill that god bestows on a lucky few, while cursing most of us with turbid tongues. It's true that some people are born with the charm of public remarks, yet it is a skill in which we all can become competent. With enough practice, we can also master the tricks to carry out conversations in the ways that would make us popular party guests, set us apart at private parties or social functions, and win us more friends.

Part One　Things to Know

01

In the field of social conversation, ancient Chinese sages have left us with the following principles. The first is to avoid arrogance, in order not to give others with disdain. The second is to avoid self-boasting, in order not to cause the disgust from others. The third is to avoid too much eloquence, in order not to hurt the self-esteem of others. The fourth is to avoid frequent interruptions without good reasons, in order not to lose personal dignity. The fifth is to avoid non-related issues, in order not to divert the main topic under discussion. The sixth is to avoid absent mindedness, in order not to spoil interests for the conversation. The seventh is to avoid excessive complementary remarks, in order not to look flattering. The eighth is to avoid mystifying things, in order not to cause confusion of the dialogue partner. The ninth is to avoid excessive body gestures, in order not to lose self-respect. The tenth is to avoid lengthy remarks, in order not to waste the time of others.

在社会交谈领域，古代先贤给我们留下了下列几项原则。一忌居高临下，以免给对方目中无人之嫌。二忌自我炫耀，以免引起对方反感。三忌口若悬河，以免伤及对方自尊心。四忌随意插嘴，以免有失风度。五忌节外生枝，以免在交谈时“跑题”。六忌心不在焉，以免对方扫兴。七忌言不由衷，以免献媚之嫌。八忌故弄玄虚，以免对方云山雾罩。九忌动作过多，以免有失自尊。十忌短话长谈，以免浪费他人时间。

02

Language communication is vital for interpersonal relations. It’s true that the art of conversation comes easy for some people, but not for others. Yet, verbal language interaction is crucial for all of us, when we’re travelling, living, studying, working or doing business overseas. According to the research findings, many of us might be comfortable having conversations in private or online, but often struggle with words at parties or business functions. This is the “short board” that we all need to patch up before it’s too late.

语言交际对增进人际关系至关重要。诚然，交谈的艺术对某些人来说很容易，但对另一些人则不然。因此，我们在海外旅行、生活、学习、工作或做生意时，良好的语言交流技能至关重要。研究发现，我们中的许多人在私下或网上交谈时可能会侃侃而谈，但在聚会或商务活动场合则会感到“茶壶煮饺子”。这是我们都需要及时补齐的“短板”。

03

When we attend large functions, we should first find out the main guests at the function. Second, we should brainstorm stories we can tell and questions we should ask, and prepare to answer possible questions. Third, we should tailor our conversations to the listeners, and place what we want to talk about on the solid ground, and avoid second-hand information or hearsay. Fourth, we should be conscious about the time, and avoid rambling on any topic.

参加重大社交活动时，我们首先需要了解参加活动的主要嘉宾，做到心中有数。其次，应当针对特定嘉宾准备相关话题，既要准备提出问题，也要准备被提问。再次，现场交谈的内容应有理有据，避免二手信息或道听途说。最后，要有时间观念，不要东拉西扯。

04

As one saying goes, we should think twice before doing anything. The same is true for social conversations with foreigners. In line with conversational etiquette and that of social activitives, we've got to understand the ground rules. On any occasions, we should do homework beforehand, in order to grasp the initiative in conversations on the spot, to demonstrate our conversational skills, and to achieve the expected goals, etc.

古训说得好，凡事三思而后行。与外国人交谈亦然。如同大多数礼仪和社交活动一样，我们必须了解基本规则。因此，在任何场合，我们事前一定要做好功课，以期把握现场交谈主动权，展示语言交际风采，实现预期的目标。

05

Social conversations are more stressful than those in the workplace. When we want to kick start a conversation with someone on the spot, we need to get to know him or her. We need to find out the common interests, values, level of education or profession, in order to start meaningful conversations. Therefore, we'd better do some homework beforehand about topics in general and the ways on how to get on a good start.

社交对话比职场对话更具有挑战性。如果想在现场与某人交谈，我们需要设法了解对方。我们需要了解共同的兴趣、价值观、受教育水平或职业，以便进行有意义的对话。因此，我们最好事先做一些功课，并准备好相关的话题以及开启对话的方式。

06

During social conversations, we need to make sure the right way to carry on a dialogue. We should also start with simple questions and move on to formal ones. When we sense the other party is hesitating on the subject matter we're talking about, we should quickly switch to a new one. We should encourage the other party to continue with the conversation by asking relevant questions. Better still, we should complement our dialogue partner and contribute what we know, which would be the catalyst to keep the conversation going.

在社会交谈中，我们需要确保以正确的方式进行对话。我们应该从简单的问题开始，慢慢进入正式的交谈。如果发觉对方对正在谈论的话题犹豫不决，应该赶紧转移话题。我们应该主动提出相关问题，以引导对方继续交谈。我们应当赞赏对话伙伴，并补充我们所知道的内容，这将是对话得以继续进行的催化剂。

07

The key to the art of conversation is not in talking, but in listening. Therefore, when we take part in social conversations, we should learn to listen, and take turns to speak, and we should be modest, flexible and pragmatic, firm but gentle, neither servile nor pushy. When we are doing the talking, we should control the speed, rhythm, tone, expressions, postures, body languages, and so on.

社会交谈艺术的关键不在于交谈，而在于倾听。因此，在社交场合，我们应学习倾听，轮流发言；出言谦逊、柔韧委婉、刚柔并举、不卑不亢。在讲话时，我们要把握讲话的速度、节奏、声调、表情、姿势及肢体语言等。

08

During the social conversation, we should manage the depth of the conversation and maintain a relaxed atmosphere, according to the age, occupation, education, gender, comprehension ability of the dialogue partners. Meanwhile, we should also demonstrate integrity of social conversation, and avoid four-letter words.

在社交场合，我们要根据交谈对象的年龄、职业、文化程度、性别、理解能力等情况，把握交谈内容深浅，营造轻松气氛。同时，我们还要展示良好的社交谈吐修养，切忌恶言伤人。

09

We need to know when and what to ask. Smart questions could arouse the interest of the dialogue partners. We should choose easy topics to start the conversation, in order for the other side to have something to respond offhand. We should choose topics that the other party has confidence to respond. We should stick to the code of conduct in conversation. We should avoid asking personal questions, and embarrassing each other. And, we have to cultivate a little mystery, leave the other party intrigued and wanting to continue with the conversation.

我们要掌握好提问的时机和内容。巧妙的提问可引发对方的交谈兴趣。我们要选择轻松的话题，以使对方有话想说；应选择合适的话题，以使对方有话可说。我们应当坚守社会交谈之道，避免询问对方隐私，以免双方尴尬。我们需要给对方留下一点神秘感，促使对方产生好奇心并想继续深入交谈。

10

We should look into the eyes of our dialogue partner, in order to show respect. Likewise, when we are talked to, we should look at him or her directly, or when we are talking to the crowd, we should shift our eye contact with each one accordingly. The worst scenario would be to bury our eyesight into our knees while we are speaking.

我们与人交谈，应直视对方眼睛，以示尊重。同样，如果有人和我们说话，我们的目光需要聚焦对方；当和一群人说话时，我们应该相应地移动目光，环视在场的每个人。最糟糕的情况是，我们在讲话时低头看膝盖。

11

In group conversations, we should have the courtsey to shift dialogue partners when appropriate. Once we find the other party is hesitating in the conversation, we should politely stop the conversation, and try to switch to a new dialogue partner. When we are talking about specific issues, we should avoid interrogative tones, or the aggressive questions. Meanwhile, we should be polite, even if we want to correct the mistakes of others.

在团体交谈场合，我们应当择机有礼貌地转换对话伙伴。我们一旦发现对方在谈吐中显露出为难情绪，应立即有礼貌地终止交谈，并酌情与其他人交谈。在讨论具体问题时，我们应避免质问语气，或攻击性的问题。即使需要纠正对方的错误，我们也要彬彬有礼。

12

During the social conversation, we should not only use verbal language, but also body gestures and facial expressions. It is because they are natural demonstration of personal emotions, while eye contact is an effective means of verbal communication.

在社会交谈中，除了用好有声语言之外，我们还需要借助肢体语言和面部表情。因为它们是个人情感的自然显露，而目光接触则是语言交际的有效手段。

13

We should keep our eyes soft and steady, and avoid focusing on the same person all the time, in order not to cause uneasiness of the other side. We should avoid looking around and giving the impression of “absent-mindedness”. And, we should keep a proper distance with the dialague partners, which is about 1 meter in principle.

我们应保持目光柔和而稳定，避免始终聚焦在同一个人，以免给人不适感；我们应避免东张西望，而给人“心不在焉”的印象。另外，应注意与对方保持适当的距离，原则上相互之间保持1米左右的距离为佳。

14

Social conversations are group projects. According to social protocol, during a paired dialogue or a group conversation, each person is to talk about anything for no more than three minutes. Therefore, anything we talk about should be clear and appropriate. Illustration of particular things should be concise and to the point, and we should avoid rambling or ambiguous expressions.

社交谈话是团体项目。依据社交礼仪，在两人对话或团体交谈期间，每个人每次说话的时间大致应控制在3分钟之内。因此，语言务求简洁明了，恰如其分。阐述任何事宜务求言简意赅，切中要害；切忌拖泥带水，模棱两可。

15

We should learn how to communicate with VIPs. One big hurdle to interact with a VIP is not knowing what to talk about. Therefore, we really need to do some homework beforehand. First, we should know how to approach him or her. Second, we should ask appropriate questions or complement what we hear, which would help to draw the attention of the VIP. Third, we should be brief in what we say or what we ask, because we are not to waste his or her time. Fourth, we should know how to end the conversation, which would leave an impression on the VIP.

我们应该学会如何与重要人物沟通。与重要人物互动的一大障碍是不知道该说什么。因此，我们真的需要提前做一下功课。首先，我们应该知道如何接近对方。其次，我们应该提出适当的问题或对听到的谈话内容加以补充，以吸引重要人物的注意力。第三，我们想说的或想问的都要简洁明了，以免浪费对方的时间。第四，要懂得如何结束谈话，以期给对方留下印象。

16

Generally speaking, the length of each topic would depend on the interests of the participants, and in principle, conversation on such occasions should not involve debate. There are no benchmarks regarding the time, space and the size of the conversational circles. Usually, we should not stay in a particular circle for too long, in order to mingle with more friends.

一般而言，每个话题交谈的时间主要取决于在场人员的兴趣，一般不作原则性争论。在时空和自由交谈的圈子大小方面都无定论可言。通常为了接触更多的朋友，我们不宜长时间停留在某个交谈圈子。

17

At large public functions, circles of social conversation are not to be very large. Therefore, we should avoid joining large groups unless some VIPs are at present. The reason is simple, we won’t get much chance to speak there. Therefore, when we want to join a particular dialogue group, we must not slip in abruptly. The correct way is to ask “May I join you” and then, move forward when we get the consent from someone in the crowd.

在大型活动场合，社交谈话圈子不会太大。因此，我们应避免加入太大的谈话圈子，除非有重要人物在场。原因很简单，在那里我们不会得到太多的发言机会。因此，我们如果想加入某个交谈圈子，切记不要生硬地贴上去。正确的做法是，以“我能加入你们吗”探路，得到在场者首肯之后再走上前去。

18

In terms of methodology, we should bring the conversation back to the central topic by asking questions, when we find someone is deviating too far away. Once we find that some guests are impolite in wording or intention, we should intervene promptly. Once the conversation is coming to the end, we should take initiative to conclude it.

从方法论上讲，我们如发现伙伴偏离主题太远，应酌情采用提问的方式将话题拉回到中心议题上来。一旦发现某个嘉宾发言有失礼貌，应及时提请其注意。一旦交谈接近尾声，应主动提议结束交谈。

19

It's true that warm, stimulating conversation can be greatest satisfactions in life. Nevertheless, not all conversations are created equal. Some are more pain than pleasure. Therefore, we need to know how to end a dull conversation by using the standard exit lines. When we are at public functions, there are also protocols on how to leave a group chat. When we want to leave a particular dialogue circle, we should apologize to the people around before withdrawing from the site.

是的，推心置腹、凌厉畅快的谈话可能给我们的生活带来最大的满足感。然而，并非所有的对话都是平等的，有些对话痛苦多于快乐。因此，我们需要知道如何用标准的说辞结束一段无聊的谈话。在公共场合，关于如何离开团组交谈也有礼仪规范。若想要离开一个特定的圈子，我们应该先向在场人员道歉，而后转身离场。

20

We should establish our networks for personal and business growth. We might be at a local meeting or at a national gathering, during which we may meet people whom we don't know. However, we should always remember to spot the possible candidates to establish our network for business relations or for friendship. Then, we should break the ice with compliments such as, "That is a great tie" or "Your watch is amazing" or "Those shoes are spectacular". And, we should manage our humor with caution. When we talk with people for the first time, we should guard against jokes or avoid being too casual. Finally, when we farewell someone, we should secure the contact information such as cell phone number or WeChat account, etc.

我们应该建立个人和业务发展所需关系网。在某个地方会议或全国性的集会上，我们可能会遇到不认识的人。但是我们要牢记，应通过社会交谈从人群中找到潜在的生意伙伴或朋友。这时候我们可以用诸如“这条领带真棒”“你的手表真漂亮”或“这双鞋真漂亮”等恭维话来开启对话。交谈期间，我们应该谨慎使用幽默，而且与人第一次交谈时切忌开玩笑或太随意。最后，我们在与某人告别时，应设法获得对方电话号码或微信等联系方式。

Part Two　Situational Dialogues

01

A: Hi, I don’t think I know you. Let me introduce myself. My name is Yang Shuai, and I’m from Renmin University of China.

嗨，我想我们不曾认识。请允许我做自我介绍。我叫杨帅，来自中国人民大学。

B: No, I haven’t had the pleasure yet. Pleased to know you. I’m Robert White, but you can call me Robert. Well, judging by the way you speak, you seem to have studied English somewhere.

恐怕不认识，我还没有这份荣幸。我也很高兴认识你。我是罗伯特·怀特，但你可以叫我罗伯特。从你说话的方式看，你好像以前留过学。

A: You’re right, but that was some twenty years ago when I was a junior staff member at the Ministry of Commerce. They sent me to University of California for two years, where I picked up my MA in History and Government.

你说得对，但那是大约20年前的事了，那时我还是商务部的一名初级职员。他们派我到加州大学学习了两年，在那里我获得了历史与政府管理专业硕士学位。

B: Well, it's coincidental that I was also there for five years when I was doing my BA and MA degrees in Corporate Finance. Nevertheless, when I graduated from the university, I was enrolled by Texas Oil, where I've been working first as a staff member, and then I worked all my way up to be the Vice President of the Board of Directors of the company. Now, what about you, please?

这么巧，我也在那里待了5年，当时我在攻读企业金融的学士和硕士学位。尽管如此，我大学毕业后受雇于得克萨斯石油公司。我一开始是一名职员，后来一路升为公司董事会的副总裁。你呢?

A: Well, when I left the University, I was lucky to pass the exam and won the opportunity to work at the Department of International Liaison for three years. Later, they sent me to the Chinese Embassy in Tanzania for two years where I was working at the Commercial Section as the Third Secretary.

嗯，当我离开大学的时候，我很幸运地通过考试进入国际联络部，在那里我工作了三年。后来，他们派我到中国驻坦桑尼亚大使馆工作两年，在商务处任三等秘书。

02

A: Welcome to my country, my friends. By the way, how was the flight?

欢迎来到我的国家，我的朋友们。顺便问一下，这次飞行怎么样?

B: Thank you for asking. It was perfectly alright until our aircraft was flying over North Atlantic Ocean, where we were caught in quite a few air pockets. And, the stewardess had to warn us to fasten our seat belts again and again.

谢谢你的关心。一切都很正常，直到飞越北大西洋时，我们遇到好几个气流。空姐一遍又一遍地提醒我们系好安全带。

A: I'm sorry to hear that, but you're a seasoned traveler, and I'm sure you could handle those little hiccups easily.

听到这个消息我很难过，但你是个经验丰富的旅行者，我相信你能轻松应对这些小问题的。

B: You're right, but not for some of my colleagues who were taking the long-distance flight for the first time. And, that was also an exciting experience for them, too. By the way, my colleagues and I are certainly appreciative for your considerate arrangement, and we know we're in your capable hand.

我当然没有问题，但对我那些第一次飞长途的同事来说就难了。不过，对他们来说这也是一次令人兴奋的旅行经历。顺便说一下，我和我的同事们非常感谢你周到的安排，我们知道你在这方面经验丰富。

A: My pleasure. Well, as I noticed in your letter, most of your team members are here in my country for the first time, I've included some cultural functions for this Saturday and Sunday, so that you will have a fresh mind to start the negotiation. I know you Chinese are all workaholic, and I promise not to keep you so busy while you're here. Well, before we get started, I'd like you to meet my colleagues. I'll let them do their own introduction, so that you could get better acquainted.

你太客气了。嗯，我从你们的来信中得知，你团队的大部分成员是第一次到访我的国家，因此我在本周六和周日加入了一些文化娱乐活动，以便诸位以轻松的心情进行谈判。我知道你们中国人都是工作狂，我想诸位在这里不用那么繁忙。好了，在我们开始之前，请先认识一下我的同事。我让他们各自做一下自我介绍，以便你们更好地相互认识。

03

A: Hi, my dear friends, we're glad you could make it here. Come in, and let me have your overcoats.
你们好，我亲爱的朋友们，很高兴你们能来这里。快请进，把大衣给我。

B: Thanks. Sorry, we're a bit late. We didn't expect the traffic would be so heavy on our way here.
谢谢。对不起，我们迟到了。没想到路上这么堵。

A: Sorry, we didn't warn you of the latest development in this part of the city. When more and more new attractions are constructed here in the area, the traffic is getting heavier day by day.
抱歉，我们没有提醒您这边城区的最新发展情况。我们这里的新建景观越来越多，交通也一天比一天拥挤。

B: I could see that, but the scenery on the way up here is beautiful indeed.
我注意到啦，但这一路上的风景确实很美。

A: It's nice of you to say so. Now, please make yourselves at home, and would you like a drink or something?
感谢您的赞美。现在，请随便坐，你们想喝点什么？

B: Brandy would be nice for me, please, but you can ask my wife what she prefers.
请给我来一杯白兰地，但你可以问我妻子她喜欢什么。

04

A: Hi, have you heard about the news? Professor Tom Wilson, the world-renowned Physical scientist died in the Army Hospital yesterday.
嗨，你听说这个消息了吗？世界著名物理学家汤姆·威尔逊教授昨天在陆军医院去世了。

B: Really? I'm so sorry to hear that. I was with him three months ago at one symposium where he was one of the key note speakers. In fact, we also shared the same panel at one subsection. I was deeply impressed by his professional analysis on the importance of bringing under control the wild spread of hazardous nuclear materials around the world.

真的吗？听到这个消息我很难过。三个月前我和他一起参加了一次研讨会，他还是主要的演讲者之一。事实上，我们还在同一个分会场分享了专业观点。他对控制有害核材料在世界范围内疯狂传播的重要性进行了专业分析，给我留下了深刻印象。

A: I also had the pleasure to have his acquaintance for the past 25 years. We often had meetings and conferences together, and we often coauthored articles in the field. And, in fact, we lived in the same residential area for the past 15 years, before he and his family moved to this city.

我也有幸与他共事长达25年之久。我们经常在一起开会，还经常联名撰写相关领域的文章。事实上，在他和他的家人搬到这个城市之前，我们曾在同一个住宅区住了15年。

B: Well, according to Margret Wilson, Mr. Wilson was already brain-dead when the family rushed him to the hospital. And, the family decided to hold the funeral for the late professor at Atlanta Cathedral at 9:00 this coming Friday. My wife and I are going to attend the funeral, and what about you?

根据玛格丽特·威尔逊的说法，当他的家人把他紧急送到医院时，他已经脑死亡了。他的家人决定于本周五9点在亚特兰大大教堂为这位已故教授举行葬礼。我和妻子要去参加葬礼，你们呢？

A: Certainly. Me and my family would not miss it for anything.

当然要去。我和我的家人也不会错过的。

B: Good, we'll be meeting at the funeral site then.

好的，那我们在葬礼现场见。

Part Three　Common Expression

- I wonder if I could have your WeChat, so that we could stay in touch.
  请问我能加你的微信吗，以便保持联系？
- I joined the WeChat group from the beginning, but pulled out soon afterwards. I was too busy to read those nonsense posts, you know.
  刚开始我入了群，但很快退了群。你是知道的，我没时间浏览那些无聊的帖子。
- I'm still in the group but only remain a silent reader, and seldom issue any posts.
  我还在群里，但通常潜在水里，很少发帖子。
- We have to kick him from the group as he posts too many junk messages.
  我们决定将他从群中剔除，因为他发的垃圾信息太多。
- You have to join our WeChat group, as we always place our weekly activities over the group.
  你一定要加入我们的微信群，因为我们会在群里通知每周的活动。
- I do read posts in the WeChat group, but seldom post or forward anything.
  我确实会阅读微信群的帖子，但很少发布或转发任何帖子。
- Please keep me posted via Facebook.
  请在脸书上与我保持联系。
- I've been staying in close touch with the host family during the past five years. They've given me not only a home to stay with, but also the opportunity to watch and learn from the family about German culture.

Now, I can proudly say that I take Germany as my second home away from my own country.

过去5年我一直与这家人保持交往。他们不仅给了我一个家，而且给了我一个观看和学习德国文化的机会。现在我可以自豪地说，德国是我离开家乡之后的第二故乡。

- They are certainly a happy married couple, and they've just celebrated their golden wedding last month. They managed to raise a family of six, and send all their kids to university. And, now they're already the proud grandparents.

  他们真是一对幸福的夫妻，上个月刚刚庆祝了他们的金婚。他们养活了一个六口之家，并把他们所有的孩子送入了大学。现在，他们已经是自豪的祖父母了。

- You need to be careful in our local politics. In order to keep in touch with local people or colleagues, it is alright to attend local rallies and events. It would be perfect for you to attend city council meetings and community activities. However, you need to be careful with the political organizations, and be selective in joining the political parties, in line with your career future. And, you should refrain from critical comments on our national leaders and their policies, and you need to be careful in donating funds for any politicians or political candidates.

  参与地方政治活动时你们要谨慎小心。为了与当地人或同事保持联系，你们可以参加当地的集会和社会活动，最好参加一些市议会和社区活动。但是，你们需要谨慎对待当地政治组织，并根据本人的职业前途选择性地加入某个政党。此外，你们应该避免对国家领导人及其政策提出尖锐的批评；在向政治家或政治候选人捐款的事宜上，一定要谨慎行事。

第二章

社交活动

*

在我们一生当中，可能会举办或参加各种各样的社交活动，包括帆船运动、露营、徒步旅行、自由漫步、摄影、骑行、烹饪、扑克游戏，以期与朋友、家人、亲戚、同事或生意伙伴交往。因此，我们需要认真准备。

Chapter Two

Social Activities

*

Throughout our life, we may host or participate in many social activities that include sailing, camping, hiking, casual walks, photography, biking, cooking, poker games, in order to mingle with peer groups friends, family members, relatives, colleagues or business partners. Therefore, we need to be fully prepared.

Part One　Things to Know

01

We may travel, live, study or work overseas at some point in our life, during which we may have chances to receive foreign visitors. And, we all have opportunities to host cross-cultural functions on many occasions, where we have to carry out conversations with English speakers. Therefore, we need to know how to get prepared, how to get started, and how to conclude our conversations.

我们一生中可能会在某个时候去国外旅行、生活、学习或工作，其间，我们可能有机会接待外国游客。同时，我们都有机会举办跨文化活动，并需要与讲英语的人交谈。因此，我们需要知道如何进行准备、如何开启谈话、如何结束交谈。

02

We should learn some basic skills. It's an art to associate with English-speaking people. As hosts, we need to show hospitality wherever possible, and we need to show our courtesy as guests. Nothing less will allow us to become international person.

我们需要学会一些基本的社会交谈技巧。与讲英语的人交往是一种艺术。作为主人，我们需要热情友好。作为客人，我们需要遵守礼仪。否则，我们很难成为国际社交达人。

03

We should regard everybody as equal association partner. In terms of protocol, we tend to believe that some people are naturally more sociable than others, but the fact is all human beings are social. With proper training and adequate practice, we all can get the hang of it.

我们应当将每个人都当成平等交际的伙伴。从交谈礼仪上讲，我们习惯认为，有些人天生比其他人更善于交际，但事实是，所有的人都乐意交际。通过适当的训练和实践，每个人都可以成为社会交谈老手。

04

We should always try to be positive at social conversations. However, some people tend to be smiling listeners at public functions, while some others tend to be passive dialogue partners, because they simply do not know how. In order to overcome that awkwardness, we need to try to take part in active social dialogues. Practice makes perfect, you know.

在社会交谈场合，我们应该始终保持积极向上的态度。然而，一些人在公共场合往往满足于充当微笑的听众，而另一些人往往成为被动的对话伙伴，主要原因是他们不知道怎么做。为了克服这种尴尬境况，我们需要积极主动参加社交活动。你知道的，熟能生巧。

05

We should avoid over-thinking, which prevents us from enjoying social conversations. Therefore, at social functions, we should focus on what may go wrong, or on how we should avoid embarrass ourselves, so that we could approach every function with natural expressions and positive attitude.

我们应当避免多虑，它会阻碍我们享受社会交谈。因此，在社会活动场合，我们应该关注在哪些地方可能会讲错话，如何避免难堪，这样，我们才能以自然的表情和积极的态度参加或主持每一次活动。

06

We should try to stay under the spotlight. It's interesting that some people tend to feel invisible, and would prefer to stay away from the spotlight. While other people would seldom talk unless they are asked on the spot. This paradox of shyness is also what prevents us from feeling comfortable when we are in front of others.

我们应该尽量待在聚光灯下。有趣的是，一些人在社交场合习惯上往后靠，宁愿远离聚光灯。另外一些人在社交场合则寡言少语，除非现场有人问他们问题。这种怯场心理往往会让我们在他人面前感到很不自在。

07

We should learn to enjoy social life. It's a simple fact that we all need to take stock from our social life. In order to feel at ease at public occasions, we need to master some basic skills, and keep practicing until we gain the confidence. The more we do, the better.

我们应当学会享受社交活动。一个简单的事实就是我们都需要充分享受社会生活。为了在公共场合轻松自如，我们需要掌握一些基本技能，并且不断练习，直到建立起信心为止。在这方面，我们做得越多，效果就越好。

08

We should readjust our habit. In order to realize that goal, we should form the habit of striking up casual conversations with the people we meet on the daily basis. We should spend some time with friends, relatives or colleagues whenever possible. And, we should always accept invitations for social or public functions, during which we could get enough chances to talk with one another.

我们应该改变我们的习惯。为了实现这一目标，我们应该养成日常与人轻松交谈的习惯。只要有可能，我们应该多和朋友、亲戚或同事来往。我们应该经常接受社会或公共活动的邀请，以期获得足够的机会与他人交谈。

09

We should be positive. We all want to be around the people who are optimistic, upbeat and happy. Even when we don't feel positive sometimes, we should at least act positive when we're talking to other people. As one saying goes, courtesy is the passport for us at the public functions.

我们需要保持乐观的态度。我们都想与乐观、积极上进的人交往。即便有时心里不痛快，至少在和别人交谈时我们应表现出友善的姿态。俗话说得好，礼貌是我们参加公共活动的通行证。

10

We should be fully engaged. If we want to appear interesting to others, we have to show interest in them, especially when we are in the middle of a conversation. When we are talking to somebody, we should listen to what they are saying, rather than worrying about what we should say next. We should make eye contact, nod our head, and ask the follow-up questions.

我们应该参与社会交谈活动。我们如果想让别人对自己感兴趣，就要向对方表现出热情，尤其是在具体谈话过程中。在与人说话的时候，我们应当关注对方在说什么，而不是担心我们接下来该说什么。我们应当进行眼神交流，或点头表示赞同对方的讲话，并提出后续问题。

11

Whether we are at family or at social functions, how we exert our body would project a message to other people. If we want to be approached by others, we should avoid standing in the corner, crossing our arms, or burying our eye sight in the Tik Tok items on our cell phones. Rather, we should make eye contact with others and smile along with them. Please remember, smile and laughter are the best enzymes for social conversations.

无论是参加聚会，还是其他社交活动，我们的肢体动作会向其他人传递一定的信息。如果想引起别人注意，我们应该避免站在角落里，交叉双臂，或把眼睛埋在手机的抖音里。相反，我们应该与他人进行眼神交流，并保持微笑。请记住，微笑和笑声是社会交谈最好的催化剂。

12

We should initiate interactions. When we just stand there waiting for people to call us or invite us to join their dialogues, we are just wasting our time. Relationships are built upon mutual outreaching. When we want to show people that we value their friendship, we have to reach out to them, and create opportunities to spend time with them. We should keep in touch with friends, even if we don't live in the same town. Once in a while, we should pick up the phone and call them, send them a WeChat text message, or e-mail them asking how they have been, etc.

我们应该主动互动。我们如果只是站在一旁，等着别人招呼或邀请我们加入他们的交谈，那么我们就是在浪费时间。人际关系建立在相互努力的基础之上。我们想要展示与对方的友谊，就必须主动接触对方，创造条件与对方共度时光。我们应该与朋友保持联系，即使我们并不居住在同一个城市。我们应该偶尔拿起电话，给对方打个电话，发个微信短信，或者发个邮件询问对方过得怎么样，等等。

13

We should grab the chances to meet with newcomers. The best way to make new friends and expand our social network is to grasp opportunities to meet with newcomers. Therefore, we should accept invitations to parties and social gatherings, take trips to new places, and talk to people in the coffee shops, on the bus, at school, on airplanes, etc. You never know when a stranger could turn out to be our new friend, business partner, or hobby partner!

我们需要抓住机会结交新朋友。结交新朋友、扩大社交圈的最好方法是与新来者交往。因此，我们应该接受聚会和社交的邀请，结伴去新的地方旅行，在咖啡馆、公共汽车上、学校里、飞机上与同路人聊天。你永远不知道什么时候其中有哪位会变成我们的新朋友、生意伙伴或拥有共同爱好的伙伴！

14

We should make notes what people may like. It is hard to remember each and every person we have met in terms of what he or she is interested in. So, when we go home after each function, we should make notes of what a particular person likes. And, when we meet them some other time, we should try to talk about it. You will be surprised to find the result!

我们应该记录朋友的喜好。我们很难记住见过的每一个人对什么感兴趣。因此，每次活动回家后，我们应记录下某个人的个人爱好，并尽量在下次有机会见面时谈论它。你会发现效果出奇得好！

15

We should be prudent in talking to strangers. When we talk with someone we don’t know very well, we should start with something in common, such as weather, sports, things at school or at work. Then, as the conversation gets further down the road, we could branch out to other topics.

我们在与陌生人交谈之际要把握分寸。在和不太熟悉的人交谈时，应该从共同感兴趣的话题开始，如天气、体育项目、学校生活或工作上的话题。稍后，随着相互交谈逐渐深入，我们可将话题扩展到其他领域。

16

We should be selective in making friends. Being social does not necessarily mean being friends with everybody. It’s impossible for us to please everybody. To start with, we should settle down with a small circle of friends, and gradually enlarge our network of association.

我们应该有选择性地交朋友。社交并不一定意味着和所有人都成为朋友。我们不可能让每个人都满意。首先，我们应该建立一个小的朋友圈，然后逐渐扩大社交圈。

17

We should refrain from sensitive topics. It is best to keep our personal views such as religion, politics, abortion out of the conversation unless the person whom we are talking with is genuinely interested. Even then, we should refrain from sensitive comments.

我们应避免敏感话题。在涉及宗教、政治、堕胎等话题时，最好不要在谈话中提及我们的个人观点，除非与我们谈话的人真的感兴趣。即使这样，我们也应该避免做出敏感的评论。

18

We should try to bring our close friends to some functions when appropriate. And, we should invite them to some family or public functions when we spot the opportunity. For one thing, with somebody at our side, we should feel more confident. For the other, it's the best way to deepen the existing friendship or partnership.

我们应该在适当的场合邀请好朋友一起参加社会活动。有机会时，我们应该邀请他们参加一些家庭聚会或公共活动。一方面，有人在身边，我们会感到更自信。另一方面，这是加深友谊或伙伴关系的最好方式。

19

We should be friendly to passers-by. We wouldn't have to talk to every person we bumper into in our daily life. Nevertheless, a nice smile, a wave of hand and a simple hello to anyone you come across would help break the barriers, and demonstrate our public image as an international person.

我们对路人应该友好相待。在日常生活中我们并不需要与每一个路人交谈。然而，一个善意的微笑、一次挥手或一个简单的问候，都有可能帮助我们打破障碍，并展示我们作为国际人士的公众形象。

20

We should join peer groups. When we feel that we don’t get enough social interactions, we should consider picking up a new hobby, joining a local club or a sports team, or volunteer for some community services. All these activities would help boost our chances to become a social person.

我们应该多参加同龄人群体活动。当我们觉得缺乏社交活动时，应该考虑培养一种新的爱好，加入当地的俱乐部或运动队，或参加社区志愿活动。所有这些活动都有助于我们成为社会人。

Part Two　Situational Dialogues

01

A: Welcome to our city, my dear friends, and welcome to our party tonight. How was your driving on the way?

亲爱的朋友们，欢迎来到我们的城市。欢迎来参加今晚的聚会。一路上开车还顺利吧？

B: It was quite a smooth drive on the whole. It took us twenty minutes longer before we got here, though, because of the weekend traffic.

总的来说，一路上开车相当顺利。但是，我们还是多花了二十分钟才到这里，因为周末的交通十分拥堵。

A: Well, we're glad you could make it here. Let me tell you, the traffic could be worse at this hour some other times. Now, please check in your things at cloak room down in the lobby, but don't forget to get your tag cards, and you'll need them to claim your things when you leave.

哦，我们很高兴你们能来。不过，其他时候这个时段的交通还要更糟糕。现在，请你们到楼下大堂的衣帽间寄存物品，但不要忘记拿你们的寄存卡，离开的时候，需要凭它们取回你们的物品。

B: Thank you, Mr. Robertson. I can see it's going to be a large turn out tonight.

谢谢你，罗伯逊先生。看起来今晚到场嘉宾会很多啊。

A: Well, we've organized this grand cocktail party, in honor of you and your family so that you could get better acquainted with your future colleagues and friends.

我们为你和你的家人举办了这次盛大的鸡尾酒会，以便你们能更好地结识未来的同事和朋友。

B: We certainly appreciate it.

我们非常感谢。

A: Well, I guess the bulk of the guests are already here, so, shall we move to the dining hall now? We're going to sit the head table in front of the podium.

好啦，我想大部分客人已经到了，我们现在去餐厅好吗？我们的座位安排在讲台前面的主桌上。

B: Thanks, and after you, please.

非常感谢，您先请。

02

A: We're very much obliged to you for your kindness to speak to us tonight. You know what, many guests came all the way across the country just to hear your talk about the Belt and Road Initiative and its progress.

我们非常感谢您今晚前来做演讲。你知道吗，很多客人是专程从全国各地赶来听您介绍“一带一路”倡议及其进展情况的。

B: It's my pleasure as well as my honor to address such a professional audience, but how much time would you allow me this time, please?

我很高兴也很荣幸能给这么专业的听众做演讲，但请问这次您能给我多少时间啊？

A: As usual, you will speak for about 30 minutes, then, I'll open the floor for questions and answers. Nevertheless, let me warn you, please be prepared for many questions because we're just fascinated about the Belt and Road Initiative based on equal footing and win-win outcome.

依据惯例，您先讲30分钟，然后，我开始安排问与答环节。不过，我想提醒您，请做好要回答很多问题的准备，因为我们对贵国以平等参与和互利互惠为基础的“一带一路”倡议非常感兴趣。

03

A: I'm curious, but when did you get to know each other?

我很好奇，你们是什么时候认识的？

B: Well, we met since we were at high school, but we went to different universities in China in 1980, and we went on our different careers later on. Therefore, we didn't meet each other again, until we both received the invitation for a national conference five years later in Beijing.

哦，我们在高中时就认识了，但是1980年我们在中国上了不同的大学，之后又从事不同的职业。因此，直到五年后我们都收到在北京的一个全国性会议的邀请，这才有机会再见面。

A: I don't want to be nosy, my dear friends, but why did it take so long for you to get married?

亲爱的朋友，我并不想多嘴，但你们为什么拖了这么久才结婚啊？

B: Well, it's a long story. We went to different industries where we had to settle down in our career before anything else.

哦，说来话长。我们去了不同的行业，在那里我们必须先忙于各自的事业。

A: We are proud of you two, but when do you plan to start a family?

我们为你俩感到骄傲，但你们打算什么时候要小孩呢？

B: Well, we haven't thought about it yet. Right now, we want enjoy our life for a while. However, we'll let you know when we come to that. To be serious though, we're still trying to save enough to pay off the mortgage and support our family yet.

嗯，我们还没想好。当下，我们想要享受我们的生活。但是，等我们准备要孩子的时候会告诉你的。说实在的，我们仍在努力攒足够的钱来还清抵押贷款，养家糊口。

A: I understand, but having a family is a life time thing, and you need to get it done before it's too late. You simply can't wait until everything is ready, you know.

我能理解，但是要孩子是一辈子的事，你们还是要趁早抓紧。你们总不能等到一切都准备好了再要啊。

04

A: Congratulations, my friend. Your speech tonight was really a treat and the audience really enjoyed it. There were still many hands in the crowd, but I had to wind up the function as many of them had to drive a long way home. It seems we'll have to organize one more speech for you to talk about the subject.

祝贺你，我的朋友。你今晚的演讲真棒，大家都很喜欢。人群中仍然有很多人举手，但我不得不结束，因为许多人还得开很远的路回家。看来我们需要再组织一次关于这个主题的演讲。

B: Thanks. I was also very much impressed by the interests from the audience on the Belt and Road Initiative, from which both our countries could take stock from the win-win cooperation. And, I'm sure there would be many opportunities for the companies between our two countries to join hands for the common development.

谢谢。在座的各位对“一带一路”倡议非常感兴趣，给我留下了非常深刻的印象，我们两国也可从中获得互利合作的机会。我相信，我们两国企业有很多机会携手参与合作发展。

A: I agree. That's what I had in mind when I made the proposal for one more talk on the subject. Perhaps, you could concentrate a bit more on the opportunities and challenges on the way forward, which would draw a much larger audience. Well, before I forget, this is a souvenir for you.

我同意。我也是这么想的，因此我提议就这个问题再请您来做一次演讲。也许，您可以重点讲一讲未来路上的机遇和挑战，这样会吸引更多的听众。哦，差点忘了，这是给您的纪念品。

B: I certainly appreciate it.

非常感谢。

Part Three　Common Expressions

- I'll start the courtesy calls as soon as I settle down here.

  我安顿下来之后就开始礼节性拜访。

- I'm calling to find out when I could pay a courtesy call to you and your office.

  我打电话想了解我什么时候方便去拜访您。

- You need to take part in the cultural programs which would allow you to mingle up with the local people.

你需要参加文化活动，以便与当地民众打成一片。

- You know what, social activities could help people manage the loneliness. Therefore, you could make new friends when you join us for more social events.

  你知道吗，社交活动通常有助于应对孤独。因此，你和我们一道多参加社交活动，一定能交到新朋友。

- Confucius said,"it's always a delight to welcome friends who come from afar". Indeed, you've come all the way from the other side of the Atlantic, and you've not only brought along your friendship, but also the rain we've been expecting, which is a blessing for farming. So, we must thank you for that.

  孔子曰："有朋自远方来，不亦乐乎。"事实上，你们从大西洋的另一边远道而来，不仅带来了你们的友谊，还带来了我们期待已久的雨水，这对农业来说是必不可少的。所以，我们应当感谢你们。

- We're lucky to have the full moon tonight and the wind is also friendly to us. Now, we could enjoy the beautiful valley view under the moon from the balcony here. When the night lights are fully on, you'll see the valley fully decorated under the night clouds.

  很幸运，今晚明月当空，晚风习习，我们从阳台上就可以欣赏到月光下美丽的山谷景色。一会儿等夜晚的灯光全都亮起来的时候，你会看到整个山谷被夜空中的云彩装饰得非常漂亮。

- Well, we've decided to throw a party for you, just to reciprocate the hospitality that you and your institution accorded us when we toured your country last November. Tonight, it's just an informal dinner, so please make yourself comfortable, and forget about the protocol.

  哦，我们决定为您举办一个晚会，以答谢去年11月我们访问贵国时您和您的机构给予的盛情款待。今晚我们只是非正式宴请，请随意，不用拘束于礼节。

- As we agreed on the phone, we’ve organized this banquet in your honor. And, we’ll find our seats and start the serving at 19:30 sharp. And, I suggest we each give a five-minute speech before they serve the main course. As a protocol, I’ll kick-start the welcome remarks, and you’ll follow up with your remarks, alright?
  正如我们在电话中所约定的，我们为您举办欢迎宴会。现在，我们去找座位，晚宴19：30准时开始。我建议我们每个人先做五分钟的演讲，然后开始上主菜。按照礼仪，我先致欢迎辞，然后你们再致答辞，好吗？
- Please forgive my impoliteness, but I’ll have to skip the coffee and movie. My colleagues and I are having an early morning flight to catch for our trip to the next city. And, they are already waiting for me at the lobby.
  很抱歉，我就不参加咖啡和电影活动了。我和我的同事明天要搭早班飞机去下一个城市访问。他们已在大厅等我了。
- Well, it’s a pity you’ve got to go now, and we’re just getting to the heat of the program. As one song verse says, the night is still young. In fact, we only organize such an art-show once a year, and you shouldn’t miss the most exciting part, you know.
  嗯，很遗憾你这就要走了，我们的节目才刚刚进入高潮。就像一首歌唱的那样，夜色尚早。事实上，这样的文艺演出活动我们每年仅组织一次，你真不应该错过最精彩的部分。
- Well, we won’t keep you any longer, since you’ve got to go. Please allow me to see to the gate. And, I do have something to discuss with you on our way out, and please make sure you’ve got everything with you.
  那好吧，既然你真的要走，我们就不耽搁你了。我送你到大门口。路上我还有些事情要和你商量，请检查一下东西都带齐了没有。

第三章

家庭生活

*

家庭生活是我们生活、成长和了解世界的第一个环境。家庭是我们学习和掌握本国文化及其价值观的第一个课堂，也是我们学会与社会成员交往的出发点。同样重要的是，家庭是我们从亲人那里获得或向其提供物质、文化、经济幸福的理想场所。

Chapter Three

Family Life

*

Family life is the very first environment through which we live, grow and learn about the world. It's the very first classroom where we learn about our culture and its values. It's the stepping stone where we learn to associate with members of the society. And, equally important, it's the ideal place where we seek or provide physical, cultural, economic happiness, from or to the family members.

Part One　Things to Know

01

Well, we grown-ups used to be the future of our parents, and kids are our hope for the future. Therefore, we parents would spare no efforts to provide kids with the best possible nurture, care and love, in order to train them to be strong in physical health, to be smart in learning, to be independent in decision making, and to be consistent in living habits. We would join hands to build a sound launching pad for our kids to grow and venture out into the society.

我们成年人曾是我们父母的未来，而孩子们是我们未来的希望。因此，作为父母，我们会不遗余力为孩子们提供最精心的培养、照顾和关爱，使他们身体健康，聪明好学，独立决策，养成良好的生活习惯。我们做父母的应携手为孩子们的成长和走向社会搭建一个良好的平台。

02

To be honest, it's been a painful learning experience for me and my wife to raise a family of six in the rural community some thirty years ago. Nevertheless, they have been our pride because it's our pleasure to see them learn and grow. Of course, they also gave us the endless headaches, because we had to try hard to give them enough training, in order to prepare them for school education and to become responsible members when they grow up.

老实说，大约30年前，我和我的妻子在农村需要抚养一个六口之家，对我们来说这是一段痛苦的学习经历。但是，孩子一直是我们的骄傲，因为看到他们学习和成长，我们感到很幸福。当然，他们也给我们带来了无尽的烦恼，因为我们必须努力对他们进行培训，让他们接受学校教育，以便他们长大后成为对社会负责的人。

03

From my personal experience, it's natural that kids may easily suffer from emotional fears, psychological tensions as well as some other behavioral disorders when they grow up. All these scenarios may become harmful for kids when they become members of the society. You may not agree but the best preschool education for kids takes place at home where parents would teach them via role model.

依据我的经验，孩子在成长过程中，很容易出现情绪恐惧、心理紧张以及其他一些行为障碍，这是很自然的现象。这些问题若不解决，将不利于孩子日后步入社会。你可能不同意，但最好的学前教育是在家里，父母应该以身作则。

04

If you ask me, it's never easy for teachers at all levels. There are both upside and downside for kids when they grow up. The upside is that young people are energetic, smart, and eager to learn. The downside is that they tend to be reckless, impatient and tend to rush into things without much reasoning.

要我说，各级学校的老师都不容易。孩子们成长期间，既有好的一面，也有不好的一面。好的一面是，年轻人精力充沛、聪明好学。不好的一面是，他们往往鲁莽、缺乏耐心，往往不假思索就仓促行事。

05

Simply said, some parents fail to bring up their kids mainly due to three reasons. The first is that they fail to teach kids to stay away from bad habits. The second is that they fail to teach them to be careful with sex. And, the third is that they fail to show kids how to behave behind the wheels. The bottom line is that they should have given a serious talk to their kids about the road safety when they give the car at their rite of passage.

简单地说，父母抚养孩子失败，主要有三个方面的原因。第一个原因是，他们没能教会孩子远离坏习惯。第二个原因是，他们没能教会孩子在性行为上小心行事。第三个原因是，他们没能教会孩子如何正确驾车。关键是，在成人礼上向孩子赠送汽车时，他们应该与孩子们进行一次关于道路安全的严肃谈话。

06

It's true that we all need love and romance in our life, of which family love is an important part. To be specific, love is the healing balm that repairs rifts in personal and family relationships. It is the bond that unites families, communities, and nations. Love is the power that initiates friendship, tolerance, civility, and mutual respect. It's also the source that overcomes divisiveness and hate.

是的，生活中我们都需要爱和浪漫，其中亲情是重要的组成部分。具体来说，爱是修复个人和家庭关系裂痕的灵丹妙药，也是连接家庭、社区和国家的纽带。爱是激发友谊、宽容、文明和尊重的力量，也是克服分歧和仇恨的动力源泉。

07

As you may find out a cohesive family would provide members with psychological strength which they need to cope with all the tough moments. Strong family ties must have open lines of communication, where all family

members feel heard and respected. The key factor to strengthen the family ties is to increase the skills of all members to speak out and listen. Until we can hear out one another, understand one another, support one another, we cannot build the lasting family ties or family love.
你可能会发现，一个具有亲和力的家庭会给所有成员精神力量，帮助其度过所有的困难时刻。牢固的家庭关系必须有开放的沟通渠道做支撑，必须去倾听和尊重每一位家庭成员。加强家庭关系的关键因素是提高所有成员的倾诉和倾听能力。除非能够彼此倾听，相互理解，相互支持，否则，我们无法建立持久的家庭纽带或家庭关爱。

08

It’s a common sense that true lovers should take pleasure in each other’s success, and be faithful to each other, admire each other, care for each other, and so on. More importantly, true lovers should always stand side by side under any circumstances, and need to console each other without regret or forgiving.
众所周知，真正的爱人应该为对方的成功感到高兴，忠诚于对方，欣赏对方，关心对方等。更重要的是，真正的爱人在任何情况下都会肩并肩地站在一起，互相安慰，而不需要后悔或请求对方原谅。

09

There’s a saying: True lovers would cement their love in marriage, which is sacred for the rest of their life. They would always treasure their marriage and stay as a couple until one of the two goes to the heaven.
俗话说得好，真正相爱的人总是会在婚姻中巩固爱情，这是他们生命中神圣的使命。他们将永远珍惜其婚姻，并作为夫妻生活在一起，直到其中一方进入天堂。

10

However, more and more young people now regard their marriage as a matter of convenience. As a result, divorce is becoming a norm. Some choose to divorce due to minor things, and some others do that for no reasons at all. They call it "no-fault" divorce. Still other choose to break up their marriage via "gentlemen agreement", simply for the sake of their kids who are still at school. In some cases, the couples would either end their marriages in court, or hold parties to mark the occasion.

然而，现在越来越多的年轻人选择结婚，仅仅是出于相互需求。因此，离婚成为一种常态。有些人因为各种小事情而选择离婚，还有一些人没有任何理由就离婚。他们称之为“无过错”离婚。还有一些人为了还在上学的孩子，通过“君子协议”结束婚姻。在另一些情况下，也有夫妻通过法律手段结束婚姻关系，或者举行聚会结束婚姻。

11

For long in the past, married life was basically about two people of different sex sharing their lives together in love or in partnership. They would go through ups and downs hand in hand, for the rest of their lives. They would stick to their obligation side by side, in order to extend their family trees and to bring honors to the family history.

很久以来，婚姻生活基本上是两个不同性别的人以爱情或伙伴关系共同生活。在余生中，他们会携手走过人生的起起落落。他们会肩并肩砥砺前行，信守各自的义务，延续他们的家谱，为门庭增辉。

12

You know what, there's really nothing right or wrong on anything between the husband and wife. And, there's nothing that one side or the other should give up altogether. Nevertheless, in the married life, both sides should learn to swallow his or her pride many times, just for the sake of the love and

marriage. As one saying goes, the couple should learn to harbor no hard feelings to each other when they wake up the next morning.
你知道吗，夫妻之间真的没有对与错之分。而且，任何一方都不应该完全放弃任何东西。然而，在婚姻生活中，夫妻双方都应该学会为了爱情和婚姻，在生活相互包容。正如谚语所说，夫妻不记隔夜仇。

13

It’s an open secret that parenting starts right from the maternity ward. For the newborn babies, nothing could be more comforting than smiling faces, loving voices, and constant kissing and hugging. The fact is that the more their parents talk to the born babies, the happier they would be. And, the more time their parents spend with them, the healthier they would become.
为人父母从产科病房开始，这是一个公开的秘密。对于新生婴儿来说，没有什么比微笑、充满爱意的声音、亲吻和拥抱更能安慰他们了。事实上，父母和新生儿交谈的越多，他们就会越快乐。而且，父母花在孩子身上的时间越多，他们就会越健康地成长。

14

We may all agree that kids are the great catalysts to cement the love and romance for the parents. They would share the excitement together, they would carry out the family duties together, and they would join hands in raising up their families with honor. More importantly, they should create conditions for their kids to have the better life and better future. What else could be more exciting and noble?
我们都同意，孩子是巩固父母爱情和浪漫的催化剂。他们会一起分享激情，一起履行家庭义务，并携手持家。更重要的是，他们应该为孩子创造条件，让他们拥有更好的生活和更好的未来。世上还有什么比这更令人感到兴奋和崇高的事吗？

15

Successful stories would tell you that parents should create amicable learning atmosphere at home for kids whenever and wherever possible. And, they should make the family life as interesting as possible, which would be the important platforms for them to learn things in the natural ways. Parents are natural teachers for the kids. It's true that kids learn things when they play and interact with their parents and relatives. They may also learn things either by exploring things on their own or by interacting with their brothers and sisters.

成功的经验会告诉你，无论何时何地，父母都应该为孩子营造友好的家庭学习氛围。他们还应该让家庭生活尽可能的有趣，这是孩子们能潜移默化学习知识的重要平台。父母是孩子天生的老师。的确，孩子们在与父母和亲戚玩耍及互动的过程中学习知识。他们也能通过独立探索或与兄弟姐妹互动来学习知识。

16

Here in my country, we parents should teach kids how to respect authority. Law-abiding awareness of citizen starts by respecting authority and elders. Therefore, we should teach our kids early so that they could form the natural instinct to respect parents, teachers, coaches and those who are in the leadership positions. We should teach them to obey the authority, follow rules and regulations, no matter they like it or not. As Confucius said, it's the fault of the parents for failing to teach their kids.

在我的国家，我们做父母的应该教孩子们如何尊重权威。公民守法意识应从尊重权威和长者开始。我们应该尽早教育孩子，引导他们养成习惯：尊重父母、老师、教练和处于领导地位的人。我们应该让他们知道，不管他们喜欢与否，都必须服从权威，遵守规章制度。孔子曾说过，子不教父之过。

17

As far as parenting is concerned, capacity building is at the core. We parents should train kids to manage their own things as early as possible. We should teach kids how to interact with people, how to share things with others, and how to control their emotions. More importantly, we should teach kids one important rule: Wanting to do something is one thing, and actually doing it is another.

就子女教育而言，能力培养是核心。我们做父母的应该尽早训练孩子的自理能力。我们应教育孩子如何与人互动，如何与他人分享，如何控制自己的情绪。最重要的是，我们应该教给孩子一条重要的规则：想做是一回事，实际做是另一回事。

18

Many of us may think that kids are our hope as well as our future. For that matter, we would do whatever possible to help them to be versatile when they’re still at the kindergartens. It’s always our dream to let the kids to be successful at the starting lines and to carry forward the family pride. However, not all kids are born to be smart, and they need painstaking training, in order to grow up and be competitive.

我们许多父母可能认为，孩子是我们的希望和未来。因此，我们会尽一切可能从孩子幼儿园开始，将他们培养得多才多艺。我们的梦想是让孩子赢在起跑线上，光耀门楣。然而，并非所有的孩子都天生聪颖，他们需要艰苦的训练，才能成才并具有竞争能力。

19

Experts say the teen years often are the time of experimentation, and sometimes that may include risky behaviors. Therefore, we parents should never avoid issues such as sex, drug, alcohol, or tobacco use, etc. We should find opportunities to discuss those tough issues openly with kids before they're exposed to any of them. We should share our family values with our teens, and talk about what we believe is right, what is wrong, and tell them why. Besides, we should outreach to the friends of our kids as well as their parents. Regular communication among parents can go a long way to create a safe environment for all our teens in a peer group. Furthermore, parents can help one another in keeping track of the peer group activities without making our kids feel that they're being watched.

有专家说，人在青少年时期通常处于探索成长期，这种探索有时会包括一些危险的行为。因此，作为父母，我们不应该回避性、毒品、酒精或烟草等棘手话题。我们应该在孩子们接触到这些问题之前，找机会与他们进行面对面的讨论。我们应该与正在发育的孩子分享家庭价值观，谈论我们认为什么是对的，什么是错的，并告诉他们为什么。此外，我们应该主动联系孩子的朋友和其父母。父母之间进行定期交流有助于为同龄孩子群体创造一个安全的环境。此外，父母之间可以相互帮助跟踪对方同龄孩子的活动，而不至于让自己的孩子感到被监视。

20

We parents should teach kids to think twice before opening their mouths or before anything. We should teach them how to do things within their capacity. We should teach them how to make friends and interact with their peer groups. We should teach them how to find the right person and fall in love. Equally important, we should teach them to love their family, to be active members to the society and be loyal to the nation.

我们应该教导孩子三思而后行。我们应该教孩子在自己的能力范围内做事。我们应该教他们如何交朋友，如何与同龄群体互动。我们应该教会孩子如何找对象和谈恋爱。同样重要的是，我们还应该教导孩子热爱家庭，成为一名积极的社会成员，忠于祖国。

Part Two Situational Dialogues

01

A: Linda, aren’t you excited to go to school tomorrow?

琳达，明天就要上学啦，你激动吗？

B: Yes, mom, but I’m a bit scared. I simply don’t know how to get along with my new teachers and classmates. Would they be nice to me?

是的，妈妈，但我有点害怕。我有点不知道如何与新老师和新同学相处。他们会对我友好吗？

A: Well, Linda, you were doing fine at the kindergarten, and you’ll just have to stick to the same routines as you did, you’ll be fine there. The only difference is that you’re growing up and your classmates are growing up, too. You know what, when you behave yourself and be nice to your classmates, you’ll soon make new friends there, believe me. When you’re not sure of something, please feel free to ask your teachers, okey?

哦，琳达，你在幼儿园表现得很好。你只要坚持像以前那样做就行了，你在那儿会没事的。唯一的区别是，你在成长，你的同学也在成长。你知道吗，只要你好好表现，友善地对待同学，你很快就会交到新朋友，请相信我。如果遇到不明白的事情，你尽管问老师，好吗？

B: Thank you, mom. I will try my best at school.

谢谢你，妈妈。我在学校会好好努力的。

A: Mind you, you'll have to watch out for the bullies, and always try to stay away from them, then you'll be fine.
还有，你需要防范横行霸道的孩子，而且应该尽量离他们远点。这样，你就没事了。

02

A: Mark, have you packed up your things yet?
马克，你的行李装好了吗?

B: Sort of, dad. I've double checked my luggage, and I'll just have to pick up one or two things when I arrive at the college, no worry.
差不多吧，爸爸。我已经检查过行李了，到了学校后我只需要再买上一两件东西就可以了，您不用担心。

A: I know, and I'm just asking. You're growing up, and you can handle all these things by yourself.
我知道，我只是问问。你长大了，能够自行处理这些事情了。

B: Don't worry, dad, you and mom just have to feel at ease, and I'll work hard at college.
爸爸，别担心，您和妈妈只管放心，我在大学一定会努力的。

A: That's what we want to hear. Nevertheless, your mom and I still have these things to remind you since you're leaving us now. You should think twice before you open your mouth or do anything. You should handle things within your capacity. You should learn to make new friends and interact with your peer group friends. And, you should learn how to find your sweet heart and fall in love. Equally important, you must stay away from all the evil habits on campus or in the local community there. Please remember, mom and dad are always your faithful friends, and you always have a home here with us, OK?
我们就等你这句话。然而，你现在要离开我们了，你妈妈和我还想提醒你几件事。开口说话或开始做事情之前，你应该三思。你应该在能力所及范围内处理事情。你应该学习如何结交新朋友，并与同龄群体互动。你应该学会如何找到心上人，并谈恋爱。同样重要的是，在校园或社区里你必须远离所有的坏习惯。请记住，妈妈和爸爸永远是你忠实的朋友，我们这里永远是你的家，好吗？

03

A: Bill, how have you been doing at school lately?

比尔，你最近在学校怎么样？

B: I’m doing fine. If there is nothing wrong, I may enter the list of top five in my grade, and I just need to get straight “A” in two major courses, in order to win the top scholarship.

我很好。如果没有差错的话，我可以进入年级前五名，我只需要两门专业课获得A就可以赢得最高年度奖学金。

A: Good on you, but you will have to keep busy until you get there, OK? Like your grandpa says, you should never be too sure of anything until it’s done.

你真棒，但你需要继续努力，直到获得奖学金为止，好吗？就像你爷爷说的那样，什么事情在尚未完成之前，你都不应该放松努力。

B: I know. You and mom promised to take me for a trip to China this summer holiday, and I need to bring an honor back home. That’s my promise.

我知道。你和妈妈曾答应我今年暑期带我去中国旅游，因此，我一定争得一份荣誉回家来。这是我的承诺。

A: Well, this is the thing we want to discuss with you tonight, son. Your mom and I have been thinking about a ten-day trip across China. And, we want to hear out what you’ve got in mind.

嗯，这正是我们今晚想和你讨论的事情，儿子。你妈妈和我一直在考虑去中国旅行十天。我们想听听你的想法。

B: Great! Talking about the trip to China, I’ve got to do three things. First, I want to climb up the Great Wall. They say one cannot be a hero unless he has scaled the top of the Wall. I must prove myself to be a true hero. Second, I've got to try the Beijing roast duck. They say the chefs there prepared the duck in a mysterious way. The third is most important. I want to go to Sichuan Province where I could visit panda park. I'll make sure to have a picture taken with some baby pandas there, may I?

太棒了！谈到中国之行，我想要做三件事。首先，我想爬上长城。人们常说，不到长城非好汉。我必须证明自己是真正的英雄。第二，我得尝尝北京烤鸭。他们说那里的厨师用一种神秘的方式烹制鸭子。第三点是最重要的。我想去四川，想去参观熊猫馆。我一定要与那里的熊猫幼崽合影，可以吗？

04

A: Congratulations, son. We're proud of you. Look, your mom is crying for joy, now.

恭喜你，儿子。我们为你骄傲。看，你妈妈都为你喜极而泣了。

B: Thank you, mom and dad. I love you both, and I miss you a lot, too. And, I'm really grateful for you to come all the way to attend my graduation ceremony.

谢谢你们，爸爸妈妈。我爱你们，也非常想念你们。我非常感谢你们不辞辛劳来参加我的毕业典礼。

A: You're welcome. Your mom and I have been planning for this great day since you were a kid. And, we knew that you would make it, and you have made our dream a reality, son.

不客气。我和你妈妈从你还是个孩子的时候就开始计划这个伟大的日子了。而且，我们坚信你会成功的，现在你已经让我们的梦想变成了现实，儿子。

B: You bet. I'm also proud to be in the family. And, you've worked hard to keep me at school all these years. Here and now, I want to tell you that it's only half way through to realize your dream yet. I'll have to try even harder to find a nice job and settle down with a family. I know you’re both eager to be grandparents.

你们说得对。我也为自己是这个家庭的一员而感到自豪。这么多年来，你们一直很努力地供我上学。此时此刻，我要告诉你们，实现梦想的道路我才走了一半。我需要更加努力地找一份好工作，成家立业。我知道你们都非常渴望成为祖父母。

A: Good on you, but first things first, we’ll be driving home right away for the big family celebration, and your grandpa and grandma have been preparing for the party since last week. We’ve invited all the relatives and friends for the occasion, you know.

太好了，但要紧的事需要先做，我们这就开车回家去参加家庭大聚会，你的爷爷和奶奶从上星期就开始准备了。你知道吗，我们邀请了所有的亲戚和朋友前来庆贺你大学毕业。

Part Three　Common Expressions

- The outfit you wear looks fabulous, especially with your hair style.

  你的衣服看起来棒极了，尤其是配上你这样的发型。

- If you ask me, your make up is not in tune with your dress. You’d better put on the other one.

  如果你问我的话，我认为你的妆容和衣着不太协调。我建议你换另一件。

- I see what your mean, but I can’t do this. I hope you would understand.

我明白你的意思，但我不能这么做。希望你能够理解。

- They say social functions and club activities are the natural ways to help you manage your homesickness. Meanwhile, they're also the ways for you to make new friends so that you would feel that this campus could be the second home away from your home.
  有人说，参加社会活动和俱乐部活动是可以帮你应对乡愁的最佳方式。与此同时，它们也是你结交新朋友的好方法，这样你就会觉得这个校园可以成为你远离家乡的第二故乡。
- We have a saying:"Do as the Romans do". Therefore, you should temporarily forget about the ways and means you did things at home, and try to live, behave, study or work the way as we do here. This is the right way for you to be an overseas student.
  我们有句谚语说："入乡随俗"。因此，你应该暂时忘记你在国内期间的为人处世方式，试着像我们这样生活、处事、学习或工作。这是你作为留学生的正确做法。
- We need to improve our personal quality. In theory, we need to build up our personality starting with understanding ourselves. We need to evaluate what traits we see in ourselves, what needs to be improved and what needs to add up. Then, we should identify and focus on the positive personality traits that would strengthen our confidence, which includes honesty, integrity, responsibility, respectfulness, compassion, kindness, tolerance, courtesy, self-discipline, courage, and sense of justice, etc.
  我们需要努力提高个人素质。从理论上讲，我们需要从了解自身出发，改进我们的个性。我们需要评估自己具有哪些特质，哪些需要提升，还有哪些需要强化。在此基础上，我们应该找到并重视我们的优势，进而修炼并增强我们的自信心，具体包括诚实、正直、责任、尊重、同情、善良、宽容、礼貌、自律、勇气、正义感，等等。
- Here in my country, we should build up our own career. As the old saying goes, there is no road in the world, but when many people walk the same

way, the road will come into being. It’s also true to our career. First, we should make our own decision, and make sure whatever we do must be a good match for our personality, interests, aptitudes, and work-related values. Second, we should measure our own success. We should learn to distinguish between our ability to handle our jobs and our satisfaction about them. Third, we should never hesitate to ask for help or help out, because it’s a win-win way to improve our career. Fourth, we should learn from our own mistakes, and never make the same mistakes. Fifth, we should remain practical to what we want to do, keep up with what we can do, and try to build up the short boards we may have, which would add new steam to improve our career.

在我的国家，我们应该建立自己的事业。俗话说，世界上本没有路，走的人多了便成了路。我们的职业生涯亦然。首先，我们应该自主选择职业，确保我们的选择与自己的个性、兴趣、天赋和与工作相关的价值观匹配。第二，我们应该正确衡量自己的成功。我们应该学会区分我们处理工作的能力和我们对工作的满意度的关系。第三，我们应该毫不犹豫地寻求帮助或帮助他人，因为这是提升我们职业生涯的双赢途径。第四，我们要善于从自己的错误中吸取教训，切不要再犯同样的错误。第五，我们应该保持良好的职业心态，坚持做好可以做好的事情，同时，努力补齐可能存在的短板，为职业生涯增添新的动力。

- We should teach kids to care for the environment. We should teach our kids not only to protect their community environment, but also the planet which they live on. We should show them that it’s important to clean up trash, and not to litter, to be kind to plants and other living things, to recycle things, and not to mistreat the property of others. All these small things would help increase their law-abiding mindset and practical skills.

  我们应该教育孩子们爱护环境，应该教导孩子不仅要保护社区环境，还要爱护他们生活的星球。我们应该向他们讲述清理垃圾的重要性，教育他们不要乱扔垃圾，善待植物和其他生物，学会回收利用，不要破坏他人的财产。所有这些小事都有助于培养他们遵纪守法的心态和实践技能。

- We should teach our kids by examples. As parents, we should be mindful of the things that we say and do while we are out with our children. Kids may copy each and every little thing that we parents do. For example, we should ensure that we don't litter, steal, run red lights, or talk on cell phones while we do the driving.
  我们应该以身作则。作为父母，在与孩子一道外出的时候，我们应该注意本人的言行举止。孩子们有可能会模仿父母做的每一件小事。因此，在孩子面前我们一定要以身作则，不乱扔垃圾，不偷东西，不闯红灯，开车时不接打电话等。
- We should teach our kids how to become law-abiding citizens. It's common that kids would make mistakes sometimes, and may break the rules once in a while. When we notice those reckless behaviors, whether at home or in public places, and we should take immediate actions to stop and correct them. More importantly, we should let them know the consequences such as time outs and other punitive measures.
  我们应该教育孩子如何成为守法的公民。孩子们有时会犯错误，有时可能会违反规则，这是很常见的现象。一旦我们注意到孩子出现那些鲁莽的行为，无论是在家里还是在公共场所，都应该立即采取行动加以制止并纠正他们。更为重要的是，我们应当让其意识到会遭受限制自由活动等惩罚。

第四章

国际旅行

*

俗话说得好，读万卷书，不如行万里路。国际旅游可促进身体健康，丰富文化生活，拓宽视野和眼界。其间，我们可以参观当地著名的历史景点，体验不同的文化，品尝不同的食物，并与不同习俗和传统的人交谈。同时，海外旅行是一个平台，我们可借以观察和学习其他国家的人如何生活、工作和与人交往，有利于我们应对文化冲突。

Chapter Four

International Travel

*

As one saying goes, it is better to travel ten thousand miles than reading ten thousand books. International tours and visits are the best way for us to promote physical health, enrich our cultural life, and broaden our views and visions about the world, during which we could visit great historical places, experience different cultures, taste different foods, and mingle with people with different customs and traditions. Meanwhile, overseas travels would be the platforms for us to observe and learn how people in other countries live, work and associate with one another, which would help us manage the cultural shock.

Part One　Things to Know

01

As one saying goes, you would always feel comfortable at home, but not when you're away from it. Therefore, when you join a package tour to other countries, you need to get yourself fully prepared. You need to prepare a list of what to do, and you need to get ready your passport, visa, basic personal documents, as well as a medical kit. Equally important, you need to read about the destination countries and cities that you're going to visit, get familiar with the famous historical sites, tourist attractions and the things to be aware of when you're on the ground.

俗话说得好，在家千日好，出门一时难。因此，你在参团出国旅游时，需要提前做好功课。你需要列一个必备物品清单，准备好护照、签证、个人证件以及一个简单的医药包。同样重要的是，你需要了解将要参访的国家和城市，熟悉那里著名的历史遗迹、旅游景点，以及到达目的地后需要注意的事项。

02

You should check with your doctor, and make sure you're fit to travel. You should make sure that you have all the required vaccinations done, and you have collected all the essential items. Also, you should ask your medical insurance provider if your policy covers the overseas emergency cases. If not,

you should add extra coverage.
你应该向医生作咨询，并确认身体状况适合旅行。你应该按规定接种疫苗，并配齐出国旅行所需用品。此外，你应该向医疗保险公司确认，你的保单是否适用于海外紧急情况。如果不适用，你应该增补额外的保险。

03

You should produce extra copies of your passport. When your passport should get stolen or lost while you are traveling overseas, you could prove your citizenship to the local authorities and get your travel document at the Chinese Embassy, in order to proceed with your trip. Meanwhile, you should leave a copy of your passport with someone you can trust. You should also make an electronic copy, and store it in your cell phone or in your email account as well.
你应该带上护照的复印件。这样，在国外旅行期间你的护照如果被盗或丢失，你可据此向当地有关部门证明你的公民身份，并在驻当地的中国大使馆补办旅行证件，确保旅途得以继续。同时，你应该将一份护照复印件留给你信任的人。你也可考虑制作电子版副本，储存在你的手机或电子邮件账户中。

04

Whenever you arrive in a country, there will be an instant message of consular advice appearing on your cell phone, which is to tell you about the security situation on the ground, and the telephone number for you to contact. Therefore, when you should come across something urgent while you’re travelling, this would make it easier for the consular officials to contact you and get you to safety.
无论何时你到达一个国家，你的手机上立即会收到一条领事信息，向你通报当地的安全情况和供你联系的电话号码。因此，你在旅行中遇到什么突发情况，领事官员可以联系到你，并提供领事保护。

05

You should get the money matter settled before you begin your trip. You should exchange some currency into the US dollars or the currency of the destination countries. And, you should find out the conversion rate between Renminbi and the local currencies. You should also remember to bring some US dollars in small denominations, in case you need to pay for some items during your trip. You know what, not all the places would accept credit cards, especially when you are on the trains or buses.

旅行前你应该准备好旅行费用。你应该到银行兑换一些美元或目的地国家的货币。您应该了解人民币与当地货币的兑换率。你还应该记得随身携带一些小额美元现金，以备旅途中临时项目开支。你知道，并非每个地方都接受信用卡支付，尤其是在火车上或公共汽车上。

06

You should make sure that your credit card will work in the country you're visiting. It would be foolish to travel with lots of cash on you, which would make you the easy target for robbery or theft. Mind you, European banks have switched completely to the more secure chip-and-pin technology, and fewer businesses abroad are accepting the outdated magnetic-strip cards.

你应该确保你的信用卡在你要访问的国家可以有效支付。旅行时携带大量现金是愚蠢的行为，这很容易使自己成为海外抢劫或偷盗的目标。请注意，欧洲银行几乎已经改用更加安全的芯片和密码技术，在国外很少有企业接受过时的磁条码信用卡。

07

You should know how to withdraw your money at a local bank or at the ATM in the country you're visiting. The money exchangers at the airport or around the city tend to be huge rip-offs. When you are in front of an ATM, please make sure that no one is anywhere near you. It pays to be cautious, you know.

你应该学会如何在当地银行或自动取款机上取钱。机场或城市周围的转换中心兑换货币往往存在汇率敲诈。你在当地自动取款机上取现金时，一定要注意周围是否有可疑的人。常言道，万事谨慎为妙。

08

You should stay in touch with your bank or credit card provider. Sometimes, they think that fraud may be occurring when it spots that too many transactions suddenly occur in a country where you were but you're now already back in China. When your bank confirms the fraud, it would suspend your card as a security measure.

你应该与你的银行或信用卡发放单位保持联系。有时，你的银行如果发现诸多交易项目突然发生在一个你曾经去过的国家，而此时你已经回到中国，他们会认为发生了诈骗事件。一旦与你核实确定发生了欺诈情况，作为安全措施，银行会暂停你的信用卡。

09

You should double check the entrance or exit fees in the countries you are visiting. Some countries require travelers to pay in order to enter or leave the country. These fees are not included in the price of your airline ticket, and they range from $25 to $200.

你应该了解拟往访国家是否收取入境或出境费用。有些国家要求旅客在入境或出境时支付相关费用。这些费用不包括在机票价格中，价格从25美元到200美元不等。

10

You should be sensitive about the weather. You should plan your trip during when the weather would be ideal in your destination countries. When you are

on the ground, you should look at the weather forecast before you venture out for the daily activities, and make sure you have something to protect you from the rain or something.
你应该关注旅行期间的天气情况。首先，你应该选择在目的地国家比较理想的季节计划出行。到达目的地之后，在进行当天游览活动之前，你首先要查看天气预报，并带上相关防护设备，以免遭受雨水或其他气候的侵扰。

11
You should learn to use guidebooks. Country specific guidebooks usually include maps, keywords or phrases, and give you enough details on certain sites so that you won't have to purchase the pamphlet when you're on the ground. Better still, you could download travel apps before you travel. All these would help you plan your trip and choose the sites beforehand, in order to enjoy the discounts on service and charges, beauties of the scenery spots, cultural sites, food and art performances, etc.
你应该学会使用旅游指南。一个国家的指南通常包括地图、关键词或短语，并为你提供关于一些地方足够详细的信息，这样你就不必在现场购买小册子。更好的做法是，你可以在旅行前下载旅行应用程序。所有这些有助于你提前计划旅行，选择观光景点，以期在服务与收费上、美丽的风景、文化景点、食物和艺术表演等方面享受优惠。

12
You should plan your daily events while you're on the ground. This would make sure you're not missing the best events in the host city, and pick the fun items such as festival celebrations, ceremonial and cultural events. Of course, you should do some research, in order to focus on some famous national dishes to try out. In so doing, you won't have to leave the country with too many regrets.
你应该规划好每天的参访活动。这样可确保你不会错过当地最好的活动，而且便于你挑选有趣的项目，如节日庆祝、传统仪式和文化活动等。当然，你还应该做些调查研究，以便找到当地著名的菜肴去品尝。这样，在离开到访国家之际你就不会留下太多的遗憾。

13

You should bring an adapter. Countries may have different plugs in size and voltages. When you want to use your iPad or laptop during the trip, make sure you can recharge it. Of course, you could ask for one adapter at your residing hotel.

你应该随身携带充电器适配器。各国可能有不同大小和电压的插头。你如果想在旅途中使用iPad或笔记本电脑，需要确保能给它充电。当然，你也可以向你所在宾馆的前台免费要一个适配器。

14

You should check out the right voltage for your electronics. Nothing could be worse than having an adapter but still not being able to use blow-dryer, simply because the voltage does not match that in the host country.

你应该确认电子产品与到访国的电压是否匹配。最糟糕的是，你携带了适配器，但仍然不能使用吹风机，仅仅是因为东道国的电压不匹配。

15

You should activate global roaming service on your phone. There’s usually a charge for doing this, but it is much less than the roaming charges you’ll get. When you are visiting the destination countries, you should turn on your Beidou or Google navigators, which would save you the trouble to ask for information at each turn.

你应该激活手机的全球漫游功能。这是收费项目，但收费标准远低于不开通产生的国际电话漫游费。在目的地国家旅游期间，你应该开启北斗或者谷歌导航，以免每到一处都需要四处询问。

16

You should download the Travel zoo app. This would help you find great deals in many of countries, and allow you to have more options such as hotel rent, rent-a-car service, airline tickets or public site admission fees, etc.

你应当下载Travel zoo应用程序。这将帮助你在不同的国家买到物美价廉的商品，并在酒店房费、租车服务、机票或公共场所的门票等方面获得优惠的服务。

17

You should learn to equip yourself beforehand. You need to pack an extra set of clothes in your carry-on bag. In case the airline mishandles your luggage, you would have something to tide over the awkward moment.

你应该事先做好应对不时所需的安排。你需要在随身行李中放置一套换洗或备用衣服。这样，航空公司万一弄丢了你的行李，你有衣服可换能度过尴尬的境况。

18

You should know how to check in your luggage. Each airline has its own set of guidelines regarding how many bags can be checked or carried on for free. Therefore, you need to check it out from the airlines , in order to avoid any incremental fees.

你应该知道如何托运行李。每家航空公司都有一套自己的客运规范，规定乘客允许托运或免费携带行李的件数。因此，你需要事先向相关航班了解清楚，以免多付费用。

19

You should bring along some snacks. Traveling abroad is fun, but eating in a foreign country can sometimes be a task. Therefore, you need to bring some snacks that will tide you over until you find that perfect restaurant or food

cart. And, you should bring a medical kit, in case something happens to you during the trip.
你应该带上一些零食。出国旅行很有趣，但在国外吃饭有时会成为一项任务。因此，你需要带一些零食充饥，直到你找到理想的餐厅或餐车。还有，你应该带一个医药包，以便在旅途中身体欠佳时应急使用。

20

Last but not least, you should take safety precautions. Here are some tips for you to take home. You should always keep things to your front. You should always look back before leaving a place. You should not wear expensive things when you are traveling. You should stay away from panhandlers as much as possible. And, you should not play the hero.
最后，你应该随时注意安全。这里有些建议供你参考。你应该随时把东西放在眼前。在离开一个地方之前，你应该回头看看。在国外旅行期间，你不应该穿戴昂贵的东西。你应该尽可能地远离乞丐。另外，你不应该逞英雄。

Part Two　Situational Dialogues

01

A: Good evening, sir, welcome on board. Here’s the menu, you can have a quick look at it and select your meals. And, we’re serving dinner when our aircraft is in the flight motion, and we’ll serve breakfast before landing.

晚上好，先生，欢迎登机。这是菜单，您可以快速浏览一下，然后选好您要的菜。待飞机进入正常飞行程序之后，我们将提供晚餐，在着陆前还会提供早餐。

B: Well, I want to take a nap for now, but please wake me up for dinner in two hours. As for breakfast, I'll have the Chinese noodles and fruits, please.
嗯，我现在想小睡一会儿，但请在两小时后叫醒我用晚饭。至于早餐，我要中国面条和水果。

A: Yes, you've got it. Breakfast is set for six o'clock so that you'll have full energy to get off the flight, and now, please enjoy your trip.
好的，就按您说的办。早餐将在6点钟供应，以便您能精神饱满地下飞机，祝您飞行旅途愉快。

B: Thanks, but could I have one more blanket, please?
谢谢，请给我加一条毯子，好吗?

A: Sure, I'll get it for you in just a minute.
好的，我马上给您拿来。

02

A: Good morning, sir, I wonder when we can board the aircraft. We've been waiting here for four hours now.
早上好，先生，请问什么时候我们可以登机。我们已经在这里等了四个小时啦。

B: We're very sorry for the delay, sir. As far as we know, the aircraft has developed some engine problems, and it's under emergency repair at Sydney International Airport. They told us that the flight would be on its way in two more hours. If not by then, they'll send a new aircraft.
关于航班延误的事我们感到很抱歉，先生。据我们所知，这架飞机的发动机出了一些问题，目前正在悉尼国际机场进行紧急维修。我们接到通知说，飞机再过两个小时可以起飞。如果到那时还不行，他们会派出一架新飞机执行本次航班任务。

A: I understand, but I'm on my way to Canberra for an international conference, which is to start on Thursday, and I need to get there by 16:00.
我理解，但是我此行是去堪培拉参加一场国际会议，会议将于星期四举行，我需要在16：00之前赶到那里。

B: Well, in that case, you should have ample time to get there for the opening ceremony. By the way, we're going to distribute dinner boxes. When you finish your dinner, the aircraft should be landing.
这样的话，您应该有足够的时间参加开幕式。顺便说一下，我们马上发盒饭。也许您吃完晚饭后，飞机就会着陆了。

03

A: Excuse me, ladies and gentlemen, all passengers please leave your seats and proceed to the waiting room downstairs in the hall. We'll inform you to re-board the plane when we finish the cleaning and disinfection.
对不起，女士们，先生们，所有乘客请离开座位并移步到楼下大厅的候车室。我们完成清洁消毒后会通知您重新登机。

B: Well, can we leave our hand-carry luggage on the plane?
那么，我们可以把手提行李放在飞机上吗？

A: No, I'm afraid not. You'll have to take everything with you when you disembark. It's for your own safety, you know.
不，恐怕不行。下飞机时，您必须把所有随身物品都带上。您知道，这也是为了您的安全。

B: I see, but how do we get the transit lounge, please?
知道了，但是请问我们怎么去转机等候大厅？

A: You just have to follow the sign, and once you get inside the hall, it's 50 meters on your right.
您只需要照着指示牌走，进入大厅后，在您右边50米的地方就到了。

04

A: Good afternoon, sir. Can I help you?

下午好，先生，我能为您效劳吗？

B: Yes, one of my suitcases is missing. It was on Flight 863 from Beijing yesterday. Here's my luggage tag. Please help me find out what happened. It contains all my personal belongs, and I must have them while I'm here in your country for the conference.

是的，我的一个手提箱不见了。我的行李昨天交由从北京起飞的863次航班托运了。这是我的行李牌。请帮我核查发生了什么事情。行李里面存放有我来贵国开会期间必须使用的所有私人物品。

A: I'm sorry to hear that. Let me have the luggage tag and your air ticket, please. I'll check out with the flight office right away. By the way, can you describe your suitcase, please?

发生这样的情况，我很抱歉。请把您的行李牌和机票存根给我。我马上向航空公司办公室询问情况。顺便问一下，您能描述一下手提箱的样子吗？

B: Well, it's light brown, and it's 40 by 60 cm. It's got my name tag and phone number.

哦，它是浅棕色的，长60厘米，宽40厘米。旅行箱上有我的名牌和电话号码。

A: Good, that would do for the time being. Now, please make yourself comfortable and have a cup of coffee, while I check with the flight office … Sorry to have kept you waiting, but I've got something positive for you. The luggage section mistakenly transferred your suitcase to another airline, and now they've found out the problem and reloaded it on the next flight here.

好吧，目前这些信息够了。现在，请安心在这里喝杯咖啡，我这就跟航空公司办公室联系……对不起，让您久等了，但我有好的消息要告诉您。北京那边的行李部门误将您的行李箱转到了另一家航空公司，现在他们发现了问题，并已将您的行李装上飞往这里的下一班飞机上了。

B: Thank you for your timely assistance, and you've really saved my day. In that case, how long do I need to wait?

谢谢你的及时帮助，你真是帮了我大忙。这样的话，我还需要等多久？

A: In accordance with the flight schedule, the flight is to arrive here in two hours. I'll let you know as soon as the flight is coming in. Again, we're sorry for the mishap.

依据航班时刻表，下一班航班预计两小时后飞抵本机场。飞机降落后我会第一时间通知您的。我们对此意外再次表示歉意。

Part Three　Common Expressions

- Please be advised that it's the best possible season to visit my country. You have three ways to get here. You can take the airline, take the continental railway or simply come in your own car. Whichever way you should choose, please let us know, and we'll pick you up at the airport or the railway station.

  请注意，现在是来我国旅游的最佳季节。你有三种途径前来我国。你可以乘坐民用航班来，或乘坐火车来，或者干脆自己开车来。无论你选择何种方式，请预先通知我们，我们会到机场或火车站接你。

- According to my experience, before you take the trip to the South Pole, you really need to do a thorough homework. You need to check out if you have any serious health conditions. In winter, temperatures can plummet to -128 degrees Fahrenheit. It would be always windy, and there are wind gusts at times. You may suffer from altitude sickness, too.

根据我的经验，在你去南极旅行之前，你真的需要做周密的安排。你需要确保没有任何严重的健康问题。在冬天，那里的气温会骤降到零下128华氏度。那里总是刮大风，还不时有阵风。你也可能会出现高原反应。

- They say, it pays to travel light, because you need to save some space for the souvenirs you may pick up during the trip. That way, you would not have to add an extra check-in luggage.

  常言道，出门旅游宜轻装，因为你需要预留行李空间，以便在旅途中购买纪念品。这样，你就不用增加托运行李了。

- I'm afraid these items are not allowed to be carried in hand luggage. So, you need to trash it yourself, or we'll have to do it for you. By the way, we allow only 20 packs of cigarettes free of duty per traveler, so you've got to pay duty for the extra, which is 200 dollars.

  恐怕这些物品不允许放在手提行李中携带。所以，你得自己扔掉，否则我们就得替你处理掉。顺便说一下，每个旅客只允许免税携带20包香烟，所以你需要为额外的部分支付200美元的关税。

- Excuse me, you've got some excessive dutiable goods in your trunk. We've got to charge you with the duty and the fine, which is 500 dollars in total, and we'll give you the receipt. I hope it's a lesson for you.

  对不起，您的行李箱里载有超额应税物品。我们必须向您收取税金和罚款，共500美元，我们会给您开收据。希望您能吸取教训。

- Sorry, sir, there's something in your check-in luggage. Would you open it for us, please? ... OK, that's what we saw on the screen, and you're clean now. Have a nice trip in my country, sir.

  对不起，先生，您托运的行李中有样东西需要检查。请您打开箱子好吗？……好了，这就是我们在屏幕上看到的东西，您现在没问题了。先生，祝您在我国旅行愉快。

- You know what, we’ll put these dutiable items in custody until you leave our country, but you need to give us a written guarantee to reship them abroad. We’re sorry about it, but it’s a rule.
  你知道吗，在你离开我国之前，我们将替你保管这些应纳税物品，但你需要给我们一份书面保证，保证在你离境时把它们转运到国外。很抱歉，但这是规定。
- When we have to travel to pandemic prevalent countries, we must take these steps to protect ourselves. First, we should check out travel restrictions in the host countries beforehand and get fully vaccinated, in line with the requirements of the host country. We should have the viral test 1~3 days before we travel and keep the test results, in case quarantine officers may ask for them. We should not travel if we get a positive test. We should wear masks when we are in public places. We should avoid crowds and stay at least 2 meters from anyone, who does not travel with you. It’s important to do this everywhere, both indoors and outdoors. We should wash our hands often or use hand sanitizer. We should bring extra supplies, such as masks and hand sanitizer. And, we should avoid contact with anyone who is sick, etc.
  我们如果必须到疾病大流行国家旅行，必须采取措施来保护自己。首先，要事先核查东道国是否有旅行限制，并按照东道国的要求全面接种疫苗。我们应该在旅行前1—3天做一次核酸测试并随身携带测试结果，以备检疫官员索要。如果检测呈阳性，我们就该放弃旅行计划。旅行期间，在公共场所我们应该戴口罩。我们应该注意避开人群，并与周围的人保持至少2米的距离。无论在室内还是室外，我们都要这样做。我们应该经常洗手或使用洗手液。我们应该随身携带口罩和洗手液等必需品。我们应避免与任何病人接触，等等。

第五章

参观游览

*

众所周知，无论是在国内还是国外，旅游观光都是我们摆脱繁忙的城市生活或工作的最好方式，也是促进身体和心理健康的有效方式。旅游观光还有助于我们拓宽视野和经历，有助于零距离欣赏东道国独特的历史、文化、习俗和传统。

Chapter Five

Tours and Sightseeing

We all know that tours and sightseeing, whether at home or abroad, are the best means to get away from the busy city life or career isolation, and are a sure way to promote our physical health as well as psychological health. This would also help broaden our visions and experience, and provide us with opportunities to enjoy the unique history, culture, customs and traditions in the destination countries at zero distance.

Part One　Things to Know

01

With modern means of transportation at your disposal, you have lots of different ways to explore a country or a city when you are there. Here are some tips for you to take home.

有了各种现代交通工具，你可以借助许多不同的方式在往访国或往访城市观光游览。这里有一些小妙招儿供你参考。

02

You should plan your sightseeing activities in advance. When you stop in a country or a city, you only have a limited time. Therefore, you need to do some homework beforehand, in order to avoid last minute rush, or missing some essential items for your trip.

你应该提前计划你的观光活动。你在一个国家或一个城市逗留的时间总是有限的。因此，你需要提前做些功课，以避免最后一刻匆匆忙忙，或错过此行必须涵盖的游览项目。

03

You could take the hop-on-and-hop-off tour bus. In many metropolitan cities, you could spend one day on the bus tour, in order to have a general view of the city. Take the bus tour in New York for example, the tour buses would give you the flexibility to visit the sites you are interested in at your own pace. All you have to do is to hop on a double decker at a bus stop nearby, and get off at an attraction site, and hop on the next bus to continue the city tour.

你可以乘坐随上随下的旅游巴士。在许多大城市，你可以花上一天时间乘坐旅游观光车，去了解整个城市的概貌。以纽约的旅游巴士观光为例，当地的旅游巴士可以让你按照自己的节奏游览感兴趣的景点。你要做的就是在附近公交车站跳上一辆双层观光车，在某个景点站点下车，就近欣赏风景，然后再跳上下一辆巴士继续下一站的活动。

04

You could take the boat trip. Many cities around the world have the major scenery spots or famous places along the river, where you could enjoy the view on a cruise ship. Take London for example, on a tour boat along the mighty river Thames, you could enjoy the famous buildings such as Tower Bridge, St Paul's Cathedral, Tate Modern, Houses of Parliament, London Eye, etc. When you should pay for the meal, you could enjoy the most relaxed sightseeing tour in London.

你可以乘船观光。世界上许多城市都有一些主要景点或著名景点坐落在河岸旁，在那里你可以乘坐游轮欣赏沿岸风景。以伦敦为例，在沿泰晤士河的游船上，你可以欣赏到著名的建筑，如伦敦塔桥、圣保罗大教堂、泰特现代美术馆、议会大厦、伦敦眼等。你如果愿意付餐费，则可享受伦敦之旅中最为轻松的观光活动。

05

Experience shows that boat trips would create bonding experiences with family members and friends. It should be a lasting-memory that you could have while on the trip. In this digital age, when you're at the office or at work, you always have to bury yourselves in the text messages or email letters.

Stress, insomnia, and depression would make it impossible for you to power down. However, when you head out for a boat trip, it should be a perfect opportunity for you to unwind, even if it's just for a few hours.

经验表明，乘船旅行可以增进与家人和朋友的感情。一次乘船旅行经历可能会给你留下永恒的记忆。在这个数字时代，你在办公室或在工作中整天需要将自己淹没在短信或电子邮件中。压力、失眠和抑郁让你无法放松下来。然而，乘船出游则是能让你彻底放松下来的最好时机，哪怕仅仅是几个小时。

06

You could take the subway trip. When you and your friends stop in large cities, it pays for you to take the subway, in order to cruise around the city and its suburbs, where you can see all the popular tourist attractions, in accordance with the time you have. Take Beijing for example, it is a traditional yet fashionable, stately yet energetic city, where ancient history meets modern times. With a city map in hand, you could easily get to Tian'anmen Square, the Forbidden City, the Great Wall, the Bird's Nest, the Water Cube, Peking University and Tsinghua University, etc. They are the prime tourist attractions, and you shouldn't miss them for anything.

你可以选择乘地铁观光。你和你的朋友在大城市旅游时，完全可以根据你们的时间乘坐地铁巡游城市和郊区，游览热门旅游景点。以北京为例，这是一座传统而时尚，庄严而充满活力的城市，是古代与现代交汇的城市。手持一张城市地图，你可以很容易地找到天安门广场、紫禁城、长城、鸟巢、水立方、北京大学和清华大学等景点。这些都是主要旅游景点，无论如何你都不应该错过。

07

You could take the railway trip. In some countries where the natural and environmental landscape is abundant, it would be worthwhile to take the train

across the wild landscape when weather permits. With a few more bucks, you could enjoy the premier service, unlimited non-alcoholic beverages to and from your destination, a nice set of snacks and desserts on your trip, a complimentary group photo, and a canvas bag, etc.
你可选择乘火车观光。在一些自然和环境景观丰富的国家，如果天气允许，很值得乘坐火车穿越茫茫的原野。只要再多花几美元，你就可以享受头等舱服务，享受往返于目的地期间无限量的非酒精饮料供应、精美的小吃和甜点套餐、一张免费的合影，还有一个帆布大手提袋等。

08

You could take the night sightseeing trip. For many travelers, the night city tour is ideal for exploring the night life. In many cities, they start the evening tour service at the sunset, and you just have to hop on an open-top double decker bus, and admire the glittering lights and sounds of commercial and cultural city life. With the tour guide by your side, you will be driving through the iconic commercial and cultural areas of the city, around a lake or along the river.
你可以选择夜间城市观光。对于许多旅游者而言，夜间观光之旅可谓观赏所在城市夜生活的理想选择！在许多城市，夜间观光车在夕阳西下之际发车，你只需跳上一辆敞篷双层巴士，即可欣赏到城市里的灯火通明，以及商业和文化景象。你可以一边聆听导游的解说，一边穿梭于城市标志性商业和文化区域，环绕湖泊或沿河岸欣赏两旁的夜景。

09

You could take a walking tour. You won’t believe, but it’s the best way to learn about a city in the downtown area. It is also a great way to rub shoulders with local people. When you’re walking around, you won’t have to compete with engines to hear the guide, and you won’t miss the details like street art, art performances or fancy restaurants along the way. You may also stop at some fancy buildings, and see things more closely, and squeeze into small alleys.

你可以徒步游览。你可能不会相信，徒步旅行是了解一个城市最好的方式，也是与当地人接触的好途径。在你四处游逛时，你不必透过引擎噪音听导游解说，也不会错过街头艺术、艺术表演或沿途高档餐厅。你还可以在一些华丽的建筑前停下脚步，更近距离地观赏，还可以挤进小街巷探秘。

10

You could do your own driving tour. In all the metropolitan cities, you could easily find public transport service, but nothing beats the convenience of having your own means of transportation. You don't have to find a bus stop, or get into a queue to hail a cab. You can go anywhere, at any time, and with anyone. Sure, car rentals don't come cheap, but they're relatively affordable. Driving in your own car would allow you to plan your routes in advance and avoid traffic jams. Furthermore, you could ride in style. Car rental companies offer a diverse collection of cars, and when you spend some extra dollars, you can choose a luxury car that will blend in nicely with the bright lights of the modern city and feel rich for a moment.

你可以自己驾车旅行。在所有的大城市，你都可以很容易地找到公共交通服务，但没有什么比拥有自己的交通工具更为方便。你不需要寻找公交车站，也不需要排队叫出租车。你可以在任何时间，和任何人去任何地方。当然，租车不便宜，但也不算贵。自己驾车可以提前规划好路线，避免交通堵塞。此外，你还可以过一把开豪华车的瘾。租车公司提供各种各样的车辆，你如果愿意多花一些钱，可以选择一辆豪华轿车，以便很好地融入当地现代城市的明亮灯光，享受短暂的富豪生活。

11

You could take a package tour. Package tour is an ideal choice when you want

to have a memorable holiday with little stress in a city. Such tours include a variety of services binding together for a single trip. Meanwhile, safety is another big advantage of tour package, which is a sure way to help you avoid the places with potential risks.
你可以参加跟团旅游。如果你想在一个城市里轻松地度过一个难忘的假期，跟团旅游是理想的选择。这样的旅行涵盖各种各样的服务。与此同时，安全是组团旅游的另一大优势，它可以确保你避开有潜在风险的地方。

12
You could try to have a bird’s eye view of the city. They say the quickest way to overlook at a city is to go to a nearby mountain top or the rooftop of the major hotels or public buildings. For example, you won’t get any better view of Johannesburg, the City of Gold, than from the top of the 50-storey Carlton Centre. The building is still the tallest in Africa, and offers fantastic views of the FNB Stadium, Gandhi Square, the skylines of Braamfontein, Hill-brow and Sandton, and much more as far as the eye can see!
你可以尝试去制高点鸟瞰所到城市。人们说，俯瞰一个城市最快的方法是去附近的山顶或主要酒店或公共建筑的顶层。例如，在50层楼高的卡尔顿中心的顶层上，你可以领略到整个约翰内斯堡黄金之城里最好的景色。这座建筑仍然是非洲最高的建筑。在这里你可以看到非洲最大的FNB体育场、甘地广场，以及布拉姆方丹、休布罗和桑顿的天际线，还有更多你目光所及之处的风景！

13
You should book tickets early. The struggle is real when you have to make decisions on the spot, while you’re traveling overseas. Therefore, smart travelers always book their tickets for the transportation, sightseeing and entertaining activities. You know what, book tickets early would make sure

you won't miss anything you have in mind. It would also allow you to strike better deals. The earlier, the better! Above all, early booking would save you many headaches, and allow you to enjoy the expected excitement and pleasure.

你应该尽早订票。你在国外旅行时，遇到必须现场做决定的情况常会令人纠结万分。因此，聪明的旅行者总是提前预订他们交通、观光和娱乐活动的票。你知道吗，早点订票能确保你不会错过你想要游览的任何项目。这还可以让你与服务商达成更好的协议。越早越好！最重要的是，提前预订可让你省去许多头疼的事，尽情享受预期的兴奋和快乐。

14

You should use the audio service. In many public places, the host would offer live tour guide, or audio guide, which is available in the following languages: Chinese, English, French, German, Spanish, Italian, Japanese, Portuguese and Russian. You just have to pay a fee to get a set, and then enjoy your tour. There is also free WIFI available on some buses and passenger cars so that you could switch to your favorite programs.

你应该使用音频服务。在许多公共场所，主办单位会提供现场导游或音频导游，有中文、英语、法语、德语、西班牙语、意大利语、日语、葡萄牙语和俄语。你只需要付费租赁一套，就可以享受旅行。有一些公共汽车和火车车厢内还会提供免费Wi-Fi，你可以选择自己最喜爱的节目。

15

You should travel safely. You have saved for your overseas trip. Therefore, you need to prepare the pack-list either for the whole trip or for the daily sightseeing trips. These are the essentials for your reference. You need to bring along a universal travel adapter, a power bank, a micro-fiber travel towel, a first aid kit, a water bottle, and the phone number of the local police station and the Chinese Embassy in the destination country.

你要安全旅行。你已经为海外旅行筹备了资金。因此，无论是全程旅行还是日常观光旅行，你都需要准备物品清单。以下必需品供你参考。你需要随身携带通用旅行适配器、电源、超轻便捷旅行毛巾、急救箱、水瓶，以及当地警察局和中国驻当地大使馆的电话号码。

16

You should avoid adventurous activities. When you are traveling overseas, you should not let any reckless behaviors spoil the whole thing. Basically, you just have to follow the safety instructions at each tour site or public place. You should never try to climb over the fences for better photo positions. You should avoid taking pictures in front of any military establishments. You should not take any pictures of anybody without the permission. And, you should abide by the time allowance. As one saying goes, limits are the limits!

你应该避免冒险活动。你在海外旅行期间，应该避免任何鲁莽的行为，以免影响整个行程。基本上，你需要遵守每个旅游景点或公共场所的安全警告。你永远不能为了寻求更好的拍摄位置而试图翻过栅栏。你应该避免在军事设施前面拍照。未经许可，你不能抓拍他人照片。你应该遵守时间限制。俗话说，禁区就是禁区，不得越线！

17

You should respect the local cultures and traditions. Visiting a foreign country and learning about a new culture can definitely be exciting. Any smart traveler should be aware of and follow the traditions and customs of the host country, especially when it comes to spiritual and cultural ceremonies. Therefore, it’s important that you should always watch your behaviors. Please remember, playing dumb can backfire.

你应该尊重当地的文化和传统。访问一个国家并学习新的文化绝对是令人兴奋的事。任何聪明的旅行者都需要了解并遵循东道国的传统和习俗，尤其是在涉及到当地精神和文化仪式的场合。因此，时刻注重自己的礼仪是非常重要的。请记住，拒绝入乡随俗会带来麻烦。

18

You should make full use of the Goggle map. In the age of information and the Internet, you must learn to use Google map as you cruise around a city, a park or a major tourist attraction. You just have to switch your phone to the "Google" navigation map, click on your location, and then create your itinerary guide. Then, enter the intended destination and your current location. With all these steps done, you can walk, cycle or drive your own car between the two destinations.

你应该充分使用谷歌地图。在信息和互联网时代，在城市、公园或大型旅游景点巡游时，你需要学会使用谷歌地图。你只需要把你的手机切换到“谷歌”导航地图，点击你的地点并创建你的旅游路线指南，然后，再输入目的地和你所在的位置即可。完成以上操作后，你就可以信步观光、骑车或驾车前行。

19

You should keep your journey diary. It pays for you to keep diary when you travel overseas. For one thing, it helps you recall the fresh memory of the daily activities. For the other, it would help you to enrich your life experience about a country many years later down the road. Therefore, you need to make use of your down time and fully utilize those quiet moments when you are in transit. As one saying goes, poor diary is better than your good memory.

你应该坚持写旅行日记。你在国外旅行期间，很有必要坚持记日记。一方面，它可帮助唤起你对当天活动的新鲜记忆。另一方面，它会帮助你在多年后回顾在一个国家的旅行经历。因此，你需要充分利用休闲时间，充分利用在旅途中转机的安静时刻。俗话说，好记性不如烂笔头。

20

You should be a law-abiding tourist. When you are travelling overseas, you’re subject to all the local laws and regulations. You’ve got to remember ignorance is no excuse for breaking the law. Local police would not accept “I didn’t know” as an excuse, either. Therefore, you need to avoid bringing along any contraband items. You need to read the travel advice for the destination countries. You need to contact your embassy or the nearby consulate generals. You need to abide by the on-site tour guidance, in order to avoid fines or legal penalty. The fact is that the laws are the laws. You have to obey them, no matter what.

你做任何事都应该遵守法律法规。当你在海外旅行时，你会受到当地法律和规章制度的约束。请记住，无知不能成为违法的借口。当地警察也不会接受“我不知道”作为借口。因此，你需要避免携带任何违禁品。你需要阅读到访国家的旅游建议。你需要联系驻往访国的中国大使馆或附近的领事馆。你必须遵守现场导游指南，以避免罚款或法律惩处。事实是，法律就是法律，无论如何你都必须服从。

Part Two　Situational Dialogues

01

A: What are you planning for the coming weekend?

这个周末你打算做什么？

B: I haven’t given it a thought yet. Have you got anything special to recommend?

我还没想过呢。你有什么项目可推荐吗？

A: Well, in that case, shall we go to the Valley Park on Saturday? But, we'll have to leave at 6:30 in the morning, in order to avoid the traffic. Since my kids are away at college, you and your wife can go with us in our car. That's a treat from us, but please bring your camera along. There are quite a few tourist attractions on our way there, and we can pull at one or two sites to take some shots. They say the fall season offers the best valley views.

哦，那样的话，我们星期六改去山谷公园好吗？但是，为了避开交通堵塞，我们必须早上6点半出发。我的孩子们都在上大学，你和你妻子可以坐我们的车一起去。这是我们的心意，但请带上你的相机。路上有很多旅游景点，我们可以在一两个景点停下来拍些照片。人们说，秋天是欣赏山谷美景的最佳季节。

B: That's great. My wife and I certainly appreciate it. Look, we will prepare all the stuff for the picnic.

那太好了。我的妻子和我都很感激你们的邀请。这么着吧，我们会准备好野餐所需的所有东西。

A: That's a deal. After the picnic, we probably could go and visit Great Lakes, where we can take a boat cruise. When we come back, we could check into a local motel for the night. By the way, please have a pair of nice walking shoes with you. We may do some evening walking along the beautiful lakeside track. How does that sound?

那就说定了。野餐后，我们或许可以去游览五大湖，在那里我们可以乘船游览湖景。游览回来后，我们可以在当地一家汽车旅馆过夜。顺便说一下，请带上一双舒适的旅游鞋。晚上我们可以沿着美丽的湖滨步道散步。你觉得怎么样？

B: That would be lovely. It would really give me a break, since I've been busy with the project for the past two weeks. As for my wife, she would be more than happy to escape the office headache for a while.

那太好了。过去两周我一直在忙科研项目，这次郊游可让我放松一下。对于我的妻子而言，她也会很乐意暂时忘掉办公室的烦恼。

02

A: Well, I’ve double checked the engine oil and the water, and I’ve put an extra tank of oil and water, just in case. In fact, I just had the annual maintenance done last week, so you can just hop in and relax. I’ll do the driving for the first hour.

嗯，我已经仔细检查了机油和水箱，我还加带了一箱油和水，以防万一。事实上，我上周才做了年度保养，所以你们尽管放心上车吧。第一个小时我来开车。

B: Good. Now, I would like you to double check the stuff for the picnic in case my wife and I forgot something.

很好。现在，我希望你再检查一下野餐的东西，以防我妻子和我忘了带什么。

A: Let me see ... Well, I think everything is in place. So, we can now fasten our seat belts, and I’ll start the engine.

让我想想，我想一切都准备好了。所以，现在我们可以系好安全带，我就发动引擎了。

B: Wait, have you switched the satellite navigator system yet?

等一下，你开启车载卫星导航系统了吗？

A: Sure, I have, and according to the GPS map, it’s 175 kilometers away from here, and it would take us about two hours to get there. Usually, the traffic in this part of the city is a bit heavy over the weekend. Now, are we all set?

当然，我已打开导航地图了。根据全球定位系统地图显示，目的地离这里有175公里，我们大约要花两个小时才能到那里。根据周末的路况，这个地区的道路通常有点拥堵。现在，我们都准备好了吧？

03

A: Now, we're heading for Highway 45. In a minute, we'll be driving through the maple tree belts along both sides of the road. Let me tell you, this is the right season to see the endless purple valley for some 30 kilometers. There are three lookouts so we can pull at one of them for some scenery shots.

我们正前往45号高速公路。马上，我们就要穿过公路两边的枫树林带了。我跟你们说，眼下正是欣赏30公里的粉红色山谷的最佳季节。一路上有三个瞭望点，我们可以顺道在其中一个点拍些风景照。

B: Well, we're lucky, I must say. It reminds me of my memory of the fall season back in Beijing when my family, and I would take a trip to the Great Wall. On top of the West Mountain, we could admire the mountain views which were fully decorated by the maple trees and other trees with reddish leaves at the same time.

我得说，我们今天很幸运。这里的景色让我想起了北京的秋天，我和我的家人去长城旅游。站在西山顶上，我们可尽情观赏被枫树和其他灌木红色树叶装点的漫山遍野的美景。

A: I know Beijing and our city here are in about the same latitude, so we could enjoy the same earthly blessings. One more thing, my family and I haven't got a chance to visit your great country. I hear there's a saying that people are not heroes or heroines unless they scale the top of the Great Wall.

我知道北京和我们的城市大约在同一纬度，所以，我们可以享受同样的天赐美景。还有一件事，我和我的家人还没去过你们伟大的国家。我听说你们有一句俗语：不到长城非好汉。

B: You bet. I now extend to you the invitation for you and your family to take a trip to Beijing when we're back in China, so that we could have the pleasure to be the hosts.

您说得对。现在，我向您正式发出邀请：等我们回国后，请您和您的家人去北京，以便我们有幸作为东道主接待你们。

A: That’s very kind of you, and we’ll stay in touch.
你太客气啦，那我们保持联系。

04

A: Wow, this is certainly a fantastic view on top of the mountain here. We can now have a wholesome view of your city, and have a glimpse of the Atlantic Ocean from afar.
哇，站在这山顶上看，景色真是太美了。我们在这里可以饱览这座城市的美景，还可以远眺大西洋。

B: Well, I did check out the weather forecast three days ago, and I knew we could enjoy the view. Now, let me show you the major landmarks of our city. From this side, that’s the municipal government area. To its left is the Great Cathedral which was built more than three hundred years ago. Behind the Cathedral is the City Tower where we could hear the clock ringing at every hour sharp.
我跟你说，三天前我看了天气预报，知道我们今天可以欣赏到美景。现在，我来为你介绍本市的主要标志性建筑。这边是市政府区域。在它的左边是300多年前建造的大教堂。大教堂后面是城楼，在那里我们每隔一个小时都可以听到钟声。

A: We’re lucky today as the weather is with us. It’s the pure blue sky dotted by the flying white clouds, which makes the city more beautiful indeed. Oh, that must be the Central Park. I could see it’s a beautiful layout with towers and mansions scattered across the downtown area.
天公作美，我们今天很幸运。蔚蓝的天空飘着点点白云，让这座城市显得更加美丽。哦，那里一定是中央公园了。看得出来，那里的城市布局很漂亮，塔楼和大厦分散在市中心地带。

B: You’re right, and we’ll take a trip there tomorrow. Now, shall we move to the other side so that I could show you some more landmarks?
你说得对，我们明天去那里旅行。现在，我们移步去另一边观赏景色好吗？我来给你介绍一下城市另一边的地标建筑。

A: Certainly. By the way, how much time do we still have for the afternoon? I think we should hurry up a little so that we could get back to the hotel in time for the welcome dinner hosted by President Wilson.

当然。顺便问一下，我们今天下午还有多少时间？我想我们应该加快点速度，以便及时回到酒店，参加威尔逊校长主持的欢迎晚宴。

Part Three　Common Expressions

- I suggest you should join the third tour group, which still has vacancies for all of you. The total cost for the trip is 2300 dollars per head.

  我建议你们参加第三个团，这个团还有足够的名额。整个行程预算是人均2300美元。

- We had to cut short our tour at the National Park as the weather forecast warned us of the pending shower, which might cause landslides on our way back. We were lucky but many others were exactly caught up in it.

  我们不得不缩短在国家公园的游览时间，因为天气预报预警即将有阵雨，这可能会在我们回去的路上引发山体滑坡。我们很幸运，但很多人都被泥石流给困住了。

- Would you recommend a place where we can watch the beautiful sunrise? We came all the way just for this, and we wouldn't miss it for anything. We're also interested in Kalapa Volcanic Park, where we could see some rare tree species and watch the traditional song-and-dance show by the

local artists. People say the local food there is unique and tasty.
你能推荐一个可以看日出的地方吗？我们大老远来就是为了看日出，我们是绝对不会错过的。我们对卡拉帕火山公园也很感兴趣，想鉴赏一些稀有的树种，还想观看当地艺术家带来的传统歌舞表演。人们说当地的菜肴非常独特可口。

- Since you’ve got one and a half days to stay with us, we could take you for a seaside trip where we could watch the beautiful sunset. They say it’s the best place to watch the sunset on the seaside around the world. After that, we could go to the barbecue dinner at a nearby restaurant, which would be open for service in the evening every day. There, we’ll enjoy the bonfire-side cultural and art performances by the local artists and musicians.
既然你在这里有一天半的时间，我们可以带你去海边观光，在那里我们可以欣赏美丽的日落。那是世界上观看海上日落的最佳地点。之后，我们可以去附近的餐厅烧烤晚餐，他们每天晚上营业。在那里，我们可以观看当地艺术家和音乐家的篝火文化艺术表演。
- Before we set out for the activities tomorrow, you need to apply some sunscreen lotion and bring along a summer hat. For those who would like to have some fun in the sea, please bring your goggles. And, those who’d like to take the cruise trip across sea to the Treasury Island, you may have to bring some seasick pills with you just in case, because the cruise ship will sail deep into the sea for four hours before we return to the shore.
明天出发参加活动之前，你们需要涂一些防晒霜，随身带上一顶夏帽。想享受水上活动乐趣的人请带上护目镜。凡是想要乘船去海上金银岛的人请带上一些晕船药，以备不时之需，因为我们返回海岸之前，游轮会在大海深处航行四小时。
- Having said this much, I’ll leave you guys on your own for the next two hours. You can enjoy whatever activities that are open and free for you. For

those who would like to try the exciting water-activities, you'll have to buy your own tickets. One last thing, you should always follow the signboard, and please refrain from getting into any areas off the limits. I don't want you to get into troubles, you know.

话不多讲了，接下来的两个小时我就不打扰你们了。你们可以享受任何开放的和免费的活动。那些想要尝试惊险刺激的水上活动的人，必须自己买票。还有一件事，大家要一直按照指示牌游览，请不要进入禁区。你们知道吗，我希望你们不要惹上麻烦。

- When we're inside the wild animal park, we should do exactly what the tour guide tells us. If we're lucky, we may bumper into some zebra and lion families on our way, and they would be either eating the leaves from the trees or laying in the shade watching us passing by. You know what, they're used to the passing-by tour groups. When you see those animals, you can take pictures but never shout out at them. That's the rule.

  在野生动物园里，我们应该严格按照导游的要求去做。如果幸运的话，我们可能会在路上撞见斑马群和狮子群。它们要么在吃树叶，要么躺在树荫下看着我们路过。你知道吗，它们已经习惯了过路的旅游团。你如果看到那些动物，可以尽情照相，但千万不要对它们大喊大叫。这一条千万记住。

- Well, here we're at the museum. The whole tour will take one hour. Since you've all got wireless ear device, you should stay close with the tour guide. Please refrain from touching any exhibits when you tour the site. Mind you, any careless behaviors would invite fines. For those who would like to tour the museum on their own, please come back to the front gate in exactly two hours, and I'll be waiting for you right there. If you lose your way, please call me, and you've got my cell phone number in your brochures. Now, let's check our time, and it's 15:30 by my watch.

  好了，我们到博物馆了。整个参观活动大约要花一个小时。既然你们都随身带着无线导游器，请紧跟当地的导游。参观期间请勿触摸展品。请注意，任何粗心的行为都会招致罚款。想独自参观博物馆的人，请在两小时后准时回到前门，我在那里等你们。如果你们迷路了，请给我打电话，你们的小册子上都有我的手机号码。现在，让我们对一下时间，我的表显示15：30。

第六章

节庆活动

*

在历史上，世界各地的民族都有很多节假日，其中一些已经成为国际节日。无论走到哪里，我们不仅可以过本国的节日，而且可以过东道国的节日。因此，我们需要了解相关的节日，知道如何准备过节、如何主持或参加相关庆祝活动。

Chapter Six

Holiday Celebrations

*

Over the history, peoples around the world have evolved many holidays and festivals, some of which have become international. Therefore, wherever we go, we may have the pleasure not only to enjoy our own holidays, but also those of the host countries. Therefore, we need to know about the relevant holidays, how to prepare for them, as well as how to host and take part in the celebrations.

Part One Things to Know

01

Ever since the human race came into being, people from different tribes, nationalities or countries gradually created numerous cultures, which were earmarked by hundreds of holidays and festivals, and became an important part of people's life and social activities. In general, they have been designated to commemorate some famous occurrences in history, honor god, honor ancestors, to celebrate the beginning of seasons, or to mark the founding of a nation or a movement, etc.

自人类诞生以来，来自不同部落、民族或国家的人们逐渐创造了无数的文化，这些风俗文化被数以百计的节假日所标记，成为人们日常生活和社会活动中的重要组成部分。一般来说，假日和节日是用来纪念历史上的著名事件、祭奠神灵、祭拜祖先、庆祝季节的开始，或庆祝一个国家的建立或某个运动的发起等。

02

For many of us, holidays are much like the gas stations for automobiles. All those occasions would not only provide us with chances to recuperate from periodical fatigue, but also recharge us physically and mentally so that we could return to whatever we do with fresh mind and strength. Meanwhile, they are also the occasions for us to realize family reunions, outreach to some

personal interests and hobbies, or renew friendship with peer group friends or business partners.
对我们许多人来说，假期就像汽车的加油站。这些节假日不仅能让我们从周期性的疲劳中恢复过来，而且还能给我们的身心充电，使我们精神饱满、精力充沛地去做任何事情。同时，节假日也是我们实现家庭团聚、拓展个人兴趣爱好，或者与同龄朋友及生意伙伴重叙友情的好机会。

03

New Year is the oldest and most celebrated holiday around the world. According to some historical findings, the ancient Babylonians observed the holiday some 4000 years ago. According to their belief, they chose to celebrate their new year on the first day of the first new moon.
新年是最古老的节日，也是世界上最著名的节日。历史发现，古巴比伦人在大约4000年前就开始庆祝这个节日了。他们依据自己的信仰，选择在第一个新月的第一天庆祝新年。

04

According to the research findings, ancient Babylonians chose the 1st day in January as the New Year’s Day, not only out of convenience for religious, political and social activities, but also out of economic consideration. They believed it would mark the beginning of spring and the right season to plant crops.
研究发现，古巴比伦人选择1月1日作为元旦，不仅为了宗教、政治和社会活动方便，也是出于经济上的考虑。他们认为，元旦标志着春天和作物种植季节的开始。

05

China is one of the four ancient civilizations in the world. Over the past 5000 years or so, Chinese people have created many festivals such as Spring

Festival, Mid-autumn Festivals, Dragon Boat Festival, many of which have beautiful stories and historical background. According to their origins, Chinese festivals mainly fall into five categories: Agricultural, sacrificial, commemorative, recreational and celebratory.

中国是世界四大文明古国之一。在过去5000年左右的时间里，中国人创造了许多传统节日，如春节、中秋节、端午节等，其中许多节日都有美丽的传说和历史背景。根据节日的起源，中国的传统节日主要分为五大类，分别是农业节日、祭祀节日、纪念性节日、娱乐性节日和庆祝性节日。

06

By far, the Spring Festival is the most celebrated traditional festival which dates back to Shang Dynasty about 4000 years ago. Initially, it began as a tradition of worshiping ancestors and deities at the beginning of the year. In order to prepare for the festival, people would give their homes and bodies a thorough cleaning one week beforehand. This ritual of spring cleaning becomes a tradition that is still popular in many parts of China today.

到目前为止，春节是最著名的传统节日，它可以追溯到约4000年前的商朝。最初，春节作为祭奠祖先和神灵的一项传统在年初进行。为了准备过年，人们在节日前一周开始彻底大扫除、沐浴。这项过节的习俗已成为传统，即使是今天，在中国的许多地方仍然流行。

07

Like any festivals, the Spring Festival is a festival with many entertainment activities, enjoyed by people of all ages. During the half-month long festival, Chinese people and those living around the world would enjoy dragon dances, fireworks or firecrackers display, street art performances, bazaars, parties and many other activities. These activities would last until the Lantern Festival, which is on the 15th day of the first Lunar month.

像任何其他节日一样，春节是一个有许多娱乐活动的节日，所有年龄的中国人都喜欢。在长达半个月的节日期间，中国人和来自世界各地的华人可以欣赏舞龙、烟花表演、街头艺术表演，游览繁华的集市，参加假日派对和许多其他活动。这些节日活动一直持续到正月十五的元宵节。

08

Of all the traditional festivals, the Spring Festival and Mid-autumn Festival are the two important events to the Chinese people. The Spring Festival used to be called New Year, which is like the Christmas in the West, while the Mid-Autumn Festival is a bit like the Thanksgiving Day in the United States. Double Ninth Festival is for the elders to promote health awareness, and Double Seventh Festival is something like the Valentine's Day in the West.

在所有的传统节日中，春节和中秋节是现代中国人的两个重要节日。春节习惯被称为中国的新年，类似西方的圣诞节，而中秋节则有点像美国的感恩节。重阳节是老年人的节日，旨在促进身体健康，而七夕节犹如西方的情人节。

09

The history of the Spring Festival can trace back to China's ancient agricultural society. However, the date for the ceremony wasn't fixed till the Han Dynasty (202 BC–220 AD), when Emperor Liu Che issued the decree to observe the Lunar Calendar. From the Shang Dynasty (17th century BC–1046 BC) to the present day, the traditional festival had several names such as Yuanchen, Yuanri and Yuandan, etc.

春节的历史可以追溯到中国古代农业社会。然而，这个仪式的日期直到汉朝（公元前202年—公元220年）汉武帝刘彻颁旨实行阴历后方才确定下来。从商朝(公元前17世纪—公元前1046年)至今，这个传统节日曾经有过几个名称，如"元辰""元日""元旦"等。

10

China was among the first few countries to move into the agricultural civilization, during which its economy heavily depended on agricultural production. Therefore, the Spring Festival began as a festival to earmark the in-coming warm weather and spring planting. Later on, when China moved into the feudal society, celebration of deities and observation of ancestors were added to the festival agenda.

中国是世界上最早进入农业文明的少数几个国家之一。其间，中国的经济主要依赖农业生产。因此，春节作为传统的节日，旨在庆祝即将到来的温暖天气和春耕季节。中国进入封建社会以后，祭奠神灵和祖先的活动相继添加到节日议程之中。

11

Chinese people have many things to do to welcome the Spring Festival. Before the noon of the New Year’s Eve, many families would paste couplets to express their new year’s wishes. Traditionally, families would honor their ancestors with ceremonial feats. When the evening falls in, families would prepare luxury family reunion dinners, and family members would travel from far-away places just for the occasion when they could afford.

中国人为迎春节有很多事情要做。在除夕夜的中午之前，许多家庭会贴春联来表达他们的新年愿望。依据传统习俗，许多家庭会摆上供桌纪念祖先。每当夜幕降临，家家户户都会准备丰盛的团圆饭，家庭成员哪怕身在天涯海角，只要有可能，都要想方设法赶赴年夜饭。

12

New Year’s Eve is now an important occasion for the family reunion, during which family members would sit around the table or in the same room to enjoy the feast. After the dinner, family members would fix up some traditional games or watch the Spring Festival Gala. The exciting part of the function would be that the elders hand out red packets filled up with lucky money. Nowadays, people mostly use WeChat to launch the lucky draw games called “grabbing red pockets”. Colleagues, friends, business partners, peer group members or relatives would take turns to throw certain amount of lucky money into to WeChat groups for everybody to grab as the token of good luck in the coming year.

除夕是家庭团聚的重要时刻。其间，家人会围坐在桌子旁或在同一间屋子里吃年夜饭。晚饭后，家人会安排一些传统游戏或收看春节联欢晚会。年夜活动最令人兴奋的部分就是由长辈们分发装有压岁钱的红包。现在，人们纷纷用微信群“发红包”“抢红包”。同事、朋友、商业伙伴、同龄人或亲友会轮流在微信群里发一定数量的好运钱，让群友抢红包，相互祝贺来年万事顺心。

13

The focus of the New Year’s Eve is that everybody in the family is to stay up late, which is one way to welcome the New Year. To the Chinese people, staying up late that night is endowed with auspicious meaning. For the old, it’s one way to cherish their past time, and for the young, it’s one way to wish their elder family members longevity. At the midnight, family members would set off firecrackers or display fireworks. It’s their firm belief that the loud sound of the firecrackers would drive away the evil spirit, and the splashing fireworks would symbolize their thriving life or business in the coming year.

除夕的焦点是全家人都在除夕夜守岁，这是中国人迎接新年到来的一种方式。对中国人来说，除夕夜熬夜被赋予了吉祥的含义。对老年人来说，这是珍惜过去时光的一种方式；对年轻人来说，这是祝愿长辈长寿的一种方式。在午夜时刻，家庭成员会燃放爆竹或烟火。这是他们的坚定信念，认为响亮的鞭炮声可以赶走恶魔，而闪亮的烟火则象征着新的一年中生活安详和生意兴隆。

14

At breakfast on the New Year's Day, family members would greet one another happy new year, wish one another longevity and good luck in whatever they would do, and enjoy dumplings. After that, people would go out to pay the New Year calls to the neighbors, watch the traditional dragon dances or lion dances, or visit the nearby temple fairs.

在新年的早餐期间，家庭成员会互致新年问候，互祝身体健康和万事顺意，享用美味的饺子。早餐过后，人们会外出走访左邻右舍，相互拜年，观看传统的舞龙或舞狮，或到附近逛庙会。

15

In order to promote economic and commercial activities, at the suggestion of the central government, the National People's Congress passed the law to make the Festival a week-long public holiday in 1990's, so that people from all walks of life could have opportunities to go for the family reunion, to do shopping or to go for the domestic and oversea tours.

为促进经济和商业活动，20世纪90年代，在国务院建议下，全国人民代表大会通过立法，将春节定为为期一周的公众假日，以便各行各业的人们有机会与家人团聚、购物，或到国内外旅游。

16

Since Han Dynasty, temple fairs have become regular events both for city dwellers and people in the rural communities across China. On those occasions, Chinese people would go to the nearby bazaars where they would give offerings to Bodhisattva, pick up good bargains, and watch local art performances. Nevertheless, the temple fairs would remain the most important commercial venues throughout the year for the people in the local communities.

自汉代以来，中国各地的城市居民和农村居民都会定期举办庙会。在那里，中国人会到附近的集市上供菩萨，购买便宜货，观看当地的艺术表演。当然，对当地社区的人们来说，庙会构成全年最重要的固定商业交易场所。

17

Along with those major festivals, there are many other traditional festivals which are observed in modern China. Ethnic groups would celebrate their own festivals with unique colors and ceremonies. For instance, people of Zhuang nationality in Guangxi Autonomous Region would celebrate the Double-Third Festival, and the Tibetans would observe the Shou Dun Festival. Therefore, apart from the ethnic, geographic, historic and linguistic ties that unite all the minority nationalities in China, traditional festivals are one of the strong bonds reinforcing the cultural identity of the Chinese nation over the history.

除了这些重大节日，现代中国还有许多其他的传统节日。少数民族用独特的色彩和仪式来庆祝他们的节日。比如，广西壮族自治区的民众会过重三节，藏族人过守墩节。因此，除了将中国各少数民族团结在一起的民族、地理、历史和语言纽带之外，传统节日也是历史上促进中华民族文化认同的最有力的纽带。

18

October 1st is the National Day, which is a public holiday for the peoples of all nationalities across China, and marks the founding of the People's Republic of China. In order to promote the holiday economy, the central government has made it the week-long holiday, so that people from all walks of life could plan their celebrations, and take trips across the country or overseas.

10月1日是国庆节，是中国各族人民的公共假日，是中华人民共和国成立的纪念日。为了促进假日经济，中央政府确定国庆假日为期一周，以便各行各业的人计划他们的庆祝活动，或到国内外旅行。

19

Christmas is an annual festival commemorating the birth of Jesus Christ, it is observed primarily on December 25 as a religious and cultural celebration among billions of people around the world. The holiday would last for twelve days. Christmas Day is celebrated by the Christians, and culturally by many non-Christians as a regular commercial and social holiday season.

圣诞节是纪念耶稣基督诞生的年度节日，适逢每年12月25日，是世界各地几十亿人的宗教和文化庆祝活动。圣诞节通常持续12天。圣诞节是基督徒举行宗教庆祝活动的节日，许多非基督徒从文化角度庆祝圣诞节，并已使之成为常规的商业和社交节日。

20

We are now moving into the commercial society, but the traditional festivals are still the occasions for us to celebrate our glorious cultural heritages and traditions. They are the special moments in our lives, during which we could share love for one another, and care for those in need or in want. More importantly, they play an important role to connect us with our families, ethnic backgrounds and national identities. They would allow us to forget about the dull routines of day-to-day schedules, renew the happiness of family reunions, and recharge our body and mind for whatever we do in the future.

我们正进入商业社会，但传统节日仍然是我们庆祝光荣的文化遗产和传统的载体，并且构成我们生命中特殊的时刻。其间，我们可以分享彼此的爱，关心那些需要帮助的人。更重要的是，节假日在我们与家人、本民族和本国保持联系的活动中扮演着重要的角色。节假日可以让我们暂时忘却枯燥的日常生活，尽享家庭团聚的幸福，并给我们的身体和精神充电，以期更好地投入到后续工作中。

Part Two Situational Dialogues

01

A: I know the Spring Festival is an important holiday in your country, but what are the interesting facts that we foreigners need to know, please?
我知道在你们国家春节是一个最重要的节日，请问有什么是需要我们外国人知道的有趣事情吗?

B: Well, there're many interesting things about this traditional holiday but these are the essentials. First, the holiday is called the Spring Festival for the simple reason that it marks the end of the cold winter days and the incoming of spring season. Second, the festival does not fall on the same date. According to the Lunar Calendar, it may fall on any day between 21st January and 20th February. For example, in 2020, the festival was on the 25th of January. Third, the festival is a day for the farmers to pray for a good harvest, for people in general to fight off monsters and ward off any misfortunes in the coming year. Fourth, it's the festival when people set off most fire crackers or light off most fireworks. Fifth, it used to be the longest traditional holiday. Over the history, it would start from the New Year's Eve all the way to the 15th of January of the following year according to the Lunar Calendar. Sixth, it's the holiday, during which people would see the largest Chinese migration in the world, as most family members would travel for the family reunion on the New Year's

Eve. Seventh, it's the only holiday that warrants a thorough body or house cleaning prior to the festival, which literally means to wash away all the bad luck of the passing year, and prepare the room and body for the good luck in the coming year. Eighth, the children would receive lucky money in the red envelopes from their elder family members, and now it's a festival for people to share good luck money via WeChat groups. Ninth, the festival warrants all family members to wear new clothes and decorate their living spaces before the festival. Last but not the least, many families would paste the couplets on the door frames of both the front door and the inner doors, which would serve as the media to dispel the evil spirits. Well, I wish these facts would make your stay in China very much interesting.

关于这个节日有很多有趣的事情，但这些都是必须了解的。首先，这个节日之所以被称为春节，原因很简单，它标志着寒冷冬天的结束和春天的到来。第二，节日不是每次都在同一天。根据农历，春节可能是1月21日到2月20日中的任何一天。例如，在2020年，中国的新年是1月25日。第三，这个节日是农民祈求丰收、普通人驱魔辟邪的日子。第四，节日时人们会放鞭炮或烟花。第五，它曾经是中国最长的节日。在历史上，春节的庆祝活动从除夕一直持续到农历来年的正月十五。第六，节日期间，你会看到世界上规模最大的中国人迁徙，因为大多数人会在除夕夜赶回家与家人团聚。第七，春节是唯一需要所有人在节前进行住所大扫除和整理个人卫生的节日，期盼洗掉过去一年的所有坏运气，为来年的好运气做好准备。第八，孩子们会从长辈那里收到装在红包里的压岁钱，而现在人们则在微信群发红包、抢红包。第九，所有家庭成员在新年要穿上新衣服，在节日前把房间装饰一番。最后，许多家庭会把对联贴在前门和屋内门的门框上，驱散鬼怪邪灵。我希望这些信息会让你们在中国的春节假日生活更加有趣。

A: Sure. My wife and my kids will look forward to an interesting Spring Festival in your country.

当然啦。我的妻子和孩子们将十分期盼在贵国过一个有趣的春节。

02

A: I know many countries have borrowed the Chinese custom of dragon boat race which falls on May 5th each year according to your Lunar Calendar. I also know it's a tradition to honor one of your national heros Qu Yuan. Could you tell us a bit more about the festival and Qu Yuan?

我知道很多国家都借用了中国农历五月初五赛龙舟的习俗。我还知道这个传统节日与纪念你们的一位民族英雄屈原有关。你能告诉我们更多关于这个节日和屈原的事情吗?

B: Well, it's certainly a long story, but let me make it short. Qu Yuan was a great patriotic poet and politician in the Warring States Period (475-221 BC). He was a nobleman with great talent in literature and politics. Nevertheless, when he was a senior official at the imperial court of the State of Chu, his outstanding policy proposals were often ignored by the emperor, and eventually he was down-graded and sent on exile to the Miluo River area in South China. Well, in 278 BC, the capital of the State of Chu was captured by the State of Qin. When Qu Yuan heard about the news, he realized that his home country had come to doom. He felt so desperate and sorrow about his country and his people that on May the fifth, he threw himself into the Miluo River, and ended his life, in order to show his love and loyalty for the motherland. When the villagers from the local communities heard the news, they immediately jumped onto the boats and raced with one another, trying to save their national hero. Meanwhile, villagers tried to wrap the rice with reef leaves and threw them into the Miluo River, in the hope that the fish and shrimps would not decompose the body of their hero. Now, we Chinese have inherited the tradition to wrap “pyramid shaped Zongzi” and hold dragon boat races in commemoration of Qu Yuan on the same day each year.

哦，这说来话长了，但我尽量长话短说。屈原是战国时期(公元前475 —公元前221年)伟大的爱国诗人和政治家。他是一个在文学和政治方面很有天赋的贵族。然而，当他在楚国担任高级官员时，他出色的政策主张常常被皇帝忽视，最终被流放到南方的汨罗江流域。公元前278年，秦国军队攻占了楚国的首都。当屈原听到这个消息，他意识到他的祖国已经灭亡。屈原怀着对国家和人民的极度悲伤之情，于农历五月初五那一天投汨罗江自尽，以表达他对祖国的热爱和忠诚。当地村民听到这个消息后，立即跳上自家的船只，争先恐后地划向出事地点，试图营救他们的民族英雄。与此同时，村民们用芦苇叶子包裹着大米扔进了汨罗江中，希望鱼和虾不要毁掉他们英雄的遗体。现在，我们中国人传承端午节的习俗，每年的这一天都要包粽子、赛龙舟，以此来纪念屈原。

03

A: This is my first Christmas holiday since I came to your country. I wonder if you could share with me something about this important holiday.

自从来到你们国家后，这是我过的第一个圣诞节。我想请你和我分享一些关于这个重要节日的事情。

B: Well, Christmas is an annual festival commemorating the birth of Jesus Christ, observed on December 25th as a religious and cultural celebration among people here in my country. Nevertheless, many families now choose to skip the gift exchange activity, and replace it with some family games or a treat at the restaurant. Some families are taking trips to some other cities or countries for a change. Some families are organizing mini-getaway trips to the lakeside, mountainside or seaside. Some families would choose to take part in volunteer services in the local communities or at senior citizen homes. Some families are building up their own fancy floats for the town parade, or organize local charity fairs. Still some other families are giving out Christmas gifts to those who really can't afford to celebrate the holiday. As I notice, these are some favorite non-traditional ways to celebrate Christmas, which are the fabulous ways for people to enjoy their holiday season!

好吧，圣诞节在12月25日，是纪念耶稣基督诞生的年度节日，是我国人民的一项宗教和文化庆典。然而，现如今许多家庭选择取消礼物交换活动，转而举行家庭游戏或到餐馆用餐。一些家庭举家到另一个城市或国家观光旅游以换换心情。一些家庭组织到湖边、山坡上或海边进行短途旅行。一些家庭选择参加当地社区或敬老院的志愿服务。一些家庭自行制作花车参加镇上游行活动，或者组织义卖活动。仍还有一些家庭选择向没钱过节的人员分发圣诞礼物。据我所知，这些都是一些国人流行的、非传统的庆祝圣诞节的方式，而且也是享受节日不错的方式！

A: Thank you for the story, but what are the other things I need to know about the holiday, please?

谢谢你的介绍，但是关于这个节日我还需要知道些什么呢？

B: To be serious though, many families, companies or institutions would have Christmas trees and other decorations in the weeks leading to the Christmas Day. Some workplaces would hold Christmas parties prior to December 25th. Festive activities would include exchanging presents, singing Christmas songs. It's a special time when children get presents from family members, friends and Santa Claus. People would send Christmas cards to one another prior to the Christmas Day. Christmas banners may be hung from street light posts and Christmas trees would be placed in the town squares or many public places. Other traditional decorations would also include bells, candles, candy canes, wreaths, and angels, etc.

说真的，在圣诞节的前几周，许多家庭、公司和单位都会布置圣诞树和其他装饰品。一些工作场所会在12月25日前举办圣诞派对。节日活动包括交换礼物，圣诞歌咏。在这个特殊时刻，孩子们可以从家人、朋友和圣诞老人那里得到礼物。人们在圣诞节前会相互寄送圣诞贺卡。圣诞横幅通常会挂在街灯灯柱上，圣诞树放置在城镇广场上或其他公共场所。其他的传统装饰包括铃铛、蜡烛、拐杖糖、花环和天使，等等。

04

A: I knew, since I was a high school student, Thanksgiving Day has been an important day in the United States, but could you tell me something more about the festival, please?

我在上高中的时候就知道，感恩节在美国是一个重要的节日，但是你能给我多讲讲关于这个节日的事情吗?

B: Simply said, in September 1620, an ocean-going ship called the Mayflower left England, carrying 102 passengers who were the religious separatists seeking new places where they could freely practice their faith and others who were lured by the promise of prosperity and land ownership in the New World. After a treacherous sail across the Atlantic Ocean for 66 days, they dropped the anchor near the tip of Cape Cod, far north of their intended destination at the mouth of the Hudson River. One month later, the Mayflower crossed the Massachusetts Bay, where the Pilgrims began to build a village. Throughout the first brutal winter, most colonists remained on the ship, where they suffered from harsh exposures, scurvy and the outbreaks of contagious diseases. As a result, only half of the passengers and crew members lived to see their first spring in New England. In March that year, the remaining settlers moved ashore, where they received a surprised visit from an Abenaki Native American who greeted the intruders with friendship. Several days later, he returned with another Native American, Squanto, a member of the Pawtuxet tribe who had been kidnapped by an English navel captain and sold into slavery, but he managed to escape to London and returned to his homeland, joining an exploratory expedition. Squanto taught the Pilgrims to cultivate corn, extract saps from maple trees, catch fish in the rivers, and distinguish the poisonous plants. He also helped the settlers to forge an alliance with the Wampanoag tribe. In November 1621, the Pilgrims successfully harvested the first corn in quantity. Governor William Bradford decided to organize a feast to celebrate the bumper harvest, and invited some representatives from the local tribe, including the Wampanoag chief Massasoit. To make the story short, that feat became the launching pad for what we know as the “Thanksgiving” tradition. Later on, we Americans carried on this tradition and turned it into a national holiday.

简单地说，1620年9月，一艘名为“五月花”的远洋船载着102名乘客从英国出发，其中包括各种各样的宗教分离主义者，他们中的一部分人想寻找一个可以自由践行信仰的新家园，而其他人则是被新大陆的繁荣和土地所有权前景所吸引。经历了66天横渡大西洋的艰险航行后，他们在科德角附近抛锚，偏离了他们预定的目的地哈德逊河口北部。一个月后，“五月花”号穿过马萨诸塞湾，清教徒们开始在河口安营扎寨。在第一个严冬里，大多数殖民者留在船上，忍受着风吹露宿，以及坏血病和传染病的暴发。结果，仅有一半的乘客和船员活着看到了新英格兰的第一个春天。次年3月，剩下的定居者搬到了岸上，在那里，他们迎来了一位名叫阿本纳吉的印第安人的意外造访。阿本纳吉友好地迎接了这些闯入者。几天后，他和另一位印第安人斯匡托一起回到这个村庄。斯匡托是波塔克西特部落的一员，曾被一名英国船长绑架并被卖身为奴隶。后来，他成功逃脱，并在伦敦踏上探险之旅，最终回到自己的祖国。斯匡托教清教徒们种植玉米，从枫树中提取汁液，在河里捕鱼以及辨别有毒植物等。他还成功推动新来者与万帕诺格部落结成联盟。1621年11月，清教徒们第一次成功地收获了大量的玉米。总督威廉·布拉德福德决定组织一场盛宴庆祝大丰收，并邀请了当地部落的一些代表人物参加，包括万帕诺格部落的酋长马萨索伊特。简而言之，这一壮举成为我们熟知的“感恩节”的起源。后来，我们美国人继承了这一传统，并使之成为全国性的节日。

A: Thank you very much for the exciting story. Now, I know how to prepare for the holiday in your country.

非常感谢你精彩的故事。现在我知道怎样在贵国过感恩节了。

05

A: Happy Thanksgiving Day, Jerry.

感恩节快乐，杰瑞。

B: Same here, Mark. By the way, have you got any plan for the day?

我也祝你节日愉快，马克。顺便问一下，你今天有什么计划吗?

A: Not really. All my friends and colleagues are somewhere for the holiday. But, what are you planning to do anyway?

还没有。我所有的朋友和同事都在某个地方度假。不过，你们有什么过节的安排吗?

B: Well, if you're interested, you can come to my house this afternoon. We're holding a family reunion, and all the family members will be here. I'm sure you'll be able to taste the delicious turkey dinner prepared by my mother.

哦，如果你有兴趣的话，今天下午可以来我家。我们会有一个家庭聚会，所有家庭成员都将来这里。我相信你会品尝到我妈妈准备的美味的火鸡晚餐。

A: Thank you for asking. I'd love to, but it's too late for me to grab a gift or something.

谢谢你的邀请。我也很想去，但太迟了，我没时间准备什么礼物了。

B: Please don't bother, and my family and I would be more than happy to have you for the occasion. After all, it's a golden opportunity for you to see how a native family would celebrate the Thanksgiving.

请不必费心啦，我和我的家人会非常高兴你的到来。你想啊，这对你是多好的机会，可以了解当地人家是如何庆祝感恩节的。

A: That would be lovely, but could you tell me about the feast, please?

那太好了，但你能告诉我晚餐都有什么菜吗?

B: It's just an annual family get-together, where we would have lots of delicious food such as yam, sweat corn, carrots and fruit pie. Of course, roast turkey is a must. After that, we would play games or watch a movie in connection with the Thanksgiving.

就是一年一度的家庭聚会，我们可以品尝到很多美味的食物，有山药、甜玉米、胡萝卜和水果派。当然，烤火鸡是必不可少的。之后，我们会玩游戏或看与感恩节有关的电影。

A: Sounds a big feast. I’m already feeling hungry, just listening to your story.
听起来真是一场盛宴。听你这么说，我都感到饿了。

B: Then, come right away, and we’ll be expecting you.
那就快点来吧，我们期待你的到来。

Part Three Common Expressions

- We Chinese have the tradition to farewell the old year and usher in the new one. Traditionally, family members would stay up all night through on the New Year’s Eve.
我们中国人素有辞旧迎新的习俗。依据传统，家庭成员喜欢在除夕夜守岁。
- The family reunion dinner has been the important family function for the Chinese to celebrate the New Year. It’s also a must for the Chinese families to prepare and eat dumplings on the New Year’s Eve, which would symbolize the good fortune or good luck in the coming year.
年夜饭成为中国人庆祝新年的重要家庭项目。包饺子和吃饺子是中国家庭除夕夜晚的必备活动，以表达对来年财运或好运的期许。
- Chinese families have the tradition to sweep tomb sites of the beloved ones the day before the Tomb Sweeping Day, which is one way to pay tribute to

the deceased.
中国家庭历来有清明节前扫墓的传统，以祭奠亡灵。

- During the Spring Festival, Chinese people would visit temple fairs to watch the traditional art performances and do fancy shopping at the bazaars.
春节期间，中国人喜欢逛庙会，观看传统文艺演出，在集市轻松购物。
- This year is my animal year. According to the tradition, people who are born in the same animal year would wear red belts or red underwear in order to pray for good health and peace.
今年是我的本命年。依据传统，本命年的人应当扎红腰带或者穿红内衣，祈盼健康和平安。
- The best part of the holiday season is the traditions that would bring people together, during which they could share their favorite traditions with one another, and enjoy the extravagant meals, festive gatherings such as the quiet games or noisy discos. All these would inspire people to celebrate, to decorate, and to be thankful.
节假日最好是人们可相互团聚。其间，人们可以与彼此分享最喜爱的节日传统，享用丰盛的大餐，进行节日聚会，如开展安静的游戏或去喧闹的迪斯科。所有这些都会激励人们去庆祝，去装饰，去感恩。
- When COVID-19 is still wide spreading, holiday and festival celebrations are no longer the same as we know before. The best thing to do is to stay at home, and do everything in line with the sanitarian check list. We should refrain from visiting elderly people unless we've had vaccine injections done and had the negative nucleic acid result. We should refrain from inviting family members or friends from the high-risk areas. The bottom line is we should stay at home and stay safe.
在新冠肺炎疫情仍广泛传播的情况下，节假日庆祝活动不再像我们知道的那样进行。最好的办法就是待在家里，按照健康检查清单安排一切。我们应该避免看望长者，除非我们已经注射了疫苗并取得阴性证明。我们应当避免邀请来自疫情高风险地区的亲友。底线是，我们应该待在家里，确保平安。

- During the pandemic season, we have to plan our feasts with precautions. When it comes to food, we should forget about buffet dinners or outdoor barbecues. We should limit the scale of the family parties. We should keep distance. We should wear masks unless we eat, ect.

  在疫情大流行季节，我们举办宴会必须有预防措施。当谈到食物时，我们应该放弃自助餐或户外烧烤。我们应该限制家庭聚会的规模。我们应该保持距离。除了吃饭我们应该都戴着口罩，等等。

第七章

人文历史

*

无论走到哪里，无论身在何处，历史都是我们在各种社交场合经常谈论的话题。因此，我们既需要了解本国的历史，也需要了解东道国的历史，这不仅有助于彰显个人文化，而且有助于体现我们的职业水平。

Chapter Seven

Human History

*

Wherever we go and wherever we are, history is always a standing topic for conversation on social occasion. Therefore, we need to know about our own history as well as that of the host country, which would define us not only in terms of culture, but also in our profession.

Part One　Things to Know

01

What is history? Simply said, history is all about what has happened in the past, which covers three areas: How mankind came into being, how people comprehend what has happened to the mankind at different times, as well as how people empower the history forward.

历史是什么？简单地说，历史就是过去发生的一切，主要涵盖三个方面：人类是如何演变和发展的、人们对不同时期人类历史的理解以及人类是如何推动历史进步的。

02

History is a mirror to any nation. Dynasties may come and go, emperors and kings may come into being and fade away, but history endures forever. In the twenty-first century, countries in the world are faced with a hard choice of whether joining hands in addressing the common challenges for the common interests and destiny, or each going its own way, which is the precondition to power the industrial civilization forward.

对于任何国家而言，历史都是一面镜子。朝代更迭，帝王更替，只有历史永存。21世纪，人类正面临着艰难选择：是携手共同应对挑战，谋求共同利益和共同命运，还是各行其是。这是推动工业文明持续前行的前提条件。

03

Every nation has its history about how its people got here, who they are and where they are going. The Chinese history is of no exception. China is an ancient civilization and has a recorded history of more than almost 5000 years and is on its way to realize national rejuvenation.

每一个国家都有关于本民族的历史，说明人们如何走到今天，他们是谁，他们将前往何处。中国历史亦然。中国是一个文明古国，自有文字记录以来有着5000余年历史，并且正走在民族复兴的路上。

04

As one saying goes, history is a book, from which later generations can both seek inspirations and draw lessons. However, in the contemporary international relations, some countries have chosen to go against the trend of human history, and seek national interests at the expenses of other countries, which the international community is yet to come up with effective means to cope with.

俗话说，历史是一本书，后人可以从中得到启示和教训。但是，在当代国际关系中，一些国家违背人类历史发展潮流，以牺牲别国利益为代价追求本国利益。对此，国际社会尚待形成有效的措施来应对。

05

Who are we? This is a question, which should be answered not only by specialists, but also by people from all walks of life. It’s because nations around the world are increasingly becoming a “global village”, where anything happens in one country would produce impacts not only on many other countries, but also on the daily life of the people across the board, via internet or industrial chains and supply chains.

我们是谁？这个问题不仅应该由专家来回答，而且应该由各行各业的人来回答。这是因为，世界各国正逐渐成为“地球村”。一个国家发生的事情不仅会通过互联网、产业链和供应链等对其他许多国家产生影响，而且会对各界民众的生活产生影响。

06

For long in the past, the idea of "man can conquer nature" has dominated people's mind, and it is true that man has been the master and doing whatever he wants for thousands of years. However, the "master" seems to be confronted with the problems that are far beyond his control, such as climate change.

"人定胜天"长期以来主宰着人们的思想。的确，几千年来，人类一直以主人的身份行事，想做什么就做什么。然而，现在这个"主人"似乎面临着无法控制的问题，如气候变化。

07

When people talk about Egypt, they would immediately think of the Pyramids, especially the Great Pyramid of Giza. This is the oldest and largest of the three pyramids in the Giza pyramid complex not far from Cairo, Egypt. It is the oldest of the Seven Wonders of the Ancient World, and the only one that still remains largely intact.

提起埃及人们就会想起金字塔，尤其是吉萨大金字塔。在埃及首都开罗附近的三座金字塔中，这是最大、最古老的一座。埃及金字塔是古代世界七大奇观之一，而且是唯一现存的、基本保持完好的古建筑。

08

Generally speaking, the ancient silk road is a broad term, which refers to the East-West transportation route that starts from ancient Chinese city Chang'an and connects countries in Europe, North Africa through Central Asia and West Asia since China's Han Dynasty 2000 years ago. Over the history, the silk road served as the bridge upon which the ancient China, India and Greece

not only offered philosophical, cultural and spiritual wisdom to each other, but also collectively provided similar enlightenment to the peoples along the ancient silk road.
一般来说，古丝绸之路是广义的，是指自2000年前的中国汉代以来，从中国古城长安出发，经中亚、西亚，连接欧洲、北非各国的东西交通路线。历史上，丝绸之路不仅是古代中国、古印度、古希腊之间相互交流哲学、文化、精神智慧的桥梁，也共同为沿线各国人民带去了相似的文明。

09

Simply said, the Maritime Silk Road refers to the maritime section of the historic silk road that connects China with countries in Southeast Asia, those on today's Indian Peninsula and Arabian Peninsula, and those in Europe. It flourished between the 2nd century BC and 15th century AD. For a long time, it was operated by the Chinese sailors and those from other countries in Southeast Asia, Tamil merchants in India, Greco-Roman merchants and by Persian and Arab traders around the Arabian Sea and beyond.
简单说来，海上丝绸之路系指历史上连接中国与东南亚、今印度半岛、阿拉伯半岛和欧洲国家的古丝绸之路海上部分。海上丝绸之路贸易于公元前2世纪到公元15世纪达到顶峰。在很长一段时间里，这条贸易大通道主要由中国水手和东南亚其他国家的水手、印度泰米尔商人、希腊—罗马商人，以及阿拉伯海周围和更远范围内的波斯和阿拉伯商人开拓和经营。

10

China enjoys a long history, whose culture can trace back to more than 4000 years ago via written record. Yan and Huang have been honored as the first ancestor of the Chinese nation. In accordance with the history, Chinese nation was officially founded in Xia Dynasty around 21th century BC.
中国历史悠久，有文字可考的中国文化可以追溯到4000多年前。炎黄被尊为中华民族的始祖。据历史记载，中国始建于公元前21世纪的夏朝。

11

In 221 BC, Emperor Qin Shihuang defeated all the warring states and founded the first unified imperial empire. Within a short span, the Qin Emperor established the unified road and transportation system, unified calligraphy, weight and length measurement standards. More importantly, the emperor managed to establish the national governing system which was inherited by all the successive emperors and all dynasties up until 1911 when the last feudal dynasty, Qing Dynasty, was overthrown by the Nationalist Party headed by Dr. Sun Yet-sen.

公元前221年，秦始皇打败了所有诸侯国，建立了第一个统一的中央帝国。在很短的时间内，秦始皇成功地建立了统一的交通运输系统，统一了文字、度量衡。更重要的是，他成功地建立了国家统治制度，这一制度后来一直延续到1911年，最后一个封建王朝被由孙中山先生领导的国民党所推翻。

12

In the history of China, Yuan Dynasty existed for less than 200 years, but it contributed greatly to the construction of the nation in many ways. The most significant achievement of Yuan Dynasty was the reunification of the whole country. Up until then, China had been a country torn apart for more than 300 years. Another significance of the Dynasty was the outstanding achievements in the natural sciences and technology. Due to the open policy implemented by the Yuan rulers, many science and technology innovations were introduced to China, especially in the field of astronomy and mathematics. In the field of foreign relations, the Yuan rulers allowed foreign trade to become the main engine for the economic growth.

在中国历史上，元朝存在不到200年，但在许多方面对国家建设做出了巨大贡献。元朝最重要的成就是再度实现了国家疆土的统一。在此之前的300多年里，中国一直是一个分裂的国家。元朝另一个重要贡献是在自然科学和技术领域。元朝统治者实行了开放政策，大量科学技术创新引入中国，尤其是在天文和数学领域。在对外关系方面，元朝统治者使得贸易成为经济发展的主要动力。

13

For more than 1000 years in the history, feudal China became the global political, economic, cultural and technological centers of the world, especially in Tang Dynasty, Song Dynasty, Yuan Dynasty and early Ming Dynasty, which contributed to more than 40% of the annual global GDP. It was also during this period that China contributed its four great inventions such as paper making, compass, gun powder and printing as well as many other inventions to the countries around the world, which provided the enlightenment to the countries in the West in terms of Renaissance and Industrial Revolution.

在长达1000余年的历史时期里，尤其是在唐朝、宋朝、元朝和明朝早期，封建中国成为世界政治、经济、文化和科技中心，对全球GDP的贡献超过40%。正是在这一历史时期，中国为世界各国贡献了造纸、指南针、火药和印刷四大技术发明以及许多其他技术，促进了相关国家的文艺复兴和工业革命的发展。

14

Over the history, human cultural revolution benefited from the printing technology originated from China. From the perspective of the sociology, mass production of printed books, periodicals and documents not only were convenient for the collection by the government and the rich families, but also benefited the readers from all walks of life. In terms of cultural heritage, wide circulation of printing technology laid a solid foundation for the emergence and development of new ideas, new knowledge, new technology and new arts, etc. At the same time, printed books and materials helped the readers sharpen their thinking, and standardized the writing of academic monographs. From the perspective of politics, the wide spread and application of printing technology contributed to the unification of national languages and the revitalization of national culture.

历史上，人类文化革命得益于中国的印刷技术。从社会学视角来看，印刷版书刊和文件资料大量生产，既便于官方和富有家庭珍藏，又可以在更大规模上惠及各界读者。从文化传承视角来看，印刷技术的广泛应用为新思想、新学问、新技术和新艺术的出现和发展奠定了坚实的文字基础。同时，印刷书刊和资料可以助力读者强化思想，规范学术专著写作。从政治角度看，印刷术的普及和应用促进了民族语言的统一，振兴了民族文化。

15

In terms of the history of relations between ancient China and the countries in the West, some great names would appear into the central stage, of which General Zhang Qian is one. Zhang Qian (164 BC-114 BC) was an extraordinary explorer, a loyal diplomat, and a determined hero of Han Dynasty. During his two Westward missions, he fought bravely against his enemies, and was at one time captured and half-imprisoned for more than a decade. He toured many regimes in an effort to lobby for the support for the Han Empire to fight against the rising Xiongnu. It was coincidental that he initiated the state sponsored trade between China and the countries in the West which included Ferghana Horse, grape, walnut, cucumber, garlic, celery, etc. Most importantly, he helped to promoted human and cultural contact between the Han Empire and regimes in the West. It was largely due to his personal endeavor that the silk road officially came into being.

在中国古代与西方国家的对外关系史上，有一些伟大的人物必然出现在舞台中央，张骞将军就是其中之一。张骞(公元前164—公元前114年)

是汉朝杰出的探险家、忠诚的外交家和坚定的民族英雄。在两次出使西域征途中，他与敌人斗智斗勇，曾一度被俘虏并被囚禁十余年。他到访了许多西域国家，努力游说后者支持汉廷对抗崛起的匈奴。巧合的是，张骞推动了汉廷与西域国家的官方贸易往来，引进了西域的良种马、葡萄、核桃、黄瓜、大蒜、芹菜等。最重要的是，他促进了汉帝国与西方政权之间的人文交流。正是由于他个人的努力，丝绸之路得以正式形成。

16

Zheng He was the navel general and diplomat of the Ming Dynasty, who helped to extend the political, cultural and commercial influence of China to the maritime neighboring countries. At the decree of the Ming Emperor, he commanded seven naval expeditions, and reached countries in today's India and sailed to the southern tip of Africa. In short, General Zheng He contributed to China in the following areas. First, he faithfully carried out the foreign policy by Ming Emperor to extend China's political influence to the neighboring countries. Second, his maritime expeditions helped to stabilize the security situation of the Ming Dynasty. Third, he managed to promote the maritime trade between China and more than 30 countries across the region. Fourth, he effectively promoted the cultural exchanges between China and the neighboring countries. Last but not least, he pioneered the maritime expeditions more than 100 years before the Western adventurers.

郑和是明朝航海家和外交家，他帮助朝廷提高了在周边沿海国家的政治和经济影响力。依据明朝皇帝的旨意，他七次统率航海舰队远征，到达了今天的印度疆域内诸多王国，并远航至非洲之角一带。总而言之，郑和将军对明代做出了以下贡献。首先，他忠实地执行了明帝的外交政策，将中国的政治影响力扩大到周边各国。二是他统率的七次远征为明廷海上安全局势提供了保障。三是他促进了中国与这些地区30多个国家的海上贸易。四是他有效地促进了中国与周边国家的文化交流。最后，他的远征活动比西方冒险家早了100多年，因而他成为海上探险的先驱。

17

Marco Polo was a Venetian merchant and adventurer, who traveled between Europe and the Yuan China from 1271 to 1295, and stayed in China for 17 years. During this period, he served in court of the Yuan Dynasty and often toured various regions of the Yuan Dynasty upon decrees from the emperor. He also traveled to the countries in Southeast Asia and South Asia by the decrees from the Yuan emperor. *The Travels of Marco Polo*, which was written based on Marco Polo's life and mission in China, introduced to the Westerners the Oriental culture as well as the political, economic and cultural development of China, greatly enriched the geographical knowledge of the Europeans, and broke the religious fallacies and the traditional theory that the "heaven is round and the earth is square". At the same time, *The Travels of Marco Polo* played a huge role in promoting the course of maritime navigation in Europe in the 15th century. With the book in hand, Columbus in Italy and many other navigators, travelers, explorers took their adventurous maritime trips to the dreamland country in the East, which helped to break the medieval Western theocracy, and greatly promoted the cultural exchanges between China and countries in Europe.

马可·波罗是威尼斯的商人和冒险家，于1271年至1295年到欧洲和中国元朝游历，在中国待了17年。其间，他在元朝朝廷中任职，经常奉命到元朝各地考察，还曾奉命出使东南亚和南亚各国。马可·波罗依据他在中国的生活和工作经历撰写了《马可·波罗游记》，向西方人介绍东方文化，介绍中国的政治、经济和文化的发展，极大地丰富了欧洲人的地理知识，打破了宗教的谬论和传统的“天圆地方”说。与此同时，《马可·波罗游记》对15世纪欧洲的航海事业起到了巨大的推动作用。怀揣着《马可·波罗游记》，意大利的哥伦布等航海家、旅行家、探险家经过海上冒险之旅来到了东方的梦幻国度，打破了中世纪西方神权统治的禁锢，极大地促进了中国与欧洲各国的文化交流。

18

However, the Ming rulers began to sleep on the economic and social achievements and the feudal culture starting from late 18th century. China closed its door to the outside world, and turned a blind eye to the Industrial Revolution and capitalist systems that were thriving in Europe and America.

然而，从18世纪末，明朝统治者开始沉醉于经济、社会成就以及封建文化。从此，中国闭关锁国，对发生在欧洲与美洲的工业革命和资本主义制度熟视无睹。

19

It’s a hard lesson for China that the slowdown in economic and social development would invite foreign invasions and conquests. Starting from the Opium War in 1840, the European, American and Japanese imperial powers jointed the forces and defeated the decaying Qing Army, and turned China into a semi-feudal and semi-colonial nation for about one century.

经济和社会发展的落后必然招致外国侵略和征服，这对中国来说是一个惨痛的教训。从1840年鸦片战争开始，欧洲、美国、日本帝国主义列强联合起来，打败了腐朽的清廷军队，使中国成为半封建、半殖民地国家，时间长达一个世纪之久。

20

In 1949, the People’s Republic of China was founded by the Communist Party of China under the leadership of Chairman Mao Zedong. The new China has been implementing the socialist system with the characteristic of political consultation. In a matter of more than 70 years, China managed to rehabilitate the war-torn country, kick-started the rapid national construction, and joined the world of nations on its own feet. Now, China has become the largest trading nation, the second largest economy and the major country in overseas investment.

1949年，在毛泽东主席的领导下，中国共产党建立了中华人民共和国。新中国实行社会主义制度，以政治协商为特色。70多年来，中国从饱受战争蹂躏的国家恢复过来，开始了快速的国家建设，并自主加入了世界民族之林。现在，中国已经成为最大的贸易国家，第二大经济体和主要海外投资国家之一。

Part Two Situational Dialogues

01

A: Hi, Wei Qiang, I've got some good news to share with you.

嗨，魏强，我有好消息要告诉你。

B: Oh, what is it then?

哦，快请讲。

A: I've received the invitation from an institute in China for a symposium on the international cooperation on the economic recovery and growth during the post era of financial crisis in Beijing late October. After the symposium, I'll be giving two lectures at Beijing University. In between, I'm planning to tour the city for two days. I wonder if you could give me some advice.

我已收到中国一家研究机构的邀请，10月下旬参加在北京举办的“后金融危机时期国际合作促进经济复苏和增长研讨会”。研讨会结束后，我将在北京大学开设两个讲座。其间，我计划在这个城市游览两天。不知道你能不能给我一些建议。

B: Sure. During the symposium there, you could sneak out for some night life in Wangfujing Street, where you could rub shoulders with local people and tourists from around the world, and taste authentic local delicacies. In between the lectures, you could visit the Forbidden City where the Ming and Qing Emperors lived and governed and the country. On your same trip, you may choose to visit the Tian'anmen Gate Tower, where you could have a wholesome picture of the Tian'anmen Square. It is surrounded by Chairman Mao's Mausoleum, the Great Hall of the People and the National Museum of China. After that, you could find a nearby restaurant for some authentic local food.

当然。在研讨会期间，你可以找时间去王府井大街感受一下中国的夜生活，在那里你可以与当地人和世界各地的游客摩肩接踵，品尝地道的当地美食。在讲座期间，你可以抽时间参观故宫，那里曾是明清皇帝生活和处理朝政的地方。在北京的旅程期间，你可以择机参观天安门城楼，在那里你可以饱览天安门广场周围的全景，如毛主席纪念堂、人民大会堂和中国国家博物馆。之后，你可以找一家当地餐馆，品尝地道的风味菜肴。

A: Thank you, but what about the Great Wall? I hear it's a must for foreigners.

谢谢，那长城呢？我听说这是外国人必须打卡的景点。

B: Of course. That's what I want to suggest for your second-day tour. The Great Wall is the longest wall in the world. It is about 6000 kilometers long, 7 meters high and 5 meters wide. The Great Wall was built more than 2000 years ago. It was very difficult to build such a great wall without any modern machines and equipment. When you return to the city, you could finish your day with a treat at Quanjude where you could enjoy the real taste of Beijing Roast Duck.

当然啦。这就是我想建议你在第二天进行的游览活动。长城是世界上最长的城墙。它大约6000公里长，7米高，5米宽，始建于2000多年前。在没有任何现代机械设备的情况下，要建造如此宏伟的长城何等困难。返回市区后，您可以在全聚德品尝正宗的北京烤鸭，并以此结束一天的行程。

02

A: Good afternoon, Liang Jun. I'm glad that you could come for the working lunch with me. I need your advice on my term paper about your country. This time, my paper is entitled *the Silk Road I Know of*.
下午好，梁军。很高兴你能来和我一起用工作午餐。有一篇关于贵国的学期论文，我想听取你的建议。这一次，我的论文题目是《我所知道的丝绸之路》。

B: Well, that's a nice topic to write about, but these are the things you need to be aware. First, you need to give some basic information about the ancient silk road, which could be downloaded from the Internet. Nevertheless, I would like to offer my own observations. You wouldn't believe it, but several thousand years ago, the ancient Chinese people and the peoples in the West had already started the barter trade in jade, potteries, tea and silk, which was carried out by the private caravan teams. However, the real trade road that linked the ancient China and the West did not come into being until about 2200 years ago, when Han Emperor Liu Che dispatched Zhang Qian on an official trip to the countries in the West. It is also coincidental that the above ancient trade route did not acquire its proper name until 2000 years later by the German geologist named F. von Richthofen.
嗯，这个主题选得不错，但有几点你需要注意。首先，你需要提供关于古代丝绸之路的基本信息，这些可以在网上找到。不过，我还是想分享一些个人观点。令人难以置信的是，早在几千年前，古代中国人和西方人就已经开始了以玉、陶器、茶叶、丝绸等为载体的易货贸易，这些交易主要由私人商队进行。然而，真正连接古代中国和西方的贸易之路，直到2200年前汉武帝刘彻派遣张骞到西方国家进行正式访问之后方才形成。同样巧合的是，直到2000多年之后，这条古老的贸易路线才被一位名叫李希霍芬的德国地质学家正式命名。

A: Thank you for the additional information, which would ensure the passage of my term paper.
谢谢您提供的补充信息，这将确保我的学期论文顺利通过。

03

A: Today, we are gathering here to discuss a very hot issue, which is how to promote the harmony between modernization and conservation on cultural and historical legacies. In this regard, we've had the pleasure to hear from Mr. Yu Jianping on how China has managed to realize its rapid urbanization while preserving the traditional architectures and historical places. Now, let me use my privilege to ask the first question: How did your government manage to deal with so many inner and outer city walls when they pushed for the urbanization over the past decades?
今天，我们相聚在这里，讨论一个非常热门的话题，那就是如何平衡现代化与文化和历史遗产保护进程。在这方面，我们很高兴听取于建平先生介绍中国是如何在保护传统建筑和历史遗迹的同时实现快速城市化的。现在，请允许我利用特权提第一个问题：在过去的几十年间，中国政府在推进城市化进程的同时，是如何处理那么多内外城墙的？

B: That's a good question. Basically, China's urbanization is a mixture of successes and failures. On the failure side, it was tragic that most ancient city walls were torn down to provide space for city modernization and expansion. On the success side, some cities managed to retain their traditional buildings and street layouts. We've had also some successful stories. The most successful story is Xi'an, which is the provincial capital of Shanxi Province. The municipal government successfully retained the old city walls, which has become a famous attraction for the domestic and overseas tourists, in conjunction with the Terracotta Warriors.

这个问题提得很好。基本上说，中国的城市化既有成就，也有教训。在教训方面，很遗憾，为推进城市现代化和城市扩张，许多古老的城墙被拆除。在成就方面，一些城市设法保留了其传统的建筑和街道布局。我们也有一些成功的案例。其中，最成功的是陕西省西安市。市政府成功地保留了古老的城墙，古城墙与兵马俑一起成为国内外游客参观游览的著名景点。

A: What about the Great Wall?

长城的情况怎么样？

B: Unfortunately, it's also a mixture of successes and failures. For long in past, the Great Wall was left in the wild, which was on the way to decay. However, since 1970s', Mr. Deng Xiaoping, then Chinese leader launched the national campaign to preserve and renovate the Walls in quite a few provinces. As of now, sections of the renovated Great Wall have become the tourist attractions. The central authorities have been using satellite technology to survey the Great Wall from one end and other end, in an effort to draw up a national plan for a long-term renovation.

不幸的是，长城保护也是喜忧参半。在过去很长时间里，长城被遗忘在荒野上，自行走向毁败。然而，20世纪70年代，时任国家领导人邓小平发起了全国性长城保护运动，在相关省份发起了保护和修复长城的工作。到目前为止，部分修复的长城已经成为旅游景点。中央政府正在利用卫星技术从东至西对长城进行勘察，以期制定一项长期修复规划。

04

A: Good evening, Ali. I need your help if you don't mind.

晚上好，阿里。如果你不介意的话，我需要你的帮助。

B: Not at all. Please tell me what I can do for you.

别客气。请告诉我，我能为您做些什么。

A: My wife and I are planning to take a trip to the Middle East. Cairo is the first stop and we will stay there for three days. Please suggest some places for us to visit.

我妻子和我计划去中东旅行。第一站是开罗，我们准备在那里待三天。请给我们推荐一些参观的地方吧。

B: Well, on the first day, you could hire a taxi to do the city tour and enjoy the beauty of the “Mother of the World”. Besides, you could visit the National Museum where you should be able to walk through the 5000 years of Egyptian history in three hours. You can also take a boat trip on the Nile, and admire the beautiful sightseeing. Of course, you should never miss your trip to the Luxor Temple and the Great pyramids.

好的，第一天你可以租一辆车游览城市，享受“世界母亲”的美丽。你可以去参观国家博物馆，在那里你可以在三个小时内浏览埃及5000年的历史。你也可以乘船沿尼罗河旅行，欣赏两岸美丽的风景。当然，你绝对不要错过卢克索神庙和大金字塔。

Part Three　Common Expressions

- The first humans emerged in East Africa around three million years ago, in a mountainous area in today’s Ethiopia. The “Out of Africa” model is currently the most widely favored explanation, accounting for the origins of modern human beings.

  人类的祖先大约在300万年前出现在东非地区，也就是今天埃塞俄比亚的山区。“人类诞生于非洲的理论模型”是当今学术界普遍接受的关于现代人类起源的假说。

- According to the historical records, China remained a global power for more than 1000 years between the Tang Dynasty and Mid Ming Dynasty. At the peak of the Ming Dynasty, the Feudal China realized its rapid economic development and social progress, and witnessed the budding of capitalism, whose annual GDP was standing more than 40% of the gobal in total.

  据历史记载，在唐朝到明朝中期之间的1000多年里，中国一直是世界强国。明朝鼎盛时期，封建制度的中国实现了经济的快速发展和社会的进步，资本主义出现萌芽，年均国内生产总值占全球40%以上。
- Culture is an umbrella term which covers the social behavior and norms found in human societies, as well as the knowledge, beliefs, arts, laws, customs, capabilities, and habits of the individuals in these groups.

  文化是一个包罗万象的术语，包括人类社会流行的行为规范，以及相关社会群体成员共有的知识、信仰、艺术、法律、习俗、能力和习惯等。
- Human advancement began more than 100000 years ago. Chinese ancestors started as hunter-gatherers, living in caves, and migrating endlessly to different places following the changes of weather and migrations of animals. However, this changed around 12000 years ago, when the early tribal people settled down for agricultural activities, giving birth to larger communities and thriving civilizations. As human population and consumption increased, the faster methods of manufacturing and processing skills came into being. Later on, the total dependence on manual labor was assisted by machines, thus ushering in Industrial Revolution.

  人类的进步始于10万年前。中国人的祖先以狩猎采集为生，住在洞穴里，随着天气的变化和动物的迁徙不断变化居住地。然而，大约在12000年前，这一切发生了改变，当早期的部落人类定居下来从事农业活动后，催生了更大的社区和文明的繁荣。随着人口和消费不断增加，更快的制造方法和加工技能应运而生。后来，原先完全依靠体力的劳动得到了机器的帮助，从而迎来了工业革命。

- The Industrial Revolution marked a period of development in the latter half of the 18th century that transformed largely rural, and agricultural societies in Europe and America into industrialized, urban ones. Goods that had once been painstakingly crafted by hand started to be produced in mass quantity by machines in factories, thanks to the introduction of new machines and techniques in textiles, iron making and other industries.
工业革命标志着18世纪下半叶的一个发展时期，欧洲和美国的农业社会在很大程度上转变为工业化的城市社会。由于纺织、炼铁和其他行业中新机器和技术的应用，曾经由工匠精心手工制作的商品开始转为工厂进行机械化批量生产。
- A Swiss historian once pointed out, history is the subject where you cannot begin at the beginning. If we have to do so, we can trace the chain of human descent back to the appearance of vertebrates, or even to the photosynthetic cells which lie at the start of life itself. We can go back further, to almost unimaginable upheavals which formed this planet and even to the origins of the universe. Yet, these are not human “history”.
一位瑞士历史学家曾经指出，历史这个话题你是无法从头说起的。如果非要这样做的话，我们可以把人类的演变追溯到脊椎动物的出现，甚至比它更早的光合细胞，这些细胞正是生命的起源。我们还可以追寻得更远，上溯到形成我们这个星球的几乎不可想象的沧桑巨变，甚至可以追溯到宇宙的起源。然而，这些都不是人类“历史”。
- As a matter of fact, history is the story of mankind, about what it has done, suffered or enjoyed. We all know that dogs and cats do not have histories, but we human beings do. Even when historians write about a natural process beyond human control, such as the ups and downs of climate, or the spread of disease, they do so only because it helps us understand why men and women have lived and died in some ways rather than others.

事实上，历史记录的是人类的故事，其所做的事情，所经受的磨难，或者所享受的幸福。众所周知，狗和猫没有历史，而人类则有之。历史学家之所以记述非人力所能控制的自然现象，如气候的变迁或疾病的传播，仅仅是因为这些自然过程可以帮助我们理解人们为什么会以这样而不是那样的方式生存和死亡。

- The unique human achievement is the remarkable level of activity, creativity and their cumulative capacity to make changes. All animals have ways of living, some complex enough to be called cultures. Human culture alone is progressive even if it has been increasingly built by conscious choices and selections by accident, under the pressure from nature, by the accumulation of experience and knowledge. In short, human beings have always only been able to make their history within limits. Those limits were so broad that it's impossible for us today to identify the first step of the human evolution.

人类的独特成就是其异常强烈的活动能力、创造能力和不断积累经验的能力。所有的动物都有自己的生活方式，有些非常复杂，可以称之为文化。只有人类文化是进步的，它是人类在大自然压力之下，通过有意识的和偶然的选择，以及经验和知识积累而逐渐建立起来的。简而言之，人类一直总是能在一定范围内创造自己的历史。从历史的角度看，这些限制范围如此广泛，乃至今天，我们很难确定人类进化的第一步。

第八章

文化事宜

*

文化是不同国家的人们相互了解、相互联系的平台，但很多人由于文化冲突而无法做到这一点。如今，来自各行各业的人有更多的机会到伙伴国家参与“一带一路”合作建设，这就不得不与东道国伙伴或同事打交道。因此，他们不仅需要了解当地的文化习俗，而且要克服文化冲突，友好相处并开展跨文化的活动，成就自己的辉煌事业，促进“一带一路”合作建设。

Chapter Eight

Cultural Activities

Culture is a platform for peoples from different countries to know one another and relate to one another, but many would fail to do so due to the cultural shock. Nowadays, people from all walks of life have more opportunities to participate in the joint construction of the Belt and Road in the partner countries where they have to live and work with partners or colleagues. Therefore, they not only need to understand the culture and customs of the host country, but also effectively overcome cultural shock, get along and conduct cross-culture activities, and successfully realize their respective career goals and contribute to the joint construction of the Belt and Road.

Part One　Things to Know

01

What is culture? Simply said, it's a set of beliefs, values, behaviors and ways. To be specific, culture includes history, philosophies, traditions, values, religions, arts and crafts, etc. All the cultural customs and traditions are the things we need to know and observe when we live, study, work or do business in any other countries, which would help us succeed in our career.

文化是什么？简单地说，它是信念、价值观、行为方式的集合。具体来说，文化包括历史、哲学、传统、价值观、宗教、工艺美术等。所有的文化习俗和传统都是我们在其他国家生活、学习、工作或做生意期间需要了解和遵守的东西，这有助于我们在事业上取得成功。

02

It's safe to say different cultures have different ways of life, which are neither right or wrong. Nevertheless, without a clear understanding of this point, we may easily fall into the trap of "cultural shock", which is the warm bed for mutual distaste, mutual suspicion and even hostility.

保险地说，不同文化背景的人有着不同的生活方式，这原本无可厚非。然而，如果不能清晰地意识到这一点，我们就很容易陷入“文化冲击”的陷阱，这是滋生相互厌烦、相互猜疑，甚至相互仇视的温床。

03

As one Chinese saying goes, families resemble nuclear countries, and a country is the cluster of millions of families. Without exception, culture starts from the family level, upon which family values would pass down from generation to generation, and become the major building blocks of any culture. They include love, trust, understanding, role model, cohesion, flexibility, economic security and communication, etc.

中国有句古训说，家是最小的国，国是千万家。毫无例外，文化从家庭开始。在这个层面上，家庭价值观世代传承，成为所有文化的主要组成部分。价值观具体包括关爱、信任、理解、行为榜样、凝聚力、灵活性、经济安全、沟通等。

04

There's no doubt that globalization has prompted the human migration from rural areas to the cities, or from a country to anther. Nevertheless, no matter how far away they are from one another, many still depend on their families for love and happiness. They still uphold family traditions and values. And, they still expect to receive the nourishment of kinsmen ship from their families or extended families.

毫无疑问，全球化已经促使人类从农村不断迁移到城市，或从一个国家移民到另外一个国家。然而，无论他们相距多远，仍然期待从家人那里获得关爱和幸福。他们仍然秉承着家族传统和价值观，仍然期望从家庭或大家族中获取血脉滋养。

05

At family level, love is the foundation, upon which members show mutual affection and care for one another. They understand each other, and trust each other. Meanwhile, they receive love and care with no questions asked.

在家庭层面上，关爱是基础。在这个基础上，家庭成员之间相互关爱，相互理解，相互信任。与此同时，他们自然地接受关心与爱护。

06

In a typical family, the elder members are to pass on their values and traditions to the younger members through role model and family rules. At the same time, the younger members are to learn, carry on and carry forward those values and traditions without prejudice or pressure. This is the precondition for the sustainability of the family tree.

在一个典型的家庭中，年长的成员需要通过行为示范和家规把价值观和传统传给年轻的成员。与此同时，年轻的成员要在没有偏见和压力的情况下学习、继承和发扬家族价值观和传统。这是家谱得以延续的先决条件。

07

Furthermore, there must be a sense of cohesion in a closely-knit family. After all, a family is just like a harbor where members could always go back for spiritual console, security, assistance, comfort, enlightenment and advice, with no questions asked. Meanwhile, the elder members would also request everybody to stay together in mind or in kind, and each member is to contribute to the family well-being with no conditions attached.

进而言之，一个和谐的家庭必须有一种凝聚力。家庭就像一个港湾，每个成员可以毫无顾忌地回那里寻求精神慰藉、安全感、帮助、安慰、启迪和建议。与此同时，家庭长辈也会要求大家在精神上或物质上紧密地团结在一起，而每个成员都要无条件地为家庭的幸福作出贡献。

08

In a harmonious family, there must be flexibility to guide the relations among members. In a sustainable family, members are obliged to pitch in for anything important, and address the common problem with one mind.

Meanwhile, cohesive families would facilitate conditions for every member to achieve his or her goals at school, at work, in business or in politics, etc.
一个和谐的家庭必须灵活地处理家庭成员之间的关系。在一个可持续发展的家庭中，每个成员都有义务为任何重要的事情作出贡献，齐心协力解决共同的问题。与此同时，有凝聚力的家庭也将为每个成员在学校、工作、经商或从政等方面实现自己的目标创造条件。

09

It’s always the case that communication remains an important precondition for a sustainable family, within which each member is free to air out his or her feelings without fear or favor. In contrast, when family members can’t speak their minds, they would soon fall into the trap of mutual suspicion, misunderstanding and distrust. Eventually, those abnormal factors might tear the family apart.
通常情况下，沟通是家庭可持续发展的重要先决条件。在这个家庭中，每个成员都可以自由地表达感受，而不用感到恐惧，不用担心亲疏有别。相反，家庭成员如果不能自由表达想法，相互之间就会陷入猜疑、误解和不信任的陷阱之中。最终，这些异常因素有可能导致家庭破裂。

10

Researches show the fundamental reason why Chinese culture has passed down through so many dynasties and emperors without interruption, which has been supported by well-documented written records. And, it is because of that, Chinese people in the 21st century can still read and understand the engravings, written or printed documents, the ancient classic creations left behind by the sages hundreds of years ago, and the famous sayings and philosophical thoughts are still the shinning guiding principles for the Chinese descendants in their career aspirations, career achievements, service to the country and even national governance. As one saying goes, written literature never dies.

研究表明，中华文化经历了这么多代王朝和帝王但却从未间断，究其根本原因，中华文化拥有有案可稽的文字记录。正因为如此，21世纪的华夏子孙依旧能够读懂数千年前各界先贤留下的雕刻、誊抄、书写或刊印的文献资料，古代经典中的格言警句迄今依旧闪烁着时代光芒，依旧成为炎黄子孙安身立命、建功立业、报效国家，乃至治国理政的智慧启迪。正如古训所说，书面文化永不消亡。

11

Confucianism is the most influential spiritual and philosophical elements in traditional Chinese culture. For more than 2000 years, it has been exerting tremendous impacts on how Chinese would live, work or relate with family or social members, on how they would carry out economic and social activities. That's why Confucianism has survived twenty-four dynasties and two republics, but still remains at the heart of the Chinese people and those around the world.

儒家思想是中国文化中最具影响力的精神和哲学元素。2000多年来，它对中国人如何生活、工作、与家庭或社会成员相处，如何开展经济和社会活动产生了巨大的影响。这就是为什么儒家思想在经历了24个朝代和两个共和国之后，依旧是中国人和全球华人的核心思想理念。

12

Over the history, Confucianism has been an important code of conduct, philosophical thinking as well as the guiding principles of personal behaviors, career endeavors, politics or national governance. For example, it strongly appeals for the people to keep learning while pursuing values and virtues. Confucius once said men must obtain qualities of a saint, a scholar and a gentleman.

历史上，儒家思想始终是一种重要的行为准则、哲学思想，同时也是个人行为、事业追求、政治抱负或国家治理的重要指导原则。例如，儒家思想强烈呼吁人们在追求价值和美德的同时要不断学习。孔子曾说，人必须具备圣人、学者和绅士的品质。

13

Over the history, Confucius has never been worshiped as god. Most Chinese people have worshiped him as a cultural sage, and many families honored him as a great teacher and philosopher. For that matter, emperors would build temples in his name.

历史上，孔子从未被当作神而受推崇。大多数中国人把他尊为文化圣人，许多家庭把他尊为伟大的老师和哲学家。因此，帝王会为他修建庙宇。

14

Buddhism values the spiritual and moral progress and awareness of human beings. The philosophy of Buddhists is to discover the truth of life and universe, according to Sakyamuni’s method of enlightenment Buddhism, and then transcend life, death and suffering, forget all earthly desires, and achieve ultimate liberation. Thus, the main feature of Buddhism is to see the nature with a clear mind, and eventually become a Buddha. Buddhism believes that Buddha-nature is human nature, and everyone has innate Bodhi wisdom, so they can all realize their nature and become Buddhas. People fail to become Buddhas simply because of their confusion. Once people forget those earthly desires, they would realize the true wisdom, and receive thorough enlightenment, see the nature with clear conscience, and become a Buddha.

佛教重视人类心灵和道德的进步和觉悟。佛教信徒修习佛教的目的在于依照释迦牟尼所悟到的修行方法，发现生命和宇宙的真谛，超越生死和烦恼，断绝一切红尘，最终得到解脱。佛教的主要特点是明心见性、见性成佛。佛教认为佛性是人的本性，人人都具有先天菩提智慧，因此都能觉悟本性而成佛。众生没有成佛，就是因为迷惑。一旦放弃欲望，真智显露，就能明心见性，内外彻悟，见性成佛。

15

Buddhist culture has become an important part of Chinese culture. Buddhist philosophy contains profound wisdom, and Buddhism and Chinese classical philosophy have jointly promoted the philosophy which puts forward new propositions and new methods. The Buddhist insight on the universe and life, the reflection on human reason and the analysis of concepts had its unique originality. In view of life, Buddhism calls on its followers to connect the liberation of their own life with the salvation of mankind. With its unique way of thinking and life, it has given new inspiration to the spiritual life of the people in the traditional Chinese society. In short, Buddhism has brought a new artistic conception, a new style and a new way of expressions to the Chinese culture, literature and art.

佛教文化已成为中国文化的重要组成部分。佛教哲学蕴藏着深刻的智慧，佛学和中国古典哲学交互影响，推动哲学提出新的命题和新的方法。佛学对宇宙和人生的洞察，对人类理性的映射以及对概念的分析，都有着深刻独到的见解。在人生观上，佛教引导信众把本人的解脱与拯救人类联系起来。它以独特的思想方法和生活方式，给予中国传统社会民众精神生活以新的启发。简言之，佛教为中国文化、文学及艺术带来了新的意境，新的风格和新的表达方式。

16

In traditional Chinese culture, Taoist culture has been alive for five thousand years. Taoism holds that no matter how high one’s spiritual cultivation is, if one cannot put it into practice and serve the public, he cannot be regarded as having acquired “Tao”. In terms of personal life, Taoism believes that the value of life does not lie in personal fame and wealth, but in respecting

“Tao”, valuing morality, and seeking “Tao” as the ultimate goal. Therefore, people must maintain a calm, unsentimental and simple thought, refrain from personal fame, wealth and other things, guard against selfish desires and uneasiness, and always maintain a “contentment” of noble sentiment. In terms of interpersonal relationship, Taoist culture advocates philosophy of saving the people, emphasizing mutual assistance and love among people, “sympathy for people’s evil, joy for people’s good, assistance to people’s urgent need, and saving people from dangers”. Taoism opposes “the strong bullying the weak”, and advocates the principle of equality and fairness. In terms of the relationship between man and nature, Taoism holds fast to the principle of “unity of man and nature”, and believes that man is only a part of nature. It emphasizes the philosophy of “Taoism follows nature”, and advocates that man should cherish nature, get along with it, and act in accordance with the objective laws of nature.

在中华传统文化中，道教文化历史上下传承泱泱五千年。道教主张不论自己的修行有多高，如果不能运用到实践中去，不能服务于人民大众，那么也不能算“得道”。关于人生价值观，道教认为，人生的价值不在于获得个人名利，而在于尊道贵德，唯道是求。为了求道，人们必须保持恬淡无欲、归真返璞的思想，不为个人名利等外物所累，不为私欲而心神不安，始终保持“知足常乐”的高尚情操。关于人际关系，道教文化则主张济世度人，强调人与人之间要互助互爱，要“悯人之凶，乐人之善，济人之急，救人之危”。道教反对“倚强凌弱”，主张人人平等且公平相待。关于人与自然的关系，道教文化则从“天人合一”的思想出发，认为人是自然的一部分，强调“道法自然”，主张人人都要呵护自然，与大自然和谐相处，顺应大自然客观规律办事。

17

Needless to say, since the reform and opening up, China has realized the profound achievements both in terms of economic growth and social progress, and people across China have been enjoying their well-to-do life. Meanwhile, the distribution of social wealth still needs to be improved. There is still competition for economic and social opportunities among people in all walks of life. There are still rooms for further improvement in the provision of public goods. The above factors have jointly created scenarios, under which some people have become nervous, anxious and impetuous, all of which are becoming the invisible “road blocks” for the construction of a harmonious society. Therefore, the Taoist practice of “double cultivation of life” is helpful in easing people’s anxiety, and calming their impetuous mentality. It is because Taoism further encourages people to adhere to the work ethic and wisdom, in order to live and work in peace and contentment, abide by the laws and regulations, and contribute to social harmony.

毋庸讳言，改革开放以来，中国经济发展和社会进步都取得了长足的进步，中国人民过上了小康生活。与此同时，社会财富分配仍需进一步完善。在各行各业的人们之间仍然存在着对经济和社会机会的竞争。公共产品供给还需要进一步改善。以上因素使一些人变得紧张、焦虑和浮躁，这些正成为构建和谐社会的“无形障碍”。因此，道家“双重修身”的实践有助于缓解人们的焦虑，平复人们浮躁的心态。这是因为道教进一步鼓励人民群众坚持勤劳智慧，安居乐业，遵纪守法，为和谐社会作贡献。

18

From the theoretical perspective, Confucius and his disciples lived in an age of great philosophical enlightenment. They strictly adhered to, studied and documented the sayings of Confucius. All these efforts were crystallized in the nine classic Chinese works, called “Four Books and Five Classics”. It is through these works that the philosophical thinking and virtues of traditional Chinese society have remained alive over the past numerous generations.

从理论上讲，孔子及其弟子生活在一个哲学启蒙的时代。他们严格遵循、学习和记录孔子的语录。所有这些共同努力的结晶都体现在中国的九部经典著作中，即“四书五经”。正是通过这些著作，中国传统的哲学思想和美德得以世代传承。

19

In conclusion, Chinese culture is based on three pillars: Taoism, Buddhism and Confucianism. Taoism believes that anything has two bodies, one is divided into two, and the two are combined into one, man and heaven are in one, different paths would lead to the same destination, affinity and tolerance, change and flexibility. The core of Confucianism is the “Doctrine of the Golden Mean”, whose main idea is “benevolence and justice”. It stresses that a gentleman should “sacrifice his life for justice, national affairs with benevolence and filial piety. It emphasizes on the right way to pursue careers”, and advocates self-cultivation. It advocates the harmonious coexistence among families, peoples, communities, nations and countries. Confucianism is centered on the cultivation of personal morality, governance on family affairs and on national affairs. Meanwhile, the core contents of Buddhism are: Precepts, determination and wisdom. It holds the belief that precepts would lead to determination, which would in turn promote wisdom. It also holds that everything is in a state of change. There are no absolute ups and downs, right and wrong, black and white, etc.

综上所述，中国文化有三大支柱：道家、佛家、儒家。道家主张，一物有二体，一物一分为二，二物合一，天人合一，不同的路径殊途同归，亲和宽容，变化灵活。儒家思想的核心是“中庸之道”，其核心思想是“仁义”。它强调君子要舍生取义，以仁孝为政，强调人的择业之道，提倡修养。它提倡家庭、人民、社区、民族、国家之间和谐相处。儒家思想的核心思想是个人道德修养、家事治理和国事治理。同时，佛教的核心内容是：戒、决、智。它相信戒律会带来决心，而决心反过来又会提升智慧。它也相信一切都在变化中。没有绝对的起伏，对与错，黑与白，等等。

20

In general, Chinese culture, which is centered exclusively on the Chinese civilization, nurtured and progressed jointly by the 56 nationalities via their personal, production and social activities. The Chinese culture entails the spirit of the time, inherits the patriotism which up holds the characteristics of not to indulge in material wealth, not to lose dignity in poverty, and not to yield to despotic power, and displays the cultural tenets of "respecting the old, the young and teachers, attaching importance to education and persistence in diligence, thrifty, self-improvement and dedication", etc.

总之，中华文化以中华文明为中心，由56个民族在共同生活、生产和社会活动中孕育而成。中国文化需要时间的精神，继承了爱国主义的特点，不沉溺于物质财富，不因贫困而失去尊严，不屈从于专制权力，并且显示“尊老爱幼、尊师重教、勤奋节俭、自我提升和甘愿奉献”等文化理念。

Part Two　Situational Dialogues

01

A: Hi, Ouyang, nice to see you.

嗨，欧阳，很高兴见到你。

B: Me, too. How have you been doing lately?

我也是。你近来情况怎么样？

A: I'm doing fine, but I've got a problem, and I think I need your help.

我很好，但是我现在遇到一个问题，需要你的帮助。

B: What is it, please?

什么问题，请讲？

A: Well, I've got an opportunity to be on an exchange program at Wuhan University for six months. Nevertheless, I need to polish my Chinese a bit before I go. And, I wonder if you could help me with my oral Chinese. Mind you, you won't have to do it for free, I'll help you with your dissertation. So, it's a swap of service, and I hope you would accept the deal.

哦，我要到武汉大学去参加一个交换项目，为期六个月。不过，在我去之前，我需要好好打磨一下我的中文。我想你能不能帮我提升一下我的口语能力。不过，你不用义务帮我，我会在论文上帮你一把。所以，这是交换服务，我希望你不会介意。

B: You bet, but when shall we start?

没问题，我们什么时候开始？

A: Shall we start from this Friday evening at the coffee bar on our campus?

我们本周五晚上在学校的咖啡吧开始，好吗?

02

A: Good morning, Wu Huaming, have you got anything booked up for this Friday evening?

早上好，吴华明，你星期五晚上有安排吗?

B: Not yet, but have you got anything in mind?

还没有，不过，你有什么想法吗?

A: Well, there will be a transnational cultural gala hosted by the Law School at 19:30. I've already booked the seats for you if you don't mind.

嗯，法学院将主办一场多国文艺晚会，19：30开始。如果你不介意的话，我已经为你订好了座位。

B: That's wonderful. In that case, we could grab a few bites at the cafeteria at about 18:00 before we move to the theatre.

那太好了。这样的话，我们可以在18：00左右去餐厅用餐，然后再去剧院。

A: Good, we'll be meeting there. See you then!

好的，我们在餐厅碰头。到时候见!

03

A: Hi, Du Dawei, I've got a favor to ask you.

你好，杜大伟，我想请你帮个忙。

B: Yes, what is it, please?

没问题，请问我能做什么?

A: Well, on the 18th of this month, there will be our regular country presentation on campus. Dean Smith would like to invite you as the key speaker. The topic for this month is on *China's Status in the Field of 5G Technology and its Ramifications for the Major Economies in the World.*

As usual, you'll give a presentation for twenty minutes, then we'll have questions and answers for forty minutes or so.

哦，这个月18号，我们将在校园进行定期的国家主题演讲会。史密斯院长想让你做主讲人。本月的主题是“中国在5G技术领域的地位及其对世界主要经济体的影响”。像往常一样，你将有一个20分钟的简短陈述，然后我们将有40分钟左右的问答时间。

B: No problem, but do I have to prepare a PPT?

没问题，但是我需要准备一个PPT吗?

A: Of course, I should appreciate it if you could let me have it by 12th at the latest.

当然，如果你最迟在12号之前给我，我会非常感激。

04

A: Hi, Mr. Wang Haiyang, I've got something to discuss with you.

嗨，王海洋先生，我有件事想和你商量。

B: Yes, what can I do for you, Professor Stanton?

是的，我能为您做什么，斯坦顿教授?

A: Sure. This semester, I'm going to teach a course entitled *Oriental Culture*, within which there is a section called China block. I wonder if you would like to be my teaching assistant.

当然。这学期，我要开一门关于《东方文化》的课程，在这门课里有一部分叫作“中国板块”。我想请你做我的助教。

B: I'd love to, but do I have the qualification for the job?

我很愿意，不过，我有资格帮忙吗?

A: Certainly. You would be more than qualified to help out in the course since you're from China. Look, we'll go over the lecture materials together so that you'll know exactly what I'm going to talk about in class, and your obligation is to take some questions from the class. I'm sure you can handle that.

当然。既然你来自中国，你完全有资格在课程中提供帮助。我们会一起准备讲课材料，这样你就清楚地知道我要在课堂上讲些什么，你的职责就是回答一些课堂上的问题。我相信你能搞定。

B: In that case, I'll take your offer, but you've got to tutor me along the way.

那样的话，我接受你的建议，不过，你需要指导我啊。

A: That's a deal.

一言为定。

Part Three Common Expressions

- You must go to the drive-in movie theater once in a while, while you're in my country. It's a continuous show, and for twenty dollars you could enjoy three movies altogether.
  在我国期间，你一定要去一次露天电影院。那里是连续放映，因此，花20美元你就可以一次性观赏到三部电影。
- There is a new play at the Imperial Theater which is about family ties among people in the city of the 21st century. It's a four-act play.
  皇家剧院正在上演一出关于21世纪城市里人们的家庭关系的新戏。这是一出四幕戏。
- I'm a true symphony lover, and I wouldn't miss it for anything.
  我很喜欢交响乐，因此，我是无论如何都要去的。
- It's my first American concert, and I'll just follow you.
  这是我第一次听美国音乐会，我听你的。

- I couldn’t help to tears when I saw so many people died in the tragedy, which reminded me of my life experience at Wenchuan Earthquake.
  目睹那么多的人在灾难中死去，我不禁潸然泪下，这让我想起在汶川地震中的经历。
- A lot of people here love Chinese Gongfu movies, and I am one.
  这里有许多人喜欢中国功夫片，我就是一个。
- Looking back at the history of human cultural development, we can see that human civilization gave birth to human culture on the earth where we live.
  回顾人类文化发展历史，在我们生活的这个地球上，人类文明孕育了人类文化。
- China boasts a written history of more than 5000 years. The Chinese culture is one of the most ancient cultures in the world, during which dynasties and emperors may come and go, but the Chinese culture has been in existence and has been moving forward. What makes it stand out around the world is the written language, which would allow the ancient Chinese philosophy, thoughts, writings, paintings, poems and creations to be transmitted from one generation to the other without interruption.
  中国拥有5000余年有记载的历史。中国文化是世界上最古老的文化之一，朝代和帝王周而复始，但中国文化始终存在并得到发扬光大。毫无疑问，书面语言使中国文化在世界上熠熠生辉，因为，它使得中国古代哲学、思想、著作、绘画、诗歌和手工艺创作代代相传，从不间断。
- Human culture started with family and grew into tribal culture and national culture. Since the industrial revolution, industrialized countries in Europe and the United States have come into being one after the other, and facilitated conditions for the industrial culture to shine brilliantly. Under the role of multinational corporations, industrial culture has always occupied a dominant position in the world culture.

人类文化始于家族，逐次升华为部落文化、民族文化。自工业革命以来，欧美工业化国家相继崛起，并推动各国工业文化大放异彩。在跨国公司作用下，工业文化在世界文化中始终占据主导地位。

- The 21st century is the century during which China will realize the great aspiration of national rejuvenation, and is also the century, during which Chinese culture will demonstrate its glory. Therefore, citizens from all walks of life, who aspire to participate in the joint construction of the Belt and Road, should not only understand the history of Chinese culture, but also that of the world culture.

  21世纪是中华民族实现伟大复兴的世纪，也是中华文化展现辉煌的世纪。凡有志于共建“一带一路”的社会各界人士，不仅要了解中华文化发展史，也需要了解世界文化发展史。

第九章

饮食文化

*

食品是连接不同文化背景和不同时代的人之间的纽带。我们可能都同意，每当我们闻到一些典型菜肴的香味的时候，就会想起我们的童年，或者在其他国家旅行时吃过的菜肴。事实上，我们甚至不用离开餐桌，不同的菜肴就能将我们的思绪带到另一个时空、另一个国家、另一种文化。进而言之，在国际场合，民族食品时常成为跨文化交流的媒介，成为促进相互了解和友谊的平台。

Chapter Nine

Food Culture

*

Food is a great media that connects people across cultures and generations. We may all agree that the moment when we smell some typical food, it would remind us of our childhood, or the dish we had during our trip to some other countries. In fact, food can literally propel our thought to another time, another country and another culture without even leaving the dinner table. Furthermore, on international occasions, national food becomes the natural media for people to carry out cross-culture exchanges, as well as the platform to promote mutual understanding and friendship.

Part One　Things to Know

01

Chinese cuisine is an important part of Chinese culture, which includes cuisines originating from different nationalities across China. The development and the diversity of Chinese food are also representing China's long history. During each dynasty, new recipes were created until the art of food preparation reached its peak during the Qing Dynasty. Now, Chinese cuisine has influenced many other cuisines around the world, with modifications made to cater to the local tastes.

中国菜是中国文化的重要组成部分，中餐涵盖了中国不同民族的菜系。中餐的发展和多样性代表了中国悠久的历史。每一个朝代都有新的食谱涌现，导致中国烹饪艺术在清代达到了顶峰。目前，中国菜已经影响了全球许多国家的餐饮，并通过调整烹饪方式，迎合当地消费者的口味。

02

On international occasions, how to handle food nutrition reflects our life quality. In our daily life, how to eat and how to maintain health relies much on our own basic knowledge on nutrition. In terms of food science, there is no bad food, but the bad combination of food for meals.

在国际场合，如何处理食品营养反映出我们的生活质量。在日常生活中，如何饮食、如何保持身体健康依赖于我们基本的营养知识。从食品科学领域看，没有不好的食物，只有不好的食物搭配。

03

Over the history, wherever people may go or live, they would show their identities through similar food patterns, and the ways they prepare the food. Immigrants from the same country often use food as a media to retain their cultural identity and family bond. Nowadays, friends, partners and peer group friends from the different cultures would bring their native food to social gatherings or parties, which would serve as the best media for connectivity and friendship.

在历史上，无论去哪里或生活在哪里，人们都会通过相似的特色菜肴和烹饪方式展现出身份。来自同一个国家的移民经常把菜肴作为媒介来维系文化身份或家庭纽带。如今，来自不同文化背景的朋友、伙伴和同龄人朋友，通常会携带各自拿手的本民族菜肴参加社交聚会，并使之成为相互沟通和建立友谊的最佳媒介。

04

In the area of food cultural exchanges, people from different countries could easily be identified by the food they eat, and the national cultural characteristics they have. For example, Italians are associated with pizza and pasta. Americans are known for their fast food such as KFC or MacDonald. However, people could literally enjoy different foods from many countries without having to leave their own cities, which shows that the world is increasingly becoming a “global food village”.

在饮食文化交流领域，人们很容易通过饮食习惯和所具有的民族文化特征来识别来自不同国家的人。例如，人们将意大利人与比萨和意大利面条联系在一起。美国人则以他们的快餐而闻名，如肯德基、麦当劳等。然而，人们不需要离开自己的城市，就可以享受到来自不同国家的食物，这表明世界正日益成为一个“全球食品村”。

05

Over the history, people from different historical and cultural backgrounds have developed different ways at the food table. Roughly speaking, out of the seven billion plus people around the world, about one third in the world use chopsticks, the second third use forks and knives, and the remaining third simply use their hands.

历史上，不同历史和文化背景的人们有不同的用餐方式。粗略地说，在全世界70多亿人口中，大约有三分之一的人使用筷子，三分之一的人使用刀叉，剩下的三分之一的人只用手抓饭。

06

Chinese food culture generally presents four characteristics. The first is the “stress on food”. There has been a saying in China since the ancient times that food is the most important thing for the people. People from all nationalities would hold feasts to welcome and farewell one another. People at disputes would hold feasts, in order to tide over the grievance. When people were in distress, they would turn to wine, in order to drown their sorrows. The second is the “stress on body health”. Chinese people attach importance to the health care, and advocate nourishing the “five viscera” with “five grains”. They also pay great attention to various food combination in diet, during which cooking is guided by the theory of *Yin* and *Yang* harmony. The third is “stress for taste”. Chinese people love the “color, aroma, taste and shape” of the on they eat. Dr. Sun Yat-sen once said, “If the food does not taste good, then the cooking is not good.” The fourth is the “stress on sentiment attachment”. Chinese people emphasize emotional communication and advocate a happy and harmonious cultural atmosphere in food-related activities. Of course, they are always plagued by “noisy culture regarding wine drinking”, such as finger guessing games and some other abnormal eating habits.

中国饮食文化一般呈现以下四大特点。其一是“重食”。中国自古有“民以食为天”之说。人际间送往迎来，大多崇尚在饭桌上表达“洗尘”或“饯行”之意；人际间调和矛盾会组织宴请；个人遇到烦心事，往往借酒消愁。其二是“重养”。中国人重视养生之道，主张以“五谷”养“五脏”；中国人在饮食上讲究各种食物搭配，以阴阳调和理论指导烹饪。其三是“重味”。中国人饮食讲究“色、香、味、形”兼而有之。孙中山先生曾经说过，“辨味不精，则烹调之术不妙”。其四是“重情”。中国人在饮食活动中强调情感交流，提倡其乐融融、和谐的文化氛围。当然，人们也始终饱受“喧闹的劝酒文化”，如猜拳游戏和其他某些饮食陋习的困扰。

07

Generally speaking, after the long-term evolution and accumulation, Western food culture has roughly formed the following characteristics. First, it attaches importance to the organic collocation of nutrition. Westerners usually arrange dishes, and cook their food according to the human needs for sugar, fat, protein, vitamins, nutrients and calories, etc. Second, they love the fine selection of dishes. Western cuisine is very careful in selecting materials. For example, in American cuisine, fruits are often used in the dishes, which are salty and sweet. Italian food is famous for pasta, which allows pasta, noodles, flowers to be part of the dishes. Third, Westerners pay attention to seasoning. However, the seasoning they use is different from that of the Chinese food, which covers mainly sour cream, cinnamon leaves, lemon, etc. Fourth, they pay attention to the color of the dishes. They attach importance to the contrast of color, luster and nutritional compatibility, in order to stimulate appetite. Fifth, Western cooking process is rigorous, and pays attention to technological process. There are many ways to cook Western food, which includes frying, braising, roasting, stewing, baking, smoking, grilling and so on. Six, they pay attention to dining utensils. Western food utilizes porcelain tableware, crystal ware, glassware and metal ware which are to attract the eyeballs of the guests with beautiful designing and colors.

概而言之，文化经过长期的演变和积淀，西方饮食文化大致形成了下列饮食文化特色。其一，重视营养有机搭配。西方人通常依据人体对糖类、脂肪、蛋白质、维生素、营养和热量的需求来安排菜肴，并进行烹饪。其二，菜肴选料精细。西餐烹饪在选料上十分精细考究。例如，美国菜肴常用水果作食材，咸里带甜；意大利菜肴则以面食闻名于世，各种面片、面条、面花都能制成美味的佳肴。其三，讲究菜肴调味。然而，西餐烹调所用的调味品与中餐不同，主要有酸奶油、桂叶、柠檬等。其四，注重菜肴色泽。西方人在色泽上讲究颜色搭配、有光泽且有营养，以期刺激食欲。其五，烹调流程严谨。西餐制作注重工艺流程。西餐烹调方法很多，常用的有煎、烩、烤、焖、焗、熏、铁扒等。其六，讲究餐饮器皿。西餐餐具包括陶瓷餐具、水晶餐具、玻璃餐具及各类金属制餐具，以精美的设计和颜色吸引食客的眼球。

08

Deeply influenced by the concept of *Yin-Yang* and Five Elements and Confucian philosophies, Chinese food culture has evolved different schools of food in different regions, shaped colorful cooking methods, and nourished the extensive and profound Chinese food culture. China has a vast territory, abundant food resources, different climate conditions and various customs, which have jointly formed distinctive flavors in the diet.

深受“阴阳五行”理念和儒家思想影响，中国饮食文化在不同地域演变出了不同饮食风尚，塑造了色彩斑斓的中国烹饪技艺，形成了博大精深的饮食文化。中国幅员辽阔、地大物博、气候各异、风俗繁多，因此造就了饮食上多种特色风味。

09

In terms of culinary arts, Chinese people like to add onions, ginger, garlic, vinegar, pepper and other condiments to enhance the taste, kill bacteria, eliminate fat, increase appetite, and help digestion. And the names of Chinese dishes can be both refined and popular. There are dishes named according to the main and supporting ingredients, seasonings or cooking methods. There are also dishes named according to the historical facts, myths and legends, celebrity food interest and dishes image, such as “general crossing the bridge” “lion head” “beggar’s chicken” “dragon and phoenix auspicious” “Dongpo Pork”, and so on. From the perspective of health preservation, Chinese diet culture is closely related to cooking techniques, the health preservation and medical care. Experienced chefs would usually follow the principle of “medicine and food share the same origrn” and “medicine and food share the same root”, and produce a variety of delicacies, by making use of the effective ingredients from certain medicinal materials, in order to benefit from the efficacy of medicinal food.

从烹饪艺术上讲，中国人喜欢添加葱、姜、蒜、醋、辣椒等佐料，以收提升口味、杀灭细菌、消除脂肪、增进食欲、帮助消化之功效。在菜肴命名方式上，中国菜肴的名称可谓出神入化、雅俗共赏。有的菜肴根据主、辅、调料及烹调方法命名，有的根据历史掌故、神话传说、名人食趣、菜肴形象命名，如将军过桥、狮子头、叫花鸡、龙凤呈祥、东坡肉等。从养生角度讲，中国饮食文化和烹饪技术与保健养生理念密切关联。经验丰富的厨师通常依据“医食同源”和“药食同根”等理念，利用部分相关药材中的有效成分烹制各种美味佳肴，以收药膳之功效。

10

Over the history, Westerners stress the concept of rational diet. No matter what color, aroma, taste and shape of a dish may appear, it must focus on nutrition, and everyone must intake enough calories, vitamins and proteins every day. They believe that the main function of diet is to supplement calories and nutrition, and they advocate "large pieces of meat", thus giving birth to dishes such as "pork chop" "steak" "lamb chop" "chicken chop" and "fish chop", etc. Whether at family dinners or at the banquets, guests would be entertained not only with lavish tableware, the professional selection of food materials and detailed service, but also the alignment of forms and colors of each dish. Nevertheless, no matter how luxury the meal is, at each course, chicken is still chicken, and steak is steak. Even if there is any match, it's only the careful arrangement of materials on the same plate, and the tastes of the main components and auxiliary components would remain distinctively apart. For example, a plate of "French lamb chops" is simply a portion of lamb chop with mashed potatoes, boiled green beans and a few slices of tomato.

历史上，西方人讲究理性饮食观念，无论色、香、味、形如何，每道菜一定要保证有营养，每人每天必须摄取足够的热量、维生素和蛋白质。西方人认为，饮食最为主要的功能是补充热量和营养，他们主张“大块吃肉”，因而催生了“猪排”“牛排”“羊排”“鸡排”和“鱼排”等菜肴。无论是在家庭餐桌上，还是在宴席上，招待宾客不仅讲究餐具、用料和服务，而且讲究菜肴原料形与色方面的相互搭配。然而，不管餐饮多么豪华，每道菜肴，鸡排依旧是鸡排，牛排依旧是牛排。纵然有搭配，也只是在盘中进行，主菜和配菜的味道始终分开的。例如，一盘“法式羊排”仅仅是在羊排旁边配上土豆泥、煮青豆和几片番茄。

11

In terms of dietary structure, Chinese people eat more vegetables every day, while Westerners eat more protein. In the kitchen, they prefer vegetable oil, while the Westerners prefer animal oil such as butter. Chinese people generally like soy milk, tofu, bean sprouts and other soy products, while Westerners tend to stay away from all of them. Chinese people like to use

liver, intestines, lungs and other animal offal as food ingredients, while Westerners would rarely touch them. They like the baked food, while Chinese prefer the fried food.
从饮食结构上看，中国人每天进食蔬菜较多，而西方人每天进食蛋白质较多；在厨房里，中国人偏爱植物油，而西方人喜欢动物油，如黄油；中国人普遍喜爱豆浆、豆腐、豆芽等豆制品，而西方人对这些却往往“敬而远之”；中国人爱用肝、肠、肺等动物内脏作食材，西方人则很少用；西方人喜欢烘烤食品，而中国人则偏爱烹炒。

12

In terms of food customs, Chinese and Westerners have both inherited their own food culture, adding their own fast-food cultures. Fast food has become staple course of many family meals because of its convenience and affordability. In terms of festival food customs, Chinese people have evolved each solar term into a corresponding holiday. On every special day, families would cook the corresponding dishes, or make related cakes to celebrate or commemorate the occasion. For example, on the Lantern Festival, families would cook and share glutinous rice balls. People would eat dumplings on the Winter Solstice, and eat moon cakes on the Mid-Autumn Festival, and so on. Meanwhile, the daily food customs of Westerners are mainly based on sandwiches and hamburgers, with beef, mutton, pork and other dishes as the main course. In addition to wine, coffee or tea are essentials at every meal. The festival food custom of Westerners is relatively less dogmatic, and they would not pay much attention to what they should eat. The most favorite holiday for Westerners is Christmas. In terms of life etiquette and custom, Westerners have a strong religious consciousness. When church members or believers attend religious ceremonies, they often hold large-scale buffet functions. On the event site, the hosts or host organization would roast turkey, suckling pigs and other food stuff to express their best wishes to God, relatives and friends, and pray that God would bless peace and tranquility, and wish everyone healthy and happy.

在饮食习俗上，中国人和西方人都在继承传统餐饮文化的基础上，增加了快餐文化。快餐既方便，又经济实惠，因而成为许多家庭餐饮的主打菜肴。在节庆饮食习俗方面，中国人将每个节气都演变成相应的节日。每逢特定节日当天，每个家庭都会烹饪相应的菜肴或制作相关糕点，以示庆祝或纪念。例如，元宵节家家户户会吃汤圆，冬至吃饺子，中秋吃月饼等。西方人的日常饮食主要是以三明治和汉堡为主，配以牛肉、羊肉、猪肉等主菜，除了饮酒之外，咖啡或茶必不可少。西方人的节日饮食风俗相对于中国较少，也没有那么多的讲究。西方人最喜爱的节日是圣诞节。在生活礼仪与习俗方面，西方人的宗教意识比较浓厚。教徒或信众在参加宗教仪式之际，往往举行大型自助餐。在活动现场，主人或主办方以烤火鸡、烤乳猪等食物来表达对上帝的敬意，对亲友及伙伴的美好祝福，祈祷上帝保佑和平与安宁，祝福所有人健康与快乐。

13

Over the history, China has evolved different cooking styles in different places, due to different geographical environments, different climatic conditions, different seasonal products, different cultural traditions and different national customs, interacting and influencing one another. It’s no wonder China has become the “paradise for the gourmets”.

在中国历史上，不同的地理环境、不同的气候条件、不同的季节产物、不同的文化传统以及不同的民族习俗相互作用，相互影响，造就了各地不同的菜肴烹饪风格。难怪中国以“美食家的天堂”闻名于世。

14

Generally speaking, there are four general flavors of the Chinese food, namely “Bashu, Qilu, Huaiyang and Yueh-Min” across China. They are further divided into eight major cuisines, such as Cantonese cuisine, Sichuan

cuisine, Shandong cuisine, Jiangsu cuisine, Zhejiang cuisine, Fujian cuisine, Hunan cuisine and Anhui cuisine.
概而言之，中国全国范围内菜肴现已形成“巴蜀、齐鲁、淮扬、粤闽”四大风味。这些风味可进一步划分为这“八大菜系”：粤菜、川菜、鲁菜、苏菜、浙菜、闽菜、湘菜和徽菜。

15

As early as 2000 years ago, China formed the concept of “medicine and food share the same origin” and “medicine and food share the same root”. According to *Tai Su of Huangdi's Inner Canon*, the food which is eaten by people with an empty is food, meanwhile, it would become medicine when it is eaten by patients”. This is all about the concept of the “medicine and food being homologous”. Historically, for the survival or for the reproduction purposes, Chinese people have been taking food according to different nutritional needs, in an effort to promote inner body metabolism.
早在2000余年前，中国就形成了“医食同源”和“药食同根”的理念。《黄帝内经·太素》中写道：“空腹食之为食物，患者食之为药物”，从而确立了“药食同源”理念。历史上，中国人的祖先为生存或繁衍后代，依据身体不同的营养需要摄取食物，以促进身体的新陈代谢。

16

It's true that the Chinese food culture advocates aesthetics, and stipulates that food image, food environment, food utensils and food color, aroma, taste, name and sound complement one another. In short, most names of the Chinese dishes are literary, exquisite, appealing to both celebrities and ordinary people.
中国饮食文化崇尚美观，强调食物形象、饮食环境、饮食器具和食物的色、香、味、名、音等相得益彰。概而言之，中国菜肴的名称大多注重文学性，精致性，雅俗共赏。

17

Chinese people attach importance to the art of dish arrangement since the ancient time. On formal occasions, chefs would demonstrate their fine textures, unique shapes, elegant and generous utensils, in order to add luster to the dishes, attract the eyeballs of the guests, and boost the appetite of the latter.

中国人自古讲究菜肴摆盘艺术。在正式餐饮场合，厨师往往使用质地精良、造型别致、典雅美观、朴素大方的器皿，以提升菜肴美观度，吸引宾客的眼球，增加后者的食欲。

18

Chinese people pay attention to the dining atmosphere, advocate the relaxing and happy banquet environment, and pursue the artistic beauty of the combination of the two. For example, when weather permits, Chinese people would entertain their guests at the beautiful scenic spots or cozy courtyards.

中国人讲究餐饮氛围，崇尚塑造轻松愉悦的宴饮环境，追求两者结合的艺术美。例如，在天气允许的情况下，中国人喜欢在优美的景点或舒适的庭院中招待宾客。

19

Chinese food culture follows the concept of "spring birth, summer growth, autumn harvest, winter storage", and pursues the tradition of "nourishing the liver in spring, nourishing the heart in summer, nourishing the lung in autumn, and nourishing the kidney in winter" via appropriate diet formations. Meanwhile, Chinese people would adjust their life style according to the different seasons, choose relevant food to eat, and cook the relevant dishes according to different seasons, so as to promote physical health.

中国饮食文化遵循中医关于“春生、夏长、秋收、冬藏”的理念，搭配合适的饮食结构追求“春养肝、夏养心、秋养肺、冬养肾”的传统。同时，中国人按季节不同调节生活方式，选择饮食种类和烹饪菜肴，以收养身健体之功效。

20

In short, Chinese food culture regards *Yin-Yang* and Five Elements as the core philosophy, which is compatible with the concept of traditional Chinese medicine in the health preservation. And, the above food culture passed down from generation to generation, and constantly adapted to the changing world, and displayed the national food aesthetic fashion with Chinese characteristics.
总之，中国饮食文化以“阴阳五行”为核心理念，与中医养生理念相兼容。上述饮食文化代代相传，并不断适应世界变化，展现了具有中国特色的民族饮食审美风尚。

Part Two　Situational Dialogues

01

A: Here we are, Ma Ming, and this is the restaurant I've been telling you about. They serve the best beef steaks here in town, and I often take my family here for a change.
　我们到了，马明，这就是我一直跟你说的那家餐厅。这里供应的牛排是全城最好的，我经常带家人来这里换换口味。

B: This is certainly a beautiful restaurant, with nice decorations and layout.
　这家餐厅的确很漂亮，装饰和布局都很好。

A: You bet. Now, shall we go and sit at a window table so that we could enjoy the nice lakeside views?

你说得对。我们坐在靠窗的桌子好吗，以便欣赏美丽的湖滨风景？

B: Yes, please. I think we're the early birds so we can pick our own seats.

好的，请。我想我们来得真早，所以可以自由选座位。

A: I agree. Now, what shall we have, Ma Ming?

我同意。现在，我们吃点什么，马明？

B: I'd like to try the roast beef this time.

这次我想尝尝烤牛肉。

A: How would you like it done? You could either have it rare or medium rare. Which way would you prefer?

你想要牛排几分熟？你可以点五分熟或七分熟的。你喜欢哪种？

B: I'll have it medium well, please.

我要七分熟的。

02

A: May I take your order now?

您现在可以点菜了吗？

B: Well, I'm just thinking of trying your set meals. I would appreciate it if you could explain the set meals you have here.

嗯，我在想尝尝你们的套餐。请您介绍一下你们提供的套餐，好吗？

A: Sure. Our set meals include appetizer, soup, salad, your choice of the main course, dessert, and coffee or tea to conclude the meal.

当然。套餐包括开胃菜、汤、沙拉，您可以选择主菜、甜点，最后还有咖啡或茶。

B: OK, thanks. I'll have the set meal of beef steak, please, and I'd finish up the meal with coffee, please.

好，谢谢。我要一份牛排套餐，最后请给我上一杯咖啡。

A: Well, please be advised that it would take 25 minutes to prepare the steak. Therefore, could I recommend lobster as the main course?

嗯，请您注意，牛排需要25分钟才能做好。所以，我想为您推荐龙虾作为主菜，可以吗？

B: That’s a good idea. I’ll take your advice, then.

好主意。那就听你的。

03

A: Here comes the fish, and it’s sweet and sour. Shall I help you with it?

鱼来了，是糖醋的。需要我帮你吗？

B: It looks nice, but I don’t eat seafood much. So, could I skip the course?

看起来不错，但是我不怎么吃海鲜。我可以不用这道菜吗？

A: Certainly, but please try some more diced chicken with chili pepper. Since you are not familiar with serving chopsticks, you could use the serving spoon.

当然可以，请多吃点辣子鸡丁。既然你不熟悉使用筷子，你可以使用勺子。

B: Yes, I will, and it’s delicious indeed.

是的，我会的，确实很好吃。

A: Now, here comes the pork. Would you like to try some?

现在，猪肉来了。你想尝尝吗？

B: Yes, please. Pork dishes are my favorite, but I haven’t had the pleasure to try the Chinese style yet. Please give me a small piece to try out.

好的。猪肉是我最喜欢的，但我尚未尝过中式做法。请给我一小块尝尝。

A: Here you are. How do you like it?

给你，味道怎么样？

B: Hmm… it’s very tasty, and I’ll certainly have some more.

嗯……味道很好，我还想再来一点。

04

A: Well, Mr. Wang Dong, how do you like our national food? I'd like to hear your comment on our food and yours.

哦，王东先生，你觉得我们这里的饭菜怎么样？我想听听你对我们两国饭菜的评价。

B: Well, I'm not a food expert, but let me give you my amateur thought. Your national food is a typical Western food. First, the ways you cook the dishes are very different from us. We Chinese tend to use stir-fry and quick-fry methods a lot, while you folks would cook the steamed or boiled dishes. We Chinese would spend much time on cooking, in order to produce the special tastes, while you folks would stress on the nutrition. For that matter, you folks would use lots of fresh vegetables for salad.

嗯，我不是美食专家，我谈谈一个业余者的想法吧。你们国家的菜肴属于典型的西餐。首先，两国厨师烹饪菜肴的方式非常不同。我们中国人多用爆炒和快炒的方法，而你们多用蒸或煮的方法。我们中国人会花很多时间在烹饪上，以便做出独特的味道，而你们西方人则注重营养方面。因此，你们会用很多新鲜的蔬菜做沙拉。

A: Good on you. Let me also contribute a bit more on the differences between Western food and Chinese food. We Westerners would use different tools for different dishes, and would not persuade guests to finish the drink all at once. Rather, we just put the wine glasses and cups in front of the guests who could enjoy soft drink, wine or spirit at their free will. Oh, I almost forgot, we also propose toast in different ways. "*Ganbei*" is the most challenging thing for us Westerners to manage, when we come to your feasts, you know.

很好。我来补充一点西餐和中餐的不同吧。我们会用不同的工具来做不同的菜，我们不会硬性劝说客人一次性喝完杯中酒。相反，我们只是把酒杯和饮料杯放在客人面前，客人可以自由选择任何软饮料、葡萄酒或烈酒。哦，我差点忘了，我们也有不同的祝酒方式。你知道吗，“干杯”是我们这些外国人参加贵国宴会最难应对的挑战。

B: I understand. It’s an outstanding feature of the Chinese wine culture.

我理解。这是中国酒文化的一个重要的特点。

Part Three Common Expressions

- I would like you to try out the authentic Chinese cuisine.
  我想请你尝尝地道的中国风味菜。
- That strawberry muffin looks tempting, but I’m on diet.
  草莓松饼看起来很诱人，但我正在节食。
- I’ll take your advice since you insist, but please have it well done.
  既然你这么客气，我就接受你的建议，但一定要全熟的。
- They say Chinese food and French food are the best in the world, but I would stick to my national food, which is more tasty and easier to prepare. Therefore, I’ll invite you to visit us soon so that you could try some local dishes. And, my wife is good at cooking, you know.
  人们说，中餐和法国餐是世界上堪称最美味的，但是我始终坚守我们的民族餐，它更美味，也更容易准备。因此，我邀请你来我们家做客，让你尝尝当地的菜肴。你知道吗，我妻子擅长烹饪。
- To tell you the truth, my staff members had to work over-time, in order to prepare this buffet dinner. There are fifteen courses altogether. As always, it’s a mixture, half Chinese and half Western, and I’m sure you’ll find something to your taste. Maybe, you could also tell one or two stories on

how those fancy Chinese dishes came about.

实话告诉你，为了准备这次自助晚餐，我的工作人员不得不加班。这次总共有15道菜。和往常一样，这是一种混合菜式，一半中国菜肴，一半西方菜肴，我相信你会找到符合你口味的菜品。也许，你也可以讲一两个关于这些中国菜肴的故事。

- Tonight, we'd like you to try our national food. Maybe you could compare it with yours. This is the best restaurant for our national food, and the chefs here are among the best in the country. They even had the privilege to cook for your national leaders when they were touring the city. I'm sure they should be able to put some smile on your face.

今晚，我们想让你尝尝我们国家的菜肴。也许你可以和你们国家的比比。这是最好的餐厅，这里的厨师是全国最好的。以前贵国领导人在本市参访期间，这些厨师曾有幸为他们提供过服务。因此，我相信他们应该能让你脸上露出笑容。

- Well, today's beef steak is very good, which is our brand dish for years. We've got several chicken dishes if chicken is your favorite. And, we also serve pretty good barbecued mutton here. For your reference, you can have bread, butter, tea or coffee free of charge, but you've got to pay for anything else.

我说，今天的牛排很好，这是我们多年来的招牌菜。如果你喜欢吃鸡肉的话，我们还有几道鸡肉菜。我们这里也有很好的烤羊肉。面包、黄油、茶或咖啡免费供应，但其他东西需要付费。

第十章

饮茶文化

*

我们都知道饮茶是人们聚会的一种方式，是一种可以分享的经历，也是人们相互联系的媒介。同时，茶文化是世界各国人民的活动和仪式的结合，包括茶道、茶德、茶精神、茶联、茶书、茶具、茶谱、茶诗、茶画、茶学、茶传说等。历史上，茶文化是中国文化的重要组成部分，也是我们在家庭或社会活动中经常遇到的话题。

Chapter Ten

Tea Culture

*

We all know that tea is one way to bring people together. It's also a shared experience and a media for people to connect with one another. Meanwhile, tea culture is the combination of activities and ceremonies by the peoples around the world, which includes tea ceremony, tea morality, tea spirit, tea couplet, tea book, tea sets, tea scores, tea poems, tea pictures, tea science, tea legends, etc. In history, tea culture is an important component part of the Chinese culture. Topics regarding to tea is always popular at family or social functions.

Part One　Things to Know

01

Tea, coffee and coco have become three major soft drinks around the world, which are playing important social and commercial functions in many countries. Meanwhile, some countries have evolved their own tea ceremonies, of which afternoon tea has become a custom with a widespread appeal.

茶、咖啡与可可已经成为世界上三大软饮料，并在许多国家发挥着重要的社会和商业功能。与此同时，一些国家逐渐形成了各具特色的茶道。其中，下午茶已成为一种广泛传播的习俗。

02

China is the place where tea was first discovered, cultivated, processed and consumed. Chinese people have a recorded history of tea tree planting, tea processing, tea making, tea serving and tea drinking for more than 3000 years. And, Chinese tea, tea culture and tea ceremonies were introduced to the neighboring countries first, and eventually to the whole world via the trade along ancient silk roads.

中国是最早发现茶叶、种植茶叶、加工和消费茶叶的国家。中国人有文字记录的种茶、采茶、制茶、奉茶和饮茶的历史有3000余年。中国的茶、茶文化和茶道首先传到周边国家，最后，通过古丝绸之路贸易传播到世界各地。

03

In terms of human history, tea is the earliest contribution by the ancient Chinese people to the world. However, at the very beginning, tea was discovered not as a drink, but as part of the food. It did not become the tea we know today until local craftsmen accidentally developed the skill to separate the tea from the food. In general, tea has a taste of cooling, mild bitterness and astringent flavor, which has not only the function of soft drink, but also the component part of the Chinese cuisine as well as part of the traditional medicine.

从人类历史的角度看，茶是古代中国人民对世界做出的最早的贡献。然而，人们最早发现茶，并没有把它作为饮料，而是作为食物的一部分。直到当地的工匠偶然发明了将茶与食物分离的技术，才有了我们今天所知道的茶。一般来说，茶口感清凉、微苦而涩，不仅具有软饮料的功能，而且也是中国烹饪的组成部分，以及传统医药的一部分。

04

Over the history, Chinese tea culture gradually extended to the areas of tea cultivation, tea processing as well as the costumes, tea sets, tea music and tea rituals in the places and around where the tea is prepared and served.

随着历史的发展，中国茶文化逐渐扩展到茶的种植、加工，以及与备茶、奉茶的场所相适应的服饰、茶具、音乐和仪式等方面。

05

China is the birth place of tea, and the world tea culture, the enzyme of human civilization as well as the catalyst for the development of human culture. Starting from China's Qin Dynasty, tea became an important media of the two-way barter trade between the ancient China and countries in the West, in conjunction with silk and porcelain.

中国是茶的发源地，是世界茶文化的发祥地，是人类文明的培养剂，也是人类文化发展的催化剂。从秦朝开始，茶与丝绸、瓷器齐名，成为古代中国与西方国家进行双向易货贸易的重要媒介。

06

However, Chinese tea culture differs from those of many countries in the world, in terms of how to harvest and process the tea, how to prepare and serve it, and how to accept and drink it. Over the history, people across China regarded tea as one of the seven necessities of their daily life, namely "firewood, rice, oil, salt, soy sauce, vinegar and tea". Consequently, tea became an important industry and financial revenue to support the Chinese economy of many dynasties.

然而，中国茶文化与世界上许多国家在茶叶的采集、加工、制作、饮用等方面都有所不同。历史上中国各地民众将茶作为日常生活的七大必需品之一，即“柴米油盐酱醋茶”。因此，茶业逐渐发展为支撑诸多朝代经济的重要产业和财政来源。

07

As is known, tea has been an important part of Chinese cultural tradition. Over the past 4000 years or more, tea production has played an important role in economic development while tea consumption has always remained a necessity of daily life for the Chinese people. It was those activities that have brought the spirit and wisdom of human beings to a higher orbit.

众所周知，茶已经成为中国文化传统的一个重要组成部分。在过去4000余年间，茶业生产推动了经济发展，茶产品的消费已经成为中国人日常生活的一部分。正是那些茶文化活动把人类的精神和智慧推向更高的层面。

08

According to the history, ancient Chinese began to use wild tea leaves as medicine, and the recorded history of tea cultivation can trace back to 1100 years BC. By the Tang and Song Dynasty, the tea culture came into being where many sages developed music and poems with tea as the focal themes. According to incomplete statistics, great sages from those two dynasties composed about 2000 tea-related poems. During the same period, tea drinking ceremonies also helped many people to divert their alcoholic habits to tea drinking habits.

据历史记载，古代中国人就开始用野生茶叶入药，茶叶种植有记录的历史可以追溯到公元前1100年。到了唐宋时期，中国已经形成了茶文化，许多先哲谱写了以茶为主题的音乐和诗歌。据不完全统计，上述两个朝代的文人墨客创作了大约2000首以茶为主题的诗歌。在同一时期，饮茶仪式促使许多人改变饮酒习惯，转而养成饮茶的习惯。

09

More importantly, tea used to play an important part in the ancient Chinese economy. With the permission of the imperial governments, local artisans processed and pressed the black tea into tea bricks, and allowed it to circulate as money in the market. Then, the traders and Western caravans carried the tea bricks back to the countries in the West, where they would be worth as much as gold bars of equal weight.

更重要的是，茶在中国古代经济中曾扮演着重要的角色。在朝廷授权下，当地工匠将红茶加工并压制成茶砖作为货币使之在市场上流通。然后，中国商人和西方商队把这些茶砖运到西方国家，茶叶在那里的市场价值相当于同等重量的金条。

10

It was also during Tang and Song Dynasty that the tea ceremony spread to the neighboring countries, especially Japan. Based on the Chinese rituels, it managed to create its own tea culture. According to one research, Japanese

tea culture came into being during the Heian Period (794-1192).
也是在唐宋时期，茶道传播到周边国家，尤其是日本。在中国茶文化的基础上，日本人形成了具有本国特色的茶道。有研究表明，日本茶道形成于平安时代(794—1192年)。

11

You wouldn't believe it, but there're hundreds of tea products across China. In general, Chinese tea can fall into green tea, black tea, Oolong tea, white tea, yellow tea, scented tea, each of which would have different physical and medical functions.
你可能不会相信，中国各地有成百上千种茶产品。一般来说，中国茶可以分为以下几类：绿茶、红茶、乌龙茶、白茶、黄茶、花茶，其中每一种茶都有不同的生理和医疗功能。

12

Research finds that green tea is processed without being fermented. As a result, both the tea leaves and tea liquid remain greenish in color. Scientists have found that green tea would dispel people's inner body heat, serve as anti-aging agent, suppress bad breath and prevent people from screen radiations, etc. Traditionally, people drink the green tea during the hot season.
研究发现，绿茶在加工过程中不采用发酵工序，因此茶叶和茶水颜色都呈绿色。科学家发现绿茶能帮助人们驱散体热，充当抗老剂，抑制口臭，抵御屏幕辐射等。人们通常在炎热的季节喝绿茶。

13

Black tea is a fermented tea, which is the most popular tea in the world. By the look of it, both the tea leaves and tea liquid are reddish in color. According to the traditional Chinese medicine, black tea is to foster the "*Yangqi*" inside the human body, warm up people's stomach, and is conducive to people's

digestive system. That’s why people tend to drink it during the cold season.
红茶是一种发酵茶，是世界上最受欢迎的茶。从外观上看，茶叶和茶水的颜色都是红色的。根据中医的说法，红茶可滋补体内的“阳气”，温暖人的胃，有利于人们的消化系统。这就是为什么人们通常在寒冷的季节喝红茶。

14

Traditional Chinese medicine believes that tea contains nutrients conductive to people’s health. And, its stimulus ingredients would help people to concentrate more on whatever they do. On top of that, tea helps to reduce thirst, purge toxins from our body, alleviate inflammations, and prevent cardiovascular diseases, etc.
根据中医理论，茶含有营养物质，有助于人体健康。茶碱有助于提高人们的专注力。除此之外，它还能解渴、排除体内毒素、缓解炎症和预防心血管疾病等。

15

Chinese tea culture has its deep roots in the ideological and cultural fertile soil nurtured by Confucianism, Buddhism and Taoism. It absorbs and integrates the essence of the ideological thought of the three religions, and enriches contents of the tea culture. For example, Confucianism believes people should motivate their minds and determination via tea ceremonies, harmonize interpersonal relations, actively integrate into the society, strive to be kind to human beings, to material beings, to the heaven, and to the earth, and contribute to a harmonious world.
中国茶文化植根于儒、释、道三教倡导的思想和文化沃土之中，吸收并融会了三教思想精华，丰富了茶文化的内涵。例如，儒家认为，人们应该通过茶道来激发自己的思想和志向，协调人际关系，积极融入社会，与人为善、与物为善、与天为善、与地为善，为和谐世界作出贡献。

16

Over the history, tea culture has nurtured more and more social functions, which in turn promoted the Chinese culture. In many places across China, tea serves as a popular agent for friendship and acquaintance. For example, on the wedding day, family members would gather to perform the tea ceremony, within which the bride and groom would put on traditional wedding costumes, and serve tea to their parents, parents-in-laws, in order to show love and respect.

历史上，茶文化孕育了越来越多的社会功能，正是这些功能推动了中华文化的发展。在中国的许多地方，茶充当一种友谊和社交活动的流行媒介。例如，在婚礼上，新郎和新娘的家人和亲友会聚集在一起举行茶礼，新娘和新郎身着传统婚礼服，向双方父母敬茶以示爱和尊敬。

17

Currently, tea processing and tea trading have become an important part of international cooperation under the Belt and Road Initiative. Back in China, in various tea producing areas, tourists could watch how tea leaves are picked up and processed, and they even participate in the above activities.

目前，在“一带一路”倡议框架下，茶叶生产和茶叶贸易已成为国际合作的重要组成部分。在中国，在不同的茶叶产地，游客可以现场观看茶叶是如何采摘和加工的，并亲自参与上述活动。

18

In the tea exhibition rooms across the country, the hosts would demonstrate the artistic rituals on how to prepare the tea sets, how to prepare the tea and how to serve it, and how to drink it. Local attendants would wear traditional costumes and the guests could watch the performance and enjoy the tea against the background of traditional Chinese music.

在全国各地的茶艺展厅，主持人向来宾展示如何备茶、泡茶、上茶，以及饮茶的艺术仪式。现场的服务员身着传统的服装，客人可以在传统的中国音乐背景下观看表演，享受杯中茶。

19

Over the years, Chinese scientists and experts are outreaching to the farmers on how to apply new production technologies, and upgrade the traditional ways of tea processing, packaging and marketing, in an effort to increase unit production, raise the product quality, and expand the market share of the end products.

近些年，中国科学家和专家纷纷走向茶农群体，教授他们如何应用茶叶生产技术，改善传统茶叶加工和制作工艺、包装和营销手段，旨在增加单位面积产量，提高产品质量，扩大终端产品的销售。

20

Under the Belt and Road Initiative, China and partner countries have listed the tea industry into the cooperation agenda. Researches find out tea farming does not involve too many high technologies, but could generate more jobs for the local people and help the relevant communities to expedite the process of fighting against poverty, and realize the 2030 Development Goals set by the United Nations.

在“一带一路”倡议下，中国和伙伴国家在茶叶产业上的合作已经提上日程。研究发现，茶业不涉及太多的高科技，但可以为当地人民创造更多就业机会，帮助相关社区加快脱贫致富，实现联合国2030年发展目标。

Part Two　Situational Dialogues

01

A: Thank you very much for the tea, which you've brought all the way from China...Well, since the guests here today know very little about the history of tea in your country, why don't you brief us about the story behind the history? It's the best time for you to do some cultural promotion, you know.

非常感谢您从中国远道带来的茶叶……哦，既然今天在座的客人对贵国的茶叶历史知之甚少，您何不给我们讲一讲这段历史背后的故事呢？这可是您做文化推广的最佳时机。

B: Thank you, Mr. Hoover. To make the story short, China was the first country to discover, plant, process and drink tea. According to the legend, around 2737 BC, the ancient Chinese Emperor Shen Nong was on a country tour with his court officials. It was a hot summer day, and the imperial contingent stopped under the trees for a break. During the break, the royal guards tried to boil some hot water with an open oven. It was coincidental that some dry tree leaves fell down from the tree and into the oven. Then and there, the pure water turned into the brownish liquid. The court officials had a taste first, to make sure it was not poisonous, and found it mysteriously tasty. Then, they presented their newly discovered liquid to the Emperor who had sip of it, paused for a while, and exclaimed it was the most delicious water he had ever had!

谢谢你，胡弗先生。简而言之，中国是最早发现、种植、加工和饮用茶叶的国家。据传，大约公元前2737年，中国古代皇帝神农和他的随行人员进行了一次乡村旅行。那是一个炎热的夏日，皇家队伍决定在树下稍作停留。其间，皇家卫队成员支起大锅烧热水纳凉。巧合的是，一些干树叶从树上掉下来，掉进了锅里。不一会儿，锅里的纯水变成了棕褐色的液体。朝廷官员先尝了尝，以确定锅里的水安全无毒，却发现被树叶染色的水具有一种神秘的口感。于是，他们把新发现的液体呈给皇帝。皇帝尝了一口，停了一会儿，惊叹道，这是他喝过的口感最好的水！

02

A: I hear that tea still remains a mainstream beverage in your country, in spite of the fact that more and more new soft drinks are pouring into the market.

我听说，尽管越来越多的新型软饮料涌入贵国市场，但茶仍然是主流饮料。

B: You're right. Back home, tea is still the regular drink at social functions, get-togethers, or even at the official functions, where colleagues, friends, partners or relatives could carry on their conversations for hours with a cup of tea in hand.

你说得对。在我国，在社交场合、聚会，甚至公务场合，茶仍然是常见饮品。同事、朋友、伙伴或亲戚手里拿着一杯茶可以滔滔不绝地谈上几个小时。

A: I'm just curious, but what accounts for the enduring popularity of tea culture in your country?

我很好奇，是什么原因推动贵国的茶文化如此经久不衰？

B: Well, according to my amateur findings, tea has long been the main refreshing media to the millions of people in my country, and now virtually worldwide. It is scientifically proven that tea is good for meditation and self-reflection, and helps to induce inner body tranquility, even to inspire imaginations.

哦，根据我的业余发现，茶一直是千百万中国人生活中的主要提神剂，现在几乎在全世界都是如此。科学证明，茶有助于冥想和自我反省，促使内心平静，甚至激发想象力。

A: Let me also contribute my humble findings. In China, people firmly believe different tea products would cater to the tastes of the different consumers. For example, the green tea is simple and light, and stands for scholasticism; black tea is mild and reserved, and is regarded as rather ladylike; Oolong tea, which is warm and persistent, is to inspire the instincts for new thinking or new artistic products; while dark tea, with its lingering aftertaste, symbolizes the wisdom of the elderly, so on and so forth.

我也说一下我的拙见。在中国，茶客坚信不同的茶产品可以满足不同消费者的口味。例如，绿茶纯净而清淡，广为学术界人士喜爱；红茶温和且内敛，被称作女士的挚爱，乌龙茶温润而持久，有助于激发创作思维或构思新艺术产品；黑茶回味悠长，象征着长者的智慧，等等。

03

A: I wonder how you folks back home to produce the Oolong tea.

我想了解你们家乡人是怎么生产乌龙茶的。

B: That's a good question, but let me give you my simple understanding of the process. The first step is the cultivation. Tea plants are grown in rows on the tea farms on the mountain slopes, where there is plenty water, sunshine and foggy moisture. The second step is harvesting. Tea leaves for Oolong Tea are typically harvested three to four times a year. The third step is withering. As soon as the tea leaves are picked up, the enzymes inside the tea leaves would immediately start the chemical reactions, thus creating the flavor and aroma profile of the final tea. The fourth step is oxidation, which would cause more chemical reactions within the tea leaves, adding new flavors of the tea. The fifth step is to kill green, which deactivates the enzymes responsible for the oxidation process, thereby stopping the chemical transformation. The sixth step is the process of rolling and drying. After the kill-green process, tea leaves destined to become Oolong Tea are rolled and dried, during which the tea leaves would be rolled into the ball shapes of various sizes. After that, Oolong leaves are roasted repeatedly, which not only removes all the water content, but also “toasts” the leaves to various degrees, transforming the flavor and consistency of the brewed tea.

这个问题提得很好，不过，我只能告诉你我对这个过程粗浅的理解。首先是茶树培植。一排排茶树种植在山坡的茶园里，那里水分、阳光和水汽湿度充足。第二步是采茶。用于生产乌龙茶的茶叶通常每年收获三到四次。第三步是萎雕。新鲜茶叶一旦被摘下，茶叶中的酶就会立即发生化学反应，从而产生出最终产品的味道和香气。第四步是氧化，会在茶叶中引起更多的化学反应，增加茶叶的味道。第五步是杀青，以便使茶叶氧化过程的酶失效，从而停止化学转化。第六步是轧制和干燥过程。经过杀青工序后，将要加工为乌龙茶的茶叶被卷起来晒干，然后被压制成球状。此后，乌龙茶的叶子被反复烘烤，去除所有的水分，经过不同程度上的“烘烤”会在冲泡后形成不同的味道和浓度。

A: Sounds too much complicated for me to understand at the moment, but you’ve inspired my curiosity to go and buy more Oolong tea.

听起来太复杂了，我现在还无法理解，但你确实激发了我的好奇心，让我想多买一些乌龙茶。

B: Please don’t bother. I’ll ask my wife to bring you some when she is visiting with me next month.

不用麻烦了，下个月我太太来探亲时，我会让她带一些给你。

A: That’s very kind of you.

你真是太客气了。

04

A: Well, while we're still on the subject, I'd like to prick your brain a little. Since my country is almost in the same latitude as yours, do you think there might be any chance to start cooperation in the tea industry?

既然我们说到这个问题，我想让您稍微开动一下脑筋。既然我国和贵国几乎在同一纬度上，您认为在茶业方面有没有机会开展合作?

B: Well, great men think alike. Since I came to your country, I have had the opportunity to tour around quite a few places where I did find similar geographical conditions suitable for the development of the tea industry.

哦，英雄所见略同。自从来到贵国，我有机会游览了不少地方，确实发现有些地方地理条件相似，适合发展茶业。

A: Good on you! Nevertheless, how could we initiate the process, please?

太好了！不过，请问我们该如何启动项目合作程序呢?

B: I think we could proceed with the project proposal in two ways. The first one is for you and your partners to approach the Chinese Embassy in your country. Officials there may give you specific advice. The other way is to raise the project proposal to your relevant government ministry which may raise the issue via bilateral consultations or annual dialogues.

我认为，我们可以有两种方法来推进项目计划。第一个是你和你的伙伴去找我国驻贵国的大使馆。那里的官员会给你们具体建议。另一种方式是向贵国相关政府部门提出项目建议书，相关部门可以通过双边磋商或年度对话机制加以推进。

Part Three Common Expressions

- Do you like your tea strong or weak?
  您喜欢浓茶还是淡茶？
- How do you like your tea?
  您觉得茶怎么样？
- I prefer strong tea.
  我喜欢浓茶。
- I would like a cup of green tea.
  我想要一杯绿茶。
- This tea tastes just right.
  这茶浓淡刚好。
- It’s just the right taste.
  茶味道刚好。
- Please be careful. The tea is very hot.
  请小心，这茶很烫。
- I’d like my tea real hot.
  我想要很热的茶。
- I always have black tea in the morning.
  我早上爱喝红茶。
- We have a lot of herbal teas in stock.
  我们这里有很多花茶现货。

- Would you take milk and sugar in your tea?
  您的茶里需要加牛奶和方糖吗?
- We have Japanese tea, English tea and herbal tea. They are listed on our menu.
  我们供应日本茶、英国茶和花茶。茶品清单上都有。
- We'd like a pot of Chinese green tea for two, please.
  请给我们上一壶中国绿茶，供我们俩人饮用。
- We serve iced milk tea and iced pearl tea.
  我们供应冰奶茶和冰珍珠奶茶。
- I'll get a large cup of iced pearl tea.
  我要一大杯冰珍珠奶茶。
- We serve coffee, tea, sandwiches, cakes and cold drinks.
  我们供应咖啡、茶、三明治、糕点和冷饮。
- I will have black tea with lemon and sugar, and a piece of apple pie.
  我想要一杯加柠檬和方糖的红茶，再要一份苹果派。
- This tea smells good. What is it called?
  这种茶味道很好闻。是什么茶?

第十一章

饮酒文化

*

古人云，无酒不成席。在历史上，无论为了生者，还是逝者，无论在公共场合，还是在私人场合，红酒或白酒始终是所有仪式或活动的重要载体。在所有社交场合，与各类酒品相关的内容均构成社会交谈的自然话题。

Chapter Eleven

Wine Culture

*

As one Chinese saying goes, feasts would never do without wine. Over the history, wine and alcohol have been serving as an important media for all ceremonies or activities, either for the living or for the dead, either for public functions or private functions. On all those occasions, wine and spirit would be the natural subjects for social conversations.

Part One　Things to Know

01

China was the first nation to brew the red wine. Over the history, wine is now intimately intertwined with almost every aspect of the Chinese culture. In Chinese, the word for alcohol “jiu” refers to all types of alcoholic beverages, from beers, liquors to grape wines, etc.

中国是第一个酿制红酒的国家。自古以来，酒与中国文化的方方面面都密不可分。在汉语中，“酒”用来指各种酒精饮料，从啤酒、白酒到葡萄酒，等等。

02

Wine is an alcoholic beverage made from grapes. The oldest known possible evidence is that the use of grapes as the wine recipe in conjunction with fermented rice and honey, came into being in China about 9000 years ago. According to the archaeological discovery, inscriptions on bones and tortoise shells as well as bronze inscriptions both preserved the written records of the people in the Shang Dynasty who worshiped their ancestors with wine.

葡萄酒是一种由葡萄制成的酒精饮料。已知的最古老的证据是，大约在9000年前，中国就出现了用葡萄和发酵的大米、蜂蜜来酿造葡萄酒的方式。依据考古发现，甲骨铭文和青铜器铭文中都有关于商代人祭祖和饮酒的文字记载。

03

According to some research findings, yellow Liquor (Huang Jiu) and White Liquor (Bai Jiu) have dominated Chinese wine culture for thousands of years. Rice wine is believed to have first been brewed by Du Kang, the sixth emperor of Xia Dynasty. In 7000 BC to 6600 BC, the local tribes from Jiahu area in the Yellow River Valley began to brew a fermented wine consisting of rice, honey and fruit, and stored it in the earthenware jars.

据研究发现，数千年来，黄酒和白酒一直是中国酒文化的主导。人们认为米酒酿造技术是由夏朝第六代皇帝杜康首先发明的。大约在公元前7000至公元前6600年之间，中国黄河流域的贾湖一带部落人酿造了一种由大米、蜂蜜、葡萄发酵而成的酒，并储存在陶罐中。

04

According to the Western history, wine is a fermented drink, usually made from the grapes. Western scholars believed that it was originated in 6000 BC to 3000 BC between the Nile and the Persian Gulf, in today’s Iran and Georgia. However, it’s still unknown how they brewed the wine.

根据西方历史，葡萄酒是一种发酵饮料，通常由葡萄制成。有学者认为，葡萄酒起源于公元前6000至公元前3000年尼罗河和波斯湾之间，今伊朗和格鲁吉亚境内。然而关于当地人酿制葡萄酒的方法，目前仍不得而知。

05

Over the history, Chinese wine had three important functions: To perform rituals, to dispel inner-body worries and to heal. In general, Chinese wine used to be called rice wine. The main ingredient was rice or some other unknown grains. It was made by steaming the grain, then leaving it to make sugar and ferment, before it was finally filtering out under pressure. The wine was mostly yellow in color, clear and transparent, with no sediments.

历史上，中国酒有三个重要的用途：仪式媒介，消除烦恼和治疗疾病。一般来说，中国酒也叫米酒，主要成分是大米或其他不知名字的谷物。其制作方法是先将谷物蒸熟，然后让其生成糖并发酵，最后在压力下进行过滤。酒体多呈黄色，清澈透明，无沉淀物。

06

In line with the traditional culture, Chinese distilled liquors were consumed together with food. Although China has a history of more than 6000 years in grape farming, and a history of more than 4000 years in wine making, it was until 20th century that Chinese wine was recognized in the West.

依据中国文化传统，中国酿制的蒸馏酒要与食物一起饮用。虽然中国有6000余年的葡萄种植历史和4000余年的葡萄酒酿造历史，但直到20世纪，中国产的葡萄酒才被西方人所认可。

07

Alcohol has long remained the main beverage and main media for human life and culture. The ancient Chinese invented a variety of wines, which were renowned at home and abroad. Now, yellow wine remains one of the oldest wines in the world. During the Shang and Zhou Dynasty, Chinese craftsmen created the fermentation method, and began to brew yellow rice wine in large quantity. Since then, wine has been playing an important role in people’s life, in literary and artistic creation, cultural entertainment, food and cooking, health care and other aspects.

酒一直是人类的主要饮料并且是人类生活与文化的主要媒介。古代中国人发明了各种各样的酒，这些酒在国内外享有盛誉。现在，黄酒仍然是世界上最古老的酒品之一。大约在商周时期，中国人发明了发酵法，并开始大量酿造黄酒。从此，酒一直在人们的生活、文艺创作、文化娱乐、饮食烹饪、保健等方面发挥着重要作用。

08

Over the history, wine was intimately connected with most Chinese men of letters. There were many famous poets or artists who crafted their master pieces when they were propelled by power of excessive alcohol. The famous poet Li Bai of Tang Dynasty was known as the “Immortal of Wine” because of his love for alcohol. Guo Moruo, a modern scholar, compiled statistics about Li’s poems throughout his life, and found 17 percent of them were related to wine drinking.

历史上，酒与大多数中国文人有着密切的联系。中国有许多著名的诗人或艺术家在“醉酒”后创作了他们的作品。唐朝著名诗人李白因对酒的钟爱被称为“酒仙”。现代学者郭沫若统计了李白一生的诗作，发现其中有17%与饮酒相关联。

09

According to the written history, wine was applied by the local doctors both in ancient India and China. In 200 BC, *Huangdi’s Inner Canon*, which was the first ever medical book appeared in China, not only classified the food and vegetables, but also systematically illustrated the application of wine in treating patients, and the prevention of certain illness and pandemics.

根据历史记载，在古印度和中国，医生都曾使用酒治病救人。在公元前200年，中国第一部医学著作《黄帝内经》问世。该书不仅对食物和蔬菜进行了分类，而且还系统地描述了酒在治疗与预防某些疾病和流行病方面的功效。

10

Currently, experts classify the wine in the following ways. First, it’s in accordance with the grape growth source. Second, it’s in line with the color of the grape. Third, it’s according to the grape content in the wine. Forth, it’s by carbon dioxide inside the wine. Fifth, it’s in accordance with the time when the wine is served. Last but not least, it is by grape varieties in the wine.

目前，酿酒业对葡萄酒的分类标准如下。一是根据葡萄的生长来源进行分类。二是依据葡萄的颜色。三是根据葡萄酒中的葡萄含量。四是依据酒中二氧化碳的含量。五是按照上酒的时间。六是根据葡萄酒中所含葡萄的原料品种。

11

From the very beginning, wine and spirit were exclusively the offerings for spiritual purposes, and later on, they became the tribute products to the emperors and the imperial families. Gradually, it was widely consumed by the senior officials and wealthy families, as the capacity to brew wine and alcohol increased year by year. Eventually, they became part of life of the ordinary people across China.

一开始，葡萄酒和烈性酒仅作为宗教活动的祭品，后来成为皇帝和皇室成员的贡品。再后来，随着当地酿酒能力逐渐提高，酒陆续供朝廷官员和豪门广泛消费，最终成为中国普通百姓生活的一部分。

12

Long before Jesus Christ, people in ancient Egypt, India and China had discovered wine had the potentials for spiritual pleasure or inner body stimulation. Famous doctors at various dynasties in the relevant countries wrote many books to praise the virtues of wine, but also cautioned the consumers for moderation. Over the history, the word banquet literally meant alcohol feast. As the Chinese sayings goes, there would be no feasts without wine, wine and cigarettes are the gifts to be shared on all occasions.

早在耶稣基督诞生之前，古埃及、古印度和中国的人们就已经发现葡萄酒具有愉悦精神或刺激感官的潜质。有关国家的历代名医都著书颂扬酒的美德，但同时告诫人们饮酒要有节制。历史上，宴会这个词的字面意思就是酒席。正如中国谚语所说，无酒不成席，烟酒不分家。

13

Traditionally, Chinese people would throw lavish banquets on many occasions. When families had new babies born, they would hold banquets. Families would do the same when their kids were one month old, 100 days old, one year old and at every 10th birthday. When young people got married or when family built up a new house, family members would throw lavish banquets to celebrate. When people should die, family members would hold “white” feasts to wish the dead live in peace in Heaven. Meanwhile, Chinese people would also throw parties to mark the start a business or to celebrate a fortune somewhere and somehow.

按照传统，中国人会在许多场合举办奢华的宴会。每当家里有婴儿出生，家人和亲友会在孩子满月、百天、一岁以及每一个10年的生日时举行酒宴。每当新人喜结良缘或新居落成，家人会举行豪华的宴会来庆祝。每当有人离世，家庭成员也会举行“白色盛宴”，借以祈祷逝者在天堂安息。同时，中国人也会举办聚会庆贺开业或庆贺获得财富。

14

Since the ancient times, Chinese people have evolved the wine culture characteristic of “wine to cure diseases, wine to provide for the aged, and wine to be ritual”. Chinese people have always loved wine, whether they are from the north or south, whether they are men or women, whether they are young or old. From the ancient time to the present day, the significance of wine drinking in China has been far more than physiological consumption, or far more than the gourmet pleasure. On many occasions, it represents a cultural symbol, a cultural consumption, and represents an etiquette, an atmosphere, a kind of interest, a state of mind and a courage to fight on the battle field. From the ancient time, alcohol and artistic creation have forged a close bond. The Dionysian spirit has inspired many celebrities to reach the peak of their literary and artistic creations.

中国人自古探索并形成了以“酒以治病，酒以养老，酒以成礼”为特色的酒文化。中国人历来尚酒，地无分南北，人无分男女老少。从古至今，中国人饮酒的意义远不止生理性消费，远不止口腹之乐；在诸多场合，酒，代表一种文化符号，代表一种文化消费，代表一种礼仪、一种气氛、一种情趣、一种心境和一种拼搏于战场的勇气。从古至今，酒与文化艺术创造结下了不解之缘。酒神精神曾激励诸多名人雅士在文学艺术创作领域达到登峰造极的地步。

15

According to the contemporary medical theory, wine and spirit are closely linked to the blood in our body. The impact of alcohol on our body starts from the moment we take our first sip. We all know that one glass of wine a day may do no harm to our overall health. Nevertheless, when we should fall into the habit, we would find it hard to stop after the first glass, then, the cumulative effects would add up. We also know that our liver is an organ which helps break down and remove harmful substances from our body, including alcohol. However, when we should become alcoholic, excessive wine or alcohol in our body would interfere with the above process, which would increase the risk for chronic liver inflammation and liver disease.

根据当代医学理论，红酒和白酒与我们身体的血液息息相关。酒精对我们身体的影响从我们喝下第一口酒开始。我们都知道，每天一杯葡萄酒对身体健康几无损害。然而，我们养成饮酒习惯之后，会发现喝完第一杯以后则很难停下来，因此，我们体内的酒精就会累积起来。我们也都知道，肝脏是帮助分解和清除酒精等体内有害物质的器官。然而，我们过量饮酒的时候，体内积累的过量酒精会干扰这一过程，从而增加患慢性肝脏疾病的风险。

16

It’s also scientifically proven that too much alcohol in our stomach can cause abnormal activation of digestive enzymes, which is produced by the pancreas. The buildup of the enzyme could lead to inflammation known as pancreas, which could become a long-term condition and cause serious complications. Meanwhile, excessive drinking would affect our long-term memories. It would also reduce our ability to think clearly or make rational decisions. Over time, it would cause our frontal lobe damage, which is responsible for our emotional control, short-term memory and judgement, etc.

科学已证明，我们胃里留存过多的酒精会导致胰腺产生的消化酶异常激活。这些酶的大量积累则可能导致炎症，即胰腺炎，进而可能形成一种长期的状况，最终导致严重的并发症。与此同时，过度饮酒会影响我们大脑的长期记忆能力，并降低我们清晰思考和做出理性判断的能力。随着时间的推移，酗酒会导致我们的大脑额叶受损，额叶是负责我们情绪控制、短期记忆和判断能力的重要器官。

17

Currently, there are three national famous spirits across China, which include Moutai, Wuliangye and Jiannanchun. According to some research findings, the history of Moutai could trace back to China’s Han Dynasty where the smart craftsmen brewed the prototype of Moutai, and it later became the tribute wine to the Han emperors.

目前，中国有三种著名白酒，分别是茅台、五粮液和剑南春。据研究发现，茅台的历史可以追溯到中国汉代。当时的能工巧匠发明、酿造出了茅台原型酒。后来，这种酒成为汉朝帝王的贡酒。

18

In the past, at public or official functions, people would not only attach importance to wine drinking, but also to the rituals. They also largely created many games to go along with drinking sessions, which would involve the knowledge of history, literature, music and poetry. However, those civil rituals are disappearing fast. Instead, people at the table are busy with pure toasts, and play simple finger-guessing games, which would lead to excessive drinking.

历史上，在传统的公务场合，人们不仅重视饮酒，还重视饮酒礼仪。他们创造了许多与饮酒相关的游戏，涉及历史、文学、音乐和诗歌等方面的知识。遗憾的是，这些民间习俗正在迅速消失。人们在餐桌不停地敬酒，划拳劝酒，往往导致过度饮酒。

19

In short, wine culture is an important part of human food culture. From the very beginning, wine became part of the material culture, and gradually evolved into diversified forms in tune with the economic and social development in the relevant countries. Now, wine and spirit have demonstrated spiritual and cultural values. As a spiritual culture, it is embodied in social and political life, literature and art creation, as well as people's attitude towards life, aesthetic taste and other aspects.

总之，酒文化是人类饮食文化的重要组成部分。酒，从一开始就成为物质文化的一部分，并随着相关国家经济和社会的发展逐渐演变成各具特色的酒文化。现在，葡萄酒和烈性酒均展现出精神和文化价值。作为一种精神文化，酒文化体现在社会政治生活、文学艺术创作以及人们对生活的态度和审美情趣等诸多方面。

20

In all cultures, drinks are classified in terms of their social meaning. At the political, social or family functions, every drink would be loaded with a symbolic meaning, and every drink would convey a message. More importantly, spirit and wine are symbolic vehicles for identifying, describing, constructing and manipulating cultural systems, values, interpersonal relationships, behavioral norms, etc.

饮料按照各自社会意义进行分类。在政治、社交或家庭场合，每一杯酒都有其象征意义，每一杯酒都传达着一种信息。更重要的是，酒品作为一种象征性的工具，用于识别、描述、构建和管理特定的文化系统、价值观、人际关系、行为规范，等等。

Part Two　Situational Dialogues

01

A: Well, before we begin the dinner, please allow me to brief you about our customs and traditions regarding the drinks, wine and spirit, which you will find very much different as compared to yours.

在开始宴请之前，请允许我简单介绍一下我们有关的风俗和传统。你们会发现这些与贵国的风俗和传统非常不同。

B: Please go ahead, and I'm all ears.

请讲，我洗耳恭听。

A: To start with, people in my country seldom force guests to take either soft drinks or the strong stuff. We would put glasses and cups for soft drinks, wine and spirit in front of every one at the table. Each one at the table is free to choose whatever to drink during the function. Whatever is decided, the waiters would take the unrelated glasses or cups away. During the function, we may symbolically toast to one another, but never force anyone to *Ganbei*. And, the waiters or hosts would refill the cup or glass when the glass or cup is down to some extent.

首先，我们国家的人很少强迫客人喝软饮料或烈性酒。我们通常在餐桌上的每个人面前放上盛软饮料、葡萄酒和烈酒的玻璃杯和杯子。宴会期间，餐桌上的每个人都可以自由选择喝什么。无论做出什么决定，服务员都会把剩下的杯子拿走。在宴会上，我们会象征性地互相敬酒，但绝不会强迫别人干杯。另外，在座者杯子里的软饮料或酒喝到一定程度之际，服务员或主人会上前续杯。

B: Thank you for the briefing. I'll take your advice.

谢谢你的介绍，我会照你说的做。

02

A: Well, Jean, I know you French folks are pretty good wine drinkers in the world. Since you've regularly traveled back and forth between Paris and Beijing in the wine business, I wonder if you could enlighten us a bit on the differences of the two.

我说，乔恩，我知道你们法国人是世界上很会喝酒的人。另外，由于您经常往返于巴黎和北京之间，做葡萄酒生意，请问您能否给我们讲讲两种葡萄酒的异同。

B: Sure. To put it simply, as a beverage, wine is infiltrated into almost all human activities, and plays an important role in the fields of politics, economy, culture and international exchanges. It is not only an objective material, but also a symbol of a national culture. Having said this, let me come back to your question, the differences between the Chinese and French wine culture could be found in quite a few areas. For your reference, they differ in geographical and climate conditions. They use the best possible raw materials to produce wines with their national characteristics. They both attach importance to the ways and means to brew their wines. They have developed different means to store the wine. They have developed different norms on how to drink and how to toast to the people around. Therefore, people from both countries must learn as much table manners as possible, in order to avoid embarrassments during the cross-cultural activities.

当然。简单地说，葡萄酒作为一种饮料，几乎渗透到人们的一切活动中，在政治、经济、文化、国际交流等领域发挥着重要的作用。它既是一种客观物质，又是一个民族文化的象征。说了这么多，我来回答你的问题，中国和法国的葡萄酒文化在很多方面都存在差异。以下想法供您参考，两国的地理和气候条件各不相同。两国都使用最好的原料来酿造具有民族特色的葡萄酒。两国都重视酿造葡萄酒的方法。两国发明了不同方法来储存葡萄酒。两国制定了不同的饮酒规范，也制定了不同的敬酒规范。因此，我们两国人民必须尽可能多地了解各自的饮酒礼仪，以免在跨文化活动中出洋相。

03

A: Since our last guest has arrived, shall we move on to the table, Mr. Jiang Weidong?

最后一位客人已经到了，我们开始用餐吧，姜卫东先生。

B: After you, please.

您先请。

A: Now, would you please sit by my right-hand side so that we could have some small talk on things of our common interests. By the way, shall we pop open one Moutai since we’re celebrating our joint research project?

现在请您坐在我的右边，以便我们就共同感兴趣的问题交换意见。顺便问一下，为庆贺我们合作的研究项目，我们开一瓶茅台，好吗？

B: Why not? I brought it all the way from China just for this occasion. Now, would you please try it out before I should fill the cup for you?

为什么不呢？我大老远从中国带来的酒，就是为了这一时刻。现在，在给你斟满酒杯之前，请您先品尝一下，好吗？

A: That’s a good idea, but before I do that, may I ask you to tell me and my colleagues something about the spirit so that we could appreciate more about your national drink?

这是个好主意，但在我这么做之前，我能请您给我和我的同事讲讲关于这种酒的故事，好吗？ 这样，我们就能更加欣赏您带来的国酒了。

B: That's my privilege. Back in China, the history about Moutai can trace back to more than 2000 years ago in Han Dynasty. And, it became internationally renowned in 1925 when Moutai won the gold medal at the International Trade Fair in Panama. However, it became world famous when President Nixon visited China in 1972 where the national drink was covered live by the media across the world. To cut the story short, Moutai is distilled from fermented sorghum, wheat and water. The taste of Moutai is very elegant, exquisite, and harmonious, and seldom goes to head. Like other famous spirits such as Cognac and Champagne, Moutai can only be produced in its birthplace. The production of Moutai relies entirely on its unique natural environment and conditions, such as the temperature, moisture, water quality, soil, rainfall, wind force and wind direction, and biological community, etc.

这是我的荣幸。在中国，茅台酒的历史可以追溯到2000多年前的汉代。1925年，茅台酒在巴拿马国际贸易博览会上获得金奖，从此畅销国际市场。然而，1972年时任美国总统尼克松访华期间品尝了茅台酒，上述视频通过卫星传遍了世界各地，茅台酒享誉全球。长话短说，茅台酒由高粱、小麦和水发酵并蒸馏出来。茅台的味道非常优雅、细腻、和谐，很少上头。与其他干邑、香槟等名酒一样，茅台酒只能在其原材料出产地酿制。这种酒的酿制主要仰仗其独特的自然环境和条件，如温度、湿度、水质、土壤、降雨、风力和风向、生物群，等等。

04

A: While we're still on the subject, I would like to prick your brain a little further. I wonder who would like to share with us the story about wine.

既然我们还在谈这个问题，我想考验一下您的智慧。我想知道谁愿意和我们分享关于葡萄酒的故事。

B: Well, since you are all so modest, let me venture to share with you what I know about the history of wine. To be specific, wine and spirit have long been the two great cultural agents for the advancement of human society. It's coincidental that the ancient Egyptians and Chinese began to settle down permanently and gradually developed their agricultural civilizations roughly at the same time. Gradually, those early settlers managed to secure surplus food supply, and developed the skill to produce pottery vessels, which were the two preconditions for the wine culture to take place. In December, 2004, archaeologists unearthed some pottery jars from the Neolithic village in Jiahu, Henan Province of China. They carried out some carbon isotope testing on the organic material remnants in the jars, and found out that the they were a mixture of fermented beverage of rice, honey and fruits of some 9000 years ago. Therefore, we can proudly say that ancient Egypt and China are both the birth places for wine.

好吧，既然你们都这么谦虚，那我冒昧地和你们分享一点关于葡萄酒的历史吧。言归正传，长期以来葡萄酒和烈性酒一直是人类社会进步的两大文化载体。巧合的是，古埃及人和中国人大约在同一时间开始定居并逐渐发展他们的农业文明。后来，各地早期移民逐渐拥有剩余的食物供应，并且发明了陶器器皿制作技术，这些构成了酒文化形成的两个先决条件。2004年12月，考古学家在中国河南省贾湖的新石器时代村落出土了一些陶罐。他们对罐子里残留的有机物质进行了碳元素同位素测试，发现这些残留物是大约9000年前的大米、蜂蜜和水果混合而成的发酵饮料。因此，我们可以自豪地说，古埃及和古代中国都是葡萄酒发源地。

A: That was really a fascinating story. Well, I don't suppose the wine in our cup would be that old, though.

那真是个令人着迷的故事。不过，我不认为我们杯子里的酒会有那么年代久远吧。

B: Of course not. Nevertheless, it is a stock for more than five years old as of now, and it's the standard product for market circulation.

当然不是。不过，这瓶酒已经窖藏了5年以上，5年窖藏是这种酒进入市场流通的基本标准。

Part Three　Common Expressions

- Let's go and grab a beer after work.
  我们下班后去喝杯啤酒吧。
- I don't drink anything with alcohol.
  我不喝任何含酒精的饮料。
- I've quit drinking for a long time. It's the doctor's order.
  我戒酒很长时间了。这是医嘱。
- Please allow me to propose a toast to you with tea.
  请允许我以茶代酒敬您一杯。
- I don't drink. Please forgive me.
  本人不胜酒力，请见谅。
- There will always be a toast to "*ganbei*" at the end of functions, so you should not leave your glass empty.
  在宴会结束时，大家总会敬酒，所以请不要让自己的酒杯空着。
- Whether you are planning a trip to a wine country or attend private or public functions, it pays for you to learn to appreciate wine. First, you

should fill a quarter of the glass with wine, and hold the glass by the stem. Second, you should take a small sniff of the wine right after opening. This is to catch a preliminary sniff of the wine so you can compare its fragrance after swirling. Third, you should tilt the glass and appreciate the color of the wine. Fourth, you should swirl the wine in your glass to let more oxygen mingle with the wine. Fifth, you should take a sip of wine and let it linger in your mouth so that your taste buds could really appreciate the wine. Sixth, you should aspirate the wine after your first taste. With your lips pursed as if you were to whistle, draw some air into your mouth and exhale through your nose, which would allow you to fully appreciate the aftertaste.

无论你计划去葡萄酒之乡旅行，还是出席私人聚会或公共社交活动，你都需要学会鉴赏和品尝葡萄酒。首先，你应该在杯中倒上四分之一的葡萄酒，并抓住杯柄。第二，你应该闻一下杯中的红酒，让你的鼻子首先捕捉葡萄酒的香味。第三，你应该倾斜酒杯，欣赏杯中葡萄酒的颜色。第四，你应轻轻旋转摇晃杯中酒，让更多的氧气与之混合。第五，你每次应该喝上一小口酒，让它在口中徘徊停留，以使你的味蕾真正感觉葡萄酒的奥妙。第六，你应该在第一次品尝后用口鼻吸呼气，噘起你的嘴唇，就像你要吹口哨一样，把一些空气吸入嘴里，然后用鼻子呼出，以便品尝葡萄酒的余味。

- French wine and champagne manufacturers often boast the importance of the geographical environment surrounding the grapes and crops, and the practices which was used to create great wine. The same applies to Moutai. The mountainous town where Moutai is brewed has long, hot summers and comparatively mild winters. Moutai Town rarely suffers from excessive rainfall or strong winds, and instead, it is defined by a warm climate and higher level of humidity, which serves as the warm bed for certain bacteria, a must for the authentic spirit. In addition, the Kweichow Moutai Co, Ltd distillery is located very close to the Chishui River, which supplies the unique source of water for the product.

法国葡萄酒和香槟制造商经常夸耀葡萄和作物周围地理环境的重要性，以及用来制造优质葡萄酒的做法。茅台酒亦然。酿造茅台酒的山区小镇夏季漫长而炎热，冬季相对温和。茅台镇很少有过多的降雨或强风，取而代之的是温暖的气候和较高的湿度，这些微观环境为某些细菌生长提供了温床，而这些特有菌种是酿制真正的茅台的必备要素。此外，贵州茅台酒厂位于赤水河附近，那里的水是酿制茅台的唯一水体。

- Like all spirits, Moutai begins its life as sorghum. Typically, it must be golden in color, with a thin skin covering a plump and hard interior. At the brewery, the process starts with fermentation in conjunction with a starter that contains yeast. The sorghum would undergo the fermentation for seven times before it is relocated to a unique and separate container to produce the pure spirit. During the next step, the spirit is placed in an earthenware jars and stored in the nearby caves for up to four years, which would allow the spirit to breathe within its enclosure and to fully embraced by the bacteria within the enclosed atmosphere. The final and most critical step is blending. The spirit from the earthenware jars at this stage is not yet worthy of carrying the famous Moutai label. Right from there, it requires the attention of master blenders, who will apply finishing touches to the distil the spirit and add depth and balance to the taste.

和所有烈性酒一样，茅台酒的生命始于高粱。一般来说，这种高粱在收割之际必须呈金黄色，薄薄的皮肤覆盖着丰满坚硬的内瓤。在酿酒厂，高粱首先与发酵剂或含有酵母的加速剂一起混合发酵。经过七轮发酵后的高粱会被转移到独特容器中酿制出纯净的酒。接下来，从上述容器中引出的透明的酒被放置在一个个陶罐中，存储在附近的洞穴中长达四年，以使陶罐中的酒液在封闭的环境中呼吸其中充满特有细菌的空气。最后，也是最为关键的一步是勾调。在这个阶段，陶罐里的酒尚不配茅台的名号，仍需要调酒大师精心勾调，以期按照不同年份茅台酒的配方，勾调出味道纯真、色彩透明、滴滴爽口的年份茅台酒。

- In addition, there are three more categories to classify wine, in line with the brewing methods. The first is the brewing wine, which includes sparkling wine and fortified wine. The second is the distilled wine which includes whisky, brandy, vodka, rum and tequila. The third is the liqueur for the medical or health purposes.

  此外，根据制造方法，还有三种方式可对葡萄酒进行分类。第一种是酿制酒，包括起泡酒和强化酒。第二种是蒸馏酒，包括威士忌、白兰地、伏特加、朗姆酒和龙舌兰酒。第三种是用于医疗保健的药酒。

- On behalf of the members of my company, I would like to express our sincere thanks to you and your institute for inviting us to this grand Christmas party. We really enjoyed the delicious food and excellent wine. Also, the music was fantastic. We enjoyed the meeting and chatting with you and your colleagues. As one saying goes, a good beginning is half done. I’m confident, under your guidance, we should complete the joint venture project in time. My colleagues and I are looking forward to having you and your colleagues at our New Year’s Day party this coming 25th. Thank you again for the wonderful party, and we are having a great time. In conclusion, I’d like to invite all of you to join me for a toast.

  To the friendship between our two countries!

  To the successful cooperation between our two companies!

  我谨代表我们公司的全体成员，诚挚感谢贵公司邀请我们参加这次盛大的圣诞晚会。我们真的很享受今晚的美味佳肴和美酒。今晚的音乐也很棒。我们很高兴与您和您的同事们见面并聊天。俗话说，良好的开端是成功的一半。我相信在您的全面指导下，我们一定能如期完成合资项目。我和我的同事非常期待您和您的同事光临我们在本月 25 号的新年晚会。再次感谢贵公司的圣诞聚会，让我们度过了一段美好的时光。最后，请各位和我一起举杯：

  为我们两国的友谊干杯！

  为我们两家公司的成功合作干杯！

第十二章

服饰文化

*

服装和饰品构成界定各国服饰文化的主要标志。我们在各种场合的穿戴，以及我们遵循的着装规范，在很大程度上表明我们属于哪个民族、我们来自哪里。另外，服装、饰品和化妆品则构成不同文化背景的人在社交活动中自然涉及的话题。

Chapter Twelve

Clothing Culture

*

Costumes and ornaments have been the main benchmarks to define clothing culture of the countries around the world. What we wear on various occasions, and what dressing code we adhere to would demonstrate who we are, and where we are from. In addition, clothing, ornaments and cosmetics are the natural topics at social functions for the people from different cultures.

Part One Things to Know

01

From the global perspective, the history of clothing making came into being from about 200000 B.C. to about 30000 B.C. During this vast period, the temperature on earth rose and fell dramatically, creating series of ice ages throughout the northern areas of Europe and Asia, where the early humans lived. However, with their compact, muscular bodies that conserved their body heat, these people managed to adapt to the freezing cold climate of that time. It was their large brains that served them best.

从全球角度看，我们所知道的人类最早制衣的历史可以追溯到大约公元前20万年到公元前3万年之间。在这段漫长的历史时期里，地球表面温度急剧上升和下降，在早期人类居住的欧洲和亚洲的北部地区形成了一系列冰河世纪。然而这些人群结实的肌肉和发达的机体保存了身体的热量，使得他们成功地适应了当时极端寒冷的气候。正是他们硕大的大脑给他们以智慧战胜严寒并生存下来。

02

Under the constant harsh pressures for survival, the early humans learned to make crude but effective tools from the stone. Tools such as spears and axes made the early humans strong hunters who could live on hairy mammoths, bears, deer, musk oxen, and other mammals that shared their environment. At

some point, some smart craftsmen discovered that the thick furry hides from these animals could keep their bodies warm and dry. By and by, they started the history of clothing.
在持续的生存压力下，早期人类学会了用石头制造粗糙但有效的工具。长矛和斧头等工具使早期人类成为强大的猎手，他们以猎杀与他们生活在同一环境中的长毛猛犸象、熊、鹿、麝牛和其他的哺乳动物为生。在某个时期，一些早期聪明的人类偶然发现这些动物身上厚厚的、毛茸茸的皮可以用来保持体温和身体干燥。渐渐地，他们开启了人类服装的历史。

03

It’s still uncertain when people first started wearing clothes. However, anthropologists give estimation that it happened between 50000 to 100000 years ago. The prototype of clothes was initially made from natural elements such as animal skins, grasses and tree leaves. At the very beginning, clothes were simply draped or tied together into one piece to cover the whole body. Later on, when some smart craftsmen learned to make needles out of animal bones, they gradually learned to sew leather pieces into fur garments, and later learned to sew pieces of shells onto the clothes, in order to make their clothing more beautiful.
关于人类从什么时候开始穿着衣服，迄今仍无从考证。但是，人类学家估计这个阶段大约开启于5万到10万年前。最初的衣服由自然界的材料制成，包括动物的毛皮、草和树叶等。初始时，人类的衣服只是简单地搭结在一起的整块批件，用以遮盖人体。后来，聪明的工匠学会了用动物骨头制作针具，继而逐渐学会了如何把皮革片缝成毛皮衣服，并学会将贝壳片缝制在皮衣上，使之更美观。

04

At about 5000 to 4000 BC, cotton growing and silk producing skills came into being in ancient India and ancient China respectively, which gradually

spread to many places around the world. New materials and skills allowed the clothing making to become a special trade, and prepared the ground for the clothing culture to become a reality.
大约在公元前5000年至4000年间，古代印度和中国分别发明了棉花种植和丝绸生产技术，并逐渐传播到世界各地。新材料和新技术使服装成为一种特殊行业，并为衣着文化的形成奠定了基础。

05

It's a consensus in the international clothing industry that the original purpose of clothing for our ancestors was not for warmth or decency, but for beauty and decoration. From then on, early craftsmen gradually renovated the clothing making and turned it into the fashion, which remains the central pillar of the modern-day garment industry in the world.
对于我们的祖先而言，服装最初的用途并非为了保暖和遮羞，而是为了美观和装饰，这一点已成为国际服装界的共识。从那时起，早期的工匠逐渐更新制衣技巧，将其转变成衣着时尚，并成为当今世界服装产业的中心支柱。

06

Over the history, ancestors of Chinese people placed the "clothing" on top of the daily necessities, namely "clothing, food, shelter and means of traveling". With the advancement of national economy and more application of technologies, clothes not only served as the means to cater to the physical needs, but also served as the media of personal beauty, political ranks, public ceremonies and social propriety, etc.
历史上，中国人的先祖将“衣着”放在生活必需品的首位，即“衣、食、住、行”。随着经济和科学技术的不断进步，服装不仅成为人们遮羞避寒的基本手段，而且成为个人美丽、政治地位、公共仪式、社会礼仪的有效载体。

07

Theoretically speaking, by the look of the clothing, we could tell for sure about the people of a particular time. Over the history, each country has developed and maintained its unique clothing culture, under which the styles would display their customs, beliefs, personal tastes, values and social statuses, etc. Indeed, some anthropologists refer to clothes as “the social skin”.

从理论上讲，依据一个人的着装，我们就可以判断这个人是某个特定时代的人。历史上，每个国家都发展并保持了各自独特的服装文化，依据这种文化，服装风格可以展示各民族习俗、信仰、个人品位、价值观和社会地位等。无怪乎，人类学家将服饰称作“社会的皮肤”。

08

Furthermore, clothing is the important heritage of human culture, and is also a sign of social and cultural development stages. In general, clothing is the need of human psychology and physiology, the need of human daily life and the human cultural life adornment. Meanwhile, it is also the protection gear for human production tool, the art of human culture, an important medium of prosperity of the national economy, and an important commodity in the international division of labor.

进而言之，服装是人类文化的重要传承，是社会和文化发展程度的标志。服装是人类心理和生理的需要，是人类文化生活的装饰品。与此同时，服装也是人类生产的防护工具，是人类文化的艺术品，是国民经济繁荣的重要媒介，也是国际劳动力分工的重要商品。

09

The history of Chinese clothing dates back to the prehistoric times. At one archaeological excavation site, scientists found some 10000-year-old artifacts such as sewing needles made of bones, stone beads and shells with holes

bored into them, which indicated that barbaric people had already acquired the prototype skills for clothing making.
中国服装制作历史可以追溯到史前时代。在一个考古发掘现场，科学家们发现了拥有大约10000年历史的手工艺品，如骨缝针、石珠和具有钻孔的贝壳，这表明这个时期的原始中国人已经掌握了初步的制衣技能。

10

Furthermore, Chinese clothing history is both ancient and modern as it varies by different regions and different times, and is constantly enriched by the technological progress in clothing making. Meanwhile, the history of Chinese clothing has also been influenced by foreigners.
进而言之，中国服装的历史是古代与现代的结合，因为在不同的地区，不同的时代，随着民族服装制作技术不断进步，中国服装文化不断得到丰富和发展。与此同时，中国服装文化在不同历史时期也受到国外服饰文化的影响。

11

China has 56 ethnic groups, each of which has its own history. Over the history, smart dress makers (or tailors) from every generation dedicated their life time in the creations of national styles of clothes and costumes, which has successfully transformed the dresses and costumes into an important component part of the Chinese clothing culture.
中国有56个民族，每个民族都有自己的历史。历史上，每一代聪明的服装制作者（裁缝）均致力于创造出民族特色的服装和服饰，并成功地使之成为中国服饰文化的重要组成部分。

12

We all agree that there is no universally accepted dress format. Even in a

country, dresses and costumes would vary drastically in materials, colors and styles, which plays an important role in defining a people or nation from any other peoples or nations.
我们都同意，并不存在全球统一的服装规制。即使在一个国家，服装在材料、颜色和风格上也会有很大的差异。这是一个民族或国家区别于其他民族或国家的重要标志。

13

In line with the international dress code, business casual is a fashion style suitable for a professional setting. It’s a style that is above the jeans but not as conservative as a business suit. To put it in another word, this dress code is meant for an informal atmosphere, because it does not require strict adherence to the formal dress code.
依据国际服饰原则，商务休闲装是一种适合专业场合的时尚服装。这是一种高于牛仔服装但又不像商务套装那么保守的服装风格。换言之，商务休闲装适合不太正式的场合穿着，因为这种情况不严格要求正式着装。

14

On cross-cultural occasions, we need to observe the international dress code, or simply wear the national dress of the host country, in order to show respect for the national culture. The reason is simple, dress code indicates conformity, a sense of belonging as well as a sense of discipline. It can also create an atmosphere of cultural uniformity.
在跨文化活动场合，我们需要遵守国际着装规范，或者干脆就穿东道国的民族服装，以体现对东道国民族文化的尊重。原因很简单，着装规范展示一致性、归属感和纪律意识。它还可以创造一种和谐的文化氛围。

15

Whether at public or social functions, international dress code forms a standard in conformity with a given environment, which is commonly seen in the military, in a school or a company, or in a cultural group. Therefore, we should avoid being under dressed or overdressed at all those functions.

无论是在公共场合还是在社交场合，国际着装规范构成与特定环境相适应的着装标准，如军队、学校、企业或文化团体成员的着装。因此，在上述场合，我们应该避免过于随便或过分张扬。

16

As one saying goes, clothes make the man. In fact, clothes not only "make the man", but also affect their facial features and body outlooks. To be specific, clothing takes the form of non-verbal expressions of each people on social occasions or public functions. Meanwhile, dress code in the workplace conveys a positive image or certain ideals and traditions of a company. At schools, dress code encourage equality among students, to ensure all students would receive equal opportunities in the classroom. Dress codes at public functions would contribute to the atmosphere.

俗话说，人靠衣装，马靠鞍。事实上，衣服不仅"装饰人"，还会影响他们的面部特征和整体外观。具体言之，服装是以个体作为社会交往工具所使用的符号形式。同时，工作场所的着装规范传达了一个公司的积极形象或某些理念和传统。在学校，着装规范鼓励学生之间的平等，确保所有学生在课堂上都有平等的参与机会。公共场合的着装则有助于营造气氛。

17

Furthermore, clothing can also reflect the disciplines and beliefs of different peer groups, ethnic groups, or people of a nation. For example, national leaders would wear national dress on formal occasions. Religious officials and church workers would wear certain uniforms in line with their dress code.

此外，服装还可以反映同龄人、民族或一个国家人们的服饰规范和信仰。例如，国家领导人在正式场合会穿国服。宗教官员和教堂工作人员会穿着符合特定规范服装。

18

Today, there are many materials with which clothes are made. People can purchase clothes made from natural origin materials, like silk, wool, and leather, but may also select one from the man-made fibers extensively used in clothes manufacturing, like nylon, polyester, Lycra and Gore-Tex. With the recent technological advancements, there is great speculation for the future clothes. In fact, the clothing electronics are just around the corner.

今天，制作衣服的材料愈益增多。人们可以选择购买由天然原料制成的衣服，如丝绸、羊毛和皮革等，但也可以从专门制作服装的人造纤维中选择，如尼龙、聚酯、莱卡和戈尔特斯等。随着近来科学技术不断发展，人们对未来服装的发展方向有了更多期待。事实上，服装电子工业正向我们走来。

19

Nowadays, more and more AI and Internet technologies have been applied to the garment industry. People can design their own dresses or outfits for the different occasions on line, and then, let the tailor shop produce their unique product, in order to show their personality.

如今，越来越多的人工智能和互联网技术在服装行业得到应用。人们可依据不同社交场合需要在网上自行设计服装或服饰，并让裁缝店制作出独一无二的产品，以展示个性。

20

Meanwhile, more and more people buy or make clothing that is comfortable and easy to care for. Others would value their outlook of the dresses they purchase. Some others would chase the yearly fashions at whatever the cost.

Still some others would prefer to sacrifice the comfort and body warmth, just to stay in style.

与此同时，越来越多的人追求舒适、容易打理的服装。另一些人则看重所购买衣服的外观。还有一些人则不惜代价追求每年的时尚。更有一些人为了彰显时尚而宁愿牺牲衣服的舒适度和保暖性。

Part Two　Situational Dialogues

01

A: Well, how time flies! Before we know it, you've been with us for three years now, and you must be ready for the farewell banquet hosted by the Dean Leahy, aren't you?

时间过得真快！不知不觉中，你已经和我们在一起三年了，你一定已经准备好参加莱希院长举办的告别宴会了，对吗？

B: Yes, but I'm not sure about the black-tie dress code for the occasion.

是的，但是我不知道在这种场合是否需要穿正式礼服。

A: Listen, these are the things you need to follow. The first thing you need to do is to go and buy a set of tuxedo strictly in line with your measurement. Then, you should select a smart white shirt in high-quality fabric. When you're there at the supermarket, you need to pick up a black bow tie. Mind you, dress shoes are a must. When you want to diversify your outfit, you could consider adding a satin scarf.

听着，以下是你需要做的几件事。第一件事就是去买一套合身的燕尾服。然后，你应该选择一件高档面料的白色衬衫。你还需要去超市选一个黑色的领结。注意，正装鞋是必须的。你如果想让你的礼服与众不同，你可以考虑搭配一条缎面围巾。

B: Sure, I'll take your advice. Nevertheless, I wonder if you could go with me to the store this Saturday morning, and I must count on your help. Look, I will drive over and pick you up at about 9:00, alright?

好的，我会听你的建议。我想知道周六上午你能陪我一起去商店吗，我必须依靠你的帮助。你看，我周六上午9点左右开车去接你，可以吗？

A: That's a deal, and I'll be expecting you on Saturday morning.

一言为定。周六上午我等你。

02

A: Hi, Liu Na, can I ask a favor of you?

嗨，刘娜，我能请你帮个忙吗？

B: Sure, what can I do for you, please?

当然可以，我能为你做什么？

A: Well, I have received the full scholarship to study at Xi'an Jiaotong University for three years, and my wife is going with me, too. I know it would be nice to buy one or two traditional suits or dresses. Now, could you give me some idea?

我获得了全额奖学金到西安交通大学学习三年，我妻子也将和我一起去。我想最好买一两套传统套装或裙子。现在，你能给我一些建议吗？

B: You could pick up a Tang suit for you and one or two "Qipao" for your wife. However, you don't have to get them here in your country, and I bet they sell the same stuff at a higher unit price. When you are at the university, you could go to the right place where you could have the measurement done, in order to pick up the right size, style and color.

你可以给自己买一件唐装，给你太太买一两件旗袍。然而，你不一定要在你们国家买，同样产品，这里单价要高得多。你可以在抵达中国后到服装店现场测量尺寸，以便买到大小、款式和颜色都合适的服装。

A: Thank you for your advice.

谢谢你的建议。

03

A: Hi, Liu Na, have you received the invitation for the New Year party yet?

嗨，刘娜，你已经收到新年宴会的邀请了吗？

B: Yes, I have, but I'm not sure about the dress code for the occasion. Since it's my first time to be overseas, I want you to give me some advice, please.

收到了，但我不太清楚着装要求。由于这是我第一次出国，我想请你给我一些建议。

A: Sure. Basically, you need to follow these principles. First, you need to wear a well-fitting pants in neutral colors. Black is a favorite color and it can be paired with any top. Second, you need to have a tailored blazer, which would make you look very nice. Third, you need to wear a short shirt which is well pressed. Fourth, you should wear casual tops with matching colors. Last but not least, you should wear court shoes, not sandals.

当然。基本上你需要遵循这些原则。首先，你需要穿一条合身的中性颜色的裤子。黑色是最受欢迎的颜色，以便与任何上衣搭配。其次，你要穿着一件剪裁合身的西装，这会让你显得非常精神。第三，你需要穿一件熨烫平整的短衬衫。第四，你应该穿颜色搭配的休闲上衣。最后，你应该穿着正装的皮鞋，而不是凉鞋。

B: Thank you for your advice. Now, I know what to do now.

谢谢你的建议。现在，我知道该怎么做了。

A: Good, see you at the party.
那好，晚会上见。

04

A: Good morning, Mr. Jiang Jianwei. How do you like your life here in my country so far?
早上好，姜建伟先生。到目前为止，你在我的国家生活得怎么样？

B: Well, I'm pretty much settled down now, and I'm ready for my portfolio at the office. Nevertheless, I need to seek your advice for my daily business attire, please.
哦，我差不多已经安定下来了，我已经准备好在办公室上班了。不过，关于日常商务着装，我想征求你的意见。

A: That's a good question. Well, we do have a sort of dress code for the office attire. Here are some points for your reference. During the working hours, you should wear suit and tucked in shirt, but with no tie. You should not wear jeans unless you manager gives you the OK. You should never wear T-shirts at the office. And, no polos, either. You should not wear sneakers or sandals at all. You should not wear casual boots, but dress boots are okay. When you stick to these rules, and you'll be fine. Mind you, you should watch how your colleagues would wear, and just follow the suit, to be on the safe side.
这个问题问得好。我们这里对办公室着装确实有一些规定。以下是你需要注意的事项。在上班期间，你应该穿西装和衬衫，但不需打领带。除非经理同意，否则你不应该穿牛仔裤。你不应该在办公室穿T恤，也不能穿运动衣。你不应该穿运动鞋或凉鞋。你不应该穿休闲靴子，而应穿正装靴。只要你遵守这些规则，你就会没事的。顺便提醒你，为了安全起见，你应该留意同事们在办公室的穿着，然后照着他们做就行了。

B: Thanks a lot for your advice.
非常感谢你的建议。

Part Three　Common Expressions

- It's your day, so you need to put on the best you have.
  今天是你的重要日子，你应当穿上最帅气的衣服。
- You seem to have put too many colors on you tonight.
  今晚你这身打扮色彩似乎多了一点。
- When we're living, working, studying, visiting or doing business overseas, we must observe the international dress code. The first is the white-tie dress code. This dress code is the most formal of all dress codes, which is commonly seen at royal or national ceremonies, international award shows, ball dancing, etc. On these occasions, men should wear a tailcoat, white vest, white shirt, and white bow tie. Meanwhile, women should wear formal long floor-length or cocktail length gowns with elaborate hairdressing and matching jewelry.
  我们在国外生活、工作、学习、访问或做生意期间，必须遵守国际着装规范。首先是白领结着装规范。这是所有着装规范中最正式的，常见于皇家或国家庆典、国际颁奖典礼、舞会等场合。在这些场合，男士应穿燕尾服、白背心、白衬衫，佩戴白色领结。与此同时，女性应该穿着及地长裙或酒会礼服，并搭配精致的发型和首饰。
- The second is the black-tie code. This is a formal dress code usually seen in formal evening functions or at weddings. On these occasions, men are to wear formal clothing such as tuxedo suits, with white shirt, black tie,

and women are to wear formal long floor-length or cocktail length gowns, usually in black color.

第二个是黑领结着装礼节。这是一种正式的着装要求，通常出现在正式的晚宴或婚礼上。在这种场合，男士应穿正式服装，如无尾晚礼服、白衬衫、黑领结；女士则应穿正式的及地长裙或酒会礼服，颜色通常为黑色。

- The third is creative black-tie dress code. Men who are attending creative black-tie functions are expected to wear a tuxedo with matching trousers to maintain a formal sense. Creativity is displayed through color choice, patterns and accessories. For example, a creative black-tie event with a cowboy theme may inspire men to combine a tuxedo with a bolo tie, a bright-colored vest or even a Stetson hat.

  第三是创意的正装着装规范。参加创意正装活动的男士应穿燕尾服外套，搭配长裤，以保持正式的感觉。通过色彩选择、图案和配饰来体现创意。例如，参加有创意的牛仔主题的正装活动需要着燕尾服，搭配波洛领带、亮色背心，甚至佩戴斯泰森帽子。

- Like their male counterparts, female guests should follow the normal dress code of creative black-tie outfits. Evening gowns and cocktail dress are expected, but creativity can be showcased through fun and trendy accessories and jewelry such as earrings, bracelets and brooches, etc. For a winter holiday event, women should wear formal regalia with a red and green colored, Christmas-inspired necklace. For a summer formal event, a fresh flower tucked behind an ear is just the right outfit.

  与男性一样，女性嘉宾也应遵循正常黑领结活动的着装规范。晚礼服和鸡尾酒会礼服符合服饰规范，但创意也可以通过有趣时髦的配饰和珠宝来展示，比如耳环、手镯和胸针。在冬季假日活动中，女性可以搭配一条红绿相间的圣诞风格项链来凸显她们的正式服饰。在夏季的正式场合，在耳后插一朵鲜花可以为整件衣服增添恰到好处的创意。

- The fourth is the business formal dress code. This code requires men to wear business suits which include a shirt, vest, tie and pants and requires women to wear formal business suits with dress skirts or a tailored dress.
  第四是商务正式着装规范。这种着装要求男士穿商务套装，包括衬衫、背心、领带和裤子，女士要穿正式的商务套装，如裙装或定制的连衣裙。
- The fifth is the semi-formal dress code. This is dress code requires men to wear a dark suit and women to wear cocktail length gowns.
  第五是半正式的着装要求。这种着装要求稍低于正式服饰：男士要求穿深色西装，女士应穿酒会礼服。
- The sixth is the business casual. This dress code requires men to wear a semi-formal clothing like casual slacks with button-down shirts and no tie. Meanwhile, women are supposed to wear semi-formal clothing, which includes dresses, pants and blouses and skirts. No jeans would be allowed.
  第六是商务休闲装。这种着装要求男士穿半正式服装，如休闲裤、带领扣的衬衫，无需打领带。与此同时，女性应该穿半正式服装，包括连衣裙、裤子、衬衫和半长裙。不能穿牛仔裤。

第十三章

体育活动

*

如今，体育不再是运动员的专有权利，我们普通人也将体育作为日常身体锻炼的一部分。有大夫说，体育运动有助于增强我们的体质，活跃我们的思想，开拓我们的视野，提高我们的精神境界。另外，通过经常性体育锻炼，我们的血液得到净化，我们的思想变得活跃，更容易接受新思想，助力我们在人生中前行。

Chapter Thirteen

Sports and Hobbies

*

Nowadays, sports are no longer the exclusive rights for the athletes, we ordinary people also take sports as a part of the daily physical exercises. Doctors say that sports help build up our body, refresh our mind, enlighten our vision, and develop our moral characters. Furthermore, through regular exercising, our blood is purified and our mind becomes more apt to receive new ideas, so that we could concentrate more on whatever we do.

Part One Things to Know

01

Nowadays, sports are becoming part of our life, and we all go for sports, one way or the other. Some take sports as a career, while many others regard them as fun activities. Still some others regard sports activities as the ways and means to associate with their peer group, friends or business partners. As one commercial saying goes, golf courts are the best possible places to seal deals.

如今，体育运动正成为我们生活的一部分，我们可以通过这样或那样的方式做运动。有些人把运动作为一种职业，而许多人则把体育运动当成乐趣。还有一些人则将体育活动看作是与同龄人、朋友或商业伙伴交往的方式。正如商界名言所说，高尔夫球场是达成交易的最佳场所。

02

We are living in a commercial society, and we all expect a healthy life because it is the key to all happiness. It's only through physical and mental exercises that we can expect to enjoy our life, and to be successful in our career. Research finds out that active exercises would help us get rid of excess fat and calories in our body. They would also help us improve the quality of our sleep.

我们生活在商业化的社会，都期待享有健康的生活，因为这是通向所有幸福的关键。只有实现身心健康，我们才能享受健康的生活，才能在职业生涯中取得成功。研究发现，积极的体育活动可以帮助我们消除堆积在身体里的多余脂肪和卡路里。运动有助于改善我们的睡眠。

03

Doctors say sports would not only promote our health, but also facilitate the conditions for us to be versatile in our life. Research shows sports would open our mind for new things at all stages of our life. They would make us more optimistic in our life and for the future. They would help build up our body, and boost our mental health. And, they would also help strengthen our sense of discipline, and help build up team spirit and brotherhood.

有医生说，运动不仅有助于促进身体健康，而且还有助于我们在生活中成为多才多艺的人。研究表明，体育运动有助于我们在人生各个阶段保持对新生事物的敏锐性；有助于我们对生活和未来保持乐观的态度；有助于我们增强体质，促进心理健康。与此同时，体育运动有助于我们增强纪律意识，发扬团队精神，增进兄弟情谊。

04

As one saying goes, “Health is wealth.” A healthy body and mind can give us physical and spiritual stimulation to move forward in whatever we do. From the perspective of physical science, sports play a vital role in the formation of our body muscles. There is no better way to keep our body healthy and active, to boost our morale in the battle for life, or to power our mind for success.

俗话说：“健康就是财富。”健康的身体和心理能激发我们身体和精神上的活力，让我们无论做什么都能勇往直前。从体育科学角度讲，运动对人体肌肉的形成起着至关重要的作用。没有什么更好的方式可以让我们的身体保持健康和积极，鼓舞我们与生命斗争的士气，或增强我们取得成功的心态。

05

Doctors say we should promote health throughout our life. As kids, we should grow up in a playful and cheerful environment. As grown-ups, we should do sports to sharpen our mind and build up our body strength and muscles. As the elderly, we should do sports to keep fit and prevent senility. Therefore, doing sports is a lifetime thing.

有医生说，我们需要终生促进身体健康。在孩提时代，我们应当在轻松愉悦的环境中成长。作为成年人，我们应当通过体育锻炼来磨砺我们的思想，增强身体力量和肌肉。作为老年人，我们应当通过体育运动保持健康，减缓衰老。因此，体育运动是一辈子的事。

06

It's true that sports are an eternal source of joy. This character is the key to our success in the struggle for life and careers. Technically speaking, training in sports is a balancing act for people. There is always competition in our life, which resembles the games we play. On many occasions, we should expect the joy of victory, disappointment of defeat, and the ability to accept it with a calm heart.

是的，运动是无尽快乐的永恒源泉。这一品质是我们争取生活和事业成功的关键。从技术上讲，体育训练对人们来说是一种平衡的行为。我们的生活中总会有竞争，就像我们玩的游戏一样。很多时候，我们可能期待胜利的喜悦，也可能陷入失败的失望，但必须能以平静的心态接受比赛的结果。

07

It's true that sports exercise are not just for the win, but the process of mental and physical exercise. To be specific, physical exercise is conducive to bodybuilding, weight loss, lowering blood sugar and blood lipids, the quality of life and longevity. At the same time, physical exercise also helps strengthen

our bone structure and improve our heart and lung functions.
是的，体育锻炼不仅仅是为了胜利，更是为了磨炼身心意志。具体而言，体育锻炼有助于健美、减肥，有利于降血糖、降血脂，有利于提高生活质量，延长寿命。同时，体育锻炼也有助于强化我们的骨骼，并且增加心肺功能。

08

It’s true that our hearts have to work day and night throughout our life. Therefore, we need to get some exercise, in order to stay healthy. You would not believe it, but our hearts pump more blood during the sports activities. Therefore, they would help lower high blood pressure, and balance our cholesterol level. Blood circulation in our body is relatively high during the play, so the nutrients could have easier access to all parts of the body. Moreover, our white blood cells would also increase their activity which would improve our immunity system.
是的，我们一生中心脏需要日夜工作，因而我们需要通过体育运动保持健康。你可能不会相信，在体育活动期间，我们的心脏会泵出更多的血。因此，体育活动有助于我们降低高血压，控制胆固醇水平。在运动过程中，我们体内的血液加速循环，可以将营养更有效地输送到我们身体的各个部位。此外，我们的白细胞运动也会有所增加，因而有助于增强免疫力。

09

It’s true that people around 40 are usually at the peak of their career, and have to be busy at the office or in business. They have to address tough problems and fence off tough challenges during the day, and they have to attend social or private functions in the evening. As a result, they may find it too much a burden to do exercises when they get home. This is the common mistake for many people in business or in politics.

是的，40岁左右的人正处于事业的巅峰，不得不在办公室或商务活动中忙碌。他们白天必须解决棘手的问题，应对艰巨的挑战，晚上还要参加社交或私人活动。因此，他们回到家后会发现做运动是个大负担。这是许多商界人士或政界人士常犯的错误。

10

It's true that sports would improve our sense of leadership. To be specific, they would teach us how to handle competition and pressure, set goals and move ahead with determination. Furthermore, playing sports would allow us to build relationships with our coaches and teammates, which would help us improve relations with people, whether we are at home, at school, at work or in business.
是的，运动有助于我们增强领导意识。具体来说，运动会让我们学会处理竞争和压力，设定目标并砥砺前行。另外，体育运动能让我们与教练和队友建立良好的关系，进而有助于我们改善人际关系，无论是在家里、学校、工作中，还是在生意场上。

11

Doctors say that we could find many ways to do physical exercise. We could go cycling, hiking, or we could visit the local gyms where we pay a reasonable price for some nice workouts. However, the most economical way is jogging.
医生建议，我们可以找到很多体育锻炼的方法。我们可以骑自行车，徒步旅行，或者去当地的健身房，在那里我们支付合理的费用就可以进行一些不错的锻炼。然而，最为经济的方法就是慢跑。

12

Doctors say we should find time to mingle up with people, no matter how busy we are. We should go to movies or join some team sports as often as possible. We should take sightseeing trips or volunteer for some social activities as much as we can afford the time. As one Buddhist saying goes, when we achieve peace at heart, we'll be able to deal with everything else with relative ease.

医生说，不管多忙，我们都应该抽时间与人交往。我们应该尽可能多地去看电影或参加团队活动。只要能抽出时间，我们应该进行观光旅行或参加志愿活动。正如一句佛教谚语所说，只要达到内心平静，我们就能相对轻松地处理所有其他事宜。

13

It's an irony that many people work hard to make money before they're forty. Nevertheless, many of them have to spend the hard-earned money to buy health for the rest of their lives. In order to avoid that vicious scenario, we all have to find some ways to unwind our physical or psychological tensions, no matter how busy we are, wherever we are, and whatever we do.

具有讽刺意义的是，许多人四十岁之前就知道努力工作挣钱，但他们中许多人将不得不用辛苦挣来的钱来购买余生中的健康。为了避免这种恶性循环，无论我们有多忙，无论我们身处何地，无论我们从事何种工作，都必须想方设法改善身体或心理紧张状态。

14

We all have to face the natural law that nobody is getting younger. Therefore, we all need to cope with the change in our body and mind when we're moving into our midlife routines. Therefore, we all need to adjust our ways at work and for our life. And, we all need to discard some old habits and adopt some new ones.

我们都需要面对这个自然规律，没有人会越活越年轻。因此，我们在步入中年以后，都需要采取措施来应对我们身体和思想的变化。谨此而言，我们都需要调整自己的工作和生活方式。我们都需要抛弃一些旧习惯，接受一些新习惯。

15

It may sound a bit scary, but we're now living in a more and more well-to-do life, many of us are developing health problems, due to too much good food, too many soft drinks, too much meat stuff, and too many careless social contacts.

听起来有点可怕，尽管我们今天的生活越来越富裕，但我们中的许多人正面临健康问题，主要是由于享用了太多的佳肴、太多的软饮料、太多肉食，或进行了太多随意的社交活动。

16

As we can see, more and more bulky people are suffering from obesity. Many reasons have contributed to this global health issue. However, one most direct reason is the prepacked food, canned soft drinks and beer of all brands. All those fancy food and drinks contain too much fat, sugar and calories, which are detrimental to our health.

正如我们所见，越来越多的人遭受肥胖困扰。造成这种全球身体健康问题的原因有很多。然而，最直接的原因就是各种包装食品、罐装软饮料和啤酒。所有这些食物和饮料都含有太多的脂肪、糖和卡路里，这些都不利于我们的健康。

17

It's an open secret that the habit of over-eating is another factor to obesity. At the parties or get-togethers, we tend to over-snack things. On many occasions, our stomachs are already full, but our mouths are still hungry. Many of us won't realize the problem until we are in trouble.

这是一个公开的秘密，暴饮暴食习惯是导致肥胖的另一个因素。在派对或聚会上，我们往往会吃很多零食。每当这个时候，我们的胃已经饱了，但是我们的嘴巴仍然觉得很饿。许多人直到身体有了麻烦时才会意识到这个问题。

18

Science has proved that heredity is also a contributing factor. Scientists say we don’t inherit the diseases, but we do inherit the susceptibility from our parents. When we happen to fall into this category, we just have to watch for that scenario. Scientists also say the lack of exercise should be one more contributing factor. So, we need to find ways to burn off the excessive calories on the regular basis.

科学证明，遗传也是一个因素。科学家说，我们并不遗传这种疾病，但我们确实可能从父母那里遗传了易感性。我们如果碰巧属于这一类人，就需要防范这种情况出现。科学家还表示，缺乏锻炼是另一个致病因素。因此，我们需要找到经常锻炼的方法，燃烧掉体内过剩的卡路里。

19

For the sake of our health, we must do something when we find ourselves over-weight, or before we’re falling into medical complications. As one saying goes, there’s no use to cry over the spilt milk. Therefore, we need to recharter the road map for our living, exercising and working modalities, in line with our health conditions.

为了健康，我们在发现自己超重或陷入并发症之前，必须采取措施加以预防。俗话说，牛奶洒了，哭也没用。为此，我们需要根据自身健康状况，重新制定生活、锻炼和工作的路线图。

20

There’s no doubt that we all have to be dedicative at work or in business. We all have to deal with problems and fence off challenges during the day, and may feel burnt out when the day is finished, but this is exactly the moment for us to do some exercises, in order to take out our body-heat. As one Taoist saying goes, our body stress may hurt, but we don’t have to get hurt.

毫无疑问，我们在工作或商业领域中必须全身心投入。白天，我们要处理问题，应对挑战，因此下班后，我们可能会感到非常疲劳，但这正是我们该做运动的时候，以便把身体中的多余热量释放出去。正如一句道家名言所说，我们的身体会有压力，但我们的精神不应受到伤害。

Part Two　Situational Dialogues

01

A: How have you been doing with your dissertation, Liang Hong?

梁红，你的论文写作进展得怎么样？

B: Thanks for asking. So far, I've drafted the outline which has got the approval by my adviser, and I've managed to collect all the reference materials for my paper. I'll start writing next week.

谢谢你的关心。到目前为止，我已经起草了大纲并得到了导师的批准，而且我已收集了与论文相关的大部分参考资料。我下周就开始论文写作。

A: Good on you. That's why I would like to take you to a football match this Friday evening. It's between our university and LA. It's their third and final match to decide which team is to be the champion of the universities in the Western Conference. I've already booked the seats for three of us.

你真行。正因为如此，我想本周五晚上带你去看一场足球赛。这是我们大学和洛杉矶大学的比赛。这场比赛将决定哪支球队会成为西部大学联盟的冠军，而且这是三场比赛的最后一场。我已经预订了三个座位。

B: That would be great. The game would be very much competitive, I guess. To tell you frankly, I was thinking of something to kill off the time this weekend since I have been busy for the past two weeks.

那太好了。我想这场比赛竞争会非常激烈。坦白地说，过去两周一直很忙，因此，我也正考虑如何打发本周末的时间呢。

A: So, that’s a deal. My wife and I are coming to pick you up at 17:30 on Friday. We’re going to have a few bites at a KFC outlet before we move into the stadium. See you then.

那就这么定了。我和我妻子周五17：30来接你。进入体育场之前，我们可以去肯德基吃快餐。周五见。

02

A: Have you got anything planned for tomorrow evening, Mark?

马克，你明天晚上有什么安排吗?

B: Not really. As usual, I’ll just bury myself in the lab, and continue with my research program, as we’re at the final stage.

没有啊。如同往常一样，我将把自己关进实验室里继续研究项目，因为我们已经到了最后阶段。

A: Come on, you’ve got to give yourself a break. Look, I’ve got a ticket to spare. It’s the football match between Italy and China. It’s the last warm-up match for the Italian team before the World Cup in the Mexico City this fall.

别这样啊，你总得放松一下自己吧。跟你说，我这里有一张多余的票。这是意大利对中国的足球比赛。这是今年秋天将在墨西哥城举办的世界杯前意大利队的最后一场热身赛。

B: That’s wonderful! I’m a staunch Chinese team supporter, you know. I’ll find out if my national team would make any substantial progress against a strong team from Europe.

那太棒了！你知道，我是一个坚定的中国队粉丝。我想看看我的国家队在面对欧洲强队时是否能取得实质性的进步。

A: Well, you'll find it out at the game. I also hope your national team would have an excellent opportunity to play against a champion hopeful team.

哦，看完比赛你就知道了。我也希望你的国家队能够有机会与有望夺冠的球队比赛。

03

A: You look great, William. You must have some secret on how to stay healthy.

你的气色很好，威廉。你一定有保健的秘诀。

B: How do you think I got to look this good at my age?

你猜为什么我在这个年纪看起来气色这么好?

A: Let me guess. You must have a lot of water every day?

让我猜猜，你每天一定喝很多水吧?

B: You are right. I drink at least eight glasses a day.

你说得对，我每天至少喝8杯水。

A: I bet you do exercise every day, too.

我猜你每天也会锻炼吧。

B: I try to walk for 40 minutes a day at least.

我试着每天至少走40分钟。

A: I don't think walking is a good way to do exercise.

我认为走路并非很好的锻炼方式。

B: No, you're wrong. Walking briskly is a great way for exercise.

不，你错啦。快步行走确实是一种很好的锻炼方式。

A: What about your eating habits?

你的饮食习惯是什么?

B: I always stay away from pre-packed food, and stick to as much non-processed stuff as possible.

我尽量少吃加工食品，多吃未经加工的东西。

04

A: Tom, you look a bit tired, I'm afraid.

汤姆，你看起来有点疲倦。

B: You're right. My colleagues and I have been working hard on the annual report for the past two weeks, which took us three revisions before the Board of Directors allowed it to pass.

你说对了。过去两周，我和我的同事们一直忙于起草年度报告，报告修改了三次才被董事会通过。

A: Well, that's not the main reason, if you ask me. You've got to find out some other reasons for your physical status. We Chinese believe that men over forty usually begin to suffer from weakening kidney functions, soft knees and insomnia, and so on. You know what, kidneys serve as our inner body filtering system, removing waste and excess water from the blood. Therefore, the abnormal working habit, over eating habit and party behaviors would all give our kidneys too much burden, which would be hitting back like boomerang. Please remember, when our kidneys should fail to function as required, they would cause all sorts of health problems.

嗯，要我说呀，那不是主要原因。你肯定还有其他的原因导致你现在的身体状况欠佳。我们中国人认为，四十岁以上的男人通常有肾功能减退、膝盖软、失眠等症状。你知道吗，肾脏作为身体的过滤系统，从血液中清除废物和多余的水分。因此，超常的工作、饮食和聚会都会给我们的肾脏带来太多的负担，造成恶性循环，就像回旋镖一样。请记住，我们的肾脏一旦不能正常工作，就会引发各种健康问题。

B: I agree. I've been falling behind my physical exercise schedule lately, and I've got too many parties as we're celebrating both the Christmas and the New Year.

我同意你的看法。最近我的体育锻炼进度一直赶不上我的计划，近来我们同时在庆祝圣诞节和新年，有太多的聚会需要参加。

A: Look, I strongly recommend that you should join the faculty sports club of our university where you would get the professional assistance from the staff. More importantly, you'll meet more colleagues and new friends, and carry out meaningful academic conversations, so you won't lose anything, you know.

听着，我强烈建议你加入我们大学的教师体育俱乐部，在那里你会得到工作人员的专业帮助。更重要的是，你会遇到很多同事和新朋友，进行专业领域交谈，所以你不会浪费时间的，你知道吗?

B: Thanks, I'll take your advice, but how could I get the membership?

谢谢。我接受你的建议，不过，我怎么才能成为会员呢?

A: That's easy. We can go together at 17:30 tomorrow, and we can go directly from our office. I'll fix up everything for you, and you just have to prepare to pay the quarterly membership fee of $100 dollars. Oh, before I forget, please bring your sportswear and the stuff.

那好办。我们明天下午5点半一起去，我们可以直接从办公室去。我会帮你办理手续，你只需要准备支付每个季度100美元的会费。哦，差点忘了，请记得带上你的运动衣物。

Part Three Common Expressions

- Chairman Mao said China should promote physical culture and build up people's health.

  毛主席说过，中国需要发展体育文化，增强人民体质。

- I have been going to the gym regularly for the past ten years. Now, we would take walks in the community park when weather permits.
  过去10年我定期去健身房。现在，只要天气允许，我们就去社区公园散步。
- I've tried several ways to lose weight with little results. Have you got any advice?
  我试着几种减肥方法，但效果不佳。你有什么高见吗？
- I stopped mountain climbing since my knees began to hurt.
  由于膝盖出了问题，我就不再爬山了。
- I stopped winter swimming three years ago, in line with my doctor's order.
  遵照医嘱，三年前我就停止冬泳活动了。
- We should not only stick to regular exercises, but also keep a balanced diet. I think we should all eat more vegetables instead of junk food, in order to stay energetic.
  我们不仅需要坚持体育锻炼，而且需要保持饮食平衡。我认为，为了保持活力，我们都需要多吃蔬菜，而不是垃圾食品。
- Whatever sports we go for, we need to do it on the regular basis. We need to draft a weekly schedule, divide it into doable blocks, and stick to it until we achieve our goals. Still taking jogging for example, we can either go for distance or for time. Whichever way we choose to go, we should get to the point where we're sweating and pleasantly tired out.
  无论我们打算做什么运动，都需要定期进行。我们需要制订每周的活动计划，将它划分为可行的几个部分，并坚持下去，直到实现目标。还是以慢跑为例，我们既能以距离为目标，也能以时间为目标。无论我们选择哪种方式，我们都应该达到流汗和轻松疲劳的程度。
- When we revisit the history of New China's sports, the most glorious event must be the 2008 Beijing Olympic Games. In just 16 days, hundreds of athletes, sports officials, politicians, ordinary spectators, media organizations from many countries converged in Beijing, China. They

gathered for the first time in a country with an ancient Oriental civilization, where they could watch at zero distance China's success in reform, opening up, economic development, social progress and creativity while watching splendid sports competitions among teams from around the world. In just 16 days, China managed to present its excellent capability to host such a spectacular international game with such an efficiency and quality. In just 16 days, Chinese athletes won 100 medals, of which 51 were gold, 21were silver and 28 were bronze. In just 16 days, the Beijing Olympic Games sent the following message to the international community: China cannot develop in isolation from the world, and vice versa. In just 16 days, the Games presented to the international community an image of China as an independent country, a stable and united country, a peace-loving country, an unyielding country, a major developing country and a major responsible country.

在新中国体育史上，最辉煌的事件必属2008年北京奥运会了。在短短16天里，来自许多国家的数百名运动员、体育官员、政治家、普通观众和媒体组织共聚中国北京。他们首次相聚在这个东方文明古国，零距离观看了中国改革开放、经济发展、社会进步和创新发展等方面的成就，也观看了来自世界各国代表队的精彩比赛。在短短的16天里，中国高效、高质量地展示了承办这一国际赛事的卓越能力。在短短的16天里，中国运动员赢得整整100枚奖牌，其中金牌51枚，银牌21枚，铜牌28枚。在短短的16天里，北京奥运会向国际社会传递了下列信息：中国的发展离不开世界，世界的发展也离不开中国。在短短的16天里，北京奥运会向国际社会集中展示了中国独立自主、安定团结、热爱和平、自强不息的形象，展示了一个发展中的大国形象和一个负责任的大国形象。

第十四章

医疗事宜

*

正如中国谚语所说，人吃五谷杂粮，难免会生病。因此，我们都需要尽早注意保护身体健康。与此同时，在国外旅行、生活、学习、工作或经商期间，我们有时也会生病，因而需要看医生或去医院。在那里，我们需要知道如何向大夫说明病情，并知道如何解除我们的病痛。

Chapter Fourteen

Medical Matters

*

As one Chinese proverb goes, we, who live on grains and vegetables, cannot escape from illnesses. Therefore, we all need to look after our health before it's too late. Meanwhile, when we're travelling, living, studying, working or doing business overseas, we may also fall sick sometimes, under which we all have to visit doctors or go to the hospitals. Therefore, we need to know how to tell our symptoms, and how to get our problems attended.

Part One Things to Know

01

Physical health is never a commodity which we can bargain with. We've got to earn it with our sweat and persistent exercise. As one saying goes, without good health, we wouldn't have much to depend on.

身体健康绝非可以讨价还价的商品。相反，我们必须用汗水和坚持锻炼获得健康。正如一句谚语所说，没有良好的体魄，我们将一无所有。

02

Many people think they know how to keep physical health. Some say it's as simple as eating more fruits and vegetables, or as easy as staying away from too much red meat. Some others would say they just have to go to the gym regularly or buy some expensive sports equipment, and do exercise at home. However, these are just parts of the story.

许多人自认为知道如何保持身体健康。有人说，只需要多吃些水果和蔬菜，或者少吃些红肉。还有一些人说，只需要定期去健身房，或者只需要买一些昂贵的运动器材在家里做运动。然而，这些仅仅是维持身体健康的一部分。

03

We're all human beings, and we may all fall sick and are prone to diseases. In

order to keep healthy, we all have to be careful with what we do, what we eat, or with whom we associate.
我们都是人，都有可能生病。为了保持健康，我们都要注意应该做什么，应该吃什么，或应该与谁交往。

04

It’s commonly agreed that many health problems are related to communicable diseases one way or the other. It’s also the consensus that when we’re living a well-to-do life, many of us are still developing health issues, either due to too much good food, too many extravagant social activities or careless contact with animal meats with deadly viruses, etc.
人们普遍认为，许多健康问题或多或少与传染性疾病有关。虽然我们已经过上小康生活，但许多人正不断出现健康问题，要么是由于食用太多的美味食物、参加太多奢侈的社交活动，要么是由于不小心接触了携带致命病毒的肉类产品等。

05

We need to balance the time we spend every day between work and leisure, and find time to do regular exercise when we are still young. As one saying goes, better late than never.
我们需要平衡每天工作与休闲的时间，趁年轻时开始进行规律的锻炼。正如一句谚语所说，晚做总比不做好。

06

Researches have proven that we develop coronary diseases when we keep building up fatty cholesterol and waste substances in our arteries. As those deposits can form plagues and clog up our arteries, we’ll suffer from heart attacks, which could cause permanent damage to our heart muscles and even death.

有研究者证明，当脂肪胆固醇和废物在血管中不断堆积时，我们就会得冠心病。随着这些沉积物不断形成并堵塞我们的动脉，我们就有可能患心脏病，进而造成心肌永久性损伤，甚至导致死亡。

07

Typical symptoms would include extreme pressure on our chests, breathlessness, trapped air and belching. It all starts from the narrowing of the arteries, which gradually leads to high blood pressure. This would eventually lead to the coronary heart disease. Doctors point out family history of heart disease, diabetes, obesity, and smoking could also increase the chances of getting heart disease.

典型的心脏病症状包括极度胸闷、呼吸困难、憋气和嗳气。这些症状都始于动脉狭窄，从而逐渐导致高血压，并最终诱发心脏疾病。医生指出，家族性心脏病、糖尿病、肥胖和吸烟都会增加患心脏病的几率。

08

Up until now, doctors are still trying hard to find out the effective cure for the coronary heart disease. However, we can certainly manage the symptoms with medication and lifestyle change. To be specific, we can use some drugs to improve the function of our hearts and reduce relevant symptoms.

到目前为止，医学界仍在努力寻找治疗冠心病的有效方法。然而，我们可以通过药物治疗和改变生活方式来控制病情。具体而言，我们可以使用一些药物来改善我们的心脏功能，减缓相关症状。

09

When we feel the symptoms beyond control even with drugs, we should go and seek surgical treatment without delay. At the hospital, surgeons would open up or replace the blocked arteries, in order to prevent fatal heart attacks and strokes.

假如我们感到有些症状用药物依旧无法控制，就应该立即寻求外科治疗。在医院里，外科医生会打开或替换堵塞的动脉，以防止致命的心脏病发作和中风。

10

The key to prevent coronary heart disease is to make sure our LDL cholesterol level remains low and HDL cholesterol remains high. In order to achieve these objectives, we need to control the saturated fat we consume every day. We should avoid egg yolks, red meat and butter as much as possible. We should grill the meat, rather than frying it. Or, we should simply trim the fat off the meat before we cook it.

预防冠心病的关键是，确保我们的低密度脂蛋白胆固醇保持在较低水平，高密度脂蛋白胆固醇保持在较高水平。为了达到这些目标，我们需要控制每天消耗的饱和脂肪。我们应该尽量避免食用蛋黄、红肉和黄油。我们应该把肉烤着吃，而不是炸着吃。或者，干脆在烹饪之前把肥肉部分去掉。

11

It’s a simple fact that men over forty tend to experience the gradual decline both in physical and mental sharpness. However, they now have to shoulder more responsibility for bringing up their kids and for supporting their parents, which warrant additional care for their body health as well as mental health.

这是一个简单的道理，男人超过四十岁后身体和精神均开始衰退。然而，他们现在既需要抚养孩子，又需要赡养父母，因而需要格外注重身体健康和心理健康。

12

People say veteran patients would become self-taught doctors. We may fall into the habit of buying some pills for some chronic diseases. However, few

people realize the real risks about self-prescribed medicine. In fact, some drugs would do us more harms than help. For example, one sleeping pill called Ambian is found to have the side effects of dream walking, dream working, and even dream driving!
俗话说，久病成医。一些慢性病发作时，我们可能会形成习惯去购买药物。然而，很少有人意识到自我开药方的风险。事实上，有些药物的副作用比疗效更大。例如，一种叫做Ambian的安眠药已经证明有引发梦游、梦中工作的风险，甚至梦中驾驶的风险！

13

Generally speaking, we all have an organ in our body called pancreas. It produces a hormone called insulin which helps to convert the sugar in our body into energy. Insulin is the only hormone in the body that lowers blood sugar. It also promotes glycogen, fat and protein synthesis.
一般来说，我们体内都有一个器官叫作胰腺。胰腺产生一种叫作胰岛素的激素；胰岛素存在于我们的身体里，它的功能就是把我们吸收到体内的糖转化为能量。胰岛素是机体内唯一能降低血糖的激素，它同时还有促进糖原、脂肪、蛋白质合成的作用。

14

For the diabetics, their pancreas would stop making insulin, so their bodies just collect all the sugar they in-take, but can’t get rid of it. This is the point where all the troubles start to appear. Gradually, people in question would lose physical strength and weight. Meanwhile, they would be rushing to the bathroom too often, simply because of the excess sugar that’s building up in the body.
对于糖尿病患者来说，他们的胰腺停止制造胰岛素，所以他们的身体只是收集摄入的糖，但不能消化。这是所有麻烦出现的原因。渐渐地，这些人会失去体力，体重下降。与此同时，他们需要时不时上卫生间，主要原因是体内不断积累了大量糖分。

15

In general, there are two types of diabetes: Type I and Type II. Type I is usually attributed to the genetic heredity, and it can happen at any age. However, nowadays more and more people begin to suffer from the disease when they’re still young, but doctors are still trying hard to find out ways and means to address the scenario.

一般而言，有两种糖尿病：I型和II型。I型糖尿病通常归因于遗传因素，任何年龄都可能发生。然而，目前越来越多的人在年轻时就开始患糖尿病，但医学界仍在努力寻找有效治疗手段。

16

Meanwhile, Type II diabetes occurs mainly because of the diet related issues. Most patients tend to have poor diets, or tend to be overweight, or tend not to do regular physical exercises, etc. All these scenarios would put much strain on the pancreas, and prevent them from producing enough insulin to digest all the food we eat every day. Eventually, it would lead to Type II diabetes.

与此同时，II型糖尿病主要是与饮食相关的病情。大多数病人饮食质量很差，体型偏胖，很少进行体育锻炼等。所有这些情况都会给胰腺增添压力，阻碍后者制造足够的胰岛素来消化我们每天摄入的食物，最终诱发II型糖尿病。

17

Meanwhile, we all have an organ in our body called liver, which is a vital organ of the human digestive system. There are over 5000 identified functions. For example, it filters all the blood in the body and breaks down poisonous substances, such as alcohol and drugs, removes the toxins from our body’s blood supply, maintains healthy blood sugar levels, and regulates blood clotting, etc.

与此同时，我们的身体里都有一个叫肝脏的器官，它是人体消化系统的重要组成部分，具有超过5000种已知的功能。例如，它能过滤体内所有的血液，分解酒精、药物等有毒物质，清除体内血液中的毒素，维持健康的血糖水平，调节血液凝块等。

18

According to the reports by the World Health Organizations, roughly about one third of the people around the world suffer from insomnia of various degrees. When we've ever had long, sleepless nights, we're suffering from insomnia. Generally speaking, trouble sleeping at night would affect our normal life, daily work and the normal socialization at day time.

根据世界卫生组织的报告，全世界大约有三分之一的人患有不同程度的失眠症。一旦出现漫漫长夜难入眠的境况，我们就可能已经患上失眠症。一般而言，晚间难以入眠会影响我们的日常生活、工作或社交活动。

19

Doctors say many reasons could cause insomnia. Things we eat or drink, which contain caffeine or alcohol, are the common causes. Too much rich or spicy food before bed is another common trigger. Doctors find out that some drugs can also cause trouble sleeping as well. In fact, any type of stimulant is likely to make our sleeping difficult.

医生说导致失眠的原因很多。我们食用或饮用含有咖啡因或酒精的食物，是常见的诱因。睡前吃太油腻或辛辣的食物是另一个常见的诱因。医生们发现，一些药物也会导致病人失眠。事实上，任何含有兴奋剂的东西都可能导致我们睡眠困难。

20

When we suffer from insomnia, there are several things we can do about it.

We could practice regular sleeping habits, such as going to bed at the same time every night. And, we should avoid taking long naps during the day. We should try to abstain from caffeine or alcohol before going to bed. In addition, when we suffer from insomnia frequently, we have to consult the doctor, who could help us pinpoint the causes of the problems and give us proper advice or medication.

我们如果被失眠困扰，可以采取一些办法加以应对。我们可以养成有规律的睡眠习惯，比如每天晚上同一时间睡觉。我们应该避免在白天长时间午睡。我们应该在睡前避免饮用含咖啡因或酒精的饮料。此外，我们如果经常出现失眠，最好去咨询医生。他们可以帮助查明具体原因，并给予适当的咨询或药物治疗。

Part Two　Situational Dialogues

01

A: Good morning! This is the Royal Army Hospital. For general information, please press “1”; for registration inquiry, please press “2”; for emergency cases, please press “3”; for on-line service, please press “4”; and for personal service, please stay on the line, one of our staff members will serve you momentarily. For the training purposes, your call will be recorded. Please be advised that our telephone service is closed on Sundays and public holidays…Yes, this is Emma speaking. Can I help you?

早上好！这里是皇家军队医院。一般信息询问请按“1”；挂号咨询请按“2”;如需挂急诊，请按“3”;如需在线服务，请按“4”;如需私人服务，请不要挂机，我的同事马上会为您服务。基于培训目的，您的电话将被录音。请注意，我院的电话服务于星期日及公众假期关闭……喂，我是爱玛，我能帮您吗?

B: Sure. I'm calling in to register for Dr. Johnson on this coming Wednesday morning.

是的。我打电话想预约翰逊大夫本星期三上午的号。

A: Let me check, and hold the line, please… Sorry, Dr. Johnson will not be available on Wednesday morning as he's still on his vocation. Shall I recommend Dr. Wilson instead? They two are both specialists in the same field.

让我看一看，请不要挂断电话……对不起，约翰逊大夫星期三上午不出诊，他还在休假。我为您推荐威尔逊大夫，好吗？他们俩都是同一领域的专家。

B: Well, in that case, I'll take your advice, and please help me confirm the appointment.

那好吧，我就听你的。请帮我确认预约吧。

A: Good. Shall I put your appointment between 10:20 and 10:40, which is the only window opportunity available that morning? Mind you, please refrain from having anything in the morning that day. I guess, Dr. Wilson is likely to arrange for you to do some lab tests, OK?

那好。我把您的预约安排在10：20到10：40之间好吗？这是威尔逊大夫那天上午唯一有空的时段。请注意，那天早上不要吃任何东西。我猜想，威尔逊医生可能会安排你做一些化验的，好吗?

B: Thanks for your advice, and I'll be there on time.

谢谢你的建议，我会及时赶到的。

02

A: Good morning, Madam!

早上好，夫人！

B: Good morning, sir. Can I help you?

早上好，先生。我能帮你忙吗？

A: I'm running a high fever and feeling terrible.

我发高烧，还流鼻涕。

B: How long have you had these symptoms?

这些状况持续多久啦？

A: Since last night.

昨天晚上开始的。

B: Have you ever been here in our hospital before?

你以前来我们医院就诊过吗？

A: No, I'm a newcomer in your country.

没有。我刚刚来到贵国。

B: I see. Now please fill in this registration card. And, I've marked out the places where you've got to fill in. If you should have any questions, please let me know.

我知道了。现在请填写登记表。我已在需要填写的地方做了标记。如果你还有问题，请告诉我.

A: Thanks a lot. Now, which department should I register with, madam?

谢谢。哦，夫人，请问我需要挂哪个科？

B: You'd better tick the Medical Department. And, the registration fee is 5 dollars please.

你最好挂内科。挂号费是5美元。

A: Sure. Now, how do I get to the Medical Department, please?

给你。请问去内科我要怎么走？

B: Take the lift to the third floor and then make a left turn. Go along the corridor until you see the sign on your right.

乘坐电梯到三楼，左转。沿着走廊一直往前走，你能在右手边看到内科诊室标志。

03

A: Good afternoon, Dr. Schumer. Sorry to trouble you again.

下午好，舒默医生。很抱歉再次打扰你。

B: No problem, my friend. How can I help you this time?

没问题，我的朋友。这次我能帮你什么忙吗?

A: Well, I've been suffering from stomachache since three days or so. At first, I didn't think much about it. I thought it probably was a temporary symptom which would go away at any time. However, I felt the increasing pain in my stomach starting from yesterday. Then, my wife became nervous about it and drove me here to see you.

嗯，我在三天前左右就一直胃痛。一开始，我并没有在意。我以为这个症状很快就会消失。但是，从昨天开始，我就感到肚子越来越疼。这下，我妻子有点紧张了，于是就开车送我来找你了。

B: I see. Now, please lay on the bed and let me do some physical exams, okey? Please tell me when you feel the touching pain.

我知道了。现在，请躺在床上，让我给你检查一下，好吗?请告诉我，你哪里有触痛的感觉。

A: Woops! It's the pain point.

哇！这儿就是痛点。

B: Well, it is the appendicitis, I'm afraid. I'll have to transfer you to the state hospital for the surgical treatment since it's too late for the conservative treatment… Here is the letter of transfer, and I'll call Surgeon Hoover who is going to take care of your problem.

听着，恐怕你得了阑尾炎。我得给你转到州立医院进行手术治疗，保守治疗太晚了……这是转院单，我会打电话给胡弗医生，他将帮你解决问题。

04

A: Good morning, you must be Mr. Lin Huiming.

早上好，您一定是林会明先生吧。

B: Yes. And, you must be Dr. Hoover.

是的。您一定是胡弗大夫吧。

A: No, I’m Dr. Johnson, assistant to Dr. Hoover. Now, please let me have all the materials and lab test results from Dr. Schumer.

不是。我是约翰逊大夫，胡弗大夫的助手。现在请把舒默医生提供的所有材料和化验结果给我。

B: Here you are. I wonder when Dr. Hoover will see me.

给你。请问胡弗医生什么时候来看我。

A: Don’t worry. Dr. Hoover will receive you as soon as I get the basic things done. I’ve already made the appointment with him on your behalf, you know.

别担心。我把你的基本情况处理好以后胡弗医生就会来看你了。你知道，我已经替你约好了。

B: That’s very kind of you.

真是太感谢你啦。

A: For your reference, surgery on appendicitis is just a routine operation. Since you’ve been suffering from the pain for the past few days, we’ve decided to treat it as emergency operation, in order to prevent it from perforation.

我跟您说，阑尾炎手术属于常规手术。考虑到您过去几天一直感到疼痛，我们决定把它作为紧急手术来对待，以防止发生穿孔。

Part Three Common Expressions

- I'm calling if you could do a home visit.
  我打电话想请问您能否上门出诊。
- Please tell me about your problems.
  请告诉我你哪儿不舒服。
- I've got the burning sensation in my stomach.
  我的胃里有灼热感。
- My stools have been from soft to watery.
  我的排便从软便已经发展到水便。
- My stool is watery with blood and mucus.
  我的排便呈水泻状且带有脓血。
- I've got serious pain when passing urine.
  我小便时感到非常疼。
- I feel heavy pressure around my front chest.
  我的前胸感到很闷。
- I'm beginning to have difficulty in breathing.
  我开始感到呼吸困难。
- I used to suffer from liver trouble when I was at college.
  我在大学期间曾经得过肝炎。
- I would feel dizzy when I get up lately.
  我近来早上起来时头总是发晕。

- Could you tell me some more about your symptoms?
  你还能说说其他的症状吗？
- Can you describe the pain?
  你能描述一下这种疼痛感吗？
- How long have you had these symptoms?
  你的这些症状有多久啦？
- Have you ever had these symptoms before?
  你以前有过这些症状吗？
- Please point out where the pain is.
  请给我指指哪里疼。
- What kind of treatments have you had before?
  你以前接受过哪些治疗？
- I'll let you do some tests before I give you the diagnosis and the prescription.
  我想让你做一些化验，然后再给你诊治并开药方。
- You do have some problems in your digestive system, but I'll let you take an Ultrasound, just to make sure.
  你的消化系统确实有问题，我想让你做一个B超，确定一下病况。
- Now, I need to take a look at the digital medical history data from your country, and then I'll ask you some questions before we proceed with some lab tests, alright?
  我需要先查阅一下你从国内发来的电子病历，然后再问你一些问题，并做一些化验，好吗？
- In your case, I'll arrange for you to check into a ward room. I'll arrange for you to do some lab tests and give you some medicine, in order to prepare you for the surgical operation.
  根据您的情况，我会为你安排入住病房。我要给你做些化验，再开些药，以为手术做准备。
- Now, please listen carefully. According to the digital case history and our

lab tests, we have confirmed that you've got pancreatic problem, which is getting worse. Therefore, we need to give you the surgery. Based on the above assumptions, you need to stay with us for about three weeks. My assistant will give you the list of total cost. You'll have to make your own decision and let us know about your decision by tomorrow, OK?
现在，请仔细听着。根据电子病历和我们的化验结果，我们确认你有胰腺问题，而且还在恶化。因此，我们需要给你实施手术治疗。基于以上假设，你需要在我们这里待上三周左右。我的助理会给你总费用的清单。请你认真考虑，并于明天之前告诉我们你的决定，好吗？

第十五章

个人理财

*

正如一句谚语所说，出门没钱，寸步难行。在这个竞争日益激烈的世界里，金钱在我们个人生活和事业中均扮演着重要的角色，其间我们需要学习一些基本的知识和技巧来管理我们的财务事务。原因很简单。理财可让我们随时了解本人的财务状况，做好策略调整，加速实现既定财务目标，并为新的目标留出财务空间。

Chapter Fifteen

Personal Finance

As one saying goes, you can't go anywhere without money. In the ever-competitive world, money plays an important role both in our personal life and in our careers, during which we've got to learn some basic knowledge and skills on how to manage our financial matters. The reason is simple. It would allow us to find out where we are standing financially, make adjustments in order to realize our financial goals, and allow rooms for new ones.

Part One　Things to Know

01

We may pursue different careers, but we all have to live within our means, and we have to build our safety net for the future. Therefore, we all have to manage our regular income with some money skills, and make the hard-earned income work harder for us.

我们可能从事不同的职业，但我们都必须量入为出，并且努力为未来构建安全保障。因此，我们都必须通过理财管理好我们的固定收入，让辛辛苦苦挣来的钱物尽其用。

02

There is an old saying: Whatever we are doing, we need to prepare for the rainy days. Likewise, we've got to balance our earnings, savings and investments, for the sake of our future. And, we should trust our regular incomes with a sound financial institution, in order to generate the best possible interests.

有句古话说得好：无论我们做什么，凡事需要未雨绸缪。同样，为了未来的财务前景，我们必须平衡分配收入、储蓄和投资。我们应该把定期收入托付给一个健全的金融机构，以期最大限度地获得收益。

03

When we’ve got enough income to spare, we should spend some of it on state bonds or stocks, in order to ensure an average plus annual return. The sure way to manage our surplus income is to earn interest on savings, but it could hardly beat the visible and invisible inflation that’s always in front of us. Therefore, we need to sit down with our financial agent.

我们手中如果拥有足够多可支配的收入，应该把一部分投资在国债或股票上，以确保平均年收益。管理手中多余收入的可靠方法就是通过储蓄获得利息，但这样做怎么也跑不赢可见的和隐形的通货膨胀。因此，我们需要和投资顾问坐下来谈一谈。

04

It’s a hidden fact that the money we entrust with the bank under the savings account or term deposits would decrease in purchasing power even though we earn the nominal interests upon maturity. So, the longer we put the money in the bank, the less purchasing power we will have with the money we own.

这是一个隐藏的事实：我们通过活期存款或定期存款将手中的钱托付给银行，即使到期后可望获得名义利息，其购买力也会下降。因此，把钱放在银行的时间越长，我们手中的钱购买力就越低。

05

For us ordinary people, the more convenient way to beat the inflation is to trust our money with some financial tools such as mutual funds and government bonds. Of course, for some long-term financial benefits, we should choose real estate as the safety net to lay our “economic eggs”.

对我们普通人来说，战胜通货膨胀更有效的方法是将我们手中的钱托付给一些金融工具，比如共同基金和政府债券等。当然，为了获得长期经济利益，我们应该将房地产作为投放手中资金的安全网。

06

It's the common practice for us middle-class people to look for some more lucrative means and ways to begin some long-term investment. And, it's only natural that we could buy stocks from the companies or institutions that are popular with the general public. The thing is that the companies we buy stocks from must be the backbone of certain industries or high-tech companies, which are likely to bring us regular or higher annual yields.

对于我们中产阶级人群而言，通常应寻找一些有利可图的方式进行长期投资。我们通常需要购买受大众欢迎的公司或机构的股票。要注意的是，我们购买股票的公司必须是某些行业的支柱企业，或者高科技公司，而且必须有望给我们带来固定的或更高的年收益。

07

The winning tip is that we should divide our investments into both high-end and low-end stocks. At the high end, we should pick stocks from high-tech companies such as AT&T Wireless or Microsoft, etc. At the lower end, we should buy stocks from companies such as Wal-Mart and Home Depo, etc. In short, when we decide to move into the risky stock market, we need to fasten our seat belts for the up turns and down turns, which might either generate more returns on the stocks we've got in hand, or wash away the little values by large amount.

成功的秘诀是，我们应该把投资分配投放到高端市场和低端市场。在高端市场，我们应该选择高科技公司的股票，如美国电话电报公司或微软等。在低端市场，我们应该购买沃尔玛和家得宝等公司的股票。简而言之，当我们决定进入有风险的股票市场之际，需要对市场的跌宕起伏保持警惕，因为股市既可能给我们手中的股票带来更多的回报，也可能会让我们手中有限的股票价值大量地蒸发掉。

08

Social security is an area where we should pay attention to. In many countries, multi-functional financial products are popular among ordinary working people. In some other countries, instruments such as old age pensions are the main tools for the middle-class families.

社会保险是我们应该关注的投资领域。在许多国家，多功能金融产品深受普通工薪阶层欢迎。在其他一些国家，养老金等金融工具是中产阶级家庭的主要工具。

09

It’s a sad fact that under the market economy, more and more people have to look after their personal or family financial future as the governments are failing in generating enough revenues to facilitate sustainable social welfare and security coverage in terms of housing, medical service or education, etc.

很遗憾，在市场经济条件下，越来越多的人必须谋划本人或家庭未来的经济保障，因为政府愈益难以筹措足够的财政收入，在住房、医疗服务或教育等方面提供可持续的社会福利和保障。

10

COVID-19 has taught us a lesson that we should maintain a comfortable cash pool with the savings account, in case some unexpected expenditures may pop up. And, when we’ve got to plan for the mid-term payments, we should choose some term deposits or three-year treasury bonds, which would allow us to withdraw savings upon maturity while earning interests.

新冠肺炎疫情给我们上了一课，那就是必须在储蓄账户里保持相对充裕的现金，以便应对不时之需。而且，我们在进行中期付款规划之际，应该选择一些定期存款或三年期国债。这样，我们就可以在存款到期时提取现金并赚取相应的利息。

11

Experts say we need to be good at money management as early as possible, which covers the following areas. First, we should identify sound ways to manage own cash incomes on the annual basis, which is to prevent our savings and investments from going down the drain. Second, we should create a personal balance sheet and cash flow statement book, which would allow us to know where we are and where we should go. Third, we should plan and implement personal budget, in order to spend the money wisely and economically. Last but not least, we should connect our money management with our lifetime goals, so that we wouldn't have to be caught unprepared in the future.

专家说，我们要尽早开启资金管理规划，主要包括以下几个方面。首先，我们应该确定一些合理的途径来管理每年的现金收入，以确保本人的储蓄和投资不会浪费掉。其次，我们应该创建一个个人资产负债表和现金流量表，以便掌控我们的现金流，控制我们的支出。第三，我们应该认真计划和执行个人预算规划，以使各项支出经济实惠。最后，我们还应该把理财规划和人生目标联系起来，以便在遇到突发情况之际不至于措手不及。

12

We may fall into the "debt trap" some time in our life, but we've got to find the way out. The first is to evaluate our debt situation, in order to implement a tangible way out. The second is to track our expenditures, in order not to further blow up the debt bubbles. The third is to plan our payments on time, in order to avoid fines. The fourth is to find new source of income, in the hope of tiding over the debt crisis. Lastly, we need to seek financial assistance from the banks or we could get it from relatives or friends, which should be avoided as much as possible.

在一生中，我们都有可能遇到"债务陷阱"，但必须找到摆脱债务困境的方法。首先是要评估我们的债务状况，以便制定和实施切实可行的解决办法。其次是节制支出活动，确保不进一步放大债务泡沫。第三是按时付款，以避免被罚款。第四是找到新的合法收入来源，以便能清偿债务。第五是向银行贷款，或从亲戚朋友那里寻求经济援助，但这一点应该尽量避免。

13

In order to put our financial future on a solid ground, we need to keep the habit of a sound financial expenditure record. First, we need to keep a record on daily expenditures, such as monthly bills. Second, we need to plan and readjust our payment routines, in line with the status of our financial income. Third, we need to keep the record of tax payment. Fourth, we need to keep the record of financial decisions. Last but not least, we need to keep the record on regular purchases.

为把个人财务建立在坚实的基础上，我们需要保持做财务支出记录的习惯。首先是记录日常支出，比如月度账单。二是根据工薪收入状况规划和调整支付事项。三是做好纳税记录。四是做好财务决策记录。最后，我们也要坚持记录常规采购。

14

In the fierce competitive commercial society, we need to form the habit of keeping personal files, in order to define ourselves as responsible individuals both at personal level and family level. To be specific, we need to establish the files in the following areas: personal employment records, money management records, tax records, financial records, credit records, major-purchase records, housing records, insurance records, investment records, honors and entitlement records, etc.

在充满激烈竞争的商业社会，我们需要养成保存个人档案的习惯，努力成为负责任的社会成员和家庭成员。为此，我们需要建立以下几个方面的档案：个人就业记录、资金管理记录、税务记录、金融服务记录、信用记录、主要采购记录、住房记录、保险记录、投资记录、荣誉和津贴记录等。

15

Against the backdrop of globalization, we're increasingly becoming mobile, which warrants us to choose cars as our first fixed assets. Therefore, we've got to do things in line with the laws and regulations, because any mistakes we make would have a negative impact on our credit rating, and will affect the interest rates and other terms of conditions when we purchase any major articles in the future.

在全球化背景下，我们自由流动的机会日益增强，其结果，我们中许多人选择将汽车作为自己名下的首个固定财产投资对象。因此，我们所进行的一切商业行为都必须遵守法律法规，因为我们所犯的任何错误不仅将对本人信用评级产生负面影响，也会对我们以后购买重大商品时的利率和其他优惠条件产生影响。

16

There're many ways for us to purchase stocks. Therefore, we would have to face both advantages and disadvantages. When we have little or no stock buying experience, we may want to start with a full-service firm, which is more expensive, but experts there may come up with professional advice. Meanwhile, when we don't want to pay higher commissions for our stock market activity, we can use online brokerage firms, which would charge us less for the service.

购买股票的方式有很多。因此，我们既需要利用机遇，也需要防范风险。如果没有或只有很少的股票购买经验，我们需要从专业公司获得专业服务。这样做，虽然要多付佣金，但那里的专家可能会提供专业的建议。与此同时，如果我们不想为股市活动支付更高的佣金，可考虑在线经纪公司，这些公司收取的代理费用相对便宜。

17

When we just want to buy stocks at smaller amounts, we could choose the direct purchase options. They come in two varieties: Direct investment plans (DIPs) and dividend reinvestment plans (DRIPs). Both plans would allow us to buy stocks without a broker. Furthermore, both options are inexpensive and easy for investors with smaller amounts of money at regular intervals.
我们如果只是想少量购买股票，可考虑直接购买方式。主要有两种途径：直接投资计划(DIPs)和股息再投资计划(DRIPs)。这些计划允许我们在不通过经纪人的情况下购买股票。此外，对定期小额投资者而言，这两种方式都是既经济又方便的购股方式。

18

When we decide to venture into more risky business, we have to find a proper institution. Whatever options we may choose, our next step is to open an account. We have to fill out some forms and deposit money in line with the benchmark requests. Then, we could just wait for the things to happen.
我们决定从事更有风险的投资时，需要找一家合适的机构开立账户。无论我们选择哪种方式，下一步都需要开通一个账户。我们将需要填写一些表格，并根据基准要求存入相应的资金。此后，我们就可坐等佳音。

19

The following things are important for us to bear in mind. When we use a full-service firm, we should pick a broker we are comfortable with so that we could share our private financial information. If possible, we should meet face to face so that we can explain our needs and goals in details. The more information we offer, the more likely the broker will serve our needs. Meanwhile, when we use a discount brokerage firm, we will need to complete some online paperwork. We may need to mail in other forms that need our physical signatures. And, we may also need to make a deposit depending on the dollar value of our initial trade.

下面这些信息很重要，我们要牢记。我们在选择全方位服务公司炒股之际，需要选择一位愿意与之分享私人财务信息的经纪人。如果可能的话，通过面对面的交流，我们可以详细阐述需求和目标。对方掌握的信息越多，就越有可能有效提供服务。与此同时，我们在使用折扣经纪公司的服务之际，需要在网上填写相关表格。凡是需要申请者签名的文件都需要通过邮寄形式送达对方。另外，我们还需要根据初始交易的金额预存相应现金。

20

Once we've set up the account, we could start our first purchase. From this point on, we need to use all the information we have to choose our first pick. When we're not so sure, we can seek help from a firm or can simply call our broker. He or she will buy the stock on our behalf. However, we need to open our account and give the latter the account number. Then, the broker will confirm our order before he or she places it into the system. Please remember brokers are humans, who can also make mistakes. And, from this point on, we need to watch our portfolio investment carefully and regularly. It is important to recognize that stocks and stock markets are both volatile. Stock values may move up and down, especially in the short term. Therefore, when we spot one of our investments consistently performs poorly, it may be the time for us to change stocks in our portfolio.

我们在开立账户之后，就可以开始进行第一次购股活动。从此刻开始，我们需要运用了解的所有信息选择我们的第一支股票。我们如果没有把握，可以向咨询公司寻求服务，或者直接打电话给我们的经纪人。他或她会为我们买股票。这时，我们需要建立账户并向经纪人提供账号。然后，经纪人会确认我们的订单，然后把它录入交易系统。请注意，经纪人也是人，也会犯错误。从现在开始，我们需要定期仔细地关注我们的投资组合。重要的是我们需要认识到，股票和股票市场都具有不稳定性。股票价值可能会上下波动，尤其是在短期内。如果我们发现投资的某个股票一直表现不佳，理当考虑改变投资组合了。

Part Two Situational Dialogues

01

A: Good afternoon, sir! Can I help you?

下午好，先生！我能帮您点什么吗？

B: Good afternoon. I would like to open a savings account.

下午好。我想开个储蓄账户。

A: Good. Would you like a current account or deposit account?

好的。请问您想要开活期的，还是定期的？

B: I’d like to have a current account to start with.

我想先开活期的。

A: Good. How much money would you like to put in with us, please?

好的。请问您想存多少钱？

B: $1500, please. Here you are.

1500美元。给你现金。

A: Thank you. Please fill in this form in places I marked out for you. When you’re not sure about something, please let me know.

谢谢。请按照我标记的地方填写这张表。您有不确定的地方，请告诉我。

B: That’s very kind of you… Now, I’ve done the format, and here you are.

谢谢。好了，表填好了。给您。

A: Thank you, but please hold on… Here is your receipt and we'll send you the pass card through mail in three working days. When you receive the new card, you need to activate it before it's effective.

谢谢，请稍等……这是您的收据，我们会在3个工作日内给您邮寄储蓄卡。收到新卡以后，您需要激活才能生效。

02

A: Welcome to the West Union, sir. Can I help you?

欢迎来到西联汇款，先生。我能帮您做什么？

B: Yes. I'd like to send $1000 to this person at this address, please.

是的。我想给这个地址汇款1000美元。

A: Sure, please fill out the format before I double check your cash.

好的。请填写汇款单，我再核对您的现金。

B: Well, it's done, and here you are.

填好了，给您。

A: Thanks. Mind you, it would take four days before your family member should get the money. Here is your receipt.

谢谢。请您注意，这笔钱需要4天方可汇达。这是收据。

03

A: Welcome to the Pacific Insurance, madam and gentleman. Can I help you?

欢迎来到太平洋保险公司，夫人和先生。我能帮你们的忙吗？

B: Yes, we're here to buy the insurance for our new house here in your city.

是的。我们来是想为在你们城市购置的新住房购买保险。

A: Good. You've come to the right company. We offer package insurance and item-specific risk insurance. Which insurance would you prefer? Now, please let me have your ID and the property transaction certificate.

好的。你们来我们公司算来对了。我们提供保险套餐和单项风险保险。你们喜欢哪种保险？现在，请出示你们的身份证和房产交易证明。

B: Here you are. And, we’re thinking about the package insurance. Please brief us about the details.

给你。我们考虑投保险套餐。请给我们介绍下细节情况。

A: Well, it is the comprehensive insurance against all risks resultant from the excessive rain, snow, flood, earthquakes and fire, etc. I want you to know it’s a package insurance, so you just have to pay a lump sum premium, which would allow you to enjoy all the benefits when your house should face all those scenarios. Here is our brochure. Please take it home and do some more reading.

好的。这是一种综合险，包括暴风雨、大雪、洪水、地震、火灾等引起的风险。这是保险套餐，你们只需要一次付清保险费，这样当你们的住房出现合同涵盖的所有情况时，就可以享受保险理赔。这是我们的宣传册，请带回家仔细阅读。

B: Thank you for the advice, but what’s the charge?

谢谢你的建议。请问综合险年度费用是多少？

A: Well, it all depends on how much you would value your house at the current market price.

嗯。这要看依据当前的市场行情你们家房子的估价情况。

B: Well, we bought the house at $1 million from one of our friends. Here is the certificate.

我们花了100万美元从一个朋友那里买了这栋房子。这是购房契约。

A: OK. In your case, the premium is $250 per year to start with.

好。依据你们的情况，初始年度保费是250美元。

04

A: Good morning, sir. Welcome to the Atlantic Insurance. What can I do for you, please?

早上好，先生。欢迎来到大西洋保险公司。我能帮您做什么？

B: I'm here to buy the car insurance for my new car.

我想为我的新车购买保险。

A: Good, please let me have your ID and the transaction certificate for your car.

好的。请给我您的身份证和购车凭证。

B: Here you are.

给您。

A: Thanks a lot. Did you take a photo of your car? We need it for the file purpose.

非常感谢。您给新车拍照了吗？我们需要存档。

B: Certainly. In fact, I took four photos from four angles. Shall I give all of them to you?

当然。事实上，我从四个角度拍了四张照片。我需要把它们都给您吗？

A: That would be nice.

那太好了。

Part Three　Common Expressions

- The key to manage the money matter for the people in their 20s is to build up their budget and bookkeeping habits, and increase their earning power. They have to strive for more income, live within their means, and accumulate funds.

对于20多岁的年轻人来说，这个时期的理财之道是养成预算和记账的好习惯，增强挣钱能力。增加收入、量入为出、积累资金。

- By the age of 30, most people have established their families, and are in the golden period of their career. They are receiving more regular income, and are building up their surplus earnings. They are also accumulating fixed assets. On the other hand, they are also increasing their mortgage and consumer spending. Therefore, they need to be more strategic in financial management, and each sum of income needs to be allocated in a diversified way.

  人在30岁时，大多数已经成家立业，并处于职业生涯的黄金时期。他们的固定收入越来越多，开始积累盈余，也开始积累固定资产。另一方面，他们也在增加抵押贷款和消费支出。因此，他们需要在财务管理方面更具策略性，每一笔收入都需要进行多元化配置。

- When people are in their 40s, they've got growing-up kids, they're at the peak of career, they've got more money to invest, and they're getting more financial income than they've ever had in their life. In terms of consumer spending, the demand for improved housing, the education of children, and the cost of living are all increasing. At this stage, the focus of financial management is to maintain risk awareness, and avoid major financial crisis.

  人们步入不惑之年后，子女渐长，事业迈进巅峰期，拥有可观的财富用于投资，财务性收入也在不断增加，这可能是一辈子中收入最多的时期。在消费支出上，改善住房的需求、子女教育、生活费用都在增加。这一时期的理财重点在于绷紧风险意识，避免陷入重大财务危机。

- When people retire, their income will consist mainly of their financial income. In terms of expenditures, besides their daily expenses and pension costs, they may face large expenditures in terms of diseases and physical aspects. At this conjuncture, they need to pay special attention to family financial management, in order to ensure the stability of the regular income. Since the retirees usually have a weak risk tolerance, fixed-return financial products become good choices.

人退休后，其收入将主要由财务性收入构成。在支出上，除了日常开支、养老费用，他们可能面临着疾病等方面的大额支出。这一时期人们需要格外注意家庭理财，以确保收入的稳定性。由于老年人风险承受力较弱，这个时期，固定收益类理财产品成为不错的选择。

- For an ordinary family, the monthly repayment of household loan should not exceed 33 percent of its immediate annual income. Monthly mortgage payments should not exceed 30 percent of its monthly income. And, the cash being put aside for saving and investment should be no less than 10% of its monthly income.

  对普通家庭而言，家庭贷款的每月偿还额不得超过即期年收入的33%。房屋分期付款的月供不能超过月收入的30%。每个月用于储蓄和投资的金额不得少于月收入的10%。

- Experts suggest that personal finance should be divided into three parts: 40 percent of monthly income should be spent on cash or quasi-cash expenses, 30 percent on venture capital and 30 percent on fixed assets investment. Nevertheless, whatever financial instruments we choose, we've got to consider their profitability, safety and liquidity.

  专家建议，个人理财应采取三分法，每月收入的40%用于现金或准现金开支，30%用于风险投资，30%用于固定资产投资。但是，不管我们选择什么理财工具，一定要考虑收益性、安全性和流动性。

- Throughout our life, we need to manage our cash flow. To be specific, financial planning would help us to increase cash flows by monitoring the spending patterns and the nature of expenses. This would help us save up the hard-earned income.

  我们一生中都需要管理现金流。具体而言，财务计划通过监控支出模式和支出性质来帮助我们增加现金流。这将有助于我们积蓄血汗钱。

- We need to spot our financial errors, which will not only help us spend wisely, but also provide us with easy fixes for our financial problems. For instance, proper financial planning would help invest our idle funds or improve our debt status.

我们需要发现理财漏洞。此举不仅有助于我们明智地花钱，还能让我们轻松发现及解决理财问题。例如，合适的理财计划有助于我们合理投资闲置资金或改善债务状况。

- We need to improve our return on investment. In general, we need to take into consideration several aspects such as investment planning, risk management, liquidity management, liability management and goal planning. With a sound financial plan, we would design our investment plan better, and live a comfortable life as we would.

  我们需要提高投资回报率。一般来说，我们需要考虑投资计划、风险管理、流动性管理、负债管理和目标规划等因素。有了良好的理财计划，我们就可以更好地安排投资计划，过上舒坦的生活。

第十六章

房屋购租

*

我们都熟悉那句谚语：金窝银窝，不如自家的狗窝。在其他国家生活、学习或工作期间，我们都会遇到住房问题。无论是买房，还是租房，我们都要处理好法律问题，以免掉入陷阱。

Chapter Sixteen

Housing Matters

*

We're all familiar with the saying: East, West, home is the best. When we're living, studying or working in other countries, we'll have to come across housing matters. Whether we would buy our own condominium or rent a house, we would have to deal with legal matters, in order to avoid pitfalls.

Part One　Things to Know

01

Nowadays, renting a place to live can be a thankless task, but it's a must for anyone who's planning to stay in a foreign country for a while. The key is to know how, and how to get things done properly.

如今，租房子住可谓是一件吃力不讨好的事，但对于任何打算在国外住上一段时间的人来说，这是必办事宜。关键是要知道相关程序，以及如何把事情办妥。

02

Basically, there are many things to do when you decide to rent a house or an apartment, but the most important thing you need to be aware is the legal procedures. You should never rush into any decision before you consult with your lawyer.

基本上，当你决定租房子或公寓时，有很多事情要做，但你最需要了解的是法律程序。在咨询律师之前，你不要匆忙做任何决定。

03

You need to find out if a residential area is safe in terms of law and order. At the same time, you should find out if it's a mature residential community where you don't have to live with neighbors from too many different cultural

backgrounds. Rather, you should choose a place somewhat close to the police station, where you could seek help in times of need.
你要做的第一件事就是找一个治安条件良好的居民区，同时，你要弄清楚这个小区是否是成熟的居民社区，以免和拥有太多不同文化背景的邻居住在一起。比较可靠的做法是找一个离警察局比较近的社区，以便在需要的时候及时寻求帮助。

04

After that, you should think of the distance between the place where you live and the place where you will be studying or work. Meanwhile, you should find out if you would have access to the nearby supermarkets and public facilities.
然后，你应该考虑你生活的地方和你将要学习或工作的地方之间的距离。同时，你还应该了解附近是否有超市和其他公共设施。

05

Before you sit down with your agent or the rental department officials, you need to visit at least three or four places, in order to compare the desirability of the places, convenience to get the service and the public transportation systems. As one saying goes, it pays to do comparison among prices before you do any serious shopping.
在与相关租房代理或租赁部门的职员坐下来谈之前，你至少需要走访三到四个地方，以便比较拟租赁房子的中意程度、获得服务的便利性以及周边的公共交通。俗话说，购物之前，要货比三家。

06

You need to balance out the house you can have for the moment and the capability to come up with monthly bills down the road. When you are still struggling in your career, you should think twice about living in expensive

residential areas, you know.
你需要平衡目前拥有的房子和未来每月支付账单的能力。你知道吗，当你还需要为事业拼搏时，需要认真考虑是否要住在高档居民区。

07

One more thing, before sealing the deal with the landlord, you should have a thorough check on the interior and exterior conditions of the house or apartment house you are to rent. And, you must make sure that the basic conditions are fully met.
还有一件事，在与房东签订合同之前，你应该全面检查拟租赁房子或公寓的内部和外部条件。另外，你还需要确保基本条件得到满足。

08

You must check out the noise environment. While checking on the physical conditions about the property, you should also find out if the walls are soundproof. You should find out about your future neighbors because you would not want to be wakened up in the heat of the night by some crazy neighbors or roaring overnight parties outside.
你应该核查住所的噪音环境。在查看拟租赁房屋的基本情况时，你还应该了解房屋墙壁是否隔音，了解你未来的邻居情况，因为你一定不想在夜深人静时被疯狂的邻居或室外吵闹的通宵聚会吵醒。

09

In addition, you need to find out if the landlord would allow you to carry out business at home, or have guest to stay for the night. In some residential areas, they have the rules to prohibit any pet animals inside the house, or they would request you to build or buy the special facility for your pets. And, it's a common practice for you as the tenants to pay for any damages done by your pets to the property or the immediate environment.

此外，你还需要了解房东是否允许房客在家里开展商业活动，或者是否允许你留客人过夜。一些居民区禁止任何宠物进入屋内，或要求你为宠物建造或购买特殊设施。通常情况下，作为房客，你要为自家宠物对房屋或周边环境造成的任何破坏买单。

10

Finally, when you conclude the deal, you should go over everything listed in the contract. Some landlords or leasing companies would include some hidden clauses in the contract, which would result in more bills for you to pick up afterwards, such as unnecessary maintenance costs or overdue bills left behind by the former tenants, etc.

最后，在签合同时，你应该仔细浏览合同条款。有些房东或租赁公司可能会在合同中加入一些隐藏条款，迫使你多付费用，比如不必要的维修费或前租客拖欠的账单等。

11

To avoid those pitfalls, you need to consult your friends or experts, and make sure the proper maintenance is done to the property before you should move in. Therefore, you need to go over the list, and make sure everything is in good order, or in sound conditions before you should accept the key. By the way, you should make sure to include the clause to allow you to end the leasing contract before it comes to maturity, due to some unexpected reasons at a negotiated cost, or allow you to end the contract when you find out some major defaults with the property at no cost to your side.

为了避免这些陷阱，你需要咨询你的朋友或专家，确保房东对拟搬进的房子进行了适当的维护。经验表明，在接受住房钥匙之前，你应认真阅读合同的所有条款，确保房屋中的设备齐全，状况良好。顺便说一下，你应该设法增加条款，如允许你在遇到一些无法预料的情况需要提前终结租赁合同时，以协商一致的价格支付费用，或你以后发现一些重大住房问题时，可以无条件免费退房。

12

When you want to buy a property, you must seek the service from a professional lawyer or an agent who would do everything on your behalf. For that matter, you need to pay a surcharge of 2~3 percent of the total purchase volume, but it would save you all the troubles when you have moved in.

你在购买房产时，需要寻求专业律师或代理的服务，他们会为你办理所有事宜。当然，你需要支付总购金额2%～3%的代理费，不过这样可避免搬进新居后所有的麻烦。

13

Once you give your agent or sales agent an asking price on any possible house or apartment with the conditions you would look forward to, he or she would move into action and come back with possible properties for you to consider. At this point, you could still change your mind without having to pay for the service. However, once you put your signature on the pre-service contract, you'll have to pay as much as what is listed in the contract.

一旦你向代理机构或销售人员提供关于理想房屋或公寓的底价后，他们就会积极行动起来，找到符合条件的房源供你考虑。截至此时，你仍然可以改变主意，不必支付服务费。但是，一旦在服务合同上签字，你就要支付合同所列项目的全部费用。

14

Before you decide to go any further from this step, you should find out if the property would include the land right underneath. If not, you should forget about the deal right there. On top of that, you must make sure the property you're to purchase is free from any legal conflicts with any persons or institutions. And, you should also make sure the property does not have any

overdue bills left over by the former owners.
在你决定采取进一步措施之前，你应该弄清楚相关房产是否包括相关的地皮。如果没有，你应该停止这笔交易。此外，你应该确保你打算购买的房产没有前住户遗留的任何法律纠纷。你还应当确保这个房产没有前房东留下的账单。

15

You must consult your lawyer at every turn. When you manage to get this far and are ready to sign the contract, you should conclude all the legal procedures with the help of your lawyer, so that you could move in and enjoy your life without having to fall into legal battles. As one saying goes, it pays for you to do anything with care.
凡事都要咨询你的律师。当你准备签合同时，你应该在律师的协助下完成所有的法律程序，以确保你在搬进新居后可以享受平静的生活，而无需陷入任何法律纠纷。正如俗语所说，凡事小心为妙。

16

You must find a reliable agent or agency. In every country or city, it’s easy to find professional agent or agencies. The critical thing is that you need to check out their commercial and professional credibility. They must have the capacity to provide honest service, and work on your behalf in line with the contract. It’s because you don’t want to move into a property with any suspicion or uneasiness on your mind.
你必须找一个可靠的代理或代理商。在每个国家、每个城市，很容易找到专业的中介机构。关键是你需要核查对方的商业和专业信誉。他们必须有能力提供诚实的服务，并按照合同条款为你服务。因为你一定不想带着任何怀疑或不安的心情住进新房子。

17

You must carry out prior property evaluation. Before you sign the contract, you need to seek the professional agency to do the property revaluation. And, you should make sure to get the maintenance records on the property, which the former owner or agent must provide, in line with the laws and regulations.

你需要对拟购房产进行价值评估。在签署购房合同之前，你需要找一家专业的机构对拟购房产进行价值评估。你应该设法拿到先前对该房产进行的维护记录。依据法律规章，前业主或交易代理必须提供相关文件。

18

You should try your luck at the town house market. Generally speaking, town houses don’t stay in the market for too long. Therefore, you need to make up your mind quickly when you come across such opportunities. For those who wish to settle down in a country, houses of this nature would be a good start.

你应该在联排别墅市场碰碰运气。一般来说，联排别墅不会在市场上停留太久。因此，当遇到这些机会时，你需要尽快下决心。对于那些想在一个国家安家落户的人，购买这种房产是一个不错的开端。

19

You should observe the market rules. When you want to move up your housing ladder or down size your house, or when you’ve got to move to a new job or new business in a new city, you do have to sell your current condominiums, town houses or houses. For that matter, you need to follow the basic rules.

你应遵循市场交易规则。如果想改善居住条件或缩小住房面积，或由于新的工作或新的业务需要搬到一个新的城市，你需要卖掉现有公寓、联排别墅或其他房产。就此而言，你需要遵循下列几项基本规则。

20

First, you need to give a facelift to the place surrounding your property, give the interior a thorough cleaning, and make sure that every facility and equipment is in the working conditions, before you turn it over to a listing agent or agency. Second, you should take some nice photos about your property, and post them out on the media, in order to attract the potential buyers. Third, you should price your property in line with the market trend. Fourth, you need to choose the best possible real estate agent or agency to sell your property. Fifth, you should ask the agent or agency to host an open house party, which is a sure way to attract more interested buyers to do the ground investigations on your property. Last but not least, you should find out ways to pop up the deal. For instance, some buyers would ask for some existing house appliances. And, some other buyers may ask the owners to replace some equipment or to improve the yard miniature, etc.

第一，你在把房子移交给房地产经纪人之前，需要把周围的环境翻新一下，对内部做彻底的清扫，并确保所有的设施和设备都处于正常工作状态。第二，你应该拍一些漂亮的照片刊登在平台上，以吸引潜在的买家。第三，你应该根据市场趋势确定售价。第四，你需要选择最好的房地产中介或代理机构来代销房产。第五，应该让你的代理或代理机构举办一个开放日聚会，以期吸引更多感兴趣的客户前来看房。最后，你应该想办法促成交易。例如，一些购房者会要求户主免费提供现有的家用电器。一些客户还可能会要求业主更换一些设备或修缮院子的景观等。

Part Two Situational Dialogues

01

A: Hi, Mike, it's Alison calling from New York. How have you been lately?

嗨，迈克，我是艾莉森，从纽约给你打电话。你们最近好吗?

B: Hi, Johnson, we are fine. Thanks for calling.

嗨，约翰逊，我们很好。谢谢你来电话。

A: We heard that you've just bought a new house.

我们听说你们刚买下一幢新房子。

B: Yes. Right now, we're giving the last touch to the interior decoration. When we finish that, we're planning a house-warming party, which is set for October 20th. And, we hope you and your wife would honor the occasion.

是的。现在，我们正在做最后的室内修饰。完成之后，我们计划在10月20日举办一个暖房聚会。我们希望你和你的妻子届时能赏光。

A: Sure. We look forward to the party.

当然。我们期待参加你们的聚会。

02

A: Good evening, Mr. and Mrs. Howard, thank you for coming to our house-warming party. Please come in and make yourselves comfortable.

晚上好，霍华德先生和太太，谢谢你来参加我们家的暖房聚会。请进，不要拘束。

B: Good evening, Lora and Mark. Congratulations for your new house, and here's the flowers and Champagne. I must say you've certainly bought a nice house.

晚上好，劳拉，马克。恭喜你们乔迁新居，这是鲜花和香槟。我必须要说你们买的房子真漂亮。

A: Thanks a lot. Can you believe it? We finally have our own house here in this community.

非常感谢。你能相信吗？ 我们终于在这个社区拥有自己的房子了。

B: Well, on our way here, we also noticed that you have a nice community, the lake water is clean and the air is so fresh.

嗯，在来的路上，我们注意到你们这个社区很不错，湖水很清澈，空气也很新鲜。

A: You're right. These are the main reasons why we chose the place.

你说得对。这些是我们选择这个社区的主要原因。

B: And, I must say you've got a nice and cozy garden.

我还想说，你们家的小花园既漂亮又舒适。

A: Thanks. In fact, we bought the house three months ago, and we had barely the time to decorate the rooms to our taste, and we're yet to find the time around to renovate the garden. We're thinking of adding a few flowery trees of different types so that we could enjoy the flowers in different seasons, you know. When we come to that part, we'll certainly ask you for advice as you two are experts in this regard.

谢谢。事实上，我们三个月前刚买下这所房子，几乎没有时间把室内布置得符合我们的品位，也没有时间来翻新花园。我们正想再栽一些不同类型的花树，这样就可以在不同的季节都可以赏花了。说到花草，到时我们一定要征求你们的意见，因为你们是这方面的专家。

B: You bet.

一定效劳。

03

A: What else should we do when we have the floors done and have moved your furniture in?

地板铺好，家具摆好之后，我们还需要做什么？

B: Well, we will redo the curtains and repaint all the walls and ceilings.

我们打算重做窗帘，重新粉刷墙壁和天花板。

A: No problem. Then, you and I have to go to the furniture city, where you could choose the right materials and patterns. I could give you some advice on the spot.

没问题，不过你和我需要跑一趟家具城。在那里你可以选择各种不同的材料和图案。我也可以在现场帮你出出主意。

B: I see. Can't we just buy the ready-made curtains?

好的。难道我们不可以买成品窗帘吗？

A: Absolutely not. The windows must be measured, and then the curtains need to be made professionally. That will take a while, though.

绝对不行。必须先量好窗户尺寸，再专门缝制窗帘。不过，这可能要花一段时间。

B: While the curtains are being made, I can start having people look at the kitchen. I can't stand that old one. And, I don't like that outdated electric stove.

做窗帘期间，我可以着手请人来测量厨房。我受不了那个破旧的厨房，我也不喜欢那个老旧的电炉。

A: In that case, you need to find an interior decoration company to redo the kitchen. I know a company that specializes in this area. Shall I get in touch with them on your behalf?

那样的话，你需要找一家室内装潢公司来整修厨房。我知道一家专门做这个的公司，要不要我替你问一下？

B: Yes, please. I think I'd like a kitchen mostly in ivory and light green.

那就劳驾啦。我想把厨房的颜色设计为象牙白和浅绿色。

A: I agree. The colors must be soft and pleasant, but you can talk to them directly.

我同意。颜色必须柔和愉悦，但这些你可以直接同装潢公司人员商量。

04

A: Do you have any vacant condominiums or apartments for letting? We have a family of four, we want to have it for two years, and we need them ready in three weeks. Could you help us out?

你们有空置的公寓房出租吗？我们一家四口，想要租两年，需要在三周内入住。你能帮我们吗？

B: Yes, you’ve come to the right place. We do have some apartments ready for our customers. Currently, we charge $800 per month for single bedroom apartments and $1000 per month for the two-bedroom apartments.

当然，你来对地方了。我们确实为客户准备了一些公寓房。目前，一居室公寓每月800美元，两居室公寓每月1000美元。

A: Wow, the rent has certainly gone up a lot.

哇，房租涨了好多。

B: You’re right, but the rates we give to our customers are still very competitive in the community. However, as a favor and in line with our company rules, I’ve got the authorization to give you a 5% discount on your monthly rate.

你说得对，但是我们向住户征收的房租在这个社区仍然很有竞争力。但是，为表示诚意，依据本公司的规定，我可以给你每月的房租打5%的折扣。

A: That’s very kind of you.

那真是太感谢你了。

B: Here is the lease contract. Please have a close look at it before we go any further. Mind you, you’ve got to pick up your own utility bills, and you should pay the bills on anything that’s not included in the contract.

这是租赁合同。请先仔细阅读，然后进入下一步。注意，你们必须自己付水电费，以及合同以外的任何服务费用。

Part Three　Common Expressions

- We're looking for a two-bedroom apartment with a den for my study.
  我们正在寻租一套带书房的两居室公寓。
- We need an apartment with three bedrooms and we would like to have it for one year.
  我们需要一套有三间卧室的公寓，租期一年。
- We can arrange for you to pay by installments.
  我们可以为你安排分期付款。
- You could pay up the total bill in 10 years.
  你可以在10年的时间内支付完购房款。
- The house you're looking at has a floor space of 250 square meters and a small yard of 80 square meters with a flowery fence.
  你参观的这套房子是250平方米，还带一个80平方米的花篱笆的小院子。
- This is the living and dining room combination. Here is the kitchen. It's a bit small but it's fully equipped. The refrigerator is new and the stove and the microwave oven are less than a year old.
  这是客厅和餐厅的组合套间。这里是厨房。虽小，但设施齐全；冰箱是新的，炉子和微波炉用了不到一年。

- By the way, the shopping center is 5 miles from the residential area and there’s a grocery just around the corner. You can have access to two buses and the metro to the downtown area.
  顺便告诉你，离小区5英里就有购物中心，小区边上有个杂货店。小区有两路公共汽车和地铁可以通往市中心。
- It’s true that this is a new residential area, but we have all the transportation access to the down town area, and we’ve built all the service facilities in the community.
  没错，这是新建的小区，但我们这里有直达市中心的交通工具，而且小区建有所有的服务设施。
- We’re mindful about the green environment, and we’ve also built green belts and flower beds in every available space, so that you could enjoy different flowers in different seasons.
  我们十分重视绿化环境，在每个可利用的空间都建了绿化带和花圃，因此，你们一年四季都可以欣赏到不同的鲜花。
- Please be advised that our community has established standard security service, and we’re just 150 meters away from the police station.
  请注意，本小区设有标准的安保机制，而且离我们小区150米就是派出所。
- In many cities, you might be lucky to buy houses off market. For various reasons, some home owners would put up “FOR SALE” posts in front of their homes to attract potential buyers. Then, you could cruise around some ideal residential communities, and stop at some homes, knock at the door and introduce yourself to the owner and talk about the possible deal.
  在许多城市，你也许有幸无需通过市场就能购买到房子。由于种种原因，一些房主会在门前插上“出售”的招牌吸引过往行人的眼球。因此，你可以在一些理想的居民小区开车巡视，并在中意的房门前停车，去敲敲门，向房主做自我介绍，探讨交易的可能。

第十七章

车辆购租

*

工业革命以来，人们越来越多地生活在车轮上。如今，我们开车上班、上学、去公司或参加活动。我们开车做生意，乘坐出租车旅行，通过多种交通工具观光旅游。同时，我们中许多人将各类车辆作为第一笔固定资产投资，或在必要时租车出行。其间，我们均需要遵循法律规章。

Chapter Seventeen

Vehicle Purchase and Lease

*

Since the industrial revolution, people have been increasingly living on wheels. Nowadays, we are driving to work, to school, to office or to functions. We conduct business via vehicles, we travel in taxi, and we do sight-seeing via many means of transportation. Meanwhile, many of us would regard vehicles as our first investment in the fixed asset, or we would rent them when necessary. However, whatever we do in the above regard, we need to follow all the laws and regulations.

Part One　Things to Know

01

For many of you, vehicles may become your first ever private property. Therefore, if you want a car, get things right from the very beginning. You've got to look for a car to your taste and at par with your financial capability. Then, you would add some features of your own choice, because nothing less would beat the thrill of sitting behind the wheels that are under your own name. However, every car comes at a price in terms of depreciation, which starts from around 20% the moment you have the key in hand.

对你们许多人而言，汽车可能成为第一件个人固定资产。因此，你若想买一辆车，从一开始就必须把事情办妥。你要在财务允许范围内寻购一辆符合您品位的车辆。然后依据个人喜好增加配饰，因为没有什么比驾驶自己的爱车更令人兴奋。不过，每辆车都有折旧问题，在你拿到钥匙之际，你的爱车就已发生了相当于总价值20%的折旧。

02

To start with, you need to cruise on the Internet or visit some car dealers and compare their offers before you should sit down with any particular dealer, in order to get the best quotation and after service. Therefore, you should prepare a thorough questionnaire beforehand, which is the sure way to go safe and to save money.

首先，你需要上网浏览或寻访不同的汽车经销商，货比三家，然后再坐下来与经销商谈判，以期获得最佳的报价和售后服务。因此，你应该事先准备一份详细的问题清单，这是既安全又省钱的购车方法。

03

Once you’re at the exhibition hall, you need to stick to the “bottom lines” such as brands, styles, colors and interior configurations. There’re occasions when the dealer would show you the vehicles that are plenty in stock. The trick is real popular brands or modals never pile up at the dealer’s bonds. One more thing, you should change the dealer when he or she should be hesitating at any questions of yours.

你抵达车行展厅后，需要在品牌、风格、颜色和内部配置等方面坚守“底线”。有时候经销商会带你看库存充足的现货车辆。经验表明，经销商绝不会将真正流行的品牌或型号车辆留在手上。还有一点，一旦发现经销商对你的问题答非所问，你应该尽快换人。

04

When you’re certain about the final vehicle you would purchase, you’ve got to test drive the vehicle, in order to find out the hand-feel and engine conditions on the road. It’s also a must that you should request the dealer to accompany you, so that the latter could tell you something more about the vehicle on the way, and you may find other issues to discuss with the latter.

确定好最终想要买的车型之后，你要先试驾，以充分了解车的手感和动力情况。要求经销商陪你一起试驾也是必要的，这样他可以向你介绍更多关于车辆的情况，也可以就你关心的问题进行进一步商讨。

05

Before you should put your signature on the contract, you need to go over all the articles that you have agreed upon. You need to make sure that everything

you want is written in the contract. The truth is that any new things or conditions you raise afterwards would be added to your final bill.
在合同上签字之前，你需要仔细核查你与经销商达成的所有条款。你需要确保你关注的事项都写进合同里。事实上，合同签署后你再提出任何新要求或新条件都需要自掏腰包。

06

You need to strike a deal that's within your financial reach. Therefore, you've got to make sure you get a good interest rate and the best possible after service package, so that you'll know what to do when you receive the monthly bills in the future.
你需要在你的财力范围之内达成交易。因此，你需要确保获得最佳的商贷利率和售后服务。这样，每月收到分期付款账单之后，你就不用犯难。

07

Here in my countries, you need to find out preferential treatments when you should buy a car. Mind you, some dealers would offer cash rebates or discounts. Some other dealers would provide customers with complimentary refueling for the first few months, as well as free car wash for a certain period. Still some others would offer free maintenance up to the first 30000 miles on the meter. Therefore, you need to find out all those possible terms of conditions, and exploit them to your advantage.
在我的国家，你在购车时需要了解相应的优惠待遇。请注意，一些经销商会提供现金回扣或折扣。另有一些经销商会在头几个月内为客户提供免费加油服务，并在一段时间内提供免费洗车服务。还有一些公司会在新车行驶达30000英里时提供免费保养。因此，你需要设法获得这些优惠，谋划应得的利益。

08

Whether you have your own car, or you are yet to have one, you may have reasons to rent a car for some short trips. When you plan to do that , you need to know that many rental companies may give you different charges. Therefore, you need to do some homework so that you will not only enjoy quality services, but also get a good bargain.

无论你已经拥有爱车，还是即将要购买一辆，你都有可能会需要租一辆车进行短途旅行。你在打算租车时需要记住，很多租车公司可以提供服务，但收费标准各不相同。因此，你需要做好功课，不仅可以争取到优质的服务，而且可以获得公道的租赁价格。

09

In some cases, you could rent a car for a long-distance trip, even though you have your own car. It’s because you could save your car from wear and tear. Perhaps, you would sell your car at a good price, as it would be a good way to preserve mileage on your car. Another reason is that it is possible to give you a better gas mileage. More importantly, you may enjoy the kind of comfort which your own car may not be able to provide.

有时候，尽管你拥有爱车，但也可以租车进行长途旅行。因为租车可以让你的爱车免于磨损。将来你想转让爱车时，还能卖一个好价钱，因为租车可以减少爱车的里程数。还有一个原因，租车可以节省每公里油耗费用。更为重要的是，你可以享受到驾驶自己车辆不大可能得到的惬意。

10

When you have a car under your name, you need to carry out the maintenance as prescribed by the car manufacturer. Some people would not bother about the maintenance until they are in trouble. As a result, they have to pay for their lessons. For instance, some car engines may break down halfway

of a trip. Or, the brake systems may suddenly fail to respond to the road conditions, etc.
你购买车辆后需要依据汽车制造商规定的时间定期进行保养。有些人懒得对爱车进行保养，直到出了问题。其结果，他们必须为自己的错误买单。例如，有的汽车引擎会在半路上熄火；有的在遇到紧急情况之际，刹车会失灵等。

11

It's cost effective and enjoyable to travel with peer groups or colleagues. There're many ways to go out in groups. For example, it would be ideal to travel together in a commuter bus, on the same trains or in the same flight, where you could have most time to have casual conversations or play games.
和同龄人或同事结伴旅行既省钱又愉快。有很多途径可以集体出行。例如，你们可一起乘通勤巴士、火车或飞机旅行，那些都是理想的选择，以便有足够的时间聊聊天或玩游戏。

12

When you do your own driving, you will likely get a ticket or to be stopped by the traffic police sometime. Minor traffic violations such as speeding or double parking are classified as "infractions", which are not punishable by jail time, you just have to pay the tickets through mail or on-line. However, for the serious traffic offenses, or when you have extra points on your license, you could face the termination of your driving license or police detention, which warrants you to consult with an attorney.
只要你自己开车，你一生中会收到罚单或被警察半路拦下盘查。对于超车或压线停车之类的"小违规"，不至于被警察拘留，你只需要通过邮寄或在网上缴纳罚款。但是，你如果严重违章且你的驾驶证上已有前科记录，那么你可能会被吊销驾驶执照或被拘留。那样的话，你就需要寻求律师的帮助。

13

Here in my country, when you approach a roundabout, you must turn on your light indicators when turning left, right or making a U-turn, and must give prompt indications to the cars in front you, which are already in the roundabout. When you’re going straight ahead, there is no need to do so. Meanwhile when you’re entering a roundabout, you must slow down and give way to any vehicles already in the loop. When you’re exiting a roundabout, whether you are turning left, right or going straight ahead, you must indicate a left turn just before you exit.

在我国，在驾车接近环岛之际，无论你需要左转、右转或掉头行驶，都需要打开转向灯，提醒已经在转盘内行驶的所有车辆。你如果只是前行，则无需打开转向灯。你在进入环岛之际，需要放慢车速，给所有已经在环岛车道上行驶的车辆让道。你如果想要离开环岛，无论是左转、右转还是直行，在离开之际都需要打开左转向灯。

14

Here are some tips for you to follow. White lines are used to separate lanes of traffic moving in the same direction. Meanwhile, the yellow lines are used to separate traffic headed in opposite directions. Whatever mistakes you make there, you’re simply asking for trouble.

以下是你需要遵守的一些交通规则。白线限制在同一车道上行驶的车辆。与此同时，黄线禁止对方车道上的车辆驶入本车道。违反以上任何一条交规，你都会遇到麻烦。

15

When you reach the location of the rent-a-car company, you will have to make payment with your credit card. You have to provide driving license and a copy of documents for identity verification purposes. In addition, you will have to provide your mobile phone number and back-up numbers which the

company can contact you with, during the rental period.
你在抵达租车公司之际，需要用信用卡支付租金。您还需要提交驾驶执照和其他文件的副本，以验明你的身份。此外，你还需要提供手机号码和其他联系方式，以便租车公司在租车期间与你取得联系。

16

In many countries, payment by credit card is still popular. For example, when you are at a rent-a-car company, you may be required to provide a security deposit, which would be used in the event of loss or damage to the rental vehicle. Therefore, the company would withhold a security deposit from your credit card.
在许多国家，用信用卡支付费用仍很普遍。例如，你在车行租车时，可能要用信用卡支付保证金。这样，在租赁车辆发生任何损失或损坏，要从保证金中相应扣除。因此，汽车租赁公司会在信用卡上扣押一定数量的保证金。

17

In the event of any damage to the rental vehicles, the rental company will use this security deposit to pay for the costs of necessary repairs or replacement. If the cost for repair or replacement of damage exceeds the amount of the security deposit, you will have to meet the balance. For your security protection, the rental company may sell you insurance. And, you would have to provide the proof of your insurance that would cover the possible damage to the rental vehicle during the contract period. Otherwise, when the rental vehicle is damaged or destroyed, while it's in your possession, you have to pay for any required insurance deductible.
所租赁车辆如果发生损坏，租赁公司将使用保证金支付必要的维修或更换零部件费用。如果损坏的修理或更换费用超过保证金的数额，你有义务支付余额部分。出于安全利益考虑，汽车租赁公司可能会要求你购买保险。你必须向租赁公司提供保险证明，证明已购保险可用以赔偿租赁车辆的毁损。否则，如果车辆在你驾驶期间出现损毁，你需要支付所有保险费用。

18

When the company releases the car to you, you have to sign the agreement, which would outline the specific rights and obligations relating to the rental car. First, it's the names of the rental car company and the renter. Second, it is the full description of the car, which includes the model, engine number, chassis number, registration number, and the date of registration. Third, it's the duration for the car hire. The fourth is the maximum distance that you may travel in the vehicle from the commencement date of the agreement. The fifth is the scope of use. You will have to specify the usage of the car, and promise to drive the vehicle on the normal road conditions. Then, you will have to comply with all the laws and regulations when the car is under you care. And, you are not to sublease the rental vehicle, etc.

租赁公司把车交给你的时候，你需要签一份合同，明确规定车辆租赁各方的权利和义务。第一，租车公司和租车人的名字。第二，对汽车的完整描述，包括型号、发动机号、底盘号、登记号码和登记日期。第三，租车的期限。第四，自协议生效日期起，你可以驾驶车辆行驶的最大距离。第五，适用范围。你必须说明车辆的具体用途，并承诺在路况正常的道路上行驶。你要在驾驶和保管车辆期间遵守所有的法律法规。不得将所租车辆转租他人等。

19

When you are on the road, you need to abide by the laws and regulations, which would keep you and your folks safe. The safety of all road users would depend on the motorists who would follow the rules to the letter.

你在驾驶途中需要遵守交通规章，以确保自己和同行人的安全。所有交通相关人员的安全取决于所有严格遵守规章制度的司机。

20

The rental agreement comes into effect the moment when the rental car is handed over to you. Therefore, before leaving the rental company, you should make sure that the car is in good condition. It should be the right model that you can easily drive. One more thing, the rental company will refuse to hire out the car to you if you've got the following issues: Failure to meet minimum age requirement; failure to provide legal driving license; under the influence of alcohol; in intoxication; having a child under the age of six without a toddler seat; with previous crime record; bad credit record, etc.

租赁公司将车辆交到你手里后，租赁协议立即生效。因此，在离开租车公司前，你应确保车况良好。你应当确认所租赁车辆属于你可以轻松驾驶的车型。还有一件事，如果存在以下问题，租赁公司将拒绝向你出租车辆：未达到最低年龄要求、未提供合法驾驶执照、体内酒精含量超标、醉酒、有六岁以下的儿童随行但没有携带儿童座椅、有犯罪前科、有不良信用记录等。

Part Two　Situational Dialogues

01

A: Good morning, madam. What can I do for you?

早上好，女士。我能为您做些什么？

B: Good morning, sir. I'm here to look for a Nissan SUV.

早上好，先生。我想购买一辆尼桑越野车。

A: Well, you've come to the right place. We're the largest dealer for Nissan vehicles in the city, and we've got all the models you can think of. Here's the brochure, please have a look at it, and find out if we have the right vehicle for you in stock. Shall I get you a cup of coffee?

哦，您算是来对地方了。我们是市内最大的尼桑汽车经销商，您能想到的所有车型我们都有。这是产品样册，请先看一看是否有您想要的现货车辆。我给您倒杯咖啡好吗？

B: Yes, please.

好的，请。

02

A: Well, madam. Now, I shall take you for a tour to our exhibition hall where you could have a look at them all, which could help you make up your mind.

哦，夫人。现在，我带您参观一下我们的车辆展厅，您可以看到所有产品，以便您做出选择。

B: Thank you very much. After you, please.

非常感谢。请带路。

A: While we're on the subject, what model you're having in mind and what is the price range that you have for the vehicle, please?

关于您购车的事，请问您想要什么型号的车，以及您的心理价位是多少？

B: Well, I'll buy the latest model with the normal configuration, but I'll add some new features of my own choice. With regard to the price, I can afford around $40000.

嗯，我想买一辆标准配置的最新款车辆，但我会要求另外添加部分新功能。关于价格，我的心理价位是4万美元左右。

A: I see. In your case, I'll recommend this model, which has the price tag of $36000 as start-off price. So, when you should add some additional features, the final price will fall within your budget.

我知道了。根据您的情况，我向您推荐这一款，它的起价是36000美元。即使您想增加一些功能，最终价格仍将在您的预算范围以内。

B: Thanks, I'll take your advice, and here is the request list.

谢谢，我会听你的建议，这是我要求添加新功能的单子。

A: Let me see… I think I can meet all your requirements, and still keep the final price within your budget. Well, for your information, we're still in the middle of the seasonal sale period, which will offer you a free maintenance up to 30000 miles and provide free car wash service for 18 months. How does it sound?

让我看看。我想我可以满足您所有的要求，并且保证最终价格仍然在您的预算之内。顺便告诉您，我们仍在进行季节性促销活动，因此，我们将为您提供长达30000英里的免费保养和18个月的免费洗车服务。您觉得怎么样？

B: That's very kind of you. Now, I'd like to have a test drive on this vehicle.

Could you accompany me so that you could brief me more about the vehicle?

你太好了。现在我想试驾一下这辆车。你能陪我一起试驾，并多介绍一些关于这辆车的情况吗？

A: Certainly, it’s my pleasure.

当然可以，这是我的荣幸。

03

A: Good afternoon, sir. What can I do for you?

先生，下午好。我能为您做些什么吗？

B: I wonder if you have any rental cars available.

请问你们是否有车辆租赁。

A: Of course. Here is the brochure, and what kind of cars would you prefer, please?

当然有。这是宣传册，请问您喜欢什么样的车？

B: I would like to have a look at the brochure before I make the decision, please.

我想先看一下宣传册，然后再做决定。

A: Sure. Please take your time. When you’ve decided, please let me know.

当然可以。您慢慢看。等您想好了，请告诉我。

B: Well, my wife and I would like to rent a wagon. How much will it cost for one week?

嗯，我妻子和我想租一辆旅行车。租一个星期要多少钱？

A: It would be 40 dollars and 120 miles per day plus 20 cents per extra mile, and here is the list of rates for different duration.

一天40美元可行驶120英里，之后每英里加收20美分。这是不同租用时间的报价表。

B: Thanks. Should we pay for the gasoline?

谢谢。我们用付汽油费吗？

A: Well, we've filled up the tank already, but you'll have to refill the tank when you're on your own expense. Please remember to fill up the tank when you drop the car at our branch office anywhere you are.

嗯，我们已经把油箱加满了油，但是再需要加油您得自行付费。在目的地向我们的分公司还车时，请记住要加满油。

B: By the way, how should I pay for the rental?

顺便问一下，我该如何支付租金？

A: We'll charge the rental fee for one week on your credit card. Now, please let me have your passport, driving license and credit card.

我们会在您的信用卡上收取一周的租金。现在请出示您的护照、驾驶执照和信用卡。

B: What should we do with the insurance, please?

请问我们该如何办理保险？

A: It's compulsory that you need to buy the insurance listed in the contract, according to the laws and regulations in my country. It's a guarantee for your personal interests, you know.

根据我国的交通法规，您必须购买合同中所列的保险。这是为了您个人利益考虑。

B: Then, what shall we do when we should have any problems on the road?

那么，我们在路上遇到问题的时候应该怎么办呢？

A: That's easy. You just have to call the number listed in the contract, then our technicians will help you out in no time.

那很简单。您只需拨打合同上所列的电话号码，我们的技术人员就会在第一时间帮您解决问题。

04

A: Good morning, sir. What can I do for you?

早上好，先生。我能为您做些什么吗？

B: Good morning, sir. I'm here to report a car stolen.

早上好，先生。我是来报案的，我的一辆车被盗了。

A: Wait a minute, and let me get the recording ready... Now, please tell me what happened.

等一下，让我把录音准备好……现在，请告诉我是怎么回事。

B: Yesterday evening, my wife and I drove to a party at our friend’s house. We parked the car just on the roadside. However, it was gone when we came out after the party.

昨天晚上，我和妻子开车去朋友家参加一个聚会。我们把车停在马路边。然而，当聚会结束后，我们的车不见了。

A: I’m sorry to hear that. Now, let us get some details about your case, and please tell me everything you know about your car.

很抱歉听到这个消息。现在，我们了解一些细节情况，请您描述一下车辆的所有情况。

B: It’s Toyota and is a 2017 model.

是丰田牌2017款。

A: What’s the plate number and the chassis number?

车牌号码和底盘号码是多少？

B: Well, to save you the trouble, I brought the photo copy of the two numbers. Here you are.

哦，为了省去您的麻烦，我把这两个号码的影印件带来了。给您。

A: Thanks, that’s better.

谢谢，这样很好。

B: What’s the color, please?

请问车是什么颜色的？

A: It’s greyish beige.

灰褐色的。

B: Well, that’s all I want to know. Please leave your name, cell phone number and residence address. My colleagues will get in touch with you when should we get any information about the car. Please also check in with us once a week.

嗯，暂时我们就需要了解这些情况。请留下您的姓名、手机号码和居住地址。我的同事一旦有了关于这辆车的消息，就会立即联系您。也请您每周与我们联系一次。

A: Please pardon my naive question, but do you think it's possible for us to get it back?

请原谅我问一个外行问题，您认为我们有可能找回丢失的车辆吗？

B: God knows. Nevertheless, I'll immediately put your case into our system, and do our best to help you out.

只有上帝知道。不过，我会立即把您的情况录入我们的系统，并尽我们最大的努力帮助您找回车辆。

Part Three　Common Expressions

- I'm looking for an economy car for daily use within the city.

  我想买一辆经济型的小汽车，供每天在城里日常使用。

- Here in my country, you need to remember three rules when you have to pull over at the instruction from the traffic police. First, you should always be courteous and polite. A bit of class and respect will make the next steps easier for you. Second, you should resist any request of the police until you're forced to oblige. Don't worry. You won't get in trouble for being arrested. You only get in trouble for being convicted of the crime you're arrested for. Third, you should not answer questions. No matter what an officer may tell you, you are not compelled to speak or answer their questions without a lawyer present.

在我的国家，根据交警的指示靠边停车时，你需要记住三条规则。首先，你应该彬彬有礼。保持风度和尊重他人会使你的下一步变得更容易。第二，除非是不得不，否则你应该拒绝警察的每一个要求。别担心，你不会因为被捕而惹上麻烦。你只会因为被逮捕的罪名而惹上麻烦。第三，你不应该回答问题。无论警官会对你讲什么，在没有律师在场的情况下，你都不要勉强作回应或回答任何问题。

- Here in my country, the moment you get into the cockpit, the first thing you must do is to fasten your seat belt, and so do the people in the passenger seat. Otherwise, you will inevitably receive a ticket from the traffic police.

  在我的国家，你坐到驾驶座上后首先要系好安全带，同车的乘客也一样。否则，必然会接到交警的罚单。

- It’s common for you to be impatient when sitting behind the steering wheels, which would very often lead you to short tempers, and even lead to car accidents. When you’re caught in those scenarios, you’re easy to fall into verbal or fist fighting. Nevertheless, the cool way is to make sure everybody is safe from life threatening situation. Then, call the police.

  在驾车期间失去耐心，这很正常，但这常会导致情绪失控，甚至车祸。每当陷入这种情绪时，你很容易与对方言语争吵或拳拳相加。然而，冷静的方法是，确保每个人的生命安全后，报警。

- On the daily basis, we constantly hear the news about road accidents, which would result in hundreds of deaths and injuries worldwide. Despite the efforts by the governments to implement the tough laws and regulations, the accidents have been increasing year after year, either because some people would recklessly drive their vehicle, or because of human and natural disasters.

  在日常生活中，我们经常听到关于交通事故的新闻，每年在全世界成百上千的人死于或伤于车祸。尽管政府努力实施严厉的法律法规，交通事故依旧逐年增加，或因为有些司机鲁莽驾驶，或因为人类和自然灾害。

- It's cool to drive our own cars or a motorcycle, which would keep us on track in our fast-paced lives and work. Nevertheless, when we do not abide by the simple safety driving procedures, we're definitely at risk. It pays for us to buckle up our seatbelts, wear our helmets, and follow the traffic lights and street signs. Once we fail to follow the traffic laws and take proper precautions, we're bound to bump into severe accidents or have trouble with the traffic police.

  自己开车或骑摩托车确实很惬意，完全符合我们快节奏的生活和工作。然而，如果不能遵守基本的安全驾驶规则，就会很危险。我们需要系好安全带，戴上头盔，遵守交通灯和路标。如果不能遵守交通法规并采取适当的预防措施，我们一定会遭遇严重的车祸或受到交警的处罚。

第十八章

留学事宜

*

有人说，学习是终身事，但只有少数幸运儿能有机会出国留学。作为一名留学生，你不仅要选好主修专业、副修专业，而且需要痛下决心学好英语，了解东道国政治、经济、文化、价值观和传统等领域的知识，以期成为多才多艺的国际人，而不是仅仅是从外国大学多获得一个学位的中国学生。

Chapter Eighteen

Overseas Studies

*

They say learning is a lifetime thing, during which studying abroad is the rare opportunity for the luck few. However, as an overseas student, you should not only exert yourself in the chosen major and minors, but also take pains in polishing up your English, learning about the politics, economics, cultures, values and traditions so that you would become a versatile international person, rather than a Chinese student with just one more academic degree from a foreign university.

Part One　Things to Know

01

Higher education is absolutely necessary for the young people in today's world. Colleges and universities are the launching pads to get young people into the competitive society, as well as the roads to their successful careers.

高等教育对当今世界的年轻人是非常必要的。大学是年轻人进入竞争激烈社会的跳板，也是通向个人事业成功的必由之路。

02

For many families, parents would bend backward in sending their kids overseas for higher education, in order to make their own dream a reality. And, for many high school students, studying abroad would be a chip on their shoulders.

对于许多家庭来说，父母会竭尽所能把孩子送到海外接受高等教育，以实现他们的梦想。对于许多高中生而言，出国留学会成为令人羡慕的荣耀。

03

Simply said, preparation for college starts with application. First, you need to draft a road map, which covers everything you need to do before you should get your scholarship from a possible foreign university or college.

简单地说，为留学做准备需要从留学申请开始。首先，你需要制定出国留学路线图，涵盖你要从国外高等院校获得奖学金所需要做的所有事情。

04

When you've decided which country to go for higher education, you need to choose the right university, and you shouldn't aim at only those top colleges or universities. Rather, you should choose the ones that are in line with your academic capability and qualifications.

你决定去哪个国家接受高等教育之后，需要选择合适的院校。你不应该只瞄准那些顶尖的学院或大学，而应该选择那些与你的能力和资格相匹配的院校。

05

You should check out the universities or colleges that best meet your expectations in terms of scholarship, faculty, the opportunity for further degree education. More importantly, you should choose the majors in terms of job opportunities, or your future career when you graduate.

你应该综合考察院校奖学金、师资、继续深造的机会。更为重要的是，你应当从就业机会或发展前景方面选择专业。

06

When all these matters are sorted out, you should tally your qualifications, and make sure your dream schools would accept your applications and contact you. In order to avoid the pitfalls, it pays for you to seek professional help from the relevant agents.

所有这些事情都考虑妥帖之后，你应该认真核对本人的资历，确保你梦想的学校会接受你的申请并联系你。为了避免掉入陷阱，你应向留学代理机构寻求专业帮助。

07

Meanwhile, you need to polish up your English. You need to catch up with the capability to tackle difficult passages, and learn to read between the lines. You need to improve your oral capability to reason, question, argue or debate. You need to build up your capability to produce quality papers in English within the deadline, etc. All these would help you overcome the language barrier when you're on the ground.

与此同时，你需要提高英语水平。你需要提高阅读理解高难度段落的能力，学会领会课文的言外之意；你需要强化思辨、提问、争论和辩论的能力；你需要增强在规定时间里完成高质量论文的能力。所有这些准备活动均有助于你入学后克服语言障碍。

08

In short, you will have to make sure that everything is under control before you should get going. You will have to get prepared both in kind and in mind, in order to avoid the last-minute rush. For example, your paperwork involves a lot of formalities, from applying for visas to getting the medical tests. These may take months to complete. And, you have to make sure your passport is valid for the entire duration of your stay overseas, and you should bring along a copy of your medical report, driving license, birth certificate and any other documents you may have.

简而言之，在出发之前，你必须确保一切都在掌控之中。为了避免最后一刻抓瞎，你必须在物质上和精神上都做好准备。例如，你的文书工作涉及很多手续，从申请签证到做体检等。这些有可能需要几个月才能办妥。你必须确保你的护照在整个留学期间都是有效的，你应记得带上医疗报告、驾照、出生证明和其他需要携带的文件复印件。

09

Finally, you should get some powerful letters of recommendation. They're

very important when you're applying for colleges and universities which have strict admission philosophies, and the admission officers there would look closely at those letters before they give you the green light.
最后，你应该设法找到有影响力的人为你写信推荐。你想要申请那些具有严格招生规章的院校，推荐信最重要，这些院校的招生官在给你开绿灯之前，会仔细查看你的推荐信。

10

Experience says life on campus is never easy for foreign students. No matter how hard you have prepared yourself, you may still come across surprises, from dorm activities to classroom rigors, or from campus routines to cultural shocks at local communities. Therefore, you need to fasten your seat belt, and prepare for anything that comes in your way, but that's part of the learning process in a foreign land, right?
经验表明，对外国人来说，校园生活从来都不容易。不管你准备得多充分，你总会遇到意料之外的事情，从宿舍活动到教室的紧张气氛，从繁琐的校园规章制度到当地社区的文化冲击。因此，你需要绷紧思想上的弦，准备应对任何意料之外的事宜，不过，这也是在异域他乡学习过程的一部分，对吗？

11

Your new life starts when you set foot on the campus of your dream college or university. There, you need to reset the clock, in line with the major you've chosen for the years to come. Whatever you do, you should avoid facing too many pending courses in the final year. You need to balance out the required courses and selective courses for each semester. And, you need to finish all the academic tasks in time, with efficiency and quality. When you're not sure about it, you should seek help from your academic advisers.
在踏上梦想中的大学校园之际，你的留学生活就正式开始了。此后，你需要根据所选择的专业重新调整你的时刻表。无论如何，你都应该避免在最后一年选修太多的必修课程。你需要平衡每学期的必修课和选修课。你需要保质保量地完成院校规定的学术任务。你如果遇到不确定的事宜，要多向学术顾问求助。

12

Please be advised your classes and lectures in overseas colleges and universities are very much interactive, which warrant your ability to learn, reason, question, argue and come to your own conclusions in English. Therefore, you should refrain from being an attentive or smiling student as you would do back in China.

请注意，国外高校的课程和讲座互动性很强，你需要培养用英语学习、思考、提问、辩论和得出结论的能力。因此，你不能像在中国那样，满足于做一个专心听讲、面带微笑的学生。

13

You should set your mind in order throughout the years when you are overseas. No one is born to be genius in any given academic subject, you know. Therefore, you need to find out what you want to achieve and what you can really do. Then, you've got to set your goals, and strive to achieve them to your level of the best. As one saying goes, donuts won't fall from the sky.

在国外留学期间，你应该整理好自己的思绪。你知道吗，在任何专业领域，没有人天生是学霸。所以，你需要弄清楚你想要实现什么以及你真正能够做到什么。然后，你需要设定目标，并尽自己最大努力去实现。正如谚语所说，天上不会掉馅饼。

14

You wouldn't believe it, but you've got to manage your required academic courses, as well as the professional skills that are important when you start

your career. Therefore, you need to take some probational training courses, and take an active part in club activities, which would foster both your “soft capability” and “hard capability”.
你可能不会相信，但你既需要掌握必修的学术课程，也需要掌握与你未来职业生涯相关的专业技能。因此，你需要参加一些培训课程，积极参加俱乐部活动，以培养你的软实力和硬实力。

15

According to some successful experiences, students from the single-child families have to do more to be independent. Therefore, it’s cool for you to make your own decisions. It’s fabulous for you to “grow up”. It’s fun for you to make new friends. It’s the right way to start your own life, and a blessing to master your own destiny.
成功的海外留学经验表明，来自于独生子女家庭的学生需要做出更多的努力才能实现独立。因此，自己做决定很酷，“独立长大”很美妙，结交新朋友很有趣。这既是你开始独立生活的正确方式，也是掌握自己命运的有效途径。

16

There are many ways to carry out interactions in the classrooms or peer group activities. When you come across something uncertain, you should raise up your hand and ask for clarifications. When the professor gives you the opportunity to speak, you should have the courage to air out what you have in mind, or write out your answer to the question on the blackboard.
在课堂上或参与同龄人活动时都有许多相互交流的方式。遇到困惑时，你应该主动举手提出并弄明白。老师如果给你机会，你应该大胆地说出你的想法，或将你的问题答案写在黑板上。

17

You should always remember that in overseas classes, your final scores for each semester on any subjects would not only include the midterm exams and the final exam, but also the involvement of class activities as well as term papers. So, you need to exert yourself on all those items.

你应该记住，在海外课堂上，每个学期任何科目的最终成绩不仅包括期中考和期末考，还包括课堂活动以及学期论文。所以，你需要在所有这些项目上努力。

18

One more thing, classroom activities are not equally open for all. You need to grab the chances. Teachers are more likely to give higher marks to those who are active in class, which makes up 40% of the scores for any particular course.

还有一点，课堂活动的机会并非人人平等，你需要主动抓住机会。老师很有可能给在课堂上活跃的学生较高分数，课堂活动表现会占任何一门课程分数的40%。

19

It's the common practice that you should plan your dissertation as soon as you officially register your major. Last minute rush would never produce quality papers. By the way, many Chinese students tend to suffer from the scenario of "dumb English", and you need to patch up this "short board" before you should venture to defend your dissertation.

通常情况下，你应该在正式注册专业后就开始规划论文写作。在最后时刻赶任务不会写出高质量的论文。顺便说一下，许多中国学生会面临"哑巴英语"的窘境。因此，在准备论文答辩之前，你一定要补齐这块短板。

20

It’s a common sense that you need to learn to communicate regularly with your course lecturers, who have the obligations to answers your questions, during which you could clarify most of the things that may bother you.

你需要学会定期与你的课程讲师沟通，这是常识。他们有义务回答你的问题，在这一过程中你可以解决困扰你的大部分问题。

Part Two Situational Dialogues

01

A: Good morning, Mrs. Liberman. I’m glad that you could receive me at such a short notice. First of all, I’ve got to apologize that I’m two days behind the schedule for registration.

早上好，利伯曼夫人。很高兴您能在这么短的时间内接待我。首先，我必须向您道歉，我比预定的注册时间晚了两天。

B: Well, it’s not really your fault, and you were smart to let us know about your pending issue so that we could reserve your case accordingly. I’m also glad you could finally make it here before the deadline. Now, let me brief you about things you need to do today. First, it’s the registration, and I can assist you, in order to save you the time.

我说，这并非你的错。你很聪明，预先告知我们你延迟的原因，这样我们就可以保留你的报到时间。我也很高兴你终于在截止日期前赶到这里。现在，让我简要地告诉你今天需要做的事情。首先是注册，我可以协助你办理相关事宜，以便节省时间。

A: That's very kind of you. I think I've filled in most of the items in these forms but there are still some blanks which I don't know for sure.

太感谢您啦。我想这些表格中的大部分条目我已经填好了，但仍有一些地方我不太确定。

B: Don't worry. We can work out the details for the missing blanks. Now, let me have a quick look at the formats you have done, just to make sure… Well, you do have some corrections to make at the lines where I've marked out in yellow color.

别担心，我们会把缺的东西补上的。现在，让我快速浏览一下你填写的表格，看看是否都填对了。嗯，你确实有些地方需要修改，我已用黄色标出来了。

A: I certainly appreciate it.

非常感谢。

02

A: Good afternoon, Mr. Wilson. I hope I'm not late to submit my registration format.

下午好，威尔逊先生。我希望我没有延误提交注册表格的时间。

B: Good afternoon, Mr. Han Fanglin. You're not late at all, and I know you Chinese guys are prompt in doing things. Now, let me have the general course plan of yours, and I'll find out if you have planned your courses evenly… Well, it seems your course outline is a bit lopsided.

下午好，韩方林先生。你一点也不晚，我知道你们中国人做事很勤快。现在，请你把大概的课程表给我看一下，让我帮你看看你的课程计划是否均衡……嗯，你的课程大纲好像有点失衡。

A: I should appreciate it if you could kindly help me to reschedule my plan accordingly. It's really new for me in this area, you know.

您能否帮我调整一下我的课程表，我将感激不尽。您知道，在这方面我是个新手。

B: Well, my advice is that you need to spread out your major courses evenly with emphasis on the courses that are closely related to your MA degree, and you should leave some space for the last year so that you could have enough time to work out your dissertation and prepare for the defense.
嗯，我的建议是，你需要均匀地安排主要课程，优先选择与你硕士学位密切相关的课程，以便为最后一年留出足够的时间，去完成你的论文并准备答辩。

A: Thank you very much, Mr. Wilson. I'll take the format back and do some more work on it, and come back to you tomorrow. Now, could I have another blank format, please?
非常感谢，威尔逊先生。我把表格拿回去再做一些修改，然后明天再回来提交。所以，请再给我一张空白表格，好吗?

B: In fact, you could download it from our website directly and fill it out on line, and then submit it to my office on line. I promise to help you double check the whole thing. When I spot something wrong, I'll let you know.
实际上，你可以直接从我们的网站上下载，在网上填写，然后在线提交到我的办公室。我一定帮你核查所有的内容。如果有问题，我会告诉你的。

03

A: Good morning, Professor Garside. Thank you very much for receiving me. As I requested on the phone, it's about my semester course arrangement.
早上好，加塞德教授。非常感谢您能接待我。正如我在电话中请求的，我想请您指导一下我这学期的课程安排。

B: You're welcome. It's my job to help you out. Now, let me have a quick look at it and see if there is anything that I can do for you… Well, you do have over-loaded yourself with the major courses. You can't swallow a donut in just one bite, you know.

不用客气。帮助你是我的职责。现在，让我快速地看一下，看看有什么我可以帮你的……嗯，你的专业课选得确实有点多。你知道吗，你不能一口吞下一个甜甜圈。

A: Well. I thought I should take as many courses as possible for the first academic year, so that I could have more time to work on my dissertation.

我原以为，第一学年我应该选尽可能多的课，这样我后面就有更多的时间撰写论文。

B: You are right, but my advice is that you should take one major course off and replace it with one selective course. You need to give yourself some time for fun. Too much academic work would make you a dull Jack, you know.

你说的有道理。不过，我建议你去掉一门必修课程，增加一门选修课。你需要给自己腾出些娱乐的时间。你知道吗，学习任务太重了会使你成为书呆子的。

A: Yes, I'll take your advice and reschedule my course. And then, I'll sign it and hand it in tomorrow.

是的，我会接受您的建议，重新规划我的课程。然后，我签好字，明天交过来。

B: Good. Please call me before coming, and I may be at a meeting somewhere or having an appointment with someone else.

好的。来之前请先打个电话，我可能正在什么地方开会或与别人有约。

04

A: Good evening, Professor Crock. May I come in?

晚上好，克罗克教授。我可以进来吗？

B: Please do, and have a seat. Can I offer you some water?

请进，请坐。我给你倒杯水好吗？

A: No, thanks. I know you are busy, and I just want to hear your advice on my term paper. As it's the first time for me to do it in English, I must have made a mess about it.

不用了，谢谢。我知道您很忙，我只是想听听您对我的学期论文的建议。这是我第一次用英语写论文，写得一定很糟糕吧。

B: Let me be frank with you. For a typical term paper, you need to concentrate on the theme subject, and leave out those descriptive sentences. Since you're new here, I'll let you rewrite your paper, but you need to turn in the revised paper in three days. Otherwise, I could only give your paper a C, which would influence your chance for the scholarship.

实话实说，对于一篇典型的学期论文来说，你需要专注于主题，忽略那些描述性的句子。因为你是新来的，我允许你重写你的论文，但你必须在三天内改好提交。否则，我只能给你的论文一个C等级，这会影响你获得奖学金的机会。

A: That's very considerate of you. I'll take your advice, and do some more work on the paper, and hand it to you as you said.

您想得真周到。我接受您的建议，会对论文再进行修改，然后按时交给您。

Part Three　Common Expressions

- Now, I'd like you to watch a clip of the video, and after that, we'll have a free discussion. First, I'll divide the class into two groups, representing Side A and Side B. You'll have a ten-minute discussion among yourselves and then, choose a representative to come to the front and air out your views. Then, everybody in class can raise questions to the two representatives. After that, I'll help you summarize the major points for you to seek reference.

现在，我想请你们观看一段录像，然后我们会自由讨论。首先，我将你们分为两组，分别代表正方和反方。你们先自己讨论10分钟，然后各组推举一位代表上台陈述各自的观点。之后，全班每个同学都可以向两位代表提问。最后，我会帮你们总结要点供你们参考。

- When you're considering taking online courses, you need to be aware of these things. First, you need to treat an online course like a "real" course. You need to have the discipline to sit down, and do everything as if you were in actual classroom.

  选修网络课程时，你需要注意下列事宜。首先，你需要像对待"真正的"课程一样对待在线课程。你需要遵守纪律，坐下来，像真的在教室里一样做事。

- Secondly, you need to manage your time. To be specific, you need to set the goals at the beginning of the semester, and check in with yourself weekly. You need to complete your semester assignments on time and with quality.

  其次，你需要管理好你的时间。具体而言，你需要在学期开始的时候设定目标，并每周检查自己的学习进展情况。你需要按时、保质保量完成学期作业。

- Thirdly, you need to stick to your time management. The flexibility to create your own schedule is often one of the biggest appeals for taking online classes. Nevertheless, that freedom can also be detrimental if you fail to manage your time.

  第三，你需要坚持管理好你的时间。你可以灵活地制定学习时间表，这是在线课程最大的吸引力之一。然而，如果你不能有效管理好时间，这种自由对你也许是有害的。

- Fourthly, you need to create a regular study space and stay organized. Whether your workspace is your kitchen table, a library seat, or the corner booth in a local coffee shop, it's important to determine what type of environment would work best for you.

第四，你需要打造一个固定的学习空间，并保持这个空间整洁。无论你的学习空间是厨房的一张桌子、图书馆的一个座位，还是当地咖啡店的某个角落，重要的是要确保哪些环境最适合你学习。

- Fifthly, you need to eliminate distractions. Wherever you are taking your classes, you need to stay away from distractions as much as possible. For example, you should switch your cell phone to flight mode or simply switch it off. You should also switch off your TV set or your Walkman.

  第五，你需要排除干扰。无论你在哪里上课，你都要尽可能远离让你分心的东西。例如，你应该将手机切换到飞行模式，或者干脆关掉它。你还应该关掉电视或随身听。

- Sixth, you need to actively participate in the on line forums relating to your course. During the discussions, you should listen carefully what other students and your professor are saying, and if you have a question, feel free to ask for clarification.

  第六，你需要积极参加与本课程相关的在线论坛。在讨论过程中，你应该仔细聆听其他同学和教授在说什么；如果你有问题，可以随时提出。

- Last but not least, you should take stock from your on line courses. They may sometimes make you feel like you are learning on your own, but this couldn’t be further from the truth. Most online courses are built around the concept of collaboration, with professors and instructors actively encouraging students to work together to complete assignments and discuss lessons. Therefore, it pays for you to create a virtual study group.

  最后，你应该积极利用网上课程。在线课程有时会让你觉得是在自学，其实并非如此。大多数在线课程都是围绕着协作的概念建立起来的，教授和讲师积极鼓励学生一起完成作业和讨论课程。因此，你们需要创建一个虚拟学习小组。

第十九章

论文事宜

*

撰写论文是你完成学业的最后冲刺阶段。这也是训练和提高你在专业或学科中应用所学知识能力的有效途径。更重要的是，这也是增强你独立思考、推理和解决学术问题能力的一种方法。

Chapter Nineteen

Thesis Matters

*

Composing dissertations is the final and critical stage before you complete your degree study. It’s also one way to train and bring up your capability in terms of applying what you have learned in a particular major or subject. More importantly, it’s also one way to help strengthen your capability to think, reason and address academic issues independently.

Part One　Things to Know

01

Generally speaking, there are three types of university degrees. They are bachelor's, master's, and doctor's degrees, each of which would demand different academic standards. Therefore, you need to carefully choose one that fits your academic and career goals. Here in my country, when you've completed a two-year associate course, you can apply for the bachelor's degree. You can further apply for other degrees until you attain a doctorate.

一般来说，大学学位有三种类型：学士、硕士和博士学位，每一种学位都有不同的学术标准。因此，你需要选择一个适合自己学术和职业目标的学位。在我们国家，你在完成两年的副学士课程之后，就可以申请学士学位。你还可以继续申请其他学位，直至获得博士学位。

02

In addition, colleges and universities here in my country also offer professional degrees which are mainly the medicine and law courses. These programs demand in-depth knowledge, accurate skills and years of experience, on top of the skills in writing out dissertations and academic papers.

此外，我国高等院校还设有医学和法学学科专业学位。这些学科需要相关学生具有扎实的知识、精准的技能、多年的经验，以及论文与相关文章的写作能力。

03

In terms of dissertations, the worst thing for you is to go alone, with the belief that you know everything. This is a sure thing to land you in trouble. Rather, you should consult the subject with your schoolmates or peer group friends, who could give you some advice. However, when you should find the real problems with your theme, you should not hesitate to talk to your tutor.
在撰写论文的过程中，最糟糕的是闭门造车，自以为什么都知道，这肯定会给你带来麻烦。因此，你需要向同学或同龄朋友咨询，他们会给你出主意。然而，你如果遇到真正的挑战，应当毫不犹豫地寻求导师的帮助。

04

You’ve got to observe the following principles when choosing the theme of your dissertation. First, you need to choose what is inspiring and interesting for you to explore the theme from a different angle with innovation. Second, you need to establish a clear structure of your dissertation which would allow you to be at par with the academic rules. Third, you need to stay impartial and objective throughout your topical research, which would allow you to illustrate your theme topic professionally. Last but not least, you need to choose the theme, which would allow you to look into your academic sources and evidences to support your arguments.
在确定论文主题时，你需要遵守下列原则。首先，你需要选择能启发灵感的有趣的主题，让自己可以从不同的角度去创新。其次，你需要为论文搭建一个清晰的结构，以期与学术规则相一致。第三，你需要在整个主题研究过程中保持公正和客观的态度，以便从专业的角度展开论述。最后，你所选择的主题要能够找到足够的学术资料来源和证据来支持你的论点。

05

It's important that a good grasp of theories and skills is a must for all undergraduates, postgraduates or even doctorate candidates before getting their degrees. Otherwise, they're bound to fail in completing their dissertations. This is the pitfall you should avoid at whatever the cost.

重要的是，掌握基本的理论和技能是所有本科生、研究生或博士生获得学位的必备条件。否则，他们的论文写作注定要失败。这个问题你一定要设法避免。

06

It's an open secret that you need to take these factors into consideration, in order to make your dissertation unique. First, the topic of your dissertation has to be appealing to the readers, in terms of theories or policy proposals. Second, your theme issues must be supported by recent researches. Third, you should provide adequate facts and materials to support your viewpoints. Fourth, you need to follow the standardized formula in composing your dissertation. Fifth, you need to ask questions and provide your own arguments. Finally, you need to use standardized language and appropriate terminologies.

这是公开的秘密，论文写作需要考虑下列因素，以使你的论文具有独创性。首先，你的论文主题必须在理论或对策建议等领域对读者具有吸引力。第二，你的论文主题必须有最新的研究成果做支撑。第三，你应该提供足够的事实和材料来支持你的观点。第四，你需要按照标准化的格式撰写论文。第五，你需要提出问题并给出自己的结论。最后，你需要使用标准化的语言和专业术语。

07

It's a golden rule that you should reserve ample time to complete your dissertation. It could be months depending on what you would choose for

your dissertation. You should provoke your instincts to do more research on the subject, in order to produce a best possible paper in your field.
你应该预留足够的时间去完成论文，这是一条黄金法则。可能需要几个月，这取决于你选择如何写论文。你应该充分发挥自己的智慧，在选定的主题上开展尽可能多的研究，以期写出本领域最好的论文。

08

Before anything else, a good theme would be the precondition to ensure the successful defense of your dissertation, and it should be conducive to your future career. To be specific, you should exert your utmost to ensure the uniqueness of your dissertation, which would ultimately define you in the field of your research, and entice defense committee members to give you the green light during your defense.
首先，一个好的主题是确保你论文答辩成功的前提，并且有利于你未来的职业生涯。具体地说，你应该尽最大的努力来确保论文的独特性，这将有利于展示你在研究领域的才华，促使答辩委员会成员在答辩期间给你开绿灯。

09

From the start, you should explore new areas in your field of study. It should allow you to conduct your own research, secure your data, and come up with some unique conclusions. This is the area where many candidates have headaches. The key is that you should choose a topic, which is already researched upon, but pursue it in a different subarea and from a different perspective.
从一开始，你就应该在自己的研究领域做出新的探索。这会促使你能够进行独立的研究，获得有效数据，并得出独特的结论。这是许多学员感到头疼的地方。关键是，你应该选择前人已经研究过的领域，但要从不同的子领域或不同的角度去展开研究和论述。

10

When you're writing your paper, you should stay within your limit. Sure, your dissertation has to abide by the academic rules and regulations of your college or university. Therefore, you need to have a good discussion with your advisor, in order to prevent you from going back to square one half way through.

在撰写论文的过程中，你应该在规定范围内写。毫无疑问，你的论文必须符合你所在学院或大学的学术要求。因此，你需要和导师认真沟通，以免半途推倒重来。

11

Among other things, you have to follow the limitation of word count or level of research. When you have accidentally chosen a very broad topic, your draft paper must exceed the required pages or word count. Or, when you have chosen a super theme, you would have difficulty in carrying out the research in totality, due to the lack of data and reference materials. In both cases, you should quickly alter the structure of your dissertation, and focus what fits your level of research.

在其他方面，你还需要遵循论文篇幅或研究水平的限制。例如，你如果在不经意中选择了一个太宽泛的主题，你的论文草稿必然会超过规定的页数或字数。或者，你如果选择了一个超级主题，由于缺乏数据和参考资料，你将很难全面展开研究。如果出现这两种情况，你都应该迅速调整你的论文结构，聚焦适合你研究水平的论文主题。

12

Experts say you should first focus your topic on the tendency of the scientific exploration, and have a clear theoretical guidance. Second, you should avoid being too superficial. Your survey and research should not only use percentage description method, but also explore the correlation and causality between

variables. Third, your theme must avoid “aiming too high”, but focus on one side of a certain theoretical topic with illustration from a different level. Fourth, your topic must avoid “only summary with no description”, and strive to extract new findings. Fifth, your subject content should cover the main progress of the related fields, and have access to the latest reference materials. Sixth, your paper should avoid the lack of professional characteristics of key words. The bottom line is that your final paper should meet the standards of an academic paper, and reflect your knowledge of the subject matter.
有专家说，其一，你的论文选题要符合科学探索的发展趋势，要具有明确的理论指导。其二，选题要避免过于肤浅，调查研究不能仅仅停留在用百分比进行描述，要尽力探究变量之间的相互关系和因果关系。其三，选题切忌“好高骛远”，要聚焦某个领域的某方面，并从不同的层次展开论述。其四，选题切忌“只综不述”，要从中提炼出新的发现。其五，选题要涵盖相关领域的主要进展，要引用最新的参考资料。其六，论文要避免关键词汇缺乏专业特征。底线是，你的论文最终要符合学术论文的标准，同时又能反映出你专业领域的知识水平。

13

Composing an academic paper in a given time is always a challenge for the degree candidates, especially for you Chinese students. The thing is that you should never leave your thesis to the last semester. As one Chinese saying goes, it would be impossible to repair the boat while it is in the middle of a river.
在规定的时间内完成学术论文，对攻读学位的人来说一直是个挑战，尤其是你们中国学生。重要的是，你绝不能把论文拖到最后一个学期。正如中国的俗语所说，船到江心补漏迟。

14

When you get to the point of writing your dissertation, you’re clearly getting

to an important stage of your educational journey. In general, you should read out the thesis guideline immediately, and make sure where to go, and how to get things done in line with the instructions. To be specific, your dissertation is to showcase your skills and capacity to conduct research in your chosen discipline, and the results. Therefore, you need to create a concrete plan and start at your early convenience.
当你开始写论文的时候，很明显你的求学旅程已经进入一个重要阶段。总而言之，你应该认真阅读论文写作指导，确定论文向，以及如何依据写作纲要完成写作。具体而言，你的论文旨在展示你的写作技巧和在所选领域开展研究的能力和研究成果。因此，你需要制定具体规划，并尽早开启写作进程。

15

Once you have a decent plan to follow, you need to follow it to the letter, as the research process can take much longer to get through than you have planned. When you've completed all your research schedule, you should make a detailed outline for your dissertation. Remember, it's only a guideline, so it does not have to be too specific at this stage.
一旦有了完善的论文写作计划，你需要严格按照计划去做，因为研究过程通常比你预期的时间更长。你在完成所有的研究之后，应该拟定详细的论文提纲。记住，这个提纲仅仅是一个写作指南，所以不需要太详细。

16

When you've got this far, it's time for you to actually compose your dissertation. On the whole, you have to focus your attention on all the relevant information, reference material, models and conclusion, and discard any irrelevant details. When you complete the first draft, you need to consult your advisor, and revise the text accordingly.

你在完成上述事宜之后，就可以真正开始撰写论文了。总的来说，你的论文需要涵盖所有相关的信息、参考资料、模型和结论，并排除所有不相关的细枝末节。论文初稿完成后，你应咨询导师的意见，并进行相应修改。

17

Let me warn you, you've got to carefully compose the executive summary on your dissertation. Metaphorically speaking, the executive summary is just like the passport of your dissertation. The main purpose of an executive summary is to highlight the important theories, facts or information from your dissertation so that the readers could see what you have written in the paper at one glance. Therefore, your executive summary must be concise, which is to cover the following items: the importance of the topical research, source of information, source of reference materials, the ways to carry out field investigations or lab tests, issues under discussion, conclusions, research findings, projection on the future trends, and theoretical and policy proposals, etc.

我要提醒你，你必须认真撰写论文摘要。打个比方，摘要就像是你论文的护照，旨在高度概括本论文的重要观点、事实和信息，以便读者对论文内容一目了然。因此，论文摘要必须简明扼要，覆盖下列事项：专题研究的重要性、信息的来源、参考资料的来源、现场调查的方法或实验流程、需讨论的问题、结论、研究成果、趋势预测以及理论和政策建议等。

18

When you've completed the draft of your dissertation, you're just half way through the process. You need to double check if you have included everything that you're supposed to write about, and make sure you've considered the arguments on both sides. And, you need to verify that you've reached most academic conclusions or policy proposals. Finally, you need to further polish your dissertation in terms of terminologies and idiomatic expressions.

论文初稿写好了，你的任务仅仅完成了一半。你需要再确认你的论文是否囊括了计划撰写的全部内容，斟酌相关论述是否涵盖正反两方面的观点。同时，你需要核查论文得出了学术结论或具体对策。最后，你需要对论文进行反复润色，以使专业术语规范化，表达自然流畅。

19

At this stage, you should not forget to edit your dissertation before you submit it. You should try your utmost to avoid technical mistakes, which would compromise your grade in the end. Therefore, you need to visit AceMyPaper, which is a perfect service to help you proofread academic papers professionally.

在这个环节，你在提交论文之前，务必认真地校阅。你要尽力避免因为一些粗心的技术错误而丢分。因此，你应该充分利用AceMyPaper网络服务功能，帮助你专业地校阅学术论文。

20

Degree thesis is the final result of your years of studying abroad. From the subject selection. subject proposal to the painstaking paper writing, you have dedicated all of your wisdom and efforts. Nevertheless, a good paper cover is to leave a deep first impression on your tutor and judges. Therefore, you'd better ask professionals to do it for you.

学位论文是你数年留学的最终成果，从选题、开题到痛苦的论文撰写，无一不凝结你的智慧和心血，但漂亮的封面包装可望给导师和评委留下深刻的第一印象。因此，最好请专业人员代为制作。

Part Two　Situational Dialogues

01

A: May I come in, Professor Gary?

我可以进来吗，加利教授？

B: Please come in and find your seat in the sofa. I'll be with you right away. Shall I get you a cup of coffee or something?

请进，自己找位置坐在沙发上吧。我马上就来。你要咖啡还是别的什么？

A: Coffee, please.

请给我来一杯咖啡吧。

B: Here you are. Now, let me see what I can do for you.

给你。现在，让我看看能为你做些什么。

A: Certainly, it's about my dissertation. I've chosen two possible themes and I'd like you to advise me which one would be more appropriate. The first one is about the IT industrial cooperation between China and your country, and the other one is about the opportunities and challenges for China in the field of IT industry.

当然，是关于我论文的事。我选择了两个主题，想请您给我一些建议哪个更合适。一篇是关于中国和贵国的信息技术产业合作，另一篇是关于中国在信息技术领域面临的机遇和挑战。

B: Well, if I were you, I'd like to pick up the first topic which would provide you with more space to work out your paper. With regard to the structure of your paper, you should abide strictly by the benchmarks of our university, which attaches importance to the academic standards for the dissertations, you know.

嗯，如果我是你，我会选第一个题目，这样你可以有更多空间展开撰写论文。关于你的论文结构，你应该严格遵守本大学的学术论文指南。咱们学校非常重视学位论文的学术标准。

A: I know. This is the area where I'm not very confident, as it's the first time for me to write such a lengthy paper in English. Therefore, I'll have to seek your professional help, language wise.

我知道。这方面我不太自信，因为这是我第一次用英语写这么长的论文。因此，我必须寻求您的帮助，尤其是语言方面。

B: You bet. I promise to help you proofread the first ten pages of your paper. Then, you'll have to handle the rest on your own. As a favor, I'll give you some suggestions on how to proceed with the academic language, and some hints on how to go ahead with your paper, alright?

没问题。我答应帮你校对论文的前十页，然后你需要自己处理剩下的论文。出于帮忙，我会在如何使用专业术语和论文写作技巧等方面给你提一些建议，好吗?

A: That would be great. Thanks a lot, Professor Gary.

那太好了。非常感谢，加利教授。

02

A: Good afternoon, Professor Benjamin. May I come in?

下午好，本杰明教授。我可以进来吗?

B: Sure, please come in, Ms. Linda Yang. You've come right on time. Now, let me see what I can do for you, my young friend.

当然可以，请进，杨琳达女士。你来得正是时候。现在，让我看看能为你做些什么，我年轻的朋友。

A: Certainly, my dear professor. As I spoke to you on the phone yesterday, I've managed to complete the draft of my dissertation. However, this is the first time for me to write the academic paper in English, so I really need your professional appraisal and guidance in this regard.

当然可以，我亲爱的教授。正如我昨天在电话中告诉您的，我已经完成了论文初稿。但是，这是我第一次用英语撰写专业论文，因此，这方面我确实需要得到您的专业评价和指导。

B: You bet. As your adviser, I'll try my best to help you out and pave the way for your successful defense of your dissertation. Now, let me be frank. As of now, you really have to fortify Chapter Three, where you have to let the readers know exactly what your original discovery is, and your own contribution to the research area. These are critical factors to guarantee the passage of your defense. With regard to the literature, you need to further polish your descriptive language, and you seem to have used too many passive voice sentences which might spoil the interests of the readers. And, please also proofread your paper, and make sure you don't leave too many technical mistakes, which would be the “eye sores”. As a favor, I'll ask my assistant to help you out. How does that sound?

没问题。作为你的导师，我会尽最大的努力帮助你，为你的论文成功答辩铺平道路。现在，我坦率地告诉你，到目前为止，你确实需要进一步充实第三章的内容，你必须让读者确切地知道你的发现是什么，你对研究领域的贡献是什么。这些都是确保答辩通过的关键因素。在语言方面，你需要进一步完善你的描述性语言，你似乎使用了太多被动语态的句子，这会影响读者的兴趣。此外，你还需要认真校阅论文，切忌留下太多的技术错误，这会成为读者眼睛中的“苍蝇”。出于帮忙，我会让我的助手帮你，怎么样？

A: Thank you very much, sir. I know I could count on you for help.

非常感谢，先生。我知道您一定会帮助我的。

03

A: Good morning, respected appraisal committee members. I'm Xiong Huimin, from the Department of Physical Biology, and a candidate for the PHD degree in physical and biological applications. And, my supervisor is Professor Cliff Franklin.

各位尊敬的评审委员会成员，早上好。我是熊慧敏，来自物理生物学系，物理与生物应用博士研究生。我的导师是克里夫·富兰克林教授。

B: Good morning, Ms. Xiong Huimin. We're pleased to assemble here to hear out your presentation of your dissertation. First, please allow me to introduce myself. I'm Professor David Linsey. Seated on my right hand is Professor Howard Johnson, on my right hand from the far side is Professor Mark Hudson. Seated on my left hand is Professor Adam Smith, and on my left hand from the far side is Professor Rick Bruce. Now, before I give you the floor, I've got some housekeeping rules for you to follow. First of all, I'll allow you 15 minutes to brief us about the main theme as well as the structure of your paper. My colleagues and I will be expecting you to share your own discovery as well as your contribution. I know this is a bit challenging for you, but you've got to walk us through all these areas in the next 15 minutes. After that, my colleagues and I will each make some comments and ask one or two questions. You should take careful notes and provide us with the answers you have in mind. Then, we'll ask you to retreat from the conference room for a while as we're going to deliberate on the performance of your defense. When that is done, we'll call you back to give you our verdict. Well, that's all I have to say. By the way, by the last two-minute mark, my assistant will ring the bell. Then, you need to complete whatever left in the remaining time. Now, without further due, the floor is yours. Good luck!

早上好，熊慧敏女士。我们很高兴聚在这里听你报告论文。首先，请允许我自我介绍一下。我是大卫·林西教授。在我右手边就座的是霍华德·约翰逊教授，最右边就座的是马克·哈德森教授。在我左手边的是亚当·史密斯教授，最左边的是里克·布鲁斯教授。在请你发言之前，我要告诉你一些答辩规则。首先，我会给你15分钟的时间来简要介绍一下论文的主题和结构。其间，我的同事和我期待你分享你在本领域的发现以及你所做的贡献。我知道这对你来说具有挑战性，但你必须在接下来的15分钟里完成这些任务。之后，我的同事和我每人会做一些评论，并问一两个问题。你要仔细地做笔记，并把你能想到的答案告诉我们。然后，我们会请你离开会议室一段时间，以便我们讨论你论文答辩的表现。最后，我们会叫你回到答辩现场，给你打分。好了，我要说的就这些。顺便说一下，在最后两分钟的时间点上，我的助手会响铃予以提醒。之后，你需要在剩余的时间里讲完内容。现在，不再耽搁时间，请你开始吧。祝你好运！

04

A: Welcome back, Ms. Xiong Huimin, and please be seated. Well, let me ask you a quick question: How did you feel about your performance this morning?

欢迎回来，熊慧敏女士，请坐。现在，我想问你一个简单的问题：你认为今天上午你论文答辩过程中的表现怎么样？

B: Thanks. To tell the truth, I was a bit nervus indeed, especially during the Q&A period, because it was the first time for me to sit in front of so many scholars and professors, you know. Nevertheless, I think I managed it.

谢谢。讲实在话，我确实有点儿紧张，尤其是在问答环节。您知道吗，这是我头一次坐在这么多学者和教授面前。不过，我想我还是完成了。

A: Well, we could see that. Now, Ms. Xiong Huimin, this is the critical moment in your life, I suppose. Let me have the privilege to announce our verdict on your defense. We penal members have heard your presentation and witnessed your performance. Based on the merits of your written paper and your performance today, we have come to the following conclusions. First, your dissertation is in line with the academic standards of our university. Second, your performance at the defense is superb, and you managed to answer our questions professionally. Good on you! Nevertheless, we've also had some suggestions for you. First, you need to balance out the contents across the paper. Second, you need to further fine tune the theoretical illustrations in some places, which are correct in grammar, but we would find them difficult to comprehend. I suppose they are some sort of Chinese English. We're confident when you work out these two issues, you'll come out with an excellent paper. Having said this much, I hereby officially announce that you have successfully passed your defense and congratulations, Ms Xiong Huiming. Now, you have the honor to have a picture with your supervisor and a collective one with us appraisal members.

你的表现我们都看到了。现在，熊慧敏女士，我想这是你一生中的关键时刻。让我荣幸地宣布我们的决定。我们评审小组全体人员认真听取了你的论文陈述，目睹了你在答辩阶段的表现。根据你的书面论文的质量和你今天的答辩表现，我们得出以下结论。首先，你的论文符合我校的学术标准。第二，你的答辩很出色，你比较专业地回答了我们提出的问题。祝贺你！不过，我们也有一些建议供你参考。其一，你需要平衡整篇文章的内容。其二，有些理论阐述你还需要进一步润色。这些句子在语法上是正确的，但我们却很费解，这也许就是中式英文吧。我们相信，解决好这两个问题，你一定会完成一篇优秀的论文。说了那么多，现在我正式宣布，你已经通过了答辩，并向你表示祝贺，熊慧敏女士。现在你有机会与你的导师合影，以及与我们的评委会成员合影。

Part Three　Common Expressions

- Good morning, distinguished professors, ladies and gentlemen! Thank you all very much for your generosity to honor my thesis defense. Please allow me to introduce myself. I'm Hu Weida from China. First and foremost, I'd like to express my sincere gratitude to my supervisor, Professor Marcos Wilkerson, for his intellectual guidance, invaluable instructions and comments on my thesis. It is with his valuable assistance that I've finally managed to complete this thesis. Now, please allow me to walk you through my thesis in an outline fashion. The subject of my dissertation is *the Characteristics of the US-China Relations under the Trump Administration*. It consists of six chapters. The first chapter gives a brief introduction to the background of the Trump administration, which endeavors to recall how Donald Trump managed to snatch the election from the experienced politician Hilary Clinton. And, the second chapter is set to probe into the policy stand by President Trump towards China. In the third chapter, the thesis tries to illustrate the China policy change by the Trump administration and its impacts on China from the perspective of domestic and foreign policies. The fourth chapter is dedicated to the policy and measures by the Chinese leaders and the government to manage the bilateral relations. The fifth chapter is to project the orientation of the bilateral relations between the first and second largest economies in the world in the mid-term. In the final chapter, the thesis intends to formulate the policy thoughts and possible roadmap for the bilateral relations for both the Chinese and US governments. That's the layout as well as the main theme of my thesis… Well, with this, I now conclude my presentation, and I'm ready to take your appraisal and I'll be more than happy to take your questions later on. Thank you!

早上好，尊敬的教授们，女士们，先生们！非常感谢你们参加我的论文答辩。请允许我做自我介绍。我是来自中国的胡伟达。首先，我要向我的导师马科斯·威尔肯森教授表示衷心的感谢，感谢他对我的学术指导，对我的论文给予的宝贵指导和建议。正是在他的鼎力帮助下，我才得以完成这篇论文。现在，请允许我给大家介绍一下论文的概要。我的论文题目是《特朗普政府时期中美关系的特点》。全文共分六章。第一章将简要介绍特朗普政府的背景，再叙唐纳德·特朗普如何从经验丰富的政治家希拉里·克林顿手中夺得大选胜利的。第二章将探讨特朗普总统对中国的政策立场。在第三章中，本文试图从中国政府内外政策的角度来说明特朗普政府对华政策变化对中国的影响。第四章是中国领导人和政府为处理双边关系所采取的政策与措施。第五章是规划世界第一和第二大经济体之间双边关系的中期发展方向。在最后一章中，本文试图为中美两国政府就双边关系提出政策思路和可能的路线图，以供双方参考。这些就是本人论文的结构和主题……好了，请允许我就此结束我的报告。现在，我准备好接受各位专家和教授的评审，并且很乐意回答诸位的问题。谢谢你们！

- Good morning, my dear appraisal committee members. I am Lin Xiaomei from the Department of Agriculture, Forest and Husbandry and my supervisor is Professor Linda Watson. With her generous encouragement and professional guidance, I've managed to come up with my dissertation which is in front of you. With your permission, I now have the privilege to briefly present to you my thesis in terms of structure and its topical theme in each chapter. The title of my dissertation is *Experiences and*

Lessons of Agricultural Development of China since 1978. I chose this as my theme topic due to the following reasons. Different countries may have different modalities in agricultural development, and there are no uniformed modalities to be copied by any other countries. However, there must be something in common. This dissertation endeavors to list some successful stories in terms of agricultural reforms which would help partner countries emancipate their productivity. For that matter, I had the pleasure to select agricultural subject for my dissertation. And, it's my firm conviction that by studying this topic, I intend to project the importance of the reforms on the traditional farming system and the agricultural production chain construction. Due to the time limit, I'll have to present my paper in the outline fashion. In short, I divided my paper into five parts. Part One covers the introduction to some relevant concepts of agricultural development and the relevant theories. Part Two dwells on the background information leading up to China's agricultural reform in the late 1970s. Part Three illustrates the process of the agricultural reforms. Part Four depicts the lessons for other countries to seek reference from. Part Five endeavors to put forward policy thoughts on how to carry out agricultural cooperation within the framework of the Belt and Road Initiative. That is all I have to say for the moment about my dissertation. Thank you very much! Now, I'm ready to take your comments and questions.

各位学位评审委员会成员，大家早上好！我是林小梅，来自农林牧系，我的导师是琳达·华生教授。在她慷慨的鼓励和专业指导下，我成功地完成了我的论文并呈现在诸位评委面前。我现在很荣幸就论文的结构和每一章的主题向你们简要介绍我的论文。本文的题目是《1978年以来中国农业发展的经验与教训》。我选择这个主题主要有以下几个原因。不同国家的农业发展方式不同，没有统一的模式可供其他国家借鉴。然而，它们之间一定有共同点。本论文试图列举一些有助于伙伴国家解放生产力的农业改革成功案例。因此，我有幸选择了农业作为我论文的主题。我坚信，通过对这一课题的研究，我应该能够展现出改革对传统耕作制度和农业生产链建设的重要性。由于时间的限制，我将以提纲的方式来展示我的论文。概而言之，我的论文分为五个部分。第一部分介绍了农业发展的相关概念和理论。第二部分论述了20世纪70年代末中国农业改革的背景。第三部分阐述了中国农业改革的进程。第四部分阐述了可供其他国家借鉴的教训。第五部分提出了在“一带一路”框架下开展农业合作的政策思路。关于我的论文，我要说的就这些。谢谢你们！现在，我准备好接受你们的点评，并回答你们的问题。

第二十章

寻找工作

*

在国外期间，无论我们是职场上的新手，还是拥有多年工作经验的专业人士，都需要寻找工作，开始或重新开始职业生涯，除非我们想自己当老板。在竞争日益激烈的劳动力市场上，越来越多的人争夺日愈稀缺的工作机会，因此，我们必须做好准备，迎接艰难的挑战。

Chapter Twenty

Job Searching

*

When we're overseas, whether we're the first timers at the job market, or a professional with years of experience under our belts, we all have to get a job, in order to start or restart our career, unless we want to be our own boss. In the ever competitive labor market where more people are competing for fewer jobs. Therefore we've got to be prepared for some tough battles.

Part One　Things to Know

01

At the labor market, there are some who would leave with smile on their faces, and others who would be otherwise. Those who follow the right job hunting methods would have more chances, and those who jump into the labor market with a blind eye are often wasting their time and energy. Generally speaking, these are the effective ways for you to be successful at the ever competitive labor market.

在劳动力市场上，总有一些人面带微笑离开，而另一些人则不然。那些遵循正确求职方法的人会有更多的机会，而那些盲目进入劳动力市场的人往往只是在浪费其时间和精力。一般而言，下列途径可助你在充满竞争的劳动力市场上找到就业机会。

02

First and foremost, you could look for job postings on the Internet by many potential employers who would offer periodical job openings with specific job descriptions. This may help you spot opportunities at any time. It works about 5% of the time on average.

首先，你可以在互联网上寻找，许多潜在雇主会在网上发布招聘信息，对空缺职位进行详细描述。这可以帮助你随时发现就业机会。这种求职方式平均成功率为5%。

03

Second, you could post or mail out your resume to the potential employers. This would get you more chances for an interview, which are the precondition to get a job you want. In order to be successful, you need to be fully prepared, though.

第二，你可以把简历直接寄给潜在的雇主。这会使你有更多参加面试的机会，这是你获得就业机会的前提。不过，为了成功应聘，你需要进行认真的准备。

04

Third, you could cruise in the local newspapers, which would carry numerous job ads. This method works somewhere between 5% and 24% on average. Those who look for low salary jobs would strike their lucks by 24%, and those who look for high salary jobs may be successful only by 5%.

第三，你可以浏览当地的报纸，上面通常会刊登大量的招聘广告。通过这种方法求职的成功率大约在5%到24%之间。那些寻找低薪工作的人有24%的几率获得成功，而那些寻找高薪工作的人可能只有5%的成功率。

05

Fourth, you could go to the private employment agencies or job search firms for help. These agencies would place almost any jobs, especially in large metropolitan cities. This method usually works between 5% and 28% of the time, depending on the attractiveness of your resume.

第四，你可以向私人职业介绍所或猎头公司寻求帮助。这些机构几乎可以协助申请者安排任何工作，特别是在大城市。这个方法的成功率在5%到28%之间，取决于你简历的吸引力。

06

Fifth, you could look for opportunities by answering ads in professional or trade journals. This method apparently works only 7% of the time. The directory of these associations and their journals can be found at *Directoryofassociations.com*.

第五，你可以从专业或行业杂志上的广告中寻找就业机会。然而，这种求职方法的成功率仅有7%。这些协会及其期刊的目录可以在*Directoryofassociations.com*网站上找到。

07

Sixth, you could try out your luck at "Job Clubs". There are hundreds of job-hunting support groups that call themselves "Job Clubs". The success rate of looking for jobs through them is around 10%.

第六，你可以去"求职俱乐部"碰碰运气。有数以百计自称为"求职俱乐部"的求职支持组织。通过这些组织寻找工作的成功率为10%左右。

08

Seventh, you could visit the government employment offices. It could be the unemployment service office, where you just have to fill in the forms and leave your resume. This method works 14% of the time.

第七，你可以去政府就业办公室碰碰运气。你可以去失业服务办公室，在那里你只需要填一些表格，留下你的简历。这种方法找工作的成功率为14%。

09

Eighth, you could go to places where employers would pick up workers directly. If you're a union member, you would have access to a union hiring hall, this method will work up to 22% of the time. Nevertheless, those jobs may last just a few days.

第八，你可以去那些雇主直接接收员工的地方。如果你是工会成员，你有可能获得进入工会招聘大厅的权限，这种方法有22%的机会找到工作。但是，这些可能是只持续几天的工作。

10

Ninth, you could go and ask for job leads. With this method, you ask family members, friends and people you know to find out if there would be any place where someone with your talents and background could have a place. It works 33% of the time.

第九，你可以通过口头线索找工作。通过这种方法，你可以询问你的家人、朋友和社区里认识的人，看对方是否知道哪里有招聘与你专业和背景相关员工的单位。这种求职方式的成功率在33%左右。

11

Tenth, you could knock on the door of any employers, offices or manufacturing plants. This method works 47% of the time, and it works best with small employers. Sometimes, you just blunder into a place where a vacancy has just developed. By knocking on the doors, you have a better chance of finding a job than just depending on your resume.

第十，你可以直接去敲老板的门，或者到办公室、制造厂登门求职。这种方法成功率为47%，对小老板最有效。有时你会碰巧走进一个刚刚出现职位空缺的单位。敲门而入，这种方法比你仅仅通过发送简历求职成功的概率要高。

12

In addition, you could look for job opportunities at specific government agencies. Many national or federal agencies regularly post their jobs on their websites. If you want to work for a specific agency or department, you just have to find its website and start the procedure as they require.

此外，你也可以到特定的政府机构寻找工作机会。许多国家或联邦机构定期在他们的网站上发布工作。如果你想为特定的机构工作，你只需要找到它的网站并按照他们的要求启动求职程序。

13

Research shows that only 27 percent of graduates have jobs waiting for them. Meanwhile, more than one in five would take seven months or longer to find a good position. Therefore, in many countries, students would immediately plan their future dreams of either entering the workforce or pursuing further education.

调查显示，只有27%的毕业生有工作在等他们。与此同时，超过1/5的人需要花7个月乃至更长的时间才能找到一份好工作。因此，在许多国家，学生刚入学就要为未来的梦想做规划，是参加工作，还是继续深造。

14

You should plan your future career the moment you step into a college or university. As college and university education is getting more and more expensive, you should study in an in-demand field, in order to increase your chances of having a solid career after graduation.

从进入大学开始，你就应该计划未来的职业生涯。大学教育越来越贵了，因此，想要在毕业后找到一份稳定的工作，你应该选择具有就业机会的热门专业。

15

You should go to professional teams for advice on your career options. Research shows many students don’t have a clear mind on what to do when they graduate. According to one survey, 75 percent of respondents said they simply didn’t know what jobs would be suitable for them. On the other hand, many employers would post vague or confusing job descriptions.

你应该去专业团队寻求职业选择方面的建议。研究表明，许多学生仍然不清楚他们大学毕业后该做什么。根据一项调查，75%的受访者表示，他们根本不知道什么工作适合自己。另一方面，许多雇主发布的招聘广告岗位描述模糊，令人困惑。

16

You should learn to produce an attractive resume. Facts show that traditional resume writing tips are no longer working anymore. Most employers rely on computerized applicant tracking systems and artificial intelligence to automatically scan resumes for the keywords. Therefore, you need to seek professional assistance from the career service staff.

你应该学会撰写吸引眼球的简历。事实表明，传统的简历写作技巧已经不再有效。大多数雇主采用网上招聘程序，并利用人工智能系统搜索应聘者简历的关键词。因此，你需要向职业服务人员寻求专业服务。

17

You should learn the skills for interviews. It’s true that the first impression is significant, but most students have no idea how to handle it. Therefore, you need to attend the interview practice sessions, and try to do some homework, in order to gain confidence when you get your chance.

你应该学习面试的技巧。的确，第一印象非常重要，但大多数学生都不知道该如何处理。因此，你需要参加面试培训课程，多做一些功课，在获得面试机会时增强自信心。

18

You should learn “soft skills”. According to one research, about 60% of managers feel that fresh graduates lack critical thinking and problem-solving skills. 50% think that first-timers lack attention to the details, while 46% believe they are poor communicators. Therefore, it pays for you to patch up

those “short boards” when you’re still working on your academic degrees.
你应该学习“软技能”。调查显示，约60%的管理人员认为应届毕业生缺乏批判性思维和解决问题的能力。50%的人认为新手缺乏对细节的关注，而46%人认为他们不善沟通。因此，当你还在攻读学位的时候，应该补齐那些“短板”。

19

You should build up your network through summer jobs. Working during the summer breaks can help you build a resume that will pay off when you graduate from colleges or universities, no matter what job you may look for. Meanwhile, you could also start building up your peer group connections which may add up your chances for future jobs.
你应该通过暑期工作建立人际关系网。不管你做什么工作，暑假打工能充实你的简历，为你毕业后找工作增加砝码。与此同时，你也可以开始建立你的社交群体，这可能会增加你未来找到工作的机会。

20

You should start networking at your early convenience. One benefit of going to college is to allow you to meet more people and form lasting relationship networks. Therefore, you should make full use of networking opportunities for your future career.
你应该尽早开始建立人脉关系网。上大学的一个好处是你有机会结识更多的人，并建立持久的关系。因此，你应该充分利用机会，为未来职业生涯构建自己的人脉网。

Part Two　Situational Dialogues

01

A: Good morning, Mr. Peng Jianhua. I'm Leahy Robertson. I hope I pronounced your name correctly. Correct me if I wasn't doing the right thing.

早上好，彭建华先生。我是莱希·罗伯逊。我希望我没有读错你的名字。要是错了，请纠正我。

B: Thank you, Mr. Robertson. You pronounced my name perfectly, and you seem to have taken some Chinese lessons.

谢谢你，罗伯逊先生。我的名字你念得很准，听起来你好像学过中文。

A: Yes, you are right. That was years ago when I was the sales manager at our branch office in Shanghai, but I haven't got the chance to practice Chinese much lately. Now, let me welcome you to the interview. Please make yourself comfortable.

是的，你说得对。那是几年前我在上海分公司做销售经理时的事了，但最近我很少有机会讲中文。现在，让我欢迎你来参加面试。请不要拘束。

B: Thank you very much. Now, I'm ready.

非常感谢。现在，我准备好了。

A: Good, as a routine, our interview would last for about twenty minutes, and I hope you can handle that. And, I hope our camera won't scare you off, but your performance is to be reviewed afterwards when we make the final considerations.

好的，按常规，我们的面试将持续大约20分钟，我希望你能自如应付。还有，我希望我们的摄像机不会吓着你，我们需要记录你的现场表现，以便最后阶段参考。

B: Yes, please, and I'll do my best.

好的，请吧，我会尽力配合的。

02

A: Let's start with your educational background. Could you briefly tell us about your college life and the academic achievements when you were there?

我们先谈谈你的教育背景。你能简要介绍一下你的大学生活和学业成绩吗？

B: Sure. As you can see in my resume, I graduated from Fudan University in Shanghai exactly four years ago, majored in business management, with minor in accounting. During the six years while I was there, I won the scholarships every year, and graduated with BA and MA degrees. I also had opportunities to be a volunteer at the Shanghai Importation Expo.

当然。正如您在简历中所看到的，四年前，我毕业于上海复旦大学，主修企业管理，辅修会计。在那六年里，我每年都获得奖学金，并取得学士和硕士学位。我也曾在上海进口博览会做志愿者。

A: That was great, Mr. Peng. Then, what did you do when you graduated from the University?

太好了，彭先生。那么，你大学毕业后做了什么？

B: I think I was lucky because of my field experience with the Expo. They offered me a position at the Department of Public Relations of the Committee of Shanghai Expo.

我觉得我很幸运，因为我有世博会实习经历。他们给我提供了在上海世博会公共关系部门供职的机会。

A: Good on you. What did you do at the department?
你很幸运。你在这个部门做什么工作?

B: Well, I started as a desk officer for two years, and then, I was promoted to the assistant to the General Manager of the department, which gave me more opportunities to liaise with exporters and importers from around the world.
哦，我先做了两年的办公室职员，后来被提升为部门总经理助理。这使我有更多的机会与世界各地的进出口商打交道。

03

A: I'm just curious, but why did you leave that seemingly promising job?
我只是好奇，不过你为什么要离开那份看起来很有前途的工作呢?

B: Well, I left my post for two reasons. First, I didn't like the seasonal crash on the routine activities. As you may know, when the Expo was over, there would be three to four months, during which I had to find something to keep me busy.
嗯，我决定离职有两个原因。首先，我不喜欢季节性活动对日常活动的冲击。也许你会理解，世博会结束后，有三到四个月的时间我必须找些事情让自己忙碌起来。

A: I see. What about the other reason as you mentioned?
我明白了。那你提到的另一个原因呢?

B: The second reason is that I didn't see any prospect for further promotion in the near future as my boss himself is only three years senior than I am. In some places, seniority would have more weight than contributions or capabilities in career promotion, you know.
第二个原因是，我看不到在不久的将来有升职的希望，因为我的老板只比我年长三岁。你知道吗，在某些地方，资历在职务晋升中比贡献重要得多。

04

A: Now, let me prick your brain a bit more. Why did you choose our company for literally the same position?

现在，让我来考考你的智慧。你为什么选择到我们公司应聘同样的职位？

B: Well, I've got several reasons. Let me start with my most important one. Your company is an outstanding transnational corporation, of which the department of public relations must be more challenging for me. For me, I am looking for a company that is people-oriented.

哦，我有几个理由。最重要的一条是贵公司是一家优秀的跨国公司，其中公共关系部门对我来说一定更具挑战性。就我个人而言，我希望找一家以人为本的公司。

A: Then, why do you think you're qualified for the position we offer here?

那么，你认为自己哪方面能胜任我们这里的职位呢？

B: Well, for one thing, this position is closely in line with my background and career aspiration. Your position requirements are at par with my academic and professional training, as well as my managerial expertise.

首先，这个职位非常符合我的背景和职业抱负。该职位的要求与我的专业和职业训练以及管理技能都很匹配。

A: Why do you think you may have any better future in our company?

你为什么认为你在本公司就职会有更好的前途？

B: It's my belief I would be able to fully apply what I learned at the university and demonstrate fully my capability when I should be given the opportunity. And, I can assure you that I'm going to build on my experience and make my contribution to the company in due time.

我相信，我如果有机会得到这份工作，我一定能充分运用我在大学所学的知识，充分展示我的能力。我可以向你们保证，我将会凭借我的经验为贵公司作出贡献。

Part Three　Common Expression

- Our company is a service-oriented institution.
  本公司坚持以服务为本。
- Please give us an example of team work.
  请举一个你参与团体合作的例子。
- Would you tell us what your greatest strength is, and what your main weakness is?
  请你说说你最大的优点和缺点分别是什么?
- What do you know about our company?
  你对我们公司有什么了解?
- What do you expect to get from your new job with us?
  你想从我们这里的新工作中得到什么?
- What would you expect from this new job?
  你对这份新工作有什么期待?
- I sincerely wish to apply for the position listed on your corporate website, as I've got all the qualifications accordingly.
  我非常希望应聘贵公司网站上列的职位，因为我具备相应的条件。
- I'm fully aware that your job opening asks for the ability to coordinate and organize team activities. And, the person in that position should be good at paper work and public relations. As I mentioned in my resume, I have all the skills and abilities for the job.

我很清楚，贵公司招聘的这个职位要求应聘者具有协调和组织团队活动的能力。在这个职位的人应该擅长文书工作和处理公共关系。正如我在简历中所提到的，我具备这份工作所需的所有技能和能力要求。

- My motto is that, as long as I set my own eyes on something, I would strive to make it. Therefore, I am confident for the position, and I would appreciate it when you should give me the chance to prove it.
  我的座右铭是，只要专注于某件事，总能成功。因此，我对这个职位充满信心，如果贵公司能给我这个机会证明，我将不胜感激。
- I'm currently the human resource manager of Anderson Pty Ltd., and I've been in this position for five years now, during which I've managed to acquire the relevant skills to handle my future portfolios in the field.
  我目前是安德森股份有限公司的人力资源经理，在此职位已经工作了五年，在此期间，我获得了相关技能，能做好该领域未来的工作。
- This letter is to inform you that you have successfully passed the interview with us, but we're now going through the last stage of evaluation on the five candidates, from which four would be selected as our employees. Therefore, we'll inform you our final decision no later than October 18th.
  这封信谨通知你，你已经成功通过了本公司的面试，但我们将要对5名候选人进行最后一轮的面试，并择优录取4位。因此，最终的结果我们最晚于10月18日通知你。

第二十一章

白领工作

进入21世纪以来，服务业已成为许多国家国民经济的支柱产业，对白领员工存在大量需求。但是，在这个领域工作的人不仅要掌握企业管理理论知识，还要掌握与他们管理工作相关的技术，因而需要学习更多的知识，进行更多的实践，积累更多的经验。

Chapter Twenty-one

White Collar Work

*

Since the 21st century, service industries have become the mainstay of national economies in many countries, where large numbers of white-collar workers are in high demand. Nevertheless, those who are in this profession not only have to equip themselves with theories in business administration, but also the technical skills related to their portfolios, which warrant more learning, more practice and more accumulation of experience.

Part One　Things to Know

01

Generally speaking, white collar workers are more educated, have better managerial skills and higher social statuses. However, when you've gone through all the trials to get your job, and when you're finally sitting in your new office, you're just half way through in terms of your career.

一般而言，白领工人受教育程度更高，管理技能更扎实，且社会阶层较高。然而，在你通过所有的面试，并终于坐在新的办公室时，你的职业生涯才刚刚开启了一半。

02

Many successful stories show that you should have some space between leaving your old job and starting a new one. Therefore, it pays for you to take some time to mentally prepare yourself for the new portfolio, and pick up some new skills accordingly, which would help recharge yourself for what's to come.

许多成功经验告诉我们，在离开上一份工作和开始新的工作之间应该留有一些时间间隔。因此，你需要花些时间为新的工作岗位做好心理准备，并学习相关新技能，以期为接下来的工作充好电。

03

To start with, you need to find out where you are. They say it’s only half way through when you’re hired, or when you’ve moved into your new portfolio. You are hired for a reason. Is it to handle a specialized portfolio? Is it to train others? Or, is it to supervise client projects? You need to find out answers to all these questions so that you could best fit in the overall business strategy of your new institution.

首先，你需要找到适合你的舞台。有人说，被单位聘用并顺利进入工作单位，这仅仅是成功的一半。你被雇用是有原因的。是承担专业的工作？是专职培训他人？还是专管客户项目？这些问题你都要找到答案，以便以最佳的状态融入新单位的整体商业发展战略。

04

You need to show your caliber. After the probational period, you would be given a portfolio in line with your skills, your experiences listed in your resume and your performance during the probational period. Nevertheless, this is the start line for you to show your potentials. However, most people in your new company or institute don’t know who you are, why you are hired, or what you would bring to the team or the office. Therefore, you need to make sure your teammates or colleagues would know about you and your caliber where appropriate.

你需要展示你的才华。试用期过后，依据你简历中的技能、经验和试用期的工作表现，你会被指派负责某项工作。然而，这是你发挥潜力的起点。问题是，公司或机构的大多数人都不知道你是谁、你为什么被雇用，或者你到底能为团队或公司带来什么。因此，你需要在适当的场合让队友或同事了解你和你的能力。

05

You need to be part of the new team. Experience says that cracking the code of company culture often comes down to simply learning how to communicate with people around you. You need to find out if your boss expects you to keep him or her informed on the details or only the big problems. You need to find out whether your boss would like to be approached with just problems or problems with the road maps to address. Meanwhile, you need to find out if your teammates or partners need to be consulted, or you can handle your portfolio with complete autonomy.

你需要融入新的团队。经验告诉我们，破解公司文化的密码归根到底就是学习如何与周围人沟通。你需要弄清楚你的老板是希望你事事向他/她报告，还是只需要报告重大问题。你需要了解你的老板是仅仅需要你报告问题，还是在报告问题时提出解决问题的方案。同时，你需要了解遇事是否需要咨询团队成员或合作伙伴，还是你有权自主处理分内工作。

06

You need to live up to the expectations of your boss fast. The key to early success in your new job is to secure early wins, which include cordial working relations with people around you, partnership relations with your immediate colleagues, your credibility among associates, and your ability to create values for your organization. More importantly, you need to gain trust of your boss, and let him or her recognize what you really have. To be specific, you should find out what your boss expects you to learn and accomplish. And, you need to make sure that your boss notices your professional values. The more clarity you build around these issues, the easier your transition will be.

你需要尽快满足老板对你的期望。在新的工作中尽早获得成功的关键是确保尽早站稳脚跟，具体包括与周围的人保持良好的工作关系，与相关的同事建立良好的伙伴关系，在同事中建立起信誉以及体现出你为公司创造价值的能力。更重要的是，你要赢得老板的信任，让他认识到你的才能。具体来说，你需要了解你的老板希望你学习和完成什么。你需要让老板注意到你的专业价值。这些问题你理得越清晰，你越容易转变角色。

07

You need to think twice before doing anything. As one saying goes, you need to walk steadily before skiing on the ice. Therefore, you need to refrain from proving your creative genius overnight. Rather, you should feel confident that you're there, and at least initially. You should listen carefully before you should open your mouth. You should find ways to highlight the strengths of your colleagues via daily routines. As for your own genius, there will be plenty of time to show it down the road. All in all, when you manage to settle down in your new place, you'll be off to a great start.

做任何事情之前，都要三思而后行。俗话说，在冰上滑行之前，你要先学会稳步前行。因此，你不要想在一夜之内证明你的创造才能。相反，你应该为来到新单位感到欣慰，至少眼下如此。在日常工作中，你应该多听，少说。你应该在日常工作中设法凸显出你同事们的优点。至于你自己的才华，将来有的是时间来发挥。总而言之，你在新地方成功安定下来，这就是良好的开始。

08

You need to reshape your habits at the new office. Simply said, your career success at a new company or institution is essentially the aggregation of your habits. Whether you could fit in your new portfolio is the result of your habits. Whether you are happy in your new work environment is also the result of your habits. And, whether you would be accepted as a loyal member in a new place is also the result of your habits. Therefore, it's more important for you to forget about your old habits, and establish the new ones in line with the new environment.

你需要在新岗位上重建工作习惯。简单地说，你在新公司或机构的成功之道需要以你的履职习惯为基础。能否适应新工作取决于你的习惯。能否愉快地融入新的工作环境取决于你的习惯。在新的工作环境中能否被认为是忠诚的一员，也是你工作习惯的结果。因此，对你来说，重要的是忘却旧习惯，建立与新环境相适应的新习惯。

09

You need to build up your seniority. To borrow a metaphor, people who come into the workplace today are just like the athletes standing at the start line. You know why? You've received the same college education, read the same books, gone to the same movies, played the same video games, and watched the same TV shows, etc. Nevertheless, it is the life experience, talents, creative ideas on renovation and the teamwork spirit that would soon set each member apart at an office.

你需要增加你的资历。借用一个比喻，刚刚步入工作岗位的员工犹如处于同一起跑线上的运动员。你知道为什么吗？你们同样都接受过高等教育，阅读同样的教科书，喜欢看同类的电影，玩同类的电子游戏，喜欢看同样的电视节目等。然而，正是生活经历、才华、革新的创意和团队精神，不久将使得每个人在工作中表现各不相同。

10

You need to have the courage to handle mistakes. Too many people believe that failure in one job is a referendum on their life and career, which is not a healthy mindset at all. Scientists say that failure is a road map for people not to fall in the same place down the road. From minor slip-ups to blind falls, all of us would face the scenario at some time in our life. The key is to learn the lesson and move on, no matter what.

你需要勇于面对错误。许多人认为，在一份工作中的一次失败有可能丢掉自己的生活和职业生涯，这绝不是一种健康的心态。科学家们说，失败是一个路标，警示我们以后别重蹈覆辙。从小失误到大失败，我们所有人都难以幸免。不管发生什么，关键是要吸取教训，继续前行。

11

You need to embrace change. When you want to move forward in your career,

it pays to remember: What has got you here today isn’t going to get where you want to be tomorrow. Those who refuse to change and hold onto what has made them successful in the past are bound to fail.
你需要拥抱改变。想要在事业上有所进步，你需要记住：你今天取得的成就和拥有的经验不能确保你明天会顺利实现目标。凡是墨守成规、固守已有成功的人，注定会遭遇失败。

12

You need to build up your uniqueness. Many people believe that it would help them move forward by adapting to the new environment 100%. Nevertheless, only those who embrace their own differences within the framework of rules and regulations would stand out eventually. The key is that once you identify what makes you different, you should build up on it. In order to be successful, you don’t have to change yourself altogether, but to show who you are.
你需要做自己。许多人认为，100%地适应新环境是职业成功之道。然而，只有那些在遵守规章制度基础上坚持个性的人，才能最终脱颖而出。关键是，你一旦发现自己有与众不同的地方，就应该有意识地加以发扬光大。为了事业成功，你不必完全改变你自己，只需彰显出真实的你。

13

You need to protect your lawful interests. There is nothing wrong to take care of your own needs, and become a healthy, versatile person. And, people who are self-focused but not self-involved would be healthier, happier, and have better working relations and better leadership caliber. In modern society, successful life and career require a person to be dedicating to personal interests while caring for those of others. It’s never the choice of an either/or.
你需要保护自己的合法利益。维护自己的利益，做一个健康、多才多艺的人，无可厚非。那些既注重保护自己的利益，但又不以自我为中心的人，方可望在心理上更加健康，生活上更加快乐，工作上拥有更好的人际关系，职业上具有更强的领导才能。在现代社会，成功的人生和事业要求每个人在关心个人利益的同时，也要兼顾他人的利益。这不是非此即彼的选择。

14

You need to dedicate to your career. Many people would feel their career ahead to be long and overwhelming, which prevents them from concentrating on their daily routines. This is a common psychological mindset by many junior workers. Therefore, when you are in that scenario, you should learn to focus on milestone issues, rather than life-time visions. In fact, milestones are everywhere: The things to do in the first semester, the first week of a new job, the first client under your portfolio, etc. These doable things would make you feel much more rewarding. As one Chinese saying goes, a long march starts from the very first step.

你需要坚持发展事业。很多人觉得自己未来的职业道路很漫长、压力很大，因而无法集中精力于日常工作。这是许多初入职场的人普遍存在的心理状态。因此，你如果处于这种思想境况，应该学会聚焦“里程碑”式的事，而不是一生的愿景。事实上，“里程碑”式的事宜无处不在：第一个学期要做的事情，新工作的第一周，你在业务中接待的第一个客户等。这些切实可行的事宜会让你觉得每天都有成就感。正如中国俗语所说，千里之行，始于足下。

15

You need to work your way up for promotion. Under the market system, no one is to stay in the same place at the same level, waiting for the award or promotion to come down to you. Rather, when there are opportunities for promotions, you should take the first available opportunity to submit your application with specific details about your contributions to the appropriate

authorities. You need to explain what you're asking for. And, you also need to identify the position you want. Of course, you need to indicate your attitude to accept whatever the final decision is by the superior in the above regard.
你需要努力争取升职。在市场体制下，没有人应该待在同一个地方的同一个水平上，等着奖励或晋级机会来找你。相反，每当遇到晋升的机会，你应该在第一时间提交申请，详细说明你对相关部门的贡献。你需要解释清楚你想要得到什么。同时，你也需要明确你想要的职位。当然，你在申请中也应该表明态度，无论上级做出何种最终决定，你都会接受。

16

You need to establish working relations with your colleagues. Many people spend more time with their colleagues than anyone else in their lives. You're of no exception as a white-collar worker. Good coworker relationships is the increase of overall job satisfaction. For example, when you look forward to mingle up with colleagues, you will go to work in a happier mood, and feel more motivated in your daily routines.
你需要与同事建立良好的工作关系。很多人一生中和同事在一起的时间比和其他人都要多。作为白领工作人员，你也不例外。建立良好的同事关系有助于提升工作满意度。试想，只有期待能与同事相处，你才会愉快地上班，并且有动力做好每一天的工作。

17

You need to build up your work environment. As you will see, starting a new job could be stressful. In addition to pleasing your boss, you should also try to outreach to your workmates. Of course, building a strong working relationship takes time, but it begins on your very first day in office. In order to get a good start, you need to be friendly to everyone you work with. When you find it difficult to make small talks, a warm smile would go a long way to invite a friendly response. You should ask questions graciously and accept help and advice when others are doing so. When you get invited for a working lunch or a party, you should go. Of course, you should remember to reciprocate it accordingly.

你需要建立自己的工作环境。你会发现，开始一份新工作可能会有压力。除了要给老板留下个好印象，你还应该努力向同事示好。当然，建立良好的工作关系需要时间，但你需要从在新工作的第一天就开始行动。为了有一个良好的开端，你需要善待每个同事。你如果不想与同事闲聊，一个善意的微笑就可能获得友好的回应。你应当大大方方地向同事请教，并虚心接受对方的帮助和建议。如果受邀参加工作午餐或聚会活动，你应该前往。当然，你也要记得适时回请对方。

18

You need to get along with your superior. Generally speaking, your immediate boss would be someone you have to work with for most of the time at the office. Therefore, you need to ask him or her for advice and input whenever possible and approach him or her with questions plus ways to address them. You should let your boss do the mentor and coach work. And, you should create conditions for him or her to compliment and appreciate your interactions as well as contributions.

你需要和你的上司好好相处。一般来说，在办公室里，大部分时间你需要和你的顶头上司打交道。因此，只要有可能，你需要向老板寻求建议和工作指导，并且在向对方提出问题时，也要提供解决问题的方法。你应该让老板做你的导师。而且，你应该创造条件让老板夸赞，或者感激你的互动或贡献。

19

You need to read the mind of your boss. Knowing how to interpret the mood and responses of your boss is also a precondition to get along with him or her.

There may be some moments when you have to spot the exact mood of him or her in taking your questions or giving you instructions, and spot the lines in between.
你需要读懂老板的心思。善于理解老板的情绪和反应也是与其相处的有效方法。有时，你可能需要发现对方的情绪，寻机让对方回答你的问题或给你指示，并且听懂话外之音。

20
You need to facilitate conditions for your boss to lead. No matter how well you get along with your boss, he or she is still your boss. In short, if you want to leave an A+ impression on your boss, you need to show that you're dedicating to the benefits or image of the office, whether or not it's within your job descriptions.
你需要为你的老板创造领导条件。无论你和老板相处得多好，他仍然是你的老板。简而言之，如果想给老板留下一个A+的印象，你需要表现出你为提高办公室的利益或形象而努力的意愿，不管这是否是你工作职责的一部分。

Part Two　Situational Dialogues

01

A: Good morning, Ms. Li Nan. I'm William Clark, your supervisor. Now, let me welcome you officially on board.

早上好，李楠女士。我是威廉·克拉克，你的主管。现在，让我正式欢迎你加入我们。

B: Thank you very much, Mr. Clark. It's my honor to work in your department, and it's my privilege to work under your guidance. I know you're an expert in marketing end.

非常感谢，克拉克先生。我很荣幸能在您的部门工作，并能在您的指导下工作。我知道您是营销方面的专家。

A: It's nice of you to say so. Well, from your resume, you also majored in marketing and you've also received your MA degree. By the way, what were your average grades in your major courses, when you were at the university?

感谢你的恭维。从你的简历上看，你的专业也是市场营销，你还获得了硕士学位。顺便问一下，你在大学期间主修课程的平均成绩是多少？

B: Not bad. I had a ninety plus on average. And, I think I could do better in some areas. It took me about two years to get accustomed to the American ways at college, you know.

还不错。我的平均成绩是90分以上。不过，我认为，我在某些方面可以做得更好。你知道，我花了两年时间才习惯在美国的大学生活。

A: Well, you don’t have to feel sorry for that. In fact, you did much better than when I was a student. I know you Chinese are always smart at exams, and always manage to get higher scores.

哦，你不必为此感到遗憾。事实上，你比我在上大学时做得好多了。我知道你们中国人很会考试，每次总能得到高分。

B: Thanks, Mr. Clark. I know what I learned at college is one thing, and here, I’ll have to start from Square One. Therefore, I have a lot to learn from you, and I’ll count on you for your guidance.

谢谢，克拉克先生。我知道我在大学的成绩是一回事，但在这里，我必须从基础做起。因此，我还有很多东西需要向您学习，并需要得到您的指导。

A: You bet.

那就说定了。

02

A: Now, let’s get to the basics you need to know, before I officially give you the specific portfolio.

现在，给你正式分配工作之前，我给你讲一讲需要注意的具体事项。

B: Please do, and I’m ready to take notes.

请讲，我已经准备好做笔记了。

A: I assume you’ve read through the brochure about our company and the “bible” of our department. So, I won’t go into the details on all those things, but you need to print them into your memory. Let me warn you that you should discharge your portfolios exactly in line with the procedures and benchmarks, and I give the full authority. Nevertheless, you’re not to make any decision on anything that’s beyond your responsibility, OK? That’s the first thing you need to know. When you’ve got to carry out tasks with your teammates, please make sure you reach the understanding beforehand. When you can't do that, please let me know. Mind you, office safety is also something you need to look after carefully, especially the files and commercial secret.

我想你已经读过我们公司的宣传手册和我们部门的条例“圣经”了。我就不详细讲这些细节了，但你需要把它们印在脑海里。我谨提醒你，你应该严格按照程序和标准来开展你的工作，我会授予你全部权限。不过，你不能做任何超出你职责范围的决定，好吗？这是你需要知道的第一件事。和同事一起执行任务时，你们务必要在行动之前先达成共识。如果你们决定不了，请告诉我。我想提醒你，办公室安全也是你需要认真关注的事宜，尤其是卷宗安全和商业秘密。

B: Thanks, I'll certainly do that.

谢谢，我一定会的。

A: Good. Now, let me brief you about our department. We've got about thirty members on the pay roll, and some more people are joining us as our company has been extending its presence in Asia, especially in China. Nevertheless, you're not going to see all of them on the daily basis, as they're constantly travelling overseas on specific assignments. Right now, I'll give you one month or two to warm up with your portfolio before I give you overseas tasks.

很好。现在，我再简单介绍一下我们部门的情况。目前，我们已经有大约30名在职员工，随着本公司在亚洲，尤其是在中国的业务发展，还有人将加入我们的团队。当然，你不可能每天都见到他们，因为他们经常出差到国外执行具体任务。眼下，在我给你布置海外业务之前，我会给你一两个月的时间来熟悉你的具体工作。

B: Yes, I will.

是的，我会的。

A: Great. I also want to tell you we do have the obligation to cover the portfolios of whoever is away from the office with my instruction. Therefore, you need to be familiar with your portfolios and your colleagues as soon as possible. I hope you would understand.

那太好了。我还想告诉你，根据我的授权，我们都有义务代管出差人员的工作。因此，你要尽快熟悉好本职工作和同事的工作。我希望你能理解。

B: I certainly will. That would give me more chances to learn something new, and I love to take challenges and handle demanding tasks.

我当然会的。这会给我更多机会学习新的东西，我喜欢面对挑战并完成高要求的任务。

A: I'm glad to hear that, and I know you would be ready for it. One more thing, you've got to absolutely abide by the code of conduct in terms of corporate security. To be specific, the commercial secret is the lifeline of our company, and we all have to do our utmost to protect it from harm.

你这么说我很高兴，我相信你会尽快适应新的工作需要的。还有一件事，你必须绝对遵守公司安全方面的行为准则。具体而言，商业秘密是我们公司的生命线，我们每个人都必须尽最大的努力保护它免受侵犯。

B: Yes, I'm fully understand.

是的，我完全明白。

A: Now, here is what you've been waiting for. For the time being, you're to pick up the portfolio formerly held by your predecessor Ms. Margret Johnson. As you know, she has to resign due to health issue, and we're sorry for that. It's a pity that you're not going to have the chance to have portfolio hand-over face to face, but Margret has left a whole lot of case files and everything is in written form. You can go over her file and get started from there. Of course, you could contact me when you have any problems during the probational period.

下面是你的工作任务。目前，你将接手你的前任玛格丽特•约翰逊女士的工作。你知道，由于健康原因她不得不辞职，对此我们很抱歉。很遗憾，你没有机会与她面对面地进行工作交接，但玛格丽特留下了很多案件记录，所有的都是书面记录。你可以仔细阅读她留下的文件资料，以便接手具体工作。当然，在实习期间如果有任何问题，你可以随时联系我。

03

A: Hi, I'm Anna Smith, and I'm pleased to meet you. And, you're supposed to take over my portfolio from today. I'm sure Manager Lindon has told you about my portfolio, so I'll just hand over all those tasks to you one by one, OK?

你好，我是安娜·史密斯，见到你很高兴。从今天开始，你应该接管我的工作。我相信林登经理已经告诉你我的职责范围了，我把具体工作一项一项地移交给你，好吗？

B: Hi, I'm Yang Lei from China, and I'm glad you've agreed to hand over your portfolio to me face to face, and stay with me for one week, so that I can count on your help while I'm settling down here at the office.

你好，我是来自中国的杨磊，我很高兴你能面对面地向我移交工作，并带我一个星期。这样，我在过渡期间就可以得到你的帮助。

A: Sure, it's my pleasure. It's our corporate procedure, and I'm just doing my last assignment before leaving for another post at the R&D Department. Now, first things first, let me show you all the files on my desk and those in the cabinet. I'll brief you to the best of my ability on things you need to know, but you can ask any questions while I'm still here.

当然，这是我的荣幸。这是我们公司的程序，这是我去研发部门工作之前要做的最后一项工作。重要的事情先做，让我给你展示一下我桌上和文件柜里的所有文件。我会尽我所能向你介绍你需要知道的事情，但既然我还在这里，你有任何问题可以来问我。

B: I certainly appreciate it, Anna. I'll try to memorize things and do as much as possible, but I'm afraid I may miss something in the days to come. Therefore, please don't be offended when I should bother you with too many questions.

非常感谢，安娜。我会尽量记住需要知道和办理的事宜，但我担心会漏掉什么。所以，如果我有太多问题打扰你，请不要见怪。

A: No, not at all. While I'm here, I'm always nearby and help you out. Well, when we conclude the paper work handover, I'm going to take you to meet some partners that you're going to contact or liaise with, OK?

不，别客气。在和你交接工作期间，我会随时帮你。对了，书面交接工作完成后，我会带你去见几个日后需要联系的伙伴，好吗？

B: That's very kind of you. I know I'm in your capable hands.

你真是太好了。我知道你是行家里手。

04

A: Hi, you must be Ms. Lina Harris. I'm Lucy from Beijing, China, and I'm taking over from Ms. Anna Smith. Nice to meet you and nice to work with you, too.

你好，你一定是莉娜·哈里斯女士吧。我是来自中国北京的露西。我将接替安娜·史密斯女士的工作。很高兴见到你，也很高兴和你一起工作。

B: Likewise. Anna has been with us for the past four years, and we've been colleagues as well as friends. We're sorry to hear that she's to be hospitalized soon, and we're going to miss her a lot.

同样。安娜已经和我们在一起四年了，我们是同事，也是朋友。我们很遗憾地听说她很快就要住院了，我们会非常想念她的。

A: Me, too. Well, since I'm new here, I'll have to rely on you and your colleagues for help when I should have any problems.

我也是。嗯，我是新来的，如果有什么问题，我将仰仗你和你的同事们的帮助。

B: Sure, we're in a team now, and we have a tradition here in the department to help one another and cover the portfolios of others when they should be

on business trip or whatever. And, we'll naturally extend the tradition to you in the future.
当然，我们现在是一个团队啦。我们这个部门有互相帮助的传统，每当有人需要出差或遇有其他事情的时候，我们都会帮忙代管他们的业务。当然，我们也会把这个传统延续给你。

Part Three Common Expressions

- They say the best way to adapt to the new environment is to do everything in line with the procedures and regulations, and you should never try to make any decisions without authorization.
  人们说，适应新工作环境的最好方法就是按照程序和规章制度去做事，同时，如果没有授权，你不能擅自做决定。
- It pays for you to keep work diary on the daily basis, so that it could be ready for reference when your own responsibility is under stake.
  每天写工作日记是有好处的，这样你就可以跟踪自己的日常事务，并在你遭受问责之际随时可以拿出来作为佐证。
- You should ask for authorization and plan your way forward. You should stick to the procedures and regulations when you carry out any assignment and go over things afterwards, in order to gain experience and avoid the mistakes.
  你应该请求授权，事先计划好路线图。在执行任务时，你要坚持按程序和规定行事，事后要复盘，以便积累经验，避免犯错误。

- They say the sure way to avoid making mistakes is not to repeat the same mistakes. Therefore, you need to think twice before you should open your mouth or jump into any conclusions.
  人们常说，避免犯错误最可靠的方式是，不要重复犯同样的错误。因此，在开口说话或下结论之前，你需要三思而后行。
- When you are new at the office, you should immediately find out about the corporate cultural norms which can cover everything from the company values to very specific action. They usually come in the form of unwritten rules. For example, you should find out if the senior leaders are approachable. You should find out if your colleagues eat lunch at their desks, or use that time to meet and build up network. You should find out if your colleagues would leave office at a reasonable hour, etc.
  你刚开始在办公室履职时，应该抓紧了解公司的文化规范，具体可能涵盖从公司的价值观到具体行动的一切事宜，通常以不成文规定的形式出现。例如，你应该弄清楚高层领导是否平易近人。你应该弄清楚你的同事是否在他们的办公桌上吃午饭，或者利用这段时间见面和社交。你应该弄清楚你的同事是否在合理的时间下班等。
- You should be open to new experience. Regardless of your most recent role, changing companies means you’re entering a new institution which would inevitably do things differently. Rather than doing things the way you’re used to, you should adopt new approaches. For example, if your new team seems to focus more on output than strategy and analysis, you should learn more about the associated business impact before trying to change direction.
  你应该对适应新环境持开放心态。不管你在先前单位担任什么角色，跳槽意味着你进入了一个新的机构，行事方式难免不同。因此，你应该采用新的工作方法，而不是沿用之前习惯的方式去做事。例如，如果你的新团队注重工作绩效，而不是战略和分析，那么你应该了解更多相关的信息，而后调整方向。

- You should build up your new network quickly. Remember, your co-workers will be the key to your success at your new portfolio. Achieving results will require knowing whom to reach out to at every level. You'll find most people are happy to share their expertise if you ask. And, you should take the time to see if you have skills and insights that would be of help to your new colleagues. It never hurts to show good will, you know.
  你应该尽快建立新的人脉关系网络。记住，你的同事将是你在新公司取得成功的关键。想要取得成绩，你需要知道在每个层次上需要同谁打交道。如果求教，你会发现大多数人都很乐意分享他们的专业知识和技巧。与此同时，你应该注意观察自己是否有对新同事有帮助的技能与见解。你知道的，礼多人不怪。

第二十二章

会务活动

*

在一生中，我们都有机会筹备或参与会议或论坛，与大家就共同感兴趣的问题相聚在一起，交流观点和信息，达成共识，促进相互理解，制定共同的政策建议等。在国际舞台上，如何组织、主持和参与公共活动成为衡量我们是否是国际人士的一个重要指标。

Chapter Twenty-two

Conference and Meetings

*

In our lifetime, we may have opportunities to organize or participate in conferences and forums where we should converge with people on subjects of common interests, in order to exchange ideas and information, reach consensuses, promote common understanding, or to formulate the common policy proposals, etc. At the international arena, it's an important benchmark to define whether we are international persons by the way how we organize, preside over or participate in all those public functions.

Part One　Things to Know

01

When you're living, working, studying or doing business in the partner countries along the Belt and Road, you'll have opportunities either participate in or preside over public gatherings or meetings. Therefore, you need to get prepared both in terms of theory and technical skills.

在"一带一路"沿线国家生活、工作、学习或经商期间，你们都有机会参与或主持公共集会和会议。因此，你需要在理论和技能上都做好准备。

02

You should formulate and implement a blueprint, which should include many things to be done before, during and after those events. Whether it is to hold the meeting or attend the meeting, you should start the preparation at your early convenience. As Sun Zi said, logistics must be in place before any military campaigns. So are preparations for large scale conferences. And, all the necessary human, material and financial resources have to be in place in time, in line with the budget, in order to avoid last-minute rush.

你需要制定和实施一份蓝图，其中包括在会议之前、期间和之后需要做的大量工作。无论是召开会议，还是参加会议，你都需要尽早准备。正如孙子所说，兵马未动粮草先行。大型会议的准备工作也是如此。所有必备的人力、物力和财力资源都必须依据预算及时到位，以避免在最后一刻抓瞎。

03

You need to establish a to-do list. To be specific, you need to have the conference venue, participant list, materials, technical support and even refreshments to think about. The key to successful conference planning is to take each task one step at a time, and keep a thorough list of what you've done and what you need to do next.

你需要罗列待办事宜清单。具体而言，你需要规划会议地点、与会者名单、材料、技术支持，甚至还有餐饮和茶点等事宜。会议计划成功的关键是逐步进行每一项任务，并且详细地记录下已办事项和待办事项。

04

You need to start planning early. Usually, you need to plan the program at least half a year in advance, even longer, if the conference will have many participants or is large in scope. Remember, enough venues and catering services must be reserved months in advance, and many participants will have to make arrangements just to be present. Furthermore, you might need sponsors from large companies which also need to come up with the budget months in advance.

你需要尽早规划。通常情况下，你需要至少提前半年规划项目，如果会议参与者多或规模大，则需要更长时间。记住，应有的场地和餐饮服务必须提前几个月预订，许多参会者也需要提前安排参会计划。此外，你可能需要取得大公司的赞助，而他们也需要提前几个月安排预算。

05

You need to form a committee, which would make all the preparation for the conference, and enroll enough people to actually pull off the details.

You need to designate a conference coordinator, who is the point person for all the major decisions and will oversight everything with your guidance. If this is the annual event, you should outreach to the previous coordinator on the committee. If he or she cannot participate, at least try to allocate the file documents from the previous year, in order to streamline your planning.

你需要成立一个组委会，统筹会议准备工作，并招募足够的人员落实各项具体工作。你需要指定一个会议协调员，负责所有重大事宜，并且在你的指导下监督一切。如果这是年度活动，你可以联系往届会议协调员。如果他或她不能参加，至少努力获得前一年会议的档案文件，以便优化你的计划。

06

You need to assemble your team quickly. You need to break up your organization committee into several sub teams and give them authorizations for the specific functions such as protocol team, logistic team, secretary team, catering team, registration team, tour activity team, the person in charge at each team, who would draft their plans and report to you on the regular basis, so that you would know the progress of each team work and coordinate their portfolios accordingly.

你需要迅速整合办会团队。你需要把组织委员会分成几个小组，并给他们特定的职能授权，如礼宾组、后勤组、秘书组、餐饮组、接待组、导游组等。你应该指定每个团队的负责人来起草他们的计划并定期向你报告，以便你随时了解每个团队的进展情况并相应地协调他们的筹备工作。

07

You need to get the full authority to organize the conference because this will shape the rest of your decisions. Then, you need to know whom to give

directions and what directions to give, and how to coordinate activities among sub-teams, in order to ease the stress of moving things forward.
你需要获得组织会议的全部权力，因为这将影响你接下来的决定。你需要知道向谁下达指令，下达什么指令，以及如何协调子团队间的活动，以减轻工作向前推进的压力。

08

You need to establish your goals. First, you need to gather and assess information including the history of same or similar events held by other organizations in the field, in order to tap into actual procedures and technical experience. Second, you need to do research on the potential event attendees, in order to finalize the conference scale. These two would help you focus your follow-up preparations.
你需要确立目标。首先，你需要查阅同行举办的同类会议的档案资料，借鉴相关流程和技术经验。其次，你需要调查潜在的与会者，以确定会议的规模。这两点均可助力你做好后续会议筹备工作。

09

You need to project the weather. There’s no doubt that weather could be a factor for holding conferences. First and foremost, you should try to avoid the extreme weather conditions. Second, you need to ensure participants would find it safe to fly back and forth. Third, you need to make sure participants would take stock from the ideal weather to do sightseeing or go for the relevant activities.
你需要预估会议期间的天气状况。毫无疑问，天气可能是影响会议的一个因素。首先，你应该尽量避免在极端天气条件下开会。其次，你需要确保参与者认为往返飞行是安全的。第三，你需要确保参会者可以利用良好的天气安排观光或开展相关的活动。

10

You need to organize the conference in the city which has easy access to the nearby airport, hotels, and an acceptable choice of sub-conference venues. It's best, too, if the city is a large metropolitan city so that people would like to visit. And, pcople on the fence about attending a conference are more likely to show up if the event is located in a tourist destination.

你应该在有机场、酒店以及合适的分会场的城市举办会议。如果会议所在地是一个大城市，人们可以顺便参观游览，那就更好了。而且如果会议地点设在旅游胜地，那些对参加会议持观望态度的人则更有可能去了。

11

You need to do research on conference attendees. First, you should invite some VIPs to honor the occasion, which would attract potential attendees. Second, you should carefully select keynote speakers, and give specific suggestions on the topic they would speak about, in order to ensure the quality of the conference. Third, you should invite professionals to speak on sub-conferences, in order to fully explore the theme. Fourth, you should set the benchmarks for the ordinary participants, in order to screen out non-related participants. Fifth, you should carefully invite the media to cover the event, in order to influence the general public.

你需要对与会者做调查研究。首先，你应该试着邀请一些贵宾参会，这将吸引潜在的与会者。其次，你应该仔细挑选主题演讲者，并对他们的演讲主题给出具体的建议，以确保会议质量。第三，你应该邀请专业人士在分议题会议上作专题发言，以确保会议主题得到充分研讨。第四，你需要设定普通参会者的标准，以筛除无关人员。第五，你应该慎重邀请媒体对会议进行报道，以影响公众。

12

You need to decide the date for the conference. In general, conferences are usually held during the particular times of the year and particular days of the week. And, they are usually held between March and June or between September and November. In any other time, people are less likely to show up. In line with international practice , major conferences tend to be held from Thursday to Friday or Monday to Tuesday.

你需要确定会议的日期。一般来说，会议通常需要在一年中的特定时间和一周中的特定日子举行，通常在3月至6月或9月至11月之间举行。在其他时间开会，参会者出席率不会很高。依据国际惯例，大型会议通常在周四至周五或周一至周二举行。

13

You need to decide the duration of the conference. It depends on how many people will participate and what needs to be accomplished at the conference. For a conference of 250~300 people, you need to plan for two full days.

你需要确定大会持续的时间。会议的时间长短取决于有多少人会参加，以及会议需要完成什么目标。对于250~300人规模的会议，会期大约需要两整天。

14

You need to have the budget in hand. It’s true that money matters to anything we do, especially to the conferences or meetings. You should know how many items you need to cover, and how much money to pay for each bill. And then, you should break that down into specific items such as conference venue, materials and speakers’ fees, etc. You also need to make sure that your assistants would adhere to the fund limits.

你需要做好足够的预算。没有预算什么事都办不成，尤其是各类会议。你需要把控所有会务项目，每个项目的付费规模。而后，你需要将预算资金分解到具体项目上去，如会议场地、材料和演讲费，等等。你还需要确保你的助手严格按照预算办事。

15

You need to seek sponsors. The budget might be influenced by whether or not you would try to recruit sponsors for the event. They pay a fee to support the conference, but also get a say in the content of the conference, which would include hosting presentations or panels with their own speakers and branding conference materials with their logos. On the plus side, sponsors pay you up front, which would give you more money to work out your plan. Meanwhile, sponsors might include local industrial leaders or philanthropists, depending on your conference themes.

你需要寻求赞助商。你能否获得赞助直接影响你的预算。赞助商支付一定费用来支持会议，同时对会议本身的内容也有了发言权，通常包括由他们的发言人主持演讲或小组讨论，或者将他们的标识印刷在会议材料上。从好的方面看，赞助商会提前支付赞助款，这样，你就有更多的资金推进办会工作。同时，赞助者还可包括当地的行业领袖或慈善家参会，这取决于你的会议主题。

16

You need to allow some attendees free of charge. Some conferences are free for the participate, while others will be charged with exorbitant fees. There are several factors to consider when setting the admission ticket price. If it is a small, local conference, you should charge little or no fees. Another option is to allow some people to attend the event free of charge, while request others to pay a small fee, in order to cover conference costs.

你需要允许部分参会者免费入场。有些会议对与会者免费开放，有些则收取较高会费。在确定票价时，有几个因素需要考虑。如果这是在本地举行的小型会议，你应该收取很少的费用或不收取费用。另一种做法是允许部分人免费参会，但要求其他人支付少量费用，以补贴会议费用。

17

You need to give flexible charges to different participants. Multi-day conferences with meals included would charge registration fees, which can vary from $30 to $200. Many conferences use a sliding pay scale for people in different stages of their careers. For example, academic conferences typically charge lower fees for students than for the faculty, or they would charge lower fees for the participants of the sponsors than for those from the general public.

你需要对不同参会者实施灵活的收费机制。提供膳食的多日会议通常会收取注册费，标准从30美元到200美元不等。许多会议对处于职业生涯不同阶段的人采用浮动收费标准。例如，学术会议对学生收取的费用通常比对教师收取的费用低，对赞助单位成员收取的费用比对普通公众收取的费用低。

18

You need to choose the right conference venue. When scouting for locations, you should keep in mind the number of participants, the convenience of location, parking and proximity to public transportation, airports and hotels, etc. Your goal is to make it as easy as possible for the participants to attend. You need to check out whether the conference venue has a convention center or hotel with convention rooms. For small conferences, you can simply rent a local church or community center.

你需要选择合适的会议地点。在实地考察会议地点时，你要记住参会者的人数，地点的便利程度，有无停车场以及附近有无公共交通工具、机场和酒店。你的目标应该是尽可能让参会者更加方便。你需要检查一下你所在的城市是否有会议中心或带会议室的酒店。举行小型会议，你可以租用当地的教堂或社区中心。

19

You need to enlist the venue staff. If you have chosen a venue that regularly holds conferences, you could tap into its invaluable resource. This is what the staff members do every day and they should be able to answer any questions or address your concerns, and provide advice when needed. Some venues even have an event planner who can handle many practical details of your conference. Of course, there will be additional fee, but it's still cheaper than hiring a full-time staff for just a few days.

你需要招募会场工作人员。你如果选择一个经常举办会议的酒店，可以放心地利用对方的宝贵资源。那里的员工熟悉每天的服务工作，能够回答任何问题，解决你的疑惑，并在需要时提供建议。有些单位甚至提供会务策划人服务，协助处理与会议相关的未料事宜。当然，这会产生额外的费用，但这仍然比在会议期间雇用全职员工划算。

20

You need to attach importance to catering service. When you plan to organize an international conference, you need to remember that participants will not want to sit all day without eating decent meals. Therefore, you will have to hire a catering service to bring in breakfast, lunch and snacks, unless the conference venue will provide food service. Please remember that participants may have dietary restrictions, allergies, and preferences that can make catering service rather difficult. Nevertheless, when you choose an experienced catering company, it would automatically create options for vegetarian, or other food preferences.

你需要重视会议饮食服务。在计划组织国际会议时，你需要记住，与会者不愿意坐一整天却没有一顿像样的餐食，而且很多人都不知道在哪里用餐。因此，除非会议场地提供餐饮服务，否则你将需要聘请餐饮服务人员提供早餐、午餐和零食服务。请记住，许多人都有饮食限制、食物禁忌和偏好，这使得饮食供应相当复杂。然而你如果选择一个有经验的服务商，他们可以自动为素食者或其他饮食偏好者提供选择。

Part Two Situational Conversations

01

A: Good morning, Mr. Johnson. Thank you for receiving me at such a short notice.

早上好，约翰逊先生。谢谢你在这么短的时间内接待我。

B: Good morning Mr. Yang Hua. It’s my pleasure to help you and your company.

早上好，杨华先生。我很乐意为您和贵公司提供帮助。

A: Certainly. We’re planning to book a venue for our annual conference for all our up-stream suppliers and down-stream customers.

当然。我们计划在你们这里租场地，召开上游供应商和下游客户年度会议。

B: How many participants are you expecting, please?

请问你们预计有多少人参加？

A: Roughly 200.

大约200人。

B: When are you planning to hold the conference?

你们打算什么时候召开会议？

A: Between September and October. What do you think?

在9月和10月之间，你们这里没有问题吧？

B: I think you've chosen the best season which would ensure the participation rate. By the way, it roughly takes $300 per guest for such events. Have you got the budget ready?

我认为，你们选择了最佳时节，可确保参与率。顺便说一下，参加这样的活动，每位参会者大概要花300美元。你把预算准备好了吗？

A: Sure, we allocated the budget late last year. What we need now is your professional assistance in drafting the program. And, I need the draft program to report to the Board of Directors at the end of this month. Can you manage it?

当然，我们去年年底就划拨了预算。我们现在需要你们从专业的角度起草方案。另外，我需要在本月底向董事会报告草案。你们能行吗？

B: No problem. Nevertheless, for your reference, I'll keep you posted while I'm working out the budget proposal, OK?

没问题。但是，我想顺便告诉你，我在制定预算提案时会随时与你保持联系，好吗？

02

A: Good morning, sir, you are…

早上好，先生，你是……

B: Good morning, I'm Wei Fengming from China. And, this is my colleague Mr. Dong Hua.

早上好，我是魏凤鸣，来自中国。这位是我的同事董华先生。

A: Welcome to the conference, gentlemen. Now, please let me have your passports.

先生们，欢迎你们参加会议。现在，请把你们的护照给我。

B: Here you are. By the way, have any other Chinese delegates arrived yet?

给你。顺便问一下，其他中国代表团成员到了吗？

A: I'm afraid not. In fact, you're the early birds. Well, here are your passports, the keys to your hotel rooms, the brochures, and your name tags. One more

thing, here are the souvenir bags for you. Have a nice day.
恐怕没有。事实上，你们是第一批前来报到的参会者。好了，这是你们的护照、房间钥匙、宣传册和胸牌。还有一件事，这是给你们的纪念品袋。祝你们度过美好的一天。

03

A: Good morning, ladies and gentlemen! I'm Professor Mark Morrison. It's my pleasant duty today to chair the annual meeting. Since most participants are here, we'll start the session right now. Well, today we are very honored to have Professor Ding Liangcheng to give the keynote speech on the Economic Reform for the Developing Countries. Professor Ding is a well-known macro-economist in China, and has witnessed and participated in the whole process of China's economic reform and opening up since 1979. Over the past forty some years, Professor Ding has been a member of a national thinks tank, and has been speaking and writing widely both in China and at the international arena. For his detailed information, you just have to google his name on the Internet. I'm sure his professional presentation on the topic will produce much food for thought. Without further due, let's welcome Professor Ding to the podium. Professor Ding, the floor is yours.
早上好，女士们，先生们！我是马克·莫里森教授。很高兴主持今天的年会。考虑到大多数与会者都已到场，我们现在开始会议。今天，我们非常荣幸地请到了丁良成教授就发展中国家的经济改革这个专题作演讲。丁教授是著名的宏观经济学家，见证并参与了1979年以来中国经济改革开放的全过程。在过去的40多年里，丁教授长期任职于一个国家智库，并在中国和国际舞台上经常发表这方面的演讲和文章。关于丁教授的详细情况，你们只要在谷歌网上输入他的名字就可找到。我相信他今天的专业演讲会为我们所有人提供很多启发。言归正传，让我们欢迎丁教授上台。丁教授，请开始您的演讲。

B: Thank you Professor Morrison for your generous introduction, and I'd also like to thank the University for the invitation. As you all knows, reform and renovation are the two vehicles for any country to proceed with its sustainable economic and social development. Over the past forty years, China, as the largest developing country, has managed to realize its rapid economic growth and social progress, and become the first nation to lift the whole nation out of poverty, and moved into a well-to-do society. And, it has now become the second largest economy in the world. You may want to ask why and how. Having said this, I'll walk you through the forty years of China's economic reform and opening up. Then, I'll share with you China's experiences and lessons from a professor's view point. After that, I'll be more than happy to take your questions. Now, with your permission, I'll move into the first part of my speech.

谢谢莫里森教授的介绍，我也要感谢学校的邀请。正如诸位所知，改革与创新是任何一个国家实现经济与社会可持续发展的两大动力。过去四十年间，中国作为世界上最大的发展中国家，实现了经济的快速增长和社会的快速进步，成为世界上第一个实现全面脱贫与小康的国家，成为世界第二大经济体。你们可能想问：这是为什么，中国如何取得上述成就。带着这些问题，我将带你们回顾中国经济改革开放40年的历程。然后，我将以一位教授的身份与你们分享中国的经验和教训。之后，我将非常乐意回答大家的提问。现在，承蒙你们同意，我将进入我演讲的第一部分。

04

A: Well, thank you very much, Professor Ding. Your speech has really ignited the interests of the audience, and I've received six written questions from the floor and so many hands are up for questions. Nevertheless, I'll use my privilege to ask you the first question. The process of your economic reform and opening up is forty some years in motion, but what is your projection of its future, and what are the new strategies and policies by your national leaders and government?

非常感谢你，丁教授。您的演讲确实激发了听众的兴趣，我已经收到了6个书面提问，还很多人举手示意想要提问。不过，我还是要利用我的特权问您第一个问题。中国的经济改革和开放已经进行了40多年，请问您对贵国改革开放的未来有什么展望？请问，贵国领导人和政府有什么新的战略和政策？

B: Thank you, Professor Morrison for your professional but politically sensitive question. From my humble perspective, no economic system can be sustainable under all circumstances, and each country must find the right economic system in line with its national situation, and remain in the driving seat in its economic development via timely renovation of its system. China has maintained its consistent economic growth and social progress via reform and opening up. Nevertheless, China today faces the “new normal”, commonly seen in many countries at different stages of development, which has prompted the Chinese leadership and government to launch the new round of reform and opening up under the theory of dual circulation economy, in conjunction with the Belt and Road Initiative. As a professor of economics, I’m fully confident that the new strategies and policies will facilitate conditions for the Chinese economy to move ahead in a healthier manner.

莫里森教授，谢谢您提出的专业但在政治上比较敏感的问题。在我看来，任何一种经济制度并非在任何情况下都是可持续的，每个国家都必须找到符合本国国情的经济发展制度，并及时推进制度革新，在经济发展中保持主导地位。中国通过改革开放保持了经济持续增长和社会进步。然而，今天的中国正面临许多国家在不同发展阶段所面临的“新常态”，因此中国领导人和中央政府制定和实施了双循环经济发展战略，并结合“一带一路”倡议启动了新一轮改革开放历史进程。作为经济学教授，我相信上述新战略和新政策将为中国经济健康发展创造条件。

Part Three Common Expressions

- Ladies and gentlemen, can I have your attention, please?… Thank you for your cooperation. On behalf of the organizing committee, I have some housekeeping announcements to make. Please listen carefully. For all the speakers, please hand in your PPT to our volunteers standing around you if you haven't done that yet. For all the participants, please switch your cell phones to the flight mode or simply switch them off. That's all I have to say. Thank you for your kind attention.

  女士们，先生们，请大家注意！……谢谢大家的配合。我谨代表组委会说两个通知，请仔细听。所有的演讲者，如果有尚未提交PPT的，请交给站在你们身旁的志愿者。所有的参与者，请把你们的手机调到飞行模式，或者干脆关机。这些就是我要说的。谢谢你们的聆听。

- Ladies and gentlemen, may I have your attention please? This is the announcement about the city tour at 19:30. Three minibuses will be waiting for you in front of the main entrance at 19:20. Please wear your name tags and bring an extra clothe, as it will be windy along the seaside. The whole trip will take about 90 minutes. Please follow the instruction of our volunteers. Mind you, when you should miss the vans at 21:30 sharp, you'll have to find your own way back to the hotel, okey?

  女士们、先生们，请大家注意一下。这是今晚7点半市内观光的通知。7点20分，三辆小面包车会在大门前恭候各位。请佩戴胸牌，并多带一件衣服，因为晚上海边风很大。整个旅程大致需要90分钟。请听从我们志愿者的引导。提醒一下，你们有哪位错过9点返程的小面包车，请自己想办法回酒店。

- Ladies and gentlemen, it’s my pleasure today to chair the annual meeting. I can see that the bulk of the participants are here. So,with your permission, we’ll start the session now. In accordance with the agenda, we are here to address this challenging issue of climate change. Without further due, Professor Wolfensohn, the floor is yours.

  女士们、先生们，我很高兴主持今天的年会。我看到大部分与会者都入座了，所以如果你们允许的话，我们现在就开始会议。根据议程，我们今天在这里讨论气候变化这一具有挑战性的问题。不再耽搁大家的时间，沃尔芬森教授，现在请您发言。

- Good morning, my dear participants, would you kindly move to the conference hall, where we could kick-start the opening session? You could bring your coffee with you, but not the desserts, please.

  各位与会者，早上好，请各位移步到会场，我们马上要举行开幕式。你们可以带上咖啡，但请不要带甜点。

- Please allow me to take the opportunity to welcome all of you to our quarterly meeting at such a short notice. And, I know two participants have given the rain checks, and one or two others are still on the way. Nevertheless, we’ll have to begin the session right away as we’ve got three break-down sessions this morning.

  请允许我借此机会，欢迎诸位在这么短的时间内应邀参加我们的季度会议。我知道有两名参与者因故不能前来，还有一两位参与者仍在路上。但是，我们必须马上开始会议，因为上午我们还有三个分议题会议要举行。

- Well, time flies! After two busy days and nights, we’ve managed to conclude the conference with your generous assistance and cooperation. Now, I have the honor to wrap up the speeches and discussions during the past two days, and I hope my humble summary would meet your expectations, and the draft summary is in front of you. Please put forward any interventions and modifications wherever you see fit, and let me know afterwards.

时间过得好快啊！经过两天两夜的忙碌，在诸位大力协助与合作下，本次会议圆满落幕。现在，我很荣幸地宣布结束这两天的演讲和讨论，并希望我简短的总结能满足大家的期望，会议通稿草稿已经分发给诸位。请提出需要修改的意见，并稍后通知我。

- Dear participants, ladies and gentlemen, now I'd like to seek your comments and interventions on the wrap up of the conference. As the draft paper was dispersed to all of you, and we also have had face to face discussions separately. Therefore, if you don't have any more questions and suggestions, I suggest we clap our hands to prove the document… Now, I would like to declare the closure of the conference and wish you a safe and sound trip back to wherever you belong. Bon Voyage!

  尊敬的与会者，女士们，先生们，现在我想请你们对本次会议的结论发表评论和意见。因为初稿已经分发给大家了，我们也分别进行了面对面的讨论。因此，如果你们没有任何问题和建议，我建议大家鼓掌通过这份文件。……现在，我宣布大会结束，并祝你们回程一路平安。祝大家一路顺风！

- Well, all good things come to an end, but before I announce the closure of our symposium, I still have some housekeeping announcements to make. The first one is that the organizing committee has generously organized the city tour at 9:00 tomorrow morning. They have arranged three vans for the tour, and I kindly request you to register your participation at the secretariat right after this session. The second is that we have agreed to cover the room and board for three days until tomorrow morning for all the participants. Therefore, those who would like to extend the stay should pick up their own bills. Last but not least, for those who would like to have their papers included in the document collection, please hand in their final version before this Friday. That’s all I’ve got to say.

好吧，天下没有不散的宴席。但是，在宣布会议结束之前，我还有一些会务通知需要讲一下。第一是组委会慷慨地组织了明天上午九点的城市旅游，一共安排了三辆面包车。请愿意参加观光活动的参会者在本次会议之后到会务处登记。第二是我们已经同意为所有的参与者提供截至明天为期三天的食宿安排。因此，凡是想延期逗留的参会者请自行到饭店前台结账。最后，凡是希望将论文收录在论文集中的参会者，请在本周五之前提交论文的最终版本。这些就是我要说的。

第二十三章

公共讲演

*

中国有句古训说得好：口能言、身能行，国之宝也。同样，无论我们从事何种职业，判断我们是否具有国际公民的素质，主要看我们的公开讲话或演讲能力。

Chapter Twenty-three

Public Speech

*

As one ancient Chinese saying goes, those who are verbally eloquent and physically able are the real talents for the state. Likewise, on public occasions, one thing that defines whether we are international citizens is our ability to handle public remarks or speeches, no matter what career we are in.

Part One　Things to Know

01

On many occasions, we've got to make remarks at social functions or give speeches at official functions. Therefore, we all have to develop our presentation skills, in order to define ourselves. We have to find time to practice, in order to increase our confidence and overcome speech anxiety. As one saying goes, practice makes perfect.

在很多情况下，我们需要在社交场合讲话，或在官方场合发表演讲。因此，我们都需要提高公共演讲技能，展示我们的风采。我们必须找时间进行练习，以期增强信心，克服演讲焦虑。正如俗话所说，熟能生巧。

02

Theoretically speaking, a good speech consists of three parts: The opening remarks, the main body and concluding remarks. A nice beginning is the cream of the crust, which is the effective media to grab the attention of your audience. The main body contains the main points you want to get across to the audience. Meanwhile, carefully thought-out concluding remarks are to wrap things up and print them to the mind of the audience, which is nothing less like a grand finale of a play.

从理论上讲，优秀的演讲由三个部分组成：开场白、主体部分和结束语。好的开头可谓皇冠上的明珠，可抓住听众的注意力。主体部分包含你真正想传达给观众的主要观点。同时，精心提炼的结束语可升华主旨，给听众留下深刻印象，这就好比一场演出的压轴戏。

03

Public speaking is an important skill for all of us, whether we are in business, science, education, or politics. Public remarks or speeches can cover a wide range of topics, which are meant to inform, educate, entertain, or influence your audience. Therefore, you need to focus on the purpose of your speech and use different theories, speech techniques and languages to fully realize your goals.

公众演讲对我们所有人来说都是一项重要的技能，无论是在商界、科学界、教育界还是政界。公开讲话或演讲主题涵盖领域广泛，其宗旨是告知、教育、娱乐或影响听众。因此，每场演讲你都需要聚焦演说目的，而后运用不同的理论、演讲技巧和语言来充分实现预期的目标。

04

Theoretically speaking, when you sit down to prepare your speeches or presentations, you should list the top three goals that you want to accomplish. First, you need to be clear who your audience is, and why it's important for them to be at the meeting. You should list the major points that you want to convey to your audience. Second, you should be clear about the tone that you want to use for your presentation. You should design the attractive opening remarks, which is to take 3~5 minutes to present your goals, clarifies the benefits of the presentation and explain the overall layout of your presentation. Third, you should focus your effort on the main body of your presentation, which is to occupy about 70% of your presentation time. Fourth, you should design a clear-cut closing remark, which is about 10% of your presentation time. Last but not least, you should leave time for questions and answers, which is about 10% of the time.

从理论上讲，当你坐下来准备演讲或报告时，你应该列出你希望达到的三个主要目标。首先，你要清楚听众是谁，以及他们参会的目的。在此基础上列出你想向听众传达的主要信息。其次，设定演讲基调。你应该设计一个引人入胜的开场白，大约花3到5分钟时间向观众阐明演讲目标，说明听众能从中受益什么，并介绍演讲的整体设计。第三，需要着力准备报告或演讲的主体部分，这部分大约占整个演讲70%的时间。第四，应该设计一个简洁明了的结尾，这大约占整个演讲时间的10%。最后，应该为回答问题预留时间，这大约占演讲时间的10%。

05

Good speeches never come easy. It would take years of practice and painstaking efforts. As a matter of fact, public speaking is a skill, which can be learned. It just takes some know-how and some efforts. To be specific, for each presentation or speech, you need to do some serious preparation. Here are some tips for you to take home.

俗话说，好的演讲来之不易，需要多年的练习和艰苦的努力。事实上，公开演讲技巧是可以练就的，需要掌握一些技巧和努力。具体而言，每次报告或演讲你都需要进行认真的准备。这里有几点供参考。

06

Based on the carefully selected topic, you should then focus on the core messages. The body of a speech covers the main ideas and key concepts. Usually, three points is the standard structure for most presentations or speeches. For example, when you want to talk about the global warming, you should select these core messages: Invest in clean energy, green technologies, reduction on harmful emissions, green production and consumption, and forestation and water conservation, etc. When you get clear on your core messages, you will find it easy to go ahead with the speech writing.

在精心选好主题的基础上，你需要聚焦核心演讲内涵。正文部分包括主要思想和关键概念。通常情况下，大多数报告或演讲的标准结构涵盖三个主要观点。例如，你想谈论气候变暖这个话题，就应当选择下列核心内涵：清洁能源投资、绿色技术研发、减少有害排放、绿色生产和消费、植树造林和节约用水等。把这些核心信息搞清楚之后，你会发现撰写演讲稿很容易。

07

Speeches won't hold water without a solid structure. Simply said, a solid speech covers three parts: An attractive opening remark, a solid main body and a sobering conclusion. At each section, your language should be concise and to the point. Your audience will likely find your speech confusing if you fail to give them clear indications.

没有稳定架构的演讲立不住脚。简而言之，一个扎实的演讲涵盖三大部分：吸引人的开场白、井井有条的主体部分、发人深省的结尾。每部分的语言力求简洁明了。如果你的演讲缺乏条理，听众很可能会觉得云山雾绕。

08

First, you should collect all the information and reference materials for your speech or presentation. It can be very time consuming to find the right statistics you need in this regard. Nevertheless, specific statistics and data could add a range of benefits to your presentation. First, numbers and data are a good way to support your focal theme. Second, impressive statistic would show you've done research, and you are knowledgeable about the subject matter. Third, important statistics will stay with your audience afterwards. Nevertheless, you need to make sure that the facts and figures you are going to quote are solid, because one careless mistake may spoil your speech.

首先，你应该收集演讲所需的所有信息和参考材料。寻找演讲所需要的统计数据花费大量时间。然而，具体的统计数据可以给你的演讲带来一系列的好处。首先，数字和数据是支撑主题的好方法。第二，翔实的统计数据表明你对相关专题做过研究，且通晓演讲或报告的主题。第三，重要的统计数据通常会在演讲结束后依然留在听众的脑海中。不过，你需要确保所引用的事实和数字是可靠的，因为任何一个粗心的错误都会使你的演讲黯然失色。

09

Meanwhile, you might need to prepare supplement materials to be distributed on the spot, such as relevant articles, reports, etc. You may hand out copies of your presentation or your speech outlines. You might use your personal computer to project the slides onto the screen. Then, you need to check out the computer system before people come into the conference room. When you provide the supplement materials during the presentation, you should make sure to pass it around after you have completed your presentation or speech.

与此同时，您可能需要准备一些补充材料，如相关文章、报告等供现场分发。你可以分发你的演示文稿或演讲提纲。你也可能使用投影仪将演讲提纲投放到显示屏幕上。因此，你需要在听众进入会议室之前检查一下电脑系统。如果想要在现场分发补充材料，你应该注意在演讲结束之后发。

10

You need to use the conversational tone to write your speech, as if you would speak to them face to face. For that matter, your speech should sound the way you would normally talk. You should include one or two small talks or humors, where appropriate. What you want to talk about must be specific. You should give examples or statistics to support relevant points. Meanwhile, you need to use short sentences, which will be easier for the audience to remember.

你需要用会话语气撰写讲稿，以便听起来好像你在同他们面对面交谈一样。具体而言，你应该用平常说话的方式演讲；你应该在适当的时候加入一两个趣闻或幽默；你演讲的内容需要有针对性。你应该举例子或引用数据来支持你的观点。同时，你要使用短句，这样听众更容易记得住。

11

You need to add up caviar to your audience. Typical events or compelling stories would rally in the heads of your audience, which would make them active participants throughout your speech.

你需要调动听众的胃口。典型的事件或引人入胜的故事会在听众脑海中形成共鸣，并促使他们成为你演讲过程中的积极参与者。

12

When you deliver your speech, there are also a few things you should follow. You should not read your speech, but please try to memorize your speech beforehand. If you cannot, it’s okay to use note cards or even your speech outline. They are just tools to pop you up, in case you get stuck somewhere during the speech.

演讲期间，你应当牢记下列事宜。绝不能埋头念讲稿，你应熟记演讲内容。如果做不到，你可使用提示卡或演讲提纲。这些工具仅仅是你在演讲中“卡壳”之际借以救场的提示工具。

13

You need to do some practice when you can afford the time. It will not only help you get more comfortable with your speech, but also help you determine how your speech fits into the time slot you’ve been given. You may need to modify your sentences or change some wordings where appropriate.

只要时间允许，你需要提前试读讲稿。这样做不仅有助于你更加轻松地演讲，而且可以帮助你确定如何在规定的时间里完成所有演讲内容。你也可能需要适当修改某些句子或调整一些措辞。

14

In terms of public relations, presentations or speeches are important occasions for you to define your capacity or professionality. Nevertheless, the immediate tool is your dress. You need to dress comfortably and professionally, which would fit in the occasion. When you're not sure how others participants will wear, please contact the organizer and ask.

从公共关系领域讲，报告或演讲是你展示个人能力与风采的重要场合。但是，最直接的载体是你的着装。你需要穿着舒适的职业装，符合演讲环境。你如果不确定其他参会人员的着装情况，可向会议组织者询问。

15

Believe it or not, many people may suffer from the fear of speech. Many speakers would temporarily have a blank mind altogether. To overcome this scenario, you need to do some mental preparations, and take some deep breaths before you stand up and move to the podium. When you take the floor, you should take a wholesome look at the audience in a radar fashion, in order to have eye contact with the crowd. These small exertions may help calm down your stage fright.

不管你信不信，许多人可能会害怕演讲。许多演讲者会暂时觉得大脑瞬间一片空白。为了克服这个问题，在站起身来走上领奖台之前，你要做一些心理准备，做一些深呼吸。在开讲时，你应该像雷达那样，环视现场听众，进行眼神交流。这些心理活动有助于减缓你的怯场心理。

16

When you start your speech, you should exert yourself and speak as naturally as possible. It's normal to be a little nervous, but you have to act as naturally as you can. Even if you make a mistake somewhere, just keep going. However, when you find out you have mispronounced some key words or key expressions, it's also allowable to repeat them on the spot in line with the protocol.

当你开始演讲时，应该尽量使用自然语调。初登讲台时有点紧张在所难免，但你得尽量表现得轻松自然。即使在某个地方出了差错，继续讲下去就行。然而，如果发现有些关键单词或概念说错了，你应当现场自我纠错，这也符合演讲礼宾规范。

17

Throughout your speech, you need to be enthusiastic. You need to have eye contact with the audience once in a while, so that to let the audience know you're talking to them, and that they are included in your thought flow. The worst thing to do is burying your nose into the speech paper from the beginning to the end.

在整个演讲过程中，你需要充满激情。你需要不时与观众进行眼神交流，以向听众表明你在和他们说话，使他们觉得你始终关注他们。最糟糕的做法莫过于从头到尾埋头于讲稿之中。

18

You need to learn to use humors. More often than not, a carefully thought-out joke would wake up the audience, and prepare the platform for you to move to your next paragraph. It would also break the ice between you and the audience, especially on some dull topics.

你要学习使用幽默的技巧。通常情况下，一个经过精心准备的笑话会唤醒听众，并为你进入下一段演讲做好铺垫。笑声可以打破你和听众之间的僵局，尤其是谈论一些比较枯燥的主题。

19

You need to use your body language while delivering your speech. This is an effective media to stress the points you're trying to print into the mind of listeners. Therefore, you should move away from the podium where appropriate, in order to redirect the attention of the audience, and find out if

they are really with you.
演讲期间，你需要善于使用肢体语言。这是一种非常有效的手段，确使你的观点留在听众脑海里。因此，你应该注意在适当的时机离开讲台，以调动听众的注意力，并弄清楚他们是否真的在听。

20

Technically speaking, you should arrive at the spot early when possible. When you stand up in a strange place in front of a new audience, you may find it nerve wracking. Therefore, you should try to get into the place and walk up on the platform for a while, in order to familiarize yourself with the layout of the environment. This should allow you to prepare yourself mentally for the speech.
从技巧上讲，你应该尽可能早地到达演讲地点。站在陌生的地方，面对新观众，你可能会感到紧张。因此，你应该尽量提前进入演讲现场，在讲台上走走，以熟悉一下会场的布局。这会有助于你为演讲做好心理准备。

Part Two Sample Speeches

01

I have a dream that one day down in Alabama, with its vicious racists, with its governor having his lips dripping with the words of interposition and nullification, one day right there in Alabama, little black boys and black girls will be able to join hands with little white boys and white girls as sisters and brothers. I have a dream today. I have a dream that one day every valley shall be exalted, and every hill and mountain shall be made low, the rough places will be made plain, and the crooked places will be made straight, and the glory of the Lord shall be revealed, and all flesh shall see it together.

——Martin Luther King

今天，我有一个梦想。我梦想有一天，亚拉巴马州能够有所转变，尽管该州州长现在仍然满口异议，反对联邦法令，但有朝一日，那里的黑人男孩和女孩将能与白人男孩和女孩情同骨肉，携手并进。今天，我有一个梦想。我梦想有一天，幽谷上升，高山下降；坎坷曲折之路成坦途，圣光披露，照亮人间。

——马丁·路德·金

02

I know that you Westerners have a great sage by the name of Jesus Christ. It is the staunch belief by the Christians from around the world that Jesus was crucified in Jerusalem which became the eternal holy place. In the Far East, there is also a great sage by the name of Confucius. His birthplace forever remains in Shandong, China, as much as what you Westerners regard Jerusalem in your heart.

我知道你们西方人有一位伟大的圣人，名叫耶稣基督。全世界的基督徒都坚定地相信，耶稣在耶路撒冷被钉在十字架上，耶路撒冷成为永恒的圣地。在远东，还有一位伟大的圣人，名叫孔子。山东是孔子的家乡，就像你们西方人看重耶路撒冷一样，山东在中国人心中占有重要位置。

03

Some forty years ago when I was a student in your great country, I heard one saying: When the winter snowfalls are gone, we shall soon welcome in the spring and sunshine. Forty years later, I came again to your great country at the head of a university delegation two days ago. Our airplane literally landed at the airport, surrounded by the ice and snow. However, when we stepped out of the lobby, we walked once again into the sunshine and your hospitality. Having said this, please allow me to take the opportunity to thank you and your institution for the considerate arrangement of our program, and for the grand party tonight, where we could outreach to one another before we begin our forum. Here and now, my colleagues and I are already feeling at home. In the short time since we came here to your great city, we've toured two universities where we held in-depth discussions on the future cooperation. We've also had the opportunity to tour some great scenic and historical places where we were deeply impressed by the legacies of your history and culture. And, we were also overwhelmed by the warm greetings in Chinese from the teachers and students on campuses, which demonstrated that the bilateral language exchange programs are paying off.

大约40年前，当我在你们伟大的国家留学时，我学过一句谚语：冬天的雪过去了，我们很快就会迎来春天和阳光。40年后，两天前，我作为大学代表团团长再次来到你们伟大的国家。我们的飞机降落在被冰雪包围的机场。然而，当我们走出大厅之际，我们再次感受到了阳光和你们的热情欢迎。说到这里，请允许我借此机会感谢您和您的机构对我们项目的周到安排，感谢今晚的盛大晚会，让我们在开始访问之前有机会相互交流。此时此刻，我和我的同事们有一种宾至如归的感觉。在贵市短暂的逗留时间里，我们参观了两所大学，并就未来的合作进行了深入讨论。我们还参观了一些名胜古迹，贵国的历史文化遗产给我们留下了深刻的印象。校园里，师生们用中文热情地问候我们，这表明双边语言交流项目取得了成效。

04

Well, how time flies! Before I realize it, I'm coming to the end of my stay here as a visiting professor. Now, when I stand on this podium for the last time, I have many people to thank. First and foremost, I'd like to acknowledge my gratitude to President Johnson and all the faculty members and colleagues who have rendered valuable guidance and generous assistance and cooperation, without which I could not have concluded my schedule with success. Meanwhile, I must express my appreciation to my wife for her sacrifice over the past two years. While I was away, she had to shoulder all the family chores and act both as the mother and father. I would also like to thank my daughter for her understanding and support.

时间过得真快啊！在我意识到之前，我在这里的访问教授生涯就要结束了。现在，我最后一次站在这个讲台上，有许多人想要感谢。首先，我要感谢约翰逊校长、全体教职员工和同事，是你们给予了我宝贵的指导、帮助和合作，没有你们，我就不可能圆满地完成我的日程安排。同时，我也要感谢我的妻子在过去的两年里做出的牺牲。当我不在的时候，她不得不承担所有的家庭琐事，同时扮演父母的角色。我还要感谢我的女儿对我的理解和支持。

Part Three　Common Expressions

- Thank you, chair. First of all, please allow me to thank you and your organizing committee to give me the invitation for the annual conference, where distinguished scholars and researchers could ponder on this important issue of environment protection, which is to have huge impacts on the future of mankind.
  谢谢主席。首先，请允许我感谢您和组委会邀请我参加年会，让杰出的学者和研究人员可以就环境保护这个对人类未来有着巨大影响的重要问题进行研讨。
- During the next 30 minutes, I shall concentrate my analysis on the possible trends of the economic globalization, which would have huge impacts on the developing countries, in terms of political, economic as well as cultural transformation. However, due to the time available, I'll be brief on the political and culture field, and focus my illustration on the economic side, which is really my area of research.
  在接下来的30分钟里，我将重点分析经济全球化的可能趋势，它将对发展中国家的政治、经济和文化转型产生巨大的影响。但是由于时间关系，我将会对政治和文化领域做一个简要的介绍，然后将我的阐述集中在经济方面，这是我真正从事研究的领域。
- Well, eight minutes would not allow any elaborations, so I'll briefly walk you through my presentation in an outline fashion, and talk a bit more on

one or two key points if time permits. Then, I'll be more than happy to answer any questions.

嗯，8分钟的时间不够做任何详细的阐述，所以，我将简要地向大家介绍一下我的演讲大纲，如果时间允许的话，我还会再讲一两个方面。我非常乐意回答任何问题。

- With your permission, chair, I'll move into my presentation. I've prepared my remarks in three parts. Part One is about the background information. Part Two is to probe into the opportunities and challenges. Part Three will focus on the policy proposals, which might bring you some food for thought.

  主席，承蒙您允许，我这就开始我的演讲。我的发言分为三个部分。第一部分是背景信息。第二部分是对机遇和挑战的探讨。第三部分将着重于政策建议，这些建议可能会给你们带来一些值得思考的东西。

- With your permission, chairperson, I'll start my speech with a brief introduction on AI industries in my country. Then, I will talk about the impacts of those technologies on the transformation of the existing manufacturing industries. At the end of my speech, I'll share with you the Chinese experiences and lessons. Nevertheless, let me warn you that your countries would find it difficult to just copy the Chinese experiences because your national situations are very much different. However, it pays for you to dig deep into the lessons, which would help your government to avoid the same “pitfalls” in your own endeavors.

  承蒙主席您允许，我想先介绍一下我国人工智能产业的发展概况。然后，我将介绍人工智能技术对现有制造业转型的影响。在演讲最后部分，我将与大家分享我国的经验和教训。但是，我要预先声明，你们国家的国情不同，机械照搬中国的经验不可取。然而，你们应该认真从我国的教训找到着力点，这将有助于贵国政府在推进相关发展战略期间避免跌入同样的“陷阱”。

- My answer to the question is both “yes” and “no”. For “yes”, I mean the

international community, especially the medical and scientific circles will research and develop vaccines to bring the pandemic under control. As for "no", I mean many countries will have to prepare for the worst before they could bring the pandemic under control. I wonder if my answer would be of some help to you.
我对这个问题的回答既"是"又"不是"。要说"是"，我的意思是国际社会，特别是医学界和科学界将研究和开发疫苗，以控制疫情。至于说"不是"，我的意思是，许多国家在控制疫情之前，必须做好最坏的打算。我不知道我的回答对你是否有帮助。

- Thank you for your question, and I envy your courage to raise such a naive question. Now, by the way you asked the question and the wrong figures you have quoted, I guess you have never been to my country. Let me tell you this: Professors and economists are supposed to judge things based on the facts and figures, rather than on hearsay or unverified information, which would down grade your professionality and credibility, you know.
谢谢你的问题，我羡慕你有勇气提出这样一个天真的问题。现在，从你问问题的方式和错误的数字来看，我猜你似乎没有访问过我的国家。让我告诉你，教授和经济学家应该根据事实和数据来判断事情，而不是根据道听途说或未经证实的信息，否则会降低你的职业水平和可信度。

第二十四章

商务谈判

*

信不信由你，在一生中，我们都要和他人进行交易。就此而言，我们需要知道相关理论、基本规则和技巧。我们需要知道如何开始谈判、如何交换筹码、如何结束谈判、如何达成交易，以及如何避免陷阱。

Chapter Twenty-four

Business Negotiation

*

Believe it or not, we all have to strike some deals with somebody, somewhere in our lifetime. Therefore, we need to know the theory, basic rules and techniques. We need to know how to get started, how to swap cards, how to wrap up negotiations, how to seal the deal, and how to avoid pitfalls.

Part One　Things to Know

01

In our daily life or work, we may strike some negotiations that aims at resolving an issue, or carry out a transaction in a way that both parties should find terms of conditions acceptable. In any negotiation, each party would try to persuade the other side to agree to its own terms of conditions, and the involving parties would try to reach some sort of compromise. Therefore, true bargains must involve some gives and takes, which would allow both or all the parties to reach an agreement as winners.

在日常生活或工作中，我们需要主持或参与商业谈判，以双方都能接受的方式解决问题或完成交易。在任何谈判进程中，每一方都会试图说服对方同意本方的条件，所有当事方都试图达成某种妥协。因此，真正的讨价还价必须互谅互让，以使双方或各方达到一致，实现共赢。

02

In theory, business negotiations are the means to resolve disputes, seal a deal, reach agreement or seek collaboration. They take place almost in all the fields and at all levels, whether it is business deals, personal deals, legal procedures or government matters, etc.

从理论上讲，商务谈判是解决争端、达成交易、商签合同或寻求合作的方式。这些谈判可能发生在各个领域的各个层次，无论是商业交易、个人交易、法律程序，还是政府事务等。

03

Technically speaking, business negotiations require a lot of homework, during which we need to ask: Why we should carry out the negotiation, who should be involved, what are the cards in hands, what are the aims of the relevant parties, and what is expected to gain from the intended negotiations, etc. Questions of this nature are the preconditions to guarantee the success of any business negotiations.

从技术上讲，商务谈判需要事先做大量准备工作。其间，有一系列问题需要搞清楚：为什么要进行谈判，应该由谁参与，各自手中的牌是什么，相关各方的目的是什么，本次谈判的期许是什么等。搞清楚这些问题是保证商务谈判成功的先决条件。

04

In principle, business negotiations should aim at win-win outcomes. In any business negotiations, there must be at least two parties. And, the parties concerned must first reach an understanding on the aims, principles and procedures. The parties concerned must be willing to arrive at an acceptable outcome, which would allow all parties to walk away from the negotiation table, feeling like the winner.

原则上，商务谈判应以双赢为目标。在任何商务谈判中，至少有两个参与方。因此，有关各方必须首先就目标、原则和程序达成一致认可。有关各方必须同意达成都能接受的结果，以使各方在离开谈判桌时均感觉本方是赢家。

05

We all know that business negotiation is a part of our daily life. In order to be a successful negotiator, we need to take stock from the following tips. First, we should let our customers know we regard the product or service safety as the priority. Second, we should let them take pride in purchasing our products or services. Third, we should let them feel that we're quoting the price at a reasonable range, which still leaves some space for bargaining. Last but not the least, we should let the other party know we're marketing our products or service with a meager margin, etc.

我们都知道，商务谈判是我们日常生活的一部分。想要成为谈判能手，我们需要遵循下列技巧。首先，应该向客户表明，本公司始终将产品或服务安全放在第一位。第二，使对方为购买本公司的产品或服务感到自豪。第三，让对方感到本公司的报价处在一个合理的范围，并且还有讨价还价的空间。最后，应该让对方知道本公司实行的是薄利多销策略。

06

As a matter of fact, emotions, luck and magic would have no place in business negotiations. Rather, it takes an iron gut, preparedness, street smarts and unblinking principle, which are the secret weapons to unlock our ability to get the best deal possible under any circumstances. Therefore, at the negotiation table, we should keep our eyes on the big picture all the time. This is all about business.

事实上，在商务谈判中，感情、运气和奇迹是没有立足之地的。相反，它需要坚强的勇气、有备而往、职业智慧和坚定的原则，这些在任何商务谈判中都是展示谈判能力、达成最佳交易的“杀手锏”。因此，在谈判桌上，我们应始终着眼大局。这是生意场的核心内涵。

07

Preparation is the key to business negotiations. When we are the supplier, we need to know about the other party that we're negotiating with, so that we could capitalize on our strengths. When we're not sure about this, we should seek advice from someone who is experienced or approach our lawyer for

help. If possible, we should talk to our business associates, who have business relations with the company before.
准备工作是商务谈判取得成功的关键。作为供应方，我们需要了解谈判方，这样我们才能充分利用己方优势。我方如果在策略上没有把握，应该向有经验的人求教，或者向律师咨询。如果可能，我们应该从生意伙伴那里了解与谈判对手打交道的经验。

08

When we are a buyer, we need to familiarize with the product or service that we intend to purchase, and we need to do homework on all the procedures and tactics. If the supplier senses that we are weak on such details, we may become the target for a bluff. Here, psychology plays a crucial role in reading the responses from the other party, and in anticipating their next move.
如果是买家，我们需要熟悉打算购买的产品或服务，需要在谈判的程序和策略方面做足功课。在谈判桌上，如果对方感觉到我方不了解细节，我们可能陷入被动。这时，心理学将发挥关键作用，我们需要读懂对方的反应，并预测对方下一步可能采取的行动。

09

We’ve got to be clear business negotiation is to focus on the price. Therefore, before sitting down at the table, we should be fully prepared for all the constraints that may surface during the negotiations. These may include budget limits, direction from the top leadership, pressure on the commercial goals and unexpected external forces, etc. Furthermore, we may have to change our tactics in anticipation of the actions by the other party.
我们必须清楚，任何商业谈判都必须聚焦价格。因此，在坐到谈判桌旁之前，我们应该对谈判过程中可能出现的各种约束做好充分准备，具体包括预算限制、来自高层的干预、谈判目标的压力和意想不到的外部力量等。此外，我们还需要预估对方可能会采取的行动，进而相应调整谈判策略。

10

Before starting the business negotiation, we must ensure that the other party has the full authority to make binding commitments. We don't want to find ourselves in a position, where we believe we've struck the deal, only to discover that the agreement has to be approved by someone higher in the chain of command.

在开始谈判之前，必须确定谈判对手具有充分授权，能够做出具有约束力的承诺。应当避免下列尴尬境况：我方以为已经达成了一致，结果却发现本合同还需要得到对方更高级别人员的批准。

11

As the buyer, we need to follow the basic principles. The first offer is usually the most important factor and the benchmark, by which all subsequent bargains will be judged against. We would never get what we don't ask for, so we need to make our first counter offer bold and aggressive. Usually, counter offer price is typically to include some margins to give away during the negotiations. When we want to take all of that and hopefully more, we must start bargaining from the price level lower than the supplier expects. Here, we should not worry about insulting the other party. As long as our offer is not ridiculous, the other side would continue with the negotiations, in the hope of settling for a price agreeable to both sides.

作为买家，我们需要坚持下列基本原则。第一个报价通常是商业谈判中最重要的因素，也是后续交易参照的基准。我们永远不可能得到没有要求的东西，因而我们需要大胆地还价。一般而言，还盘价格包括本方的底价以及在谈判过程中需要让步的空间。我们如果想要守住还盘价格并获得更多的利益，必须从低于卖方预期的价格开始还价。在这里，我们不必担心侮辱对方。只要我方给出的报价不太离谱，对方就会继续进行谈判，并希望达成双方都能接受的价格。

12

We should not disclose our budget or other limitations. A common ploy of salesmen is to sell us a less-branded product by reshuffing the product specifications, schedule to deliver the goods or services, and other parameters, in order to fit our budget.

我们不应该透露己方的预算或相关条件。供货方最擅长的策略就是不断调整产品规格、供货时间表和其他参数，以便用次等品牌的产品或服务来满足我们的采购预算。

13

As the supplier, we should always have something to give away without hurting our negotiation position. To be specific, when we're submitting an offer, we must consider inserting decoys and red herrings for the other party to find. For example, when we are bidding a project, we should consider including some nice-to-have items that aren't critical to the success of the project. We could also include some spare parts that may or may not be needed in the end. When the buyer takes those items out, we haven't lost anything. Furthermore, these tactics would help to divert the other party from attacking the meat of our proposal.

作为供货商，我们应该在不损害本方谈判立场的情况下，适当做出一些让步。具体而言，在提交报价建议时，我们需要考虑涵盖一些诱饵和转移对方注意力的东西，以备与对方讨价还价。例如，我们在竞标一个项目时，应该考虑包括一些对项目成功并不太重要的东西。我们还可以在合同里包含一些最后可能需要也可能不需要的备用设备。如果买家把这些备用条款拿掉，我方则不会有任何损失。进而言之，这些技巧有助于防止对方在我方报价核心条款上讨价还价。

14

We should make full use of technical skills. We should be prepared to suspend or even cancel the negotiations, when we feel that things are getting nowhere, or the other party seems stuck in their position. We should then indicate our reluctance to continue with the negotiation under those conditions, and leave the other side with the impression whether we would ever come back to the negotiation table. When they are on the hook to cut a deal, they would have to move forward under our pressure. Meanwhile, we should be patient even when the other party isn't. The last thing we want is for the other party to think we're to conclude the deal under the smoking gun.

我们应该充分利用谈判技巧。我方如果觉得谈判进展不大或对方似乎坚守既定立场，我方应建议暂停或取消谈判。同时向对方表明我方不会同意在现有条件下继续谈判，并让对方揣摩我方是否还会回到谈判桌上来。对方如果仍期盼达成协议，则会在我方的压力之下松动原先的立场。与此同时，即使对方正失去耐心，我方也应该坚持立场，不能让对方认为，我方会迫于压力而同意达成交易。

15

In accordance with the procedure of business negotiation, a counteroffer automatically rejects all previous offers. Once an offer is made, we should expect an acceptance or rejection from the other side, or a counteroffer that would keep the negotiation open. When our offer is rejected and we are asked to submit a new offer, we should do not fall into that trap. That would be tantamount to a total failure.

依据商务谈判规范，对方的还价会自动拒绝以前的所有报价。因此，我方一旦提出报价，对方可能会接受、拒绝，或者还价，以使谈判得以继续。如果我方报价被拒绝并被要求提交新的报价，我们不应该轻易退让。此举无异于宣告谈判的失败。

16

We should exploit weakness of the other party, and maximize our advantage. When we are the only supplier available for a particular product or service, we would have tremendous leverage across the board. When what we’re selling is in high demand or in low supply, we would have more bargaining power. When we are the buyer in a depressed economy, we would normally have the advantage in receiving better price and better after service.

我们应当充分利用对方的不利地位，最大限度地发挥我们的有利地位。如果我们是某个产品或服务的唯一供应商，我们则在谈判时拥有巨大的主动权。如果我们的商品在市场上需求大于供给，那么我方有更多的价格优势。我方如果在经济萧条时期进行采购，则可从供应商那里获得较好的报价和售后服务。

17

We should aim at a win-win outcome. Throughout the negotiation, we should not only stick to the key interests that are to be included into the contract, but also be mindful about those of the other party. This is a sure way to build up the business relations. The bottom line is when we construct our offer, we should put ourselves into the shoes of the other side, and try to cater to their priority interests which would facilitate conditions for a win-win contract.

我们应该寻求双赢的结果。在整个谈判过程中，我们既要坚持合同中涉及的关键利益，也要注意对方的利益。这是建立商务关系的可靠方法。最重要的是，我们在制定报价时，也应该站在对方的角度考虑，尽量满足对方的优先利益诉求，以为达成双赢的合同创造条件。

18

We should refrain from extracting the last pound of flesh from the other side. This is especially true when we are negotiating with the same party on a recurring purchase deal. Once the negotiation is completed, we want to be able to work with other party during the contract implementation. If the other party is threatened and pounded into submission, they probably won't negotiate with us again, and possibly cut off any future business deals. While heated confrontation is a common scenario during the negotiations, at some point, collaboration and compromise are also needed, so that both parties could finally shake hands and seal the deal.

我们应该避免从对方那里榨取最后一磅肉。在与回头客进行谈判时尤其如此。一旦谈判完成，我们希望在合同履行过程中与对方合作。如果对方受到威胁，被迫签“城下之盟”，对方很可能终止谈判，并且不会再与我们保持生意往来。毋庸置疑，激烈的语言博弈在谈判中时常发生，但在某些时候，合作和妥协也是必要的，以期双方最终握手并签署合同。

19

Successful negotiation is like horse-trading. We should have a strong sense of timing, creativity, keen awareness and the ability to anticipate the other party's next move. Negotiation is also like Chinese chess, during which each move should be designed to set the stage not only for the next move, but several moves down the line. Therefore, as we carry out our negotiation strategy, we must be prepared at some point to split the remaining difference, in order to seal the deal in the preagreed time framework.

成功的谈判犹如马场交易，需要交易者具有紧迫的时间感、优秀的创造力、敏锐的意识和预测对方下一步行动的能力。商务谈判也像国际象棋，双方所下的每一步棋不仅要为下一步棋着想，而且需要确保本方在接下来的几步棋中都处于有利地位。因此，我们在制定谈判策略之际，必须准备好在某些条款上达成一致，以便在规定的期限内签署合同。

20

Whether we're negotiating on behalf of our firm, we'll do better when we manage to avoid some common pitfalls. We must make detailed plans and be

prepared. We must know our bottom line and our walkaway point. In addition, we need to understand time constraints. We need to count the cards we have in hand and those of our opponent. We should learn the tactics of cross-cultural negotiations. We should watch the anchors and where they are set. We should not cave in, and make the deal too quickly. Finally, when we've cut a sweet deal, we should not do the dance of joy in public.
无论我们是代表本公司进行谈判，如果能避免下面的陷阱，我们一定会做得更好。我们必须制订详细的计划，并做好准备。我们必须知道本方的底线，并知道在何时需要停止谈判。此外，我们需要清楚时间限制。我们需要数一数手上的牌和对手的牌。我们应该掌握跨文化商务谈判策略。我们应该把握好需坚守的底牌，切不要屈服压力而过快地达成交易。最后，我们在达成一笔不错的交易之际，切忌不要在公众场合得意忘形。

Part Two　Situational Dialogues

01

A: Hello! Welcome to the International Import and Export Fair.

　你好！欢迎光临进出口交易会。

B: Thank you. I' m Eric Johnson from Canada. Here is my business card.

　谢谢。我是艾利克·约翰逊，来自加拿大。这是我的名片。

A: Glad to meet you, Mr. Johnson. Is this your first trip to my country?

　约翰逊先生，幸会。请问，这是您第一次到访我的国家吗？

B: Sure, this is my first visit to the Fair. Everything is new to me, and you've got so many people and so many showrooms. Now, would you please show me around?

是的，这是我第一次参加进出口交易会。这里一切都很新鲜，你们这里客商很多，展厅也很多。因此，你能带我参观一下吗？

A: Sure. The Fair is a big gathering which takes place once every year. Businessmen from more than one hundred countries and regions come here to trade with us. By the way, what business is your company in?

当然。这个交易会每年举行一次，100多个国家和地区的商人云集于此，同我们谈生意。顺便问一下，你们公司从事哪方面业务？

B: Our company specializes in exporting leather products. My bank of deposit is Bank of China, which has long standing international credibility.

我们公司专营皮制产品出口。我公司的开户银行是中国银行，并享有良好的商业信誉。

A: I've heard about your company. Now, would you let us have the product brochure, please?

我听说过贵公司。您能给我们提供产品宣传册吗？

B: Sure. Here you are.

当然。给你。

02

A: Well, we've had the pleasure to show the sample products, and we've also let you try out our products. I'm sure you must be satisfactory about the products. Therefore, shall we get down to business?

我们有幸向贵方展示了产品样本，并请贵方试用相关产品。相信贵方一定对本公司产品十分满意。因此，我们可以敲定生意了吧？

B: Certainly. However, before we sign the contract, we need to get some basic things fixed up. First, are you charging us the FOB price or the CIF price? Second, are these wholesale prices or retail prices?

当然了。不过，签订合同之前，我们需要就一些基本问题达成一致。第一，你们采用离岸价格还是到岸价格？第二，贵方的报价是零售价还是批发价？

A: All right. On your first question, we always give our customers the FOB price, which is the standard way in my country. With regard to your second question, we always offer the wholesale price when our customers purchase by large quantity. As we have come this far in the negotiation, we would propose the last price at $150 per unit. How does it sound?

好的。关于你的第一个问题，我们一直给客户离岸价格，这是我们国家标准的报价方式。关于你的第二个问题，我们的客户如果大量购买，我们始终提供批发价。既然关于交易的谈判已进展到这个地步，我们提议最终单价为150美元。怎么样？

B: Well, we appreciate it a lot for your product demonstration and your kindness to let us try out your product at your own expense. However, with regard to the unit price, I have to be frank with you. My colleague have cruised on the Internet, and compared the product quality as well as the prices. I'm afraid you still have to do something about the price.

嗯，非常感谢贵公司展示样品，并让我们免费试用相关产品。但是说到报价，我必须坦率地告诉你。我的同事在网上搜索，对比了产品质量和价格。恐怕你们还需要调整报价。

A: Please be advised that, considering the high quality as compared to the similar products from other companies, our price is very reasonable. Let me also be frank with you. As the prices for materials and man power keep going up, this is the best possible price we can offer for now.

请注意，与其他公司的同类产品相比，我们的产品质量非常高，因此，我们的价格是非常合理的。让我也坦白地告诉你，由于材料和人力的价格不断上涨，这是目前我们能提供的最佳报价。

03

A: Well, we've been talking for the past two hours. Shall we break up for a quick lunch so that we could have new energy to resume our negotiation?

我们已经谈了两个小时了。我们休息一下简单吃个午饭，以便积累能量继续谈判，好吗？

B: That' a good idea. In fact, we had to leave early in the morning just to be here in time. We really treasure this business opportunity, you know.

好主意。事实上，为了及时赶到这里，我们不得不一大早就出发。你知道，我们真的很珍惜这次商机。

A: Well, same here. So far, we've exchanged the ideas and information, and reached the agreement on the major articles in the contract. When we come back, we just have to get some details fixed up before we sign the deal. Would you agree to that?

哦，我们也一样。到目前为止，我们已经交换了意见和信息，并就合同的主要条款达成一致了。等我们回来后，只需要解决一些细节问题就可以签合同了。你说呢？

B: Certainly. So, let's move to the dining room before the food turns cold.

当然可以。那么，在食物变冷之前，我们赶紧去餐厅吧。

04

A: Well, we seem to have exhausted all our efforts. Through our painstaking efforts, we've exchanged information about our companies. We've come to know better about the capability in the supply chain. And, we have both realized the stakes to take. It's a pity that we still couldn't seal a deal this time.

看来我们已经竭尽全力了。通过我们不懈的努力，我们交换了关于公司的信息。我们已经对供应链的能力有了更好的了解。我们都意识到其中的利害关系。很遗憾这次我们还是没能成交。

B: We are sorry for this, too. However, we've seen the cards from the other side, and we’ve both agreed to stay in touch.

我们对此也感到抱歉。然而，我们已经看到了彼此手中的牌，都同意继续保持联系。

A: I couldn’t agree more. So, shall we wind up our conversation and stay in touch?

我完全同意。那么，我们来结束我们的谈话，并保持联系吧。

B: You bet.

一定的。

Part Three Common Expressions

- We reserve our right to take any measures to protect our interests. So, please do your best to clear the mess. For the sake of our partnership, we’ll give you two days to fix the problem.

  我们将保留权利，采取一切措施保护我们的利益。所以，请您尽最大努力清理混乱。为了我们的合作关系，我们给你两天时间来解决问题。

- You may have reasons to explain away your responsibility, but you’ve got to honor your contract obligations, and we’re asking nothing less than that. Let me also make it clear that we reserve our right to take further actions, should our legitimate interests not be compensated accordingly.

  你可能有理由开脱责任，但你必须履行合同的义务，我们的要求不会少于这些。我还想指出，如果我们的合法利益得不到相应补偿，我们保留采取进一步措施的权利。

- Whatever you do, we should get the new shipment of our spare parts as indicated in the contract. And, my secretary Mr. Yong Lin is going to get in touch with you. You can reach him at this number… Here you are. I just want you to know that you're a professional manufacturer. I don't suppose we should settle the case in court. And, please be advised that our patience is running thin.

  无论如何，我们都应该按照合同上的要求获得新的备件。我的秘书林永先生会与您联系。您打这个电话就能找到他，给您。我只是想让您知道，您是专业的制造商。我认为我们不应该上法庭来解决这个案子。请注意，我方的耐心是有限的。

- Well, we've heard your complaints, but don't you think it's fair for both parties to join hands, in order to prevent the breakdown of our commercial relations? Having said this, let me also make it clear that my side would not endorse your claim, and my company always stick to the principle of "first come, first serve". Nevertheless, we're not to blame for anything that's beyond the contract obligation, you know.

  好了，我方已听到贵方的投诉，但您不认为我们双方应该联手防止我们的商业关系破裂吗？话说到这里，我也想明确一点，我方不接受贵方的投诉，我公司一直坚持“先到先得”原则。但是，你需要知道，超出合同义务的事宜本公司概不负责。

- Are you suggesting that my office is to blame for the fault? Let me remind you that it's too early to jump into any conclusions before the police end the investigation. So, shall we be a bit more patient, since we've agreed not to bring the case to the court? For your reference, you should have a close look at the contract, especially at Article 5 and 6, please.

  你是说我方应该为此负责吗？让我提醒你，在警方结束调查之前下结论还为时过早。既然我们已经同意不把这个案子告上法庭，我们能不能再耐心一点？另外提醒一下，请贵公司仔细查阅一下合同，尤其是第5条和第6条。

- Well, if what you said is a challenge, we're ready for it. Regarding this on-going dispute, our side has been conciliatory, in an effort to address the differences through good-will talks. Since your side would not budge, our lawyer will be ready to talk to you from now on. Now, farewell.
  如果你所说的是一个挑战，我们接受你们的挑战。在这场存在争议的纠纷中，我方一直采取和解的态度，并努力通过友好谈判解决分歧。既然你方不肯让步，从现在起由我方的律师与你们对话。好了，再见。
- As always, we treasure our century old corporate philosophy that quality service stands above anything else. With this in mind, we've designed and manufactured the equipment in accordance with the benchmarks listed in your letter of intention. I'm sure it's time for your side to honor your obligation, and come up with the prompt payment and clearance of the products that are still piling up here in our warehouse.
  我们一如既往地坚守本公司百年的企业理念：优质服务高于一切。考虑到这一点，我们已经按照贵方意向书中列出的基准设计和制造了设备。现在该贵公司履行合同义务了，请及时付款、清关，以免这些产品继续堆积在我们的仓库里。
- Look, here are the best possible terms of conditions that we can offer. We're going to send the experts to carry out the design, in accordance with your specifications. We're going to manufacture the equipment, in line with the benchmarks of our standing procedures to ensure the quality. We're to do the delivery as specified in the contract. And, more importantly, we're to offer the after service for three years at our own expense. I'm sure these offers would please you enough to seal the deal.
  我说，这是我们所能提供的最好条件了。我们将派专家按照你们的要求进行设计。我们将按照我们的标准程序来生产设备，以确保质量。我们将按合同规定交货。更重要的是，我们将自费提供三年的售后服务。我相信这些报价一定会让您满意并与我公司签署合同。
- We don't want to be fussy about our deal, but we do need your company

to dispatch an engineer to our factory during the installation and trial operation, so that he or she could give technical advice on the spot, and help train the workers and the technicians. Of course, we can share the costs, out of courtesy.

我们不想对我们的交易过分挑剔，但是在安装和试运行期间我们需要贵公司派遣一名工程师到我们工厂，这样就可以当场给予技术建议以及帮助培训工人和技术人员。当然，为表示诚意，我们可以分摊费用。

第二十五章

法律事务

*

法治是现代社会的关键要素。市场经济亦然。目前，“一带一路”倡议作为开放的、共同发展的平台，正在向尽可能多的伙伴国家延伸。作为中国公民，我们在伙伴国家生活、工作、学习和经商的机会越来越多。其间，无论我们做什么，都必须遵守法律规章，确保生活、工作和生意安全，有效维护合法利益，实现我们的理想。

Chapter Twenty-five

Legal Matters

*

Rule of law is the key element of the modern society. So is the market economy. Now, the Belt and Road Initiative, which is an open platform for common development, is outreaching to as many partner countries as possible. As Chinese citizens, we have more opportunities to live, work, study or do business in the partner countries, during which we all have to do anything in accordance with the laws and regulations, in order to ensure safety in life, work or business, effectively protect our legal interests and realize our aspirations.

Part One　Things to Know

01

No matter where you are, laws and regulations are the best tools to protect you against any mishaps. For that matter, you should never take anything for granted, and you need to strictly abide by the laws and regulations wherever you travel, live, study, work or do business.

无论你身在何处，法律规章都是保护自身免遭不幸的最好工具。就此而言，你永远不要把任何事情视为理所当然，无论你到哪里生活、学习、工作，还是经商，都需要严格遵纪守法。

02

It's a must that when you're travelling or driving overseas, you should always remember to bring your driving licenses, IDs, credit cards, your insurance policy numbers, as well as your social security numbers. These are the sure means to protect your personal safety and your legal rights.

在国外旅行或开车期间，你必须记得随身带上你的驾驶执照、身份证、信用卡、保险单号码以及社会保险号。这是保护自身安全和合法权益的可靠方式。

03

As one old saying goes, it takes caution to sail a boat. Therefore, you need

to establish the following self-protection awareness. No matter you’re in a country, in an industry, or on a job, you should always put the risk prevention in the first place. You should be aware of the risks you may encounter, and take precautions accordingly. When you’re in trouble or in danger, you should call the police, or notify the Chinese Embassy.
有一句古训说得好，小心驶得万年船。概而言之，你需要确立下列自我保护意识。无论在一个国家，在一个行业，还是从事任何工作，你都要做到风险防范在先。你需要事先了解可能会遇到的各种风险，并且采取预防措施。在遇到麻烦或危险时，你需要及时报警，或向我国驻东道国大使馆求救。

04

You need to abide by the rules and regulations, and carry out anything in a peaceful mind, which are the sure ways to avoid legal troubles when you’re abroad. You know what, the cost of seeking justice in foreign countries is high. It is morally right for you to seek fair judgement on everything, but it is not a wise choice. Rather, when you decide to take legal actions on some trivial matters, it would land you into the legal battle and put you into the real harm’s way.
你需要遵守规章制度，心平气和地做任何事情，这是在国外避免法律纠纷的可靠途径。你知道吗，在国外，伸张正义的代价很高。“凡事讨个说法”在道义上是正确的，但并非明智的选择。你如果在一些琐事上动用法律手段，那可能使自己陷入法律纷争，进而使自己陷入真正的伤害之中。

05

It’s a must that you safeguard your right by all means. Signing contracts is the most effective means for self-protection, and also an effective certificate for safeguarding your rights when you are caught in legal cases. At the same time, abiding by the contracts and fulfilling the contract duties consciously can help you avoid any legal issues due to your own negligence. When you really need to safeguard your rights via administrative or legal means, you must do it in a rational, beneficial and restrained manner, and you must get help from your lawyer.

你必须运用法律手段维护权益。签订合同是自我保护最为有效的方式，也是在你遇到法律案件时进行维权的有效凭证。与此同时，信守合同、自觉履约有助于避免因己方过失而招致的法律麻烦。你如果确实需要通过行政或法律手段维权，一定要做到有理、有利、有节，并咨询律师的意见。

06

It's a common practice that if you should be caught up in a traffic accident, you should remain cool and try to find out if anybody is seriously hurt physically. Everything else could wait. Then, you and the other party should swap relevant information, such as owner's name, contact numbers, insurance policy numbers, etc.

通常情况下，在遭遇交通事故时，你需要保持头脑冷静，首先确认是否有人受重伤。其他的事情可以等一等。然后，你和当事另一方应该交换相关信息，如车主的姓名、联系电话、保险单号码，等等。

07

If you should be caught in some unexpected scenarios when you live, travel, study or work in a foreign country, you should learn to refrain from saying anything until you meet your lawyer. The reason is simple, whatever you say could be used as the evidence against you in court. Therefore, at the first available moment, you need to get in touch with the Chinese Embassies or the nearest Consulate General.

你在国外生活、旅行、学习或工作期间，如果遇到一些意想不到的情况，你应该学会在见到律师之前保持沉默。理由很简单，你说的任何话都可能在法庭上构成对你不利的证据。因此，你应当在第一时间与我国驻该国大使馆或最近的总领事馆取得联系。

08

Here in my country, you’ve got to use the laws to protect your legal rights, even in your daily life. For that matter, you have to hire or get in touch with a lawyer, when you venture out to do anything serious or conduct any important activities.

在我的国家，你必须学会运用法律手段保护自身合法权益，即使在你的日常生活中也是如此。因此，在办理任何重要事宜或进行重大活动时，你都需要聘请或咨询律师。

09

Here in my country, you need to exert yourself in the following areas, in order to be a good citizen. First and foremost, it’s patriotism which warrants you to dedicate to the nation. You need to adapt to the cultural traditions and values. Second, you need to exert yourself in improving your personal quality, which includes honesty, integrity, responsibility, respectfulness, compassion, kindness, tolerance, courtesy, self-discipline, moral courage, and love of justice, etc.

在我的国家，你需要遵守以下几个方面，以成为一名好公民。首先，爱国主义要求你对国家要有奉献精神。你需要加快适应文化传统和价值观。第二，你要努力提升个人品质，包括诚实、正直、负责、尊重、同情、善良、宽容、礼貌、自律、道德勇气、热爱正义等。

10

Third, you should contribute to the nation by being productive in whatever you are doing. You can be a productive employee, a business owner, an artist, a public servant, and so on. In general, good citizens share their skills, talents,

and abilities with others. And, they would make positive contributions to their family, the community, the institutions they belong to, and the nation at large.
第三，无论做什么，都要积极努力，为国家作贡献。你可以成为高效的雇员、企业家、艺术家、公务员等。一般而言，优秀的公民会与他人分享自己的技能、天赋和能力。与此同时，他们乐于为家庭、社区、所属的机构和国家作出贡献。

11

Fourth, you need to be active in the community activities. You should actively participate in the social functions. You should look for ways and means to make your communities a better place to live, in terms of your time or money.
第四，积极参加社区活动。你应该积极参加社会活动。你应该适当贡献时间或金钱，为所在社区建设出一份力。

12

Fifth, you need to keep abreast with the world affairs so that you know about the important issues facing your nation. To be specific, you need to have access to various news sources that cover local, national and global news. You need to read about the history, in order to know where you came from, where you are, and where you are going.
第五，你需要关心天下大事，以便了解你的国家所面临的重要事情。具体而言，你需要浏览本地、全国和全球性的各种新闻资讯。你需要读一些历史书，以便知道你从哪里来，你在哪里，你要去哪里。

13

Sixth, you need to be vigilant. Authority is never perfect in keeping civilians safe from crime. Therefore, it's up for the ordinary people to take proper measures to protect personal safety. First, you need to do everything in accordance with the laws and regulation. Second, you should always remain vigilant on any possible evil or harmful things that may occur to you, and take appropriate measures to defend yourself or call the police when you are in trouble. Third, you should deal with the trouble makers carefully, in order not to put yourself in a more serious scenario. Fourth, you should attend some training classes for self-defense.

第六，你需要保持警惕。政府在保护平民免受犯罪侵害方面始终存在短板。因此，有时需要人们自己采取适当的措施来保护自身安全。首先，凡事你都要遵守法律法规。第二，你应该时刻提防任何可能发生在你身上的邪恶或有害的事，当遇到麻烦时，采取适当的措施来保护自己，或报警。第三，在应对麻烦制造者时一定要谨慎行事，以免自己陷入更严重的境况。第四，你应该参加一些自我防卫培训班。

14

Seventh, you need to be politically active in the host country. For example, you should attend rallies and events, go to the city council meetings, join a political organization, volunteer for political campaign activities, exercise your right to elect capable and civic minded leaders, etc.

第七，你需要在东道国积极参与政治活动。例如，参加集会和活动，参加市议会会议，加入政治组织，自愿参加政治竞选活动，行使你的权利，选举有能力、有公民意识的领导人等。

15

Eighth, you need to be mentor for the civic-minded children. When you have time, you need to talk to your own kids about civic awareness, and teach them to be good citizens. You need to join a school-based mentoring program and tutor kids who aren’t doing well academically.

第八，你需要成为孩子们的导师。如果时间允许，你需要和孩子谈论公民意识，教育他们成为好公民。你需要参加由学校组织的辅导项目，辅导学习成绩不佳的孩子。

16

Ninth, you need to be both productive and all-rounded. You need to have the knowledge necessary to be a productive social member, such as technical skills, legal skills, medical skills, and so on. Meanwhile, you need to be a well-rounded social member who would make contributions to not only the national GDP, but also to the cultural wealth of the nation.

第九，你需要成为既高效又全面的社会成员。你需要拥有高效社会成员所必需的知识，例如技术技能、法律技能、医疗技能等。同时，你需要成为一个全面发展的社会成员，不仅要为国家的GDP作出贡献，也要为国家的文化财富作出贡献。

17

Tenth, you need to create order starting from you home. You need to dedicate to your family wellbeing. You need to dedicate to your career. You need to dedicate to your nation. As the Chinese philosopher Confucius said, "to put the world in order, you must first put the nation in order; to put the nation in order, you must first put the family in order; to put the family in order, you must first cultivate your personal life, which calls for you to set your heart right."

第十，你需要从你的家庭开始构建秩序。你需要为家庭福祉作贡献。你需要致力于自己的事业。你需要献身于自己的国家。正如中国哲人孔子所说：欲明德于天下者，先治其国；欲治其国者，先齐其家；欲齐其家者，先修其身；欲修其身者，先正其心。

18

Here in my country, you've got to use legal weapons to protect your legal rights, even in your daily life. Generally speaking, you should protect your legal rights in three stages. Before you do anything serious, you've got to hire a lawyer or get in touch with a lawyer. When you're doing anything, you should abide by the laws and regulations, and keep the records or sign the contract.

When your legal rights are violated, you should never rush into any actions, until you know exactly where you stand and what options you may have. In some extreme circumstance, you should have the gut to take legal actions and settle your cases in court, but you should seek advice from your lawyer.
在我的国家，你要学会运用法律武器来保护自身合法权益，在日常生活中亦然。一般而言，你应该在三个阶段注意维权。在做任何严肃的事情之前，你都需要雇用律师或者向律师咨询。在做任何事情期间，你都要遵守法律法规，都要做好记录或签订合同。当自身合法权利被侵犯之际，不要着急采取任何行动，你应当清楚地知道你的立场是什么，你有什么可行的举措。在一些极端情况上，在自身正当利益受到侵害时，你要在律师指导之下拿起法律武器，同对手“打官司”。

19

Here in my country, you need to be a law-abiding citizen. As one saying goes, you should not harbor any intentions to harm others, but you must take precautions at every turn. Therefore, you should learn about the laws and regulation relating to your life and career. You should insist on signing contract on any meaningful commercial or business transactions. You need to request and keep the receipts for daily commercial purchases.
在我的国家，你需要做一个守法的公民。俗话说，害人之心不可有，防人之心不可无。因此，你应该了解与你的生活和职业有关的法律规章。在进行任何有意义的商业活动时，你应该坚持签署合同。你需要获取并保存日常商业采购收据。

20

Oh, one more thing, when you’re staying in my country, it pays for you to ask when you’re not sure about something. It would be too bad for you to rush into things as you would back home. The laws and regulations in our two countries may be different, you know.

噢，还有一件事，你在我国逗留期间，遇到没有把握的事，最好先征求他人的意见。最糟糕的莫过于你按国内的方式行事。你知道吗，我们两国的法律规章可能不一样。

Part Two　Situational Dialogues

01

A: Good morning, Raymond. Thank god you're here. I don't know what to say, but let me tell you what happened exactly.

早上好，雷蒙德。谢天谢地，你终于来了。我不知道该说什么，但让我告诉你到底发生了什么。

B: Yes, please. First, let me turn on my recorder... Now, I'm ready, and please go ahead.

好的，请吧。我先打开录音笔……好了，我已准备好了，请开始讲吧。

A: Well, it's all about the contract dispute that we had with supplier Johnson Pty Ltd. One week ago, they failed to deliver the spare parts in line with the contract. When we raised the complaint, they sent the follow-up shipment in three days but about 15% of the articles had false functions. Worse still, they put our production line on hold for three days and caused the hiccups of the production plan for the whole month. Here are the documents and memos that my company had with the supplier. Please have a quick look at the documents, and give us some advice on how to pursue the case.

好的，都是关于我公司与合同供应商约翰逊有限公司的合同纠纷。一个星期前，他们未能按照合同交付我们订购的配件。当我们提出投诉后，他们在三天后补发了短缺的货物，但其中大约15%的物品功能不全。更糟糕的是，他们的违约行为导致我公司的生产线停工了三天，并使得我公司当月生产计划无法顺利完成。这是我公司和供应商之间的相关文件和备忘录。请您快速浏览一下这些材料，而后就如何处理该案向我们提供建议。

B: Alright. I'll bring these materials back to my office, but then get back to you with some specific questions just to connect the dots vis-a-vis your case.
好的。我会把这些材料带回我的办公室，但我会再问你更多问题，以便将与贵公司案子相关的信息串联起来。

A: Sure, we're also going to double check the details, and provide you with more information if there is still anything left. You can call me anytime in the coming days.
当然，我们也会再次核实细节，如果还有遗留事宜，我们会及时提供给你。接下来几天你可以随时给我打电话。

02

A: Well, that's all I can tell you about the case, and I've got all the documents and materials you requested on the phone. I hope they would help you to construct your defense strategy.
好了，关于这个案子我能告诉你的就这些了，你电话里要的文件和材料我都带来了。希望它们能帮助你做出辩护方案。

B: Sure. Since you are new here in my country, and you don't know much about the criminal laws, I'll have to get a thorough look at your briefing and backup documents. I may ask for more information, in order to defend the case on your behalf.
当然。由于你刚到我的国家，对刑法又不太了解，我得详细看一看你的简报和备份文件，我可能会需要你提供更多信息，以便为你的案子制定正确的辩护策略。

A: Please do. And, please feel free to contact me and ask for any additional information or documents you may request. I know we can count on you for the professional service, and we're in your capable hands now.
那就有劳了。您如果还需要其他信息或文件，请随时与我联系。我知道我们可以依赖你们的专业服务，案子交给你，我们就放心啦。

B: That's very kind of you to say so. Nevertheless, it's too early to be confident yet, you know.
你太客气了。你知道，现在给你们打包票还为时尚早。

A: I know, but please do your best. As for the bill, please prepare the contract. I'll sign it when I have a look at it.
我知道，但请尽力而为。至于律师费用，请准备一份合同。我看过后就可以签字。

03

A: Your Honor, as you're fully aware, this case has been dragging on for months now. Up until today, the prosecution has failed to come up with any tangible evidence to convince the grand jury. Therefore, I hereby formally request Your Honor to acquit the case.
法官大人，你很清楚，这个案子已经拖了好几个月了。直到今天，控方还没有拿出任何确凿的证据来说服大陪审团。因此，我在此正式请求阁下立即宣告终止审理本案。

B: Your intervention is rejected. You've got the right to say that, but we've got the right to let the procedure take its full effect. Therefore, until we exhaust all the procedures, we're not going to take any legal verdict upon the conclusions and recommendation from the grand jury.
你的建议被拒绝了。你有权利提出请求，但是我们也有权利让这个程序继续往下进行。在完成所有程序之前，我们不会根据大陪审团的结论和建议做出任何法律裁决。

A: We fully respect your professional integrity, but please go ahead with your

procedures at your convenience so that we can get the right verdict from Your Honor. Mind you, my client has been in custody for four months now.
我们完全尊重你的职业操守，但请您在方便的情况下加快审理程序，以便我们能尽快从法官大人那里得到公正的判决。请注意，我的当事人已经被拘留长达四个月了。

B: I heard you loud and clear, but procedures are procedures. Both you and I have to respect the rules in court. I’m sure you know both parties are to take legal responsibilities.
我明白，但程序就是程序。你和我都必须尊重法庭的规则。我相信你知道本案双方都要承担法律责任。

04

A: Your Honor and respected jury members, as you can see, it’s the hard fact that the suspect stabbed into the neck and shoulder of my client four times altogether, and caused the severe physical and psychological injuries. The forensic experts have double-checked and confirmed the initial report by the forensic experts. Therefore, I hereby formally request Your Honor to do the justice, in line with the criminal laws.
法官大人，尊敬的陪审团成员们，正如你们看到的那样，嫌疑人向我当事人的颈部和肩部共行刺了四刀，并造成了严重的身体和心理伤害，这是一个残酷的事实。法医已经对医院的初步报告进行了复核并予以确认。因此，我在此正式请求法官大人，依据刑法，秉公量刑。

B: Well, with due respect, sir, we’re still collecting information relating to the case. Let me remind you that we’re both professionals, and we’ve got to manage our portfolios professionally. For that matter, shall we let the lawyers from the other side do the talking before I could receive the conclusions and legal recommendation from the grand jury, and then decide which side has to take the main responsibility.
恕我直言，法官大人，我们还在收集与此案有关的信息。提醒你一点，我们都是专业人士，我们必须专业地行使我们的职责。就这一点而言，在我得到结论和大陪审团建议之前，应当让对方的律师进行辩护陈词，再决定由哪一方承担主要责任。

A: Well, let me also remind, Your Honor, that we simply find it difficult to see why it has taken so long to conclude the court hearing, and give the final verdict. We're also very disappointed at your comment on my client.

好吧，我还要提醒您，法官大人，我们只是觉得很难理解为什么要花这么长时间才结束庭审并做出最终裁决。我们对您关于我当事人的评价也很失望。

B: Your intervention is denied. Please observe your code of conduct, and watch out your choice of words.

你的陈述不能接受。请你遵守法庭的行为规范，并注意你的语言措词。

Part Three Common Expressions

- Well, now I've got to rely on you for help, and here are all the background information and relevant documents. Please take a close look at them, and let us know how you're going to help us out.

  好吧，这次我得依靠你的帮助了，这是所有的背景资料和相关文件。请仔细看看，并让我们知道你如何打赢这场官司。

- Before we get started, let me brief you on the things leading up to the case. And, please help me sort out the way forward, since you're the expert.

  开始之前，请让我简单介绍一下这个案子的经过。您是专家，请您帮我理一下思路。

- I’ve brought some additional documents for your reference, and I’ve also talked to some of my colleagues who would like to testify in court. Maybe, you should talk to them soon, in order to consolidate your position to defend the case on our behalf.
  我带来了其他文件供您参考，我也和一些同事谈过了，他们愿意出庭作证。也许，你应该尽快和他们面谈，以强化你的立场，更好地为本案辩护。
- Well, as I promised, I’ll do my best to protect your legal interests and bring the case to a best possible conclusion. Therefore, you need to take my advice to the letter, and make sure what to say in court at each session. Whenever you’ve got something which you’re not sure, you can always ask me, and I’ll give you advice accordingly. Please remember, whatever you say will count in terms of your case.
  我答应过你，会尽我最大的努力保护你的合法权益，让案子得到最理想的判决。因此，你需要认真听取我的建议，并明确每次开庭时要说些什么。你有不确定的事情，可以随时问我，我会给你相应的建议。请记住，你说的每一句话都会直接影响到案子的判决结果。
- Now, my friend, here is the status of your case. I’ve done my homework, and you now have three choices. First, we could go through private negotiations, in order to address the case amicably. The second is to go through arbitration, but it’ll depend on whether the other side would agree to the proposal. The third is to go through the court procedures, which would cost you a fortune, I’m afraid. Therefore, you need to think it over, and give me the definite answer at your early convenience.
  现在，我的朋友，这是关于你的案子的情况。我已经做了功课，你有三种选择。首先，我们可以通过私下谈判，友好地解决问题。第二种方案是通过仲裁，但这要看对方是否同意这个方案。第三种方法是通过法律程序，但恐怕这会花掉你一大笔钱。因此，你需要仔细考虑一下，并尽快给我明确的答复。

- Well, I've got some good news for you. The court has agreed to set your bail for $100000. I wonder if you can come up with that much cash in two days. If so, let me have the access to your bank account. I need to have the money ready when I meet the court officials in two days.
  哦，我有个好消息要告诉你。法院已同意你以10万美元保释。我想知道你能否在两天内拿出这笔现金。如果可能的话，请把你的银行账户给我。我两天后会见法庭官员时需要把钱准备好。
- Mind you, when your trial gets under way in court, the prosecution will ask you all sorts of questions, many of which will bite into your private life. Therefore, you've got to reply to any questions to the best of your ability, even though some of them may hurt your feelings and public image deeply. This is the cost you've got to pay, in order to win the case, so you'd better prepare yourself for the scenarios.
  请注意，法庭在对你进行审判时，控方会问你各种各样的问题，有很多会涉及到你的私生活。因此你必须尽全力回答相关问题，即使其中一些可能会深深地伤害你的感情和你的公众形象。为赢得这场官司，这是你要付出的代价。你需要做好心理准备，应对尴尬的提问。
- My friend, this is as far as we can go on your behalf. According to the criminal laws here in my country, the penalties for the similar offence would warrant a fixed imprisonment all the way up to life imprisonment. Nevertheless, in your case, you're probably to get three-to-five years in prison, but we may have to prepare for a harsher sentence from the judge.
  我的朋友，我们只能为你做这么多了。根据我国刑法，类似的犯罪将被判处有期徒刑，直至终身监禁。不过，就你的情况而言，你可能会被判三至五年监禁，但我们可能得准备好接受法官更严厉的判决。

第二十六章

科学技术

*

当今世界，科学技术的作用无所不在。几乎我们周围看到的一切都是科学技术的馈赠。具体来说，科学技术对我们的日常生活非常重要。它们正使我们的生活更简单、更快捷、更方便和更安全，并正成为工业发展、城市化和国家发展的主要动力。此外，科学技术是我们在社会活动中经常遇到的话题。

Chapter Twenty-six

Science and Technology

*

In today's world, science and technology are indispensable. Almost everything that we see around us is the gift of science and technology. To be specific, they are extremely important in our daily life. They are making our life simpler, faster, more convenient and more secure. And, they are becoming the main engine for industrial development, urbanization and national development. Furthermore, they are frequent topics that we encounter during social functions.

Part One　Things to Know

01

We're now living in the age of digital data and remote controls, where science and technology largely decide what we think, what we see, and what we do. It's also true that they've become the main engine to propel the globalization, and quickly transform the countries around the world into a "global village".

我们生活在一个电子和遥控时代。科学和技术在很大程度上决定我们的所思所想、所见所闻和所作所为。与此同时，科学技术也成为推动全球化的主要动力，并迅速地将世界各国变成一个“地球村”。

02

It's a sad fact that green-house effect has caused many islands and cities along the coasts of many countries in danger of being submerged. And, the holes of the ozone layer have made the earth worse for people to live; the phenomena of EL Nino and La Nina have been resulting in serious floods and droughts, and the diseases, caused by pollution are increasing at an incredible speed. And, I can go on with the list.

令人悲哀的是，温室效应已经导致许多国家沿海的多座岛屿和城市处于被淹没的危险之中;臭氧层的空洞已使地球上人类的居住条件恶化；厄尔尼诺和拉尼娜现象已经导致了严重的洪水和干旱，污染造成的疾病正在以令人难以置信的速度蔓延。这样的事实不胜枚举。

03

Based on all these scenarios, we all have to face the fact: We are not the masters of nature. Man-made and human disasters have taught us a lesson: We are just normal members of the big family of mother nature. As we have been mistreating the nature for too long, we're receiving its revenge just like the boomerang.

基于这些情况，我们不得不面对这样一个事实：我们并非大自然的主人。人为的灾难都给了我们一个教训：我们人类仅仅是大自然这个大家庭中的普通成员。由于我们人类掠夺式开发已久，正受到大自然的报复，就像回旋镖一样。

04

Nevertheless, it doesn't mean that we should give a sudden stop to any development, simply because that would add up the threat to the human society and environment. Rather, governments, companies, organizations and we individuals have to observe the same principle of living in harmony with the nature. We should learn to develop natural resources in the scientific way. We should protect the environment, conserve natural resources, and repair the damage whenever possible.

但是，这并不意味着因为会威胁到人类社会和环境的存在，我们就应该突然停止任何发展。相反，政府、公司、组织和个人必须遵循同样的原则，与自然和谐相处。我们应该学会科学地开发自然资源。我们要保护环境，节约自然资源，修复遭到破坏的环境。

05

It's an encouraging trend that, at the global level, more and more people have come to the consensus that living in harmony with nature is the only way to realize continuous progress and prosperity. That's why *the Paris Accord* has become the common agenda for the countries around the world in terms of

environment protection.
在全球范围内，越来越多的人已经达成共识：与自然和谐共处是实现持续进步与繁荣的唯一途径，这是一个备受鼓舞的趋势。这就是《巴黎协定》成为世界各国环境保护的共同议程的主要动因。

06

Where modern science and technology are concerned, we ordinary people are just laymen. Nevertheless, when we pull our thoughts together, we might come up with some food for thoughts for our political and business leaders in addressing the common challenges, and facilitate conditions for the sustainable development. As one Chinese saying goes, two heads are better than one.
在现代科学技术领域，我们普通人都是门外汉。但是，我们这些外行如果集思广益，就可以为各国政府和商业领导人应对共同的挑战提供一些思路，为实现可持续发展创造条件。中国有句俗语，三个臭皮匠，胜过一个诸葛亮。

07

You wouldn't believe it, but science and technology have changed many means through which we conduct our business, give and seek education, provide and seek medical service, provide and seek service in finance, etc. From the global perspective, they've changed the traditional modalities of economic development for many countries in terms of trade, investment and industrial cooperation.
你也许不会相信，但是科学和技术已经在开展贸易、给予和寻求教育、提供和寻求医疗服务、提供和寻求金融服务等方面改变了我们的很多方式。从全球角度看，它们在贸易、投资和产业合作等领域改变了许多国家传统经济的发展模式。

08

They say the rapid progress of science and technology has much to do with research and development, which is based on the painstaking efforts of many scientists to collect miles of information, and turn out yards of data. When new science and technologies join hands with existing and new industries, they would become the powerful engines for the new economic development and social progress.

有人说，科学技术的快速进步与研究和发展有很大关系。研发是建立在许多科学家的艰苦努力基础上的，他们收集大量的信息，才能得出了少量的数据。无论何时，新科技与现有新兴产业的结合，必将成为经济发展和社会进步新的强大动力。

09

Since the fourth industrialization, developed countries and emerging countries are benefiting from the new industries, new technologies, new products and new services, which have been providing steam for their national development. However, for many developing countries, they have to pay more to import the new technologies while catching up with the third industrial revolution, which would widen not only the existing “development divide”, but also the “digital divide”.

第四次工业化以来，发达国家和新兴国家正从新产业、新技术、新产品、新服务中受益，为本国发展提供动力。然而，对于许多发展中国家来说，在追赶第三次工业革命趋势的同时，他们还需要付出更多的代价来进口这些新技术。这不仅将拉大现行“发展鸿沟”，而且将造成新的“数字鸿沟”。

10

It’s increasingly clear that computers are the crystallization of modern science and technology, which have helped to create more new things than we could imagine. In many ways, they're the vehicles for us to carry out our daily life, to pursue our career, to do business, or to conduct social functions.

越来越明显的是，计算机是现代科学和技术的结晶，帮助我们创造了比想象中更多的新事物。在众多领域，它们是我们日常生活、职业生涯、商业活动和社交活动中的载体。

11

It's well known that traditional energies are on their way to depletion in various degrees, which has become the driving force for the major countries to compete for the rights over the exploitation, production on what is left around the world. China, as the largest population and the second largest economy, is especially under the pressure for the sustainable development in terms of energy supply.

众所周知，传统能源正在不同程度上走向枯竭，这已成为世界各大国争夺开发和生产剩余资源的焦点。中国作为世界上人口最多、经济总量第二大的国家，在能源供应方面尤其面临着可持续发展的压力。

12

Against the above background, major economies have locked themselves in the race to produce renewable energies as well as the new technologies and the market shares, in order to facilitate conditions for the economic development in the energy field in the 21st century.

在上述背景下，各主要经济体正加紧开发可再生能源、新技术，争夺市场份额，以期为21世纪的经济发展提供能源支撑。

13

Theoretically speaking, nuclear power provides an ideal alternative energy source, which has become a main pillar of the energy sector in many countries. However, the nuclear incidents at the power stations in Ukraine and

Japan have caused the international community to take a second look at the environmental disasters.

从理论上讲，核能是一种理想的替代能源，已成为许多国家能源部门的主要支柱。然而，发生在乌克兰和日本核电站的事故已经引起国际社会对环境灾难的重视。

14

Consequently, scientists in many countries have been developing hydrogen power as a new source of clean energy, as there’s still a great potential in many countries. According to some reports, the 21st century might become the hydro-economy century as it’s relatively easy to produce and friendly to the environment.

结果，许多国家的科学家正将水电作为清洁能源开发新方向，因为许多国家仍有巨大潜力尚待开发。有报道称，21世纪可能会成为水电经济的世纪，因为水电相对容易开发且环保。

15

New trends in the climate change have demonstrated one simple fact that, in spite of the rapid progress of science and technology, mankind still can’t win the endless battles over natural disasters. They still come and go at their own free will, and inflict heavy tolls on human lives and properties like never before.

气候变化的新趋势表明了一个简单的事实：尽管科学技术进步迅速，但人类在与自然灾害进行无休止的斗争中仍无法取得胜利。自然灾害依旧自由来去，给人类的生命和财产造成前所未有的巨大损失。

16

Due to the ever-growing global population and depletion of natural resources, countries around the world have been pushing for economic development at

the expense of the environment, which has resulted in the fierce revenge by the nature. History has taught us again and again that the more aggressively we put the nature into harm's way, the harder it would hit back. This is the law of nature.
由于全球人口不断增长和自然资源走向枯竭，世界各国一直在以环境为代价推动经济发展，这已导致自然的强烈报复。历史一再向我们表明，我们对自然的破坏越大，自然的反击就会越猛烈。这就是自然规律。

17

The international community has come to the conclusion that, as the next generation of mobile communications technology, 5G and AI technologies will bring ground-breaking services to the consumers and businesses alike. It will be one important engine for the economic growth and social progress over the next two decades, generating millions of new, high-pay jobs.
国际社会已经得出结论，5G和人工智能技术作为下一代移动通信技术，将给消费者和企业带来颠覆性服务，并将在未来的20年里成为驱动经济增长与社会进步的重要动力，可望衍生出更多高薪工作机会。

18

At the family level, we depend more and more on reliable connectivity for living, work, education, or social activities. Thanks to the lock-downs and social distancing, families and friends are meeting and socializing with one another via cell phones or WeChat groups. In the business field, new technologies have democratized retail business, and we are now spending more of our lives online than ever before. Today, when we want to find something out, it's no more than a couple of clicks on the keyboards or on the cell phones.
在家庭层面，我们的生活、工作、教育或社会活动越来越依赖于可靠的联系。由于封锁和社交距离，家人和朋友之间正通过手机或微信群保持联系或相互交谈。在商业领域，技术使零售业务大众化，我们现在比以往任何时候更加愿意从网上采购。今天，你想要找什么东西，只要在键盘上或手机上点击几下就可以找到。

19

In the manufacturing field, industries in connection with 5G networks will be able to quickly compile and compute data, and become more efficient and effective in their daily operations. In the health and security sectors, 5G and AI technologies will enable real-time responses for mission-critical services, such as enabling surgeons to consult virtually on surgeries, and enabling the government to carry out emergency search-and-rescue operations. All in all, these technologies will enable companies to further liberate productivity. In agriculture, quicker and more efficient data transmission will also support precision farming, and enable farmers to increase crop yields as well as annual income.

在制造业领域，与5G网络相关的行业将实现快速汇编和计算数据，提高日常运营效率。在医疗保健和安全领域，5G技术和人工智能技术将为紧急任务服务提供实时响应。例如，外科医生可以通过视频远程指导外科手术，政府可进行搜索并提供紧急救援。总之，这些将使公司企业进一步解放生产力。在农业方面，更快、更有效的数据传输也将支持许多国家发展精准农业，使农民能够提高作物产量，增加年收入。

20

Since the 21st century, the most far-reaching progress of science and technology is the development of the AI technology, which is to further promote economic development, improve industrial efficiency and provide better service for people in the world. Therefore, governments are joining hands with universities, institutions and companies, in order to develop more AI technologies for the existing economic sectors, which would bring more benefits to customers who have access to the new service systems.

21世纪以来，科学技术领域最显著的进步莫过于人工智能技术的发展，这种新技术将进一步推动经济发展，提高工业效率，并为每个社会成员提供更好的服务。正因为如此，各国政府正与大学、机构和公司携手合作，为现有经济部门研发更多的人工智能技术，并且为任何有机会接触到人工智能服务系统的消费者提供更多的福利。

Part Two　Situational Dialogues

01

A: Now, I've got a question for Professor Ma Dongsheng. The question is: How should the major countries carry out their responsibilities in promoting the harmony between sustainable development and environment? We all know Professor Ma comes from the country which has gone through rapid development while carrying out its commitment in *the Paris Accord* over the past few years. Please be brief, Professor.

现在，我有一个问题要问马东生教授。我的问题是：主要国家如何承担起促进可持续发展与环境和谐的责任？我们都知道马教授来自过去几年来认真履行《巴黎协定》承诺，并正在快速发展的国家。请简要介绍一下，教授。

B: Thank you, sir, for letting me take the floor. In 2015, President Xi Jinping assured the international community that, by 2030, China would reduce CO_2 emission by 60%~65% based on the 2015 level. China would strive for the balance of economic growth and sustainable environment. Over the past few years, China has been moving forward faster in realizing the ambitious goals. As a professor of economics, I can testify that, across China, the water systems are cleaner, and people have been enjoying more blue skies than before. There has been the drastic growth of the green belts across the country. More importantly, the harmful emissions have been reduced ahead of the schedule. To realize the above goals, China has implemented tougher laws and regulations, which warrant the enterprises to pursue green production and the people to outreach to the green life. Under the master plan of Belt and Road Initiative, Chinese government has upgraded the green benchmarks in trade, investment, industrial cooperation with the partner countries and stake holders.

谢谢你给我发言的机会。2015年，习近平主席向国际社会承诺，到2030年，中国将在2015年的基础上减少60%~65%的二氧化碳排放。中国政府全力促进经济与环境均衡发展。在过去几年间，中国在实现这一宏伟目标方面取得了很大的进展。作为一名经济学教授，我可以证明，在中国各地，水系统更加清洁，人们享受着比以前更多的蓝天。全国各地的绿化带都在迅猛发展。更重要的是，中国境内的有害排放已经大大减少。为实现上述目标，中国执行了更严格的法律法规。企业要依法推行绿色生产，人民群众要自觉走向绿色生活。在“一带一路”的总体规划下，中国政府与伙伴国家和利益相关方正在提升贸易、投资、产业合作的绿色基准。

02

A: We all know that 5G technology has been developing at high speed since 2014 and has become a global economic driver. We also know that China has become the first developing country to lead the 5G technology development and application, and has become one major rule maker in the industry. My question for Dr. Ma Dongsheng is: How 5G technologies are serving the Chinese people and their economic development?

我们都知道，2014年以来5G技术一直在高速发展，已经成为全球经济的驱动力。我们也知道，中国已经成为第一个引领5G技术开发和应用的发展中国家，并真正成为本行业主要规则的制定者。我想请问马东生博士的问题是：5G技术是如何服务于中国人民和其经济发展的？

B: Thank you for your question, but it would really take an expert to answer your question. Nevertheless, please allow me to give you my amateur response. As you know, China was an absolute follower during the 1G, 2G and 3G period, but managed to catch up in the 4G period. However, when the world ushered in the 5G technology, China managed to stand at the start line in both R&D and industrial applications. China has even managed to become one of the rule makers. With regard to the industrial and social application, 5G technology has become the main engine for the development of Internet of things, artificial intelligence, online games, virtual classrooms, virtual economy, smart cities, intelligent farming, tele-medicine, smart homes, driver-less vehicles and helicopters, remote control equipment and machines, etc. According to the projection, 5G technology will generate even greater steam for Chinese economy and people's life, in conjunction with the AI technology and quantum technology. I can tell you that the Belt and Road Initiative has incorporated the 5G technology into the framework of cooperation between China and the partner countries.

谢谢你的问题，但是这真的是一个需要专家来回答的问题。不过，请允许我给你一个业余的回答。如你所知，在1G、2G和3G时代，中国绝对是一个跟随者，但在4G时代，中国成功地赶了上来。然而，当世界迎来5G技术时，中国在研发和工业应用上都站在了起点。中国甚至成功地成为了该领域的主要规则制定者。在工业和社会应用方面，5G技术已成为物联网、人工智能、网络游戏、虚拟教室、虚拟经济、智慧城市、智能农业、远程医疗、智能家居、无人驾驶汽车和直升机、远程控制设备和机器等发展的主要动力。据预测，5G技术与人工智能技术和量子技术相结合，将对中国经济和人民生活产生更大影响。我可以告诉你，“一带一路”倡议已经将5G技术纳入了中国与伙伴国家的合作框架。

03

A: Thank you, chairperson, for letting me ask the question. To my knowledge, the Belt and Road Initiative has been alive for years now, and has won more and more approval and support from the international community. Now, my question to Director General Yang Lin is: What functions have the science and technology been playing in the joint construction of the Belt and Road among the partner countries?

主席，谢谢你给我提问题的机会。据我所知，“一带一路”倡议至今已有年头了，并且得到了国际社会越来越多的肯定和支持。现在，我想问杨林局长，科学技术在“一带一路”合作建设中对伙伴国家发挥了什么样的带动作用?

B: Well, it's certainly a very challenging question, sir, but let me give you my personal response. From the very beginning, China assured the stakeholders that the Belt and Road Initiative was not just going to build up more projects or more joint venture enterprises, or the mere extension of the Chinese production chains or supply chains. The ultimate goal is to promote common development, and bring benefits to the people of the partner countries. I can tell you that China has listed technology as an important area of bilateral cooperation. From my perspective, the joint construction should help the latter to increase their capability in foreign trade, elevate productivity and increase their capability to compete both at home and at the international market. In addition, the essence of the win-win cooperation would be carried out with the proper technical assistance and technology transfer on the commercial basis. On top of that, Chinese companies would join hands with the competent partners in the host countries in terms of R&D projects in the areas of common interests.

这确实是一个很有挑战性的问题，先生，不过请允许我讲一些个人的想法。从一开始，中方就向利益相关方保证，“一带一路”不仅仅是建设更多的项目、更多的合资企业，也不仅仅是延伸中国的生产线、供应链。其最终目的是促进共同发展，造福伙伴国家的人民。我可以肯定地告诉你，中国已经把技术列为双边合作的重要领域。在我看来，合作建设有助于后者提高对外贸易能力，提高生产力，增强在国内和国际市场的竞争能力。总之，上述双赢合作建设的实质将是在商业基础上提供技术援助和技术转让。此外，中国企业还将与有能力的合作伙伴在有共同利益的行业或领域开展研发项目合作。

04

A: To my knowledge, the “brain drain” is becoming the stumbling block for China and the partner countries in carrying out the joint construction of the Belt and Road. I wonder if the Chinese side has any concrete policies to address the issue. If so, what are they?

据我了解，“人才流失”正成为中国与伙伴国开展可持续共建“一带一路”的绊脚石。我想知道，中方是否有具体的政策来解决这个问题。如果有，请问都有哪些政策？

B: Yes, this is certainly the headache that China and the partner countries have to face squarely. It’s an open secret that sustainable joint construction of the Belt and Road depends largely on the availability of the contingent of engineers and technicians. For that matter, my government has joint hands with the relevant stakeholders in this regard from the very beginning. It has signed quite a lot of bilateral or multilateral agreements to bring up engineers and technician by the joint establishment of colleges and universities, in order to bring up tailor-made candidates for the joint construction. It has been offering more and more scholarships for the partner countries to send their young people to receive higher education in the relevant majors. Meanwhile, it has been organizing more and more training courses for the government officials and professionals to receive project training in China. On top of that, it has been encouraging and supporting the Chinese companies to organize technical training programs for the local staff members and those who are working at the workshops or production lines.

是的，这是中国和伙伴国家面临的令人头痛的问题。共建“一带一路”能否持续发展，很大程度上取决于是否有一支有能力的工程技术人员队伍，这是一个公开的秘密。为此，我国政府从一开始就与相关利益方在这方面携手合作。中国政府已经签署了许多双边或多边协议，通过共同开办高等院校的方式来培养工程技术人员，为有关领域的共同建设定向培养人才。中国政府越来越多地向伙伴国提供奖学金，帮助后者的青年接受相关专业的高等教育。与此同时，中国政府一直在为伙伴国家政府官员和专业人士组织越来越多的培训课程，让其在中国接受项目培训。此外，中国政府一直鼓励和支持本国企业为当地员工和车间、生产线上的工人举办职业技能培训。

Part Three　Common Expressions

- It's an open secret that when you are bilingual, you would find it easy to get a job at the transnational corporations.
  会说两种语言会让你更容易在跨国公司找到工作，这是公开的秘密。
- At many foreign companies, bilingual staff members or professionals will get more salaries and more chances for promotion. Therefore, it pays for you to prepare yourself accordingly.
  在许多外国公司，会双语的员工或专业人士会得到更高的薪水和更多晋升机会。因此，你有必要让自己做好相应的准备。
- In the English-speaking countries or countries where English is the official language, you need to have a good grasp of English, in order to settle down and make it in your career, regardless of your ethnic background.
  在讲英语的国家或以英语为官方语言的国家，无论你的种族背景如何，若想在那里定居或是在事业上取得成功，你都需要具有良好的英语表达能力。
- To be an international person, you need to improve your English, and learn to use English confidently in the fields of science and technology, especially oral English.
  要想成为一个国际化的人，你需要提高自己的英语技能，学会在科技领域更自信地使用英语，尤其是你的英语口语。
- With the further development of science and technology, English for

science and technology has become more and more popular among people from all walks of life. Therefore, many universities and colleges have established majors for science and technology which are conducted in English.

随着科技的深入发展，科技英语在各界人群中越来越重要。因此，许多大学和学院设立了用英语授课的科技专业。

- Since the First Industrial Revolution some 400 years ago, developments in science and technology have been altering the means, by which people live, connect, communicate and transact, and have produced profound effects on economic development and social progress. To be specific, industrial development has enabled governments to tackle inequalities among and within countries either developed or developing, accelerate structural industrial transformation and social mobility, provide new jobs and additional income, and reduce social exclusions.

  自400多年前第一次工业革命以来，科学技术的发展不断改变着人们的生活、联系、交流和交易方式，对经济发展和社会进步产生了深刻影响。具体来说，工业发展使各国政府能够解决南北方国家之间和国家内部的不平等问题，加快工业结构转型，促进社会流动，创造新的就业机会和额外收入，减少社会分化。

第二十七章

国内经济

*

有些人认为，经济学太难懂了，与普通人距离太遥远。其实，这是最大的误解。简而言之，经济学涉及商品和服务的生产、分配以及消费，这些对我们的生活、学习、工作、商业，乃至政治活动都有直接影响。此外，经济事宜是社会交谈期间经常出现的话题。因此，我们需要了解相关理论和概念。

Chapter Twenty-seven

Domestic Economy

*

Some think that economics is a subject which is too difficult to learn, and it's too far away from us ordinary people. Nothing could be more misleading. Simply said, economics is a social science that deals with the production, distribution, as well as consumption of goods and services, which has immediate impacts on our life, educational, career, commercial or political activities. Furthermore, economic issues are common topics at social functions which warrant us to learn about the relevant theories and concepts.

Part One Things to Know

01

History has proven that demographic production is a deciding factor in the national development, and it's also the fundamental factor for social progress. Currently, demographic dividend is still an important endowment for many developing countries in terms of economic development. At the same time, the aging of population has become a new challenge to the developed countries and emerging countries alike.

历史证明，人口生产是国家发展的决定因素，也是社会进步的根本动力。当前，人口红利仍构成许多发展中国家经济快速发展的重要要素。同时，人口老龄化已成为发达国家和新兴国家面临的新挑战。

02

Market economy is the dominant economic system across the world, under which the decisions regarding investment, production and distribution are driven by the forces of supply and demand. The major characteristic of the market economy is that the factors market plays the dominant role in allocating the factors of production. Accordingly, companies and people from all walks of life will have to adapt to the above economic environment, and abide by the relevant rules and regulations when they live, study, work or carry out business operations in the host countries along the Belt and Road.

市场经济是世界上占主导地位的经济体系。在这个体系中，所有关于投资、生产和分配的决定均受价格信号驱使。市场经济的主要特征是要素市场在资本和生产要素配置中起主导作用。因此，公司和各界人士在“一带一路”沿线国家生活、学习、工作或经商期间，都要适应上述新的经济环境，遵守相关的法律规章。

03

Against the backdrop of globalization, economic indicators are the main benchmarks to judge the development status of a country, of which the Gross Domestic Products（GDP） remains the key factor. To be specific, GDP is the total economic output of a country for each fiscal year, which covers four components: Social and personal consumption, business investment, government spending and net exports. In most cases, the retail and service industries are critical component parts of the developed economies where consumer spending comprises more than 65% of the annual GDP. For example, consumer spending contributed to more than 80% of the total US production in 2019, which stood at $13.28 trillion.

在全球化条件下，经济指标是衡量一个国家发展状况的重要标准，国内生产总值（GDP）仍然是衡量一个国家发展状况的关键因素。简单地说，GDP系指一个国家一个财政年度的经济总产出，具体包括四个组成部分：社会和个人消费、企业投资、政府支出和净出口。在大多数情况下，零售业和服务业是发达国家经济的重要组成部分。在这些国家，消费者支出占年度GDP的65%以上。例如，消费者支出占2019年美国总产量的近80%，总额为132800亿美元。

04

For the governments, companies and ordinary consumers alike, GDP is the immediate economic indicator for them to implement or readjust their economic policies, decisions on investment, consumption and savings. For all the stakeholders, when the GDP falls for two quarters in a row, the national economy is surely heading to a recession, which would mean less revenues, more market contractions, more business closures, more pay freezes and fewer jobs. When the national GDP is on the rise, there would be more economic growth, more revenues, more public goods and services, more business opportunities, more jobs available, better salaries, more pay rises, etc. Therefore, nothing around us is too far away from economics.

对于政府、企业和普通消费者来说，GDP是他们制定或调整经济政策、投资、消费、储蓄的主要经济指标。对所有这些利益相关方而言，当GDP连续两个季度出现负增长，表明全国经济走向衰退，意味着财政收入减少、市场疲软、企业倒闭、工资冻结和失业增多。反之，当GDP处于增长期时，经济呈现增长状态，收入增多，公共产品和服务会更多，商机更多，就业机会也更多，更高的薪水和工资涨得更多等等。因此，我们周围的一切都离经济学不远。

05

From the perspective of methodology, there are three ways to calculate GDP, namely, the production method, the income method and the expenditure method, which reflect the results of national economic production activities from different angles. To be specific, the production method is to measure the newly created values contributed by the permanent economic entities during a fiscal year in terms of production. In another word, we deduct the intermediate product value invested in the production process from the total product value produced by various sectors of the national economy during the accounting period, then we could get the added value. The accounting formula is: GDP = total output - intermediate input. Income method is an accounting method that reflects the final result, according to the income shares that the factors of production deserve in the production process from the perspective of creating income during the production process. And, the accounting formula is: GDP=

labor remuneration+ net production taxes + depreciation of fixed assets + operating surplus. The expenditure method measures the final destination of products and services in the accounting period from the perspective of final use of goods and services. The so called accounting formula is: GDP = final consumption + expenditure + capital formation + net exports.

从方法论上讲，计算GDP有三种方法，即生产法、收入法和支出法，旨在从不同角度反映国民经济生产活动的结果。具体来说，生产法是指从生产的角度来衡量永久性经济实体在一个财政年度内新贡献的价值。也就是说，我们从国民经济各部门生产的产品总值中扣除生产过程投入的中间产品价值，就可以得到增加值。具体计算公式是：GDP=总产出－中间投入。收入法是从生产过程中创造收入的角度，按照生产要素在生产过程中应得的收入份额来反映最终结果的一种会计方法。具体计算公式是：GDP=劳动报酬+生产税净额+固定资产消耗+营业盈余。支出法从商品和服务的最终使用角度来衡量特定会计年份期间产品和服务的最终目的地。具体计算公式是：GDP=最终消费+支出+资本形成总额+净出口。

06

Furthermore, macroeconomic factors are important economic indicators, of which GDP nominal and GDP PPP are the two key indicators. The key difference between the two data is that the former is the GDP unadjusted for the effects of inflation at current market prices, whereas the latter is the GDP converted to US dollars using purchasing power parity and divided by total population. Apparently, GDP PPP is used to describe and compare the living standards of the peoples between or among countries. As you can see, one US dollar stretches much longer in China than in the United States.

此外，宏观经济因素是重要的经济指标，其中，名义GDP和GDP（PPP）是两个关键指标。具体而言，上述两者的关键区别是，前者是未经通货膨胀调整的GDP，以当前市场价格为基准，而后者是GDP转换为美元，使用购买力平价并除以总人口。显然，GDP（PPP）主要用来描述和比较两个国家之间民众的生活水平。如你所见，一美元在中国的购买力要比在美国强得多。

07

From the perspective of theory, GDP is the building block of the macroeconomics, because modern-day macro economics is about the government making policies to promote better performance of the national economy. Governments extensively use the GDP index to design and implement national development strategies and industrial policies. Secondly, GDP is not only used to identify the development status of a country, in line with the three worlds theory, but also to identify the current state of the national economy—boom and bust. Thirdly, GDP is serving as the benchmark for national strategy and policy readjustment. Governments would mainly use GDP to diagnose the problems with the national economy, and adopt policy measures to correct them, in order to promote the steady and healthy economic growth. Fourth, GDP indicators can be used to make cardinal and ordinal comparison between economies. We can rank the economies of the nations or regions by comparing their GDP indicators. We can also draw conclusions about the relative size of the economy of different nations based on the same indicators. For example, we can say that the economy of China was roughly 5 times larger than that of India in 2019.

从理论上讲，GDP是宏观经济学的基石，因为现代宏观经济学是关于政府制定政策促进国民经济有效运行的学科。目前，各国政府广泛采用GDP指数来制定和实施本国发展战略和产业政策。其次，GDP不仅可依据三个世界理论衡量国家的发展状态，而且被用来判断国家经济发展现状——繁荣或萧条。第三，GDP是战略和政策调整的参考依据。政府主要用GDP指标来诊断经济运行中出现的问题，并采取措施加以纠正，促进国民经济稳定健康增长。第四，GDP指标还可以用于诸多经济体的全球排位。我们可以根据一国或地区的GDP指标对其经济发展状况进行全球排名，并根据相关国家的GDP指标研究各国经济的相对规模。例如，我们可以说，2019年中国经济的规模大约是印度的5倍。

08

To be specific, the three major industries, namely primary, secondary and tertiary industries, are important indicators for us to observe the economic structure and development stage of any country. Gross Domestic Product tracks the health of a country's economy. Governments would use this data to regulate the economic growth via currency value and interest rates. Economists would use GDP data to determine whether an economy is healthy in development. Investors would use the data to decide whether or not to make investments in the target country. We ordinary people would use this same data to calculate how much to consume, how much to save, and how much to invest in a given year.

具体来说，第一、第二、第三这三大产业是我们观察一个国家经济结构和发展阶段的重要指标。国内生产总值旨在跟踪一个国家的经济健康状况。政府会利用这些数据，通过货币汇率、利率来调节国民经济增长。经济学家们主要用GDP来判断一个经济体的发展是否健康。投资者则运用GDP来决定是否对目标国家进行投资。我们普通人则依据这个指标来计算某个年度可能消费多少、储蓄多少、投资多少。

09

From the demand side, governments would utilize the revenue and monetary tools to promote economic growth. They would use tax cuts or tax rebates to put more money back into the pockets of the relevant manufactures and consumers. Ideally, they would spend the money on business renovation or expansion or daily consumption. To be specific, when companies and enterprises have more cash in hand, they would procure new machines and

equipment, renovate technology, expand production, etc. All these measures would help increase productivity, and competitiveness of the national economy, and contribute to the national revenues.
从供给领域考察，政府通过税收和金融政策促进经济增长。他们通过减税和退税把更多的钱放回相关制造商和消费者的口袋里。理想的情况下，他们会把新增的收入用于企业改造或业务拓展，或者日常消费。具体而言，公司和企业拥有更多现金之后，通常会购买新的机器和设备，革新技术，扩大再生产等。所有这些举措均有助于提高生产力、国家经济竞争力，有助于增加国家财政收入。

10

From the supply side, governments would provide various incentive policies for the companies and enterprises to renovate their production lines, develop practical technologies or import new technologies, in an effort to expand productions, enlarge economic of scale, emancipate productivity, and increase competitiveness. All these policy measures would help increase the national capacity to turn out more products and services, promote social progress and improve people's livelihood, and add new steam for the economic growth.
从供给方考察，政府将提供各种激励政策，为公司和企业更新其生产线、开发实用技术或进口新技术提供便利条件，以便进一步发展生产、扩大经济规模、解放生产力和提高竞争力。所有这些政策措施都有助于国家生产更多产品和转化更多服务，促进社会进步和改善民生，为经济增长增添新的动力。

11

Meanwhile, governments would make sure that the new technologies and industries must not exert too much new pressures on the already fragile environment. They should also attach importance to the balanced growth of different regions and industries, and ensure equal distribution of benefits from

the national development, because the social divide will eventually hit back at the political and social stability with equal ferocity.
与此同时，各国政府应确保新技术和新产业不给本已脆弱的环境带来新的压力。政府也应该促进不同地区、不同行业均衡发展，确保国家发展的利益平等分配，因为社会分化最终会对政治和社会的稳定产生同等反作用。

12

From the perspective of consumption, in order to make wise decisions on how to live, work or do business, we need to know about the economic trend in the host country. To be specific, there are four stages: Expansion, peak, contraction, and recession. During the expansion phase, the national economy would experience relatively rapid growth, during which interest rates tend to be low, production increases, and inflationary pressures would gradually build up. The peak of a cycle is reached when the growth hits its ceiling. Rapid economic growth typically creates imbalances in the economy that needs to be corrected. This would be followed by the economic contraction, during which economic growth would slow downs, employment would fall, and commodity prices would fluctuate. At the end of the circle, the trough of the cycle is reached when the national economy hits the bottom, which would set the stage for the economy to rebound.
从消费的角度来看，为了更好地生活、工作或开展营商活动，我们需要了解东道国的经济周期规律，具体分为四个阶段：扩张、高峰、收缩和衰退。在扩张阶段，经济增长相对较快，商业利率往往较低，生产持续增加，通货膨胀压力增大。当国民经济增长达到极限，就处于周期的顶峰。此时，通常会出现一些需要纠偏的经济失衡状态。此后，国民经济呈现收缩状态，具体而言，进入经济增速放缓，就业下降，物价停滞的收缩时期。最终，在本轮经济周期中，国民经济衰退探底，为经济复苏创造条件。

13

From the perspective of macro economic management, market economy is an economic system, within which the decisions regarding investment, production and distribution are guided by the forces of supply and demand. The major characteristic of the market economy is that market plays a dominant role in allocation and distribution of the factors of production, as the capital would flow naturally to the industries or economic sectors which would generate more profits.

从宏观经济领域考察，市场经济是一种经济体制。其间，投资、生产和分配活动主要由价格信号所引导。市场经济的主要特征是市场在生产要素配置进程中发挥主导作用。这是因为资本总是流向可获得更多利润的产业或经济部门。

14

Based on the above analysis, the role of government is to act as an agent of economic development and social progress via laws and industrial regulations. They have to provide the transparent legal and social framework, promote and maintain the fair competition, provide public goods and services, promote national defense, facilitate equal distribution of benefits of economic development via income, budgetary appropriation and social welfare, promote domestic and foreign economic relations, and stabilize national economy, etc.

基于以上分析，政府的作用是依法承担经济发展与社会进步的代理人作用。它们必须提供透明的法律和社会框架，促进与维护公平竞争，提供公共产品和服务，增强国防建设，通过预算拨款改善社会福利以促进经济发展利益平等分配，促进国内外经济关系，稳定国家经济等等。

15

With regard to industrial development, governments would design and implement their national strategy as well as industrial policies, which would facilitate condition for the growth of manufacturing and processing industries. Simply said, they would draft and implement the industrial development guidelines, which would cover the future goals and time framework. They would issue policies and regulations to influence the allocation of the factors of production, and promote the stable economic growth. And, they would readjust the existing strategies and policies, in line with the changing domestic and external situations.

在工业发展方面，各国政府依法制定和实施国家战略和产业政策，为制造和加工产业发展创造条件。简单地说，它们必须起草并实施工业发展指导方针，其中包括对未来目标的展望和时间规划，必须出台一整套影响生产要素配置的政策和制度，促进经济稳定增长。同时，政府必须根据国内外形势的变化调整现有的战略和政策。

16

With regard to the wealth distribution, it's the ultimate goal of national governments to facilitate conditions for the sustainable economic growth and social progress, which would include national strategies, in line with the national situation, industrial policies to modernize national economy, financial and monetary policies to balance domestic and foreign economic relations, and the foreign policies to effectively participate in the regional or international economic integration.

在财富分配领域，中央政府的最终目标都是为可持续的经济增长和社会进步创造条件，这包括符合国情的国家战略、促进国民经济现代化的产业政策、平衡国内外经济关系的财政和货币政策，以及有效参与区域或国际经济一体化的外交政策。

17

With regard to the economic and social environment, national and local governments would joint hands with the private sector and foreign

stakeholders, in order to build up or upgrade the physical structures. Economists believe that investment in infrastructure could serve as a catalyst. Top-notch national infrastructure network would not only help build up the national market, but also help companies and enterprises to expand production scales, increase productivity, and find easier access to the neighboring markets.
在经济与社会环境领域，中央和地方政府将与私营部门和外国利益攸关方共同努力，建立或升级基础设施结构。经济学家认为，基础设施支出可以作为经济催化剂。一流的基础设施不仅有助于建立国内市场，也有助于国内企业扩大生产规模，提高生产力，并为进入邻近国家市场创造条件。

18

With regard to economic theory, inflation is a trend of price rise in a country over a period of time, resulting in a sustained drop in the purchasing power of the money in circulation. When the general price level of a country keeps rising, the same amount of money would buy fewer goods and less services. Therefore, inflation represents an invisible knife to deeply cut into the consuming power of the ordinary people, and also hinders the smooth implementation of the national strategies and policies.
根据经济理论，通货膨胀是指一个国家的价格水平在一段时间内持续攀升，导致流通货币的购买力持续下降的现象。一个国家的总价格水平如果持续上升，单位货币可购买的商品和获得的服务就会相应减少。因此，通货膨胀是一把无形的刀，不仅会严重影响普通民众的消费能力，而且也会阻碍国家发展战略和政策的顺利实施。

19

With regard to the economic governance, national governments would implement the strategies and industrial policies, in order to influence the price fluctuation, and indicate the orientation of the economic developments. Traditionally, the central governments would implement policy measures such as price ceilings, in an effort to prevent companies from seeking monopoly by price hiking.

在经济管理方面，各国经济政府将执行国家战略和产业政策，调控价格波动，并指引经济发展的方向。传统上，中央政府通常会实施限价等政策，以防止企业通过涨价来寻求垄断。

20

With regard to green economy, governments are to promote economic and social development in harmony with the environment. Furthermore, sustainable development aims at economic growth and social progress without compromising the ability of future generations to meet their own needs. At the global level, the international community is to jointly realize common development and collectively address the global challenges, including poverty, inequality, climate change, environmental degradation, peace and justice, etc.

在绿色经济方面，政府必须促进经济和社会的发展与环境相协调。进而言之，可持续发展的目标是在不损害后代满足其自身需要能力的情况下实现经济增长和社会进步。在全球层面，国际社会应携手实现以共同发展为目标的可持续发展，共同应对贫困、不平等、气候变化、环境恶化、和平与正义等全球性挑战。

Part Two　Situational Dialogues

01

A: Good morning, Wallace. How have you been?

早上好，华莱士，你最近怎么样？

B: Not bad. I've just settled down here at the university, and I've been working hard on my major now.

不错。我已在大学安顿下来，现在我正忙于我的专业课程。

A: Good for you. Well, since you're to complete your MA degree in about one year, have you got any plan for your future yet?

很好。你既然要在一年内完成你的硕士学位，那么你对未来有什么打算吗？

B: I guess I'll return to my country and get a job at the Ministry of Commerce, since they sent me here to specialize in business management.

我想我将回中国并在商务部工作，因为是他们派我来这里攻读商务管理专业的。

A: Good! That would give you the opportunity to involve yourself with the bilateral relations between our two countries. Since the joint construction of the Belt and Road is well under way, the bilateral trade is set to grow more rapidly in the years to come.

很好！那你就有机会参与我们两国的双边关系。“一带一路”建设正在顺利推进，未来几年两国间的双边贸易将以更快的速度增长。

B: Sure, but the only thing I worry about is the increasing deficit. I wonder if you would have anything to offer in addressing the issue.

当然，但我唯一担心的是不断增加的赤字。请问，关于这个问题，您是否有什么好的对策？

A: Well, for a start, it is a problem. My country used to face the same problem forty some years ago. However, when more and more joint venture companies set up the production lines in the industrial parks here in the capital, they would soon turn out more goods and service for the domestic market, and export the products to China as well as to the neighboring countries. This will gradually balance out your trade in a comprehensive way.

首先，这确实是一个问题。40多年前，我的国家也曾面临同样的问题。但是，随着越来越多的合资企业进驻贵国首都工业园区建立生产线，它们很快就会为国内市场提供更多的产品和服务，并将相关产品出口到中国和周边国家。这将逐渐助力贵国全面地去平衡对外贸易。

02

A: Hi, Simba, I've got some good news to share with you.

你好，辛巴，我有好消息要告诉你。

B: What is it, please?

什么好消息？

A: I've just received the assignment by the Board of Directors to be the General Manager of the subsidiary company in your country for three years. Nevertheless, I have been away from your country for six years now, but how is the economic situation going in your country, now?

我刚被董事会任命为驻贵国分公司的总经理，为期三年。然而，我已经离开贵国六年了，贵国目前的经济情况怎么样？

B: Well, we've just had a new government which is more friendly to China, and the economic growth has been steady for the past few years, thanks to the close cooperation between our two countries. More roads have connected the major cities across the country, which have helped to consolidate the domestic market, and have been attracting more FDI from China and other countries. However, the economic structure of my country is still lopsided, during which the mining sectors has long been dominated by the transnational corporations from the West. They just produced and exported the primary products, which would not generate much spillover benefits for the government and the local people.

嗯，我们刚刚选举出了新政府，会对中国更友好。由于我们两国的密切合作，过去几年经济一直稳步增长。越开越多的道路将全国主要城市连接起来，这有助于巩固国内市场，并吸引了来自中国和其他国家的外商直接投资。然而，我国的经济结构仍不平衡，采矿部门长期以来一直被由西方的跨国公司所控制。他们仅仅只是生产和出口第一产业的产品，这不会给政府和当地民众带来太多的溢出效应。

A: I understand. That's why Chinese companies have been concentrating on the infrastructure and manufacturing sectors, which are certainly to generate more jobs for the local people, and help your country to boost the productivity and export.

我明白了。这就是为什么中国企业一直专注于基础设施和制造业，这肯定会为当地人民创造更多就业机会，帮助贵国提高生产能力和增加出口。

03

A: Thank you, chair, for giving me the opportunity to ask questions. My question is simple and for Professor Yu Wenhua. For many years in the past, my country has been flooded with the less-quality products from China. What do you think would be the effective ways to address this hot issue?

主席，谢谢您给我这个提问的机会。我的问题很简单，想请问余文华教授，在过去的许多年里，我的国家充斥着来自中国的低质量产品。您认为解决这个棘手问题的有效方法是什么？

B: Thank you for your question. In fact, it’s not a simple question at all, and it would really take a comprehensive approach. The truth is that Chinese government has long banned the export of less-quality products, in line with the international practice. Let me tell you why there are still those goods at your national market. It’s my guess that, in order to make easy profit, importers from your country have been roaming around the local Chinese markets for the suppliers and managed to sneak through Customs inspections and quarantine verification at the border of both countries. Therefore, our two government institutions must join hands to implement tougher control over the borders. There must be a tight control of the flows of less quality products. Those who involve in the “grey trade” must be dealt with accordingly. More importantly, our two governments must expedite the efforts to fully utilize the National Trade Center in your capital, so that local consumers could get the authentic Chinese products at reasonable prices right here in your country.

谢谢你的问题。事实上，这不是一个简单的问题，它需要采取全面措施加以解决。事实是根据国际惯例，中国政府早就禁止出口质量较差的产品。让我告诉你为什么在你们国家市场上这种产品仍然存在。我想，贵国的进口商为了获取更多利益，一直在中国市场上四处走访游荡，寻求提供你提到的商品，继而设法绕过两国边境的海关检查与防疫。因此，我们两国政府机构必须携手在边境实施更严格的管制；必须严格控制低质量产品的流通。那些参与“灰色交易”的人必须得到相应的处理。更重要的是，两国政府必须充分利用国家商品贸易中心，让当地消费者可以以合理的价格在本国市场上买到正宗的中国商品。

04

A: Well, my question relates to the COVID-19, which has been rampaging around the world, and has been inflicting disasters to all the countries indiscriminately. However, this time around, the major developed countries have almost stepped back from their historical responsibilities to help the less developed countries, my country included. My question is for the Chinese officials on the podium: What has your government been doing in this regard?

我想问的是，当前疫情正在全球肆虐，给各国普遍带来了灾难。然而，这一次，主要发达国家几乎放弃了帮助包括我国在内的欠发达国家的历史责任。我想问在座的中方官员，中国政府在这方面实施了什么政策？

B: Thank you for your question. As you know, China was the first to face the challenge from the pandemic, and the whole country was united closely behind the national leaders and central government. Therefore, China managed to bring the coronavirus epidemic under control in a matter of three months. Meanwhile, the government organized the national campaign to race against the time to research and developed the drugs and vaccines. Up till now, four vaccines have managed to undergo Stage Three test, in conjunction with more than 10 countries. These vaccines have realized the effective protection rate of 80% plus. President Xi Jinping has assured the WHO that the Chinese vaccines, once available, would be public goods for the developing countries, and China would share the products with friendly countries at affordable prices, and China would also provide free supplies of vaccines to the least developed countries in conjunction with the WTO via the development assistance programs. Meanwhile, relevant institutions of the Chinese government have been bending backward in exchanging information and experience with their counterparts in many countries in terms of pandemic prevention and the treatment of the patients. And, the Chinese government has been running production lines three shifts a day and seven days a week, in order to provide the badly needed machines, equipment and products to the countries on the commercial basis or via emergency assistance programs.

谢谢你的问题。你知道，中国是第一个面对疫情挑战的国家，全国上下紧密团结在国家领导人和中央政府的身后。因此，中国仅用了3个月时间就控制住了疫情。与此同时，政府组织了全国抗疫运动，与时间赛跑，研发药物和疫苗。目前，与10多个国家合作推动4种疫苗完成了第三阶段试验。这些疫苗已实现80%以上的有效率。习近平主席向世界卫生组织承诺，一旦中国研制的疫苗获准上市，将作为公共产品向发展中国家提供，中方将以合理的价格提供给友好的国家，并将与世界卫生组织合作，透过发展援助计划向最不发达国家免费提供。与此同时，中国政府相关机构正尽其所能在疫情防控和患者救治方面与许多国家的同行交流信息和经验。此外，中国的生产线正每周7天、每天三班倒，全力生产抗疫急需的机械、设备和产品，并在商业基础上向相关国家供货，或通过紧急抗疫项目提供援助。

Part Three　Common Expressions

- Domestic trade, different from international trade, is the exchange of goods and service within the boundaries of a country. This may be sub-divided into two categories, wholesale and retail. Wholesale trade is relating to buying goods from manufacturers, dealers or producers in large quantities, and selling them in smaller quantities to the retailers or consumers.

  与国际贸易不同，国内贸易是指一个国家境内的货物与服务交换。具体可以再细分为两类，批发和零售。批发贸易是指从制造商、经销商或生产商那里大批量购买商品，然后再小量卖给零售商，甚至消费者。

- You wouldn't believe it, but foreign trade has long been an important factor in promoting economic growth and social progress in both developed and developing countries. Especially for the countries in the South, foreign trade has been the locomotive to pull many countries out of the absolute poverty line, and realize the 2030 Development Goals set forth by the United Nations.
  也许你不会相信，但发达国家和发展中国家的对外贸易长期以来一直是促进其经济增长和社会进步的重要因素。尤其是对南方国家来说，对外贸易一直是长期推动各国摆脱绝对贫困、实现联合国制定的2030年发展目标的火车头。
- In economics, GDP is used to calculate the total value of the goods and services produced within a country's borders, while GNP is used to calculate the total value of the goods and services produced by the residents of a country, irrespective of their locations.
  在经济学中，GDP主要用来计算一个国家境内生产的商品和服务的总价值，而GNP则被用来计算一国居民生产的商品和服务的总价值，无论他们身在哪里。
- From the research perspective, GDP looks into the amount of economic activity within a nation's economy, while GNP looks at the value of the economic activity generated by the people of a nation no matter where they are. This means that GNP will count the economic activities of expatriates and citizens outside the country, but GDP will not. Meanwhile, GDP will consider the activities of non-citizens within those borders, but GNP will not.
  从研究的角度来看，GDP本质上是指一国经济中经济活动的总量，而GNP则是指一国人民所创造的经济活动的价值。这意味着GNP将计算在国境之外的侨民和其他公民的经济活动，但GDP不会。GDP将包含各国境内非其公民的活动，但GNP不会。

- Policymakers rely on Gross National Product（GNP） as one of the important economic indicators to oversight and regulate national economy. GNP produces crucial information on manufacturing, savings, investments, employment, production outputs of major companies and other economic variables. Therefore, policymakers would use this information to prepare policy papers that legislators use to make laws.
  政策制定者将国民生产总值作为监管国家经济重要的经济指标之一。国民生产总值提供关于制造业、储蓄、投资、就业、主要公司的生产产出和其他经济变数的重要资料。因此，政策制定者依据这些信息来准备政策文件，供立法部门制定法律时参考。
- Under the market economy, both governments and business communities are very much co-dependent. Therefore, they are to influence and complement each other in line with the laws and regulations for the welfare of the national economy. To be specific, governments would shape the business practices directly and indirectly by both economic tools and industrial policies, which dictate what organizations can and cannot do. Meanwhile, business community would demand their governments to create level-playing fields and provide public goods, etc.
  在市场经济条件下，政府和企业界相互依赖。因此，为了经济和国家的福利，他们要按照法律法规相互影响和补充。具体而言，政府试图通过经济杠杆和产业政策直接和间接地规定组织能做什么、不能做什么，确定商业条例。同时，商界会要求政府创造公平竞争的环境，并提供公共产品，等等。

第二十八章

国内政治

*

如今，政治不再仅仅是政治家、经济学家和教授关注的专业。事实上，我们普通民众也日益成为业余的政治家。而且，我们似乎比政府公职人员更加了解政治与社会问题及其解决方案。为此，我们都需要熟悉相关理论、政策、专业术语和表达。

Chapter Twenty-eight

Domestic Politics

*

Nowadays, politics is no longer the subject reserved for politicians, economists and professors. As a matter of fact, we ordinary people are becoming amateur politicians. And, we seem to have more visions and solutions to political and social problems than those in government or in office. For that matter, we all have to be familiar with relevant theories, policies, technical terms and expressions.

Part One　Things to Know

01

Whether we like it or not, government plays an overriding role in our daily lives, ranging from the amount of tax we pay for our commodities, to the services we're to buy. When we're living, working or doing business in another country along the Belt and Road, we have to know about its political system, party politics, laws and regulations, industrial policies, and know how those legislative processes work. We need to know who make these laws, and how they would impact us. When we can manage all these issues, we would be able to determine the best actions to take for ourselves, for our family, for our career, and for our institutions.

不管我们喜欢与否，政府在我们的日常生活中始终扮演着极其重要的角色，从我们购物需要支付的税款，到我们购买的服务，政府的影子可谓无所不在。因此，我们在“一带一路”伙伴国家生活、工作或做生意期间，必须了解该国政治制度、政党政治、法律法规、产业政策，并且了解其运作过程。我们需要知道由谁制定这些法律，这些法律对我们有什么影响。只有弄清楚所有这些问题，我们才能够为自己、为家庭、为事业、为所属机构发展制定最好的行动方案。

02

It's an international norm that sound economic and social development depend very much on three pillars. The first is the shared commitment to the market economy, which would give full play to the private-sector-led economic growth. The second is the sound stewardship of the natural and human resources, so as to ensure that the social wealth from the national development would be shared by the people across the board. The third is the tangible social progress, which would effectively promote peoples' living standards, and ensure their rights to participate in national politics.

依据国际范例，良好的经济和社会发展很大程度上取决于三大支柱。其一是坚持对市场经济的共同承诺，充分发挥私营部门主导的经济增长。其二是对自然资源和人力资源的合理开发和应用，确保国民经济发展的财富惠及全国人民。其三是切实的社会进步，有效提高人民的生活水平，并保障他们参与国家政治活动的权利。

03

There are many democracies around the world, but a true democracy must be at par with three benchmarks. First, the government must facilitate conditions for the sustainable economic growth and social progress. Second, it has to consistently improve people's living standards. Third, it is to maintain its economic competitiveness both at home and abroad.

世界上有许多民主国家，但一个真正的民主国家必须符合下列三个标准。第一，政府必须为可持续经济增长和社会进步创造条件。第二，政府必须努力提高人民的生活水平。第三，政府必须保持在国内外经济的竞争力。

04

It's becoming a consensus by the international community that a good political system has to be, in line with the national situation. It must be built on the foundation of governance, transparency and the rule of law. It must

ensure the interests from the national development would benefit people at large, and the smooth transfer of national power in line with the constitution.
国际社会正在逐渐形成共识：一个良好的政治制度必须符合本国国情，必须建立在良政、透明和法治的基础之上，必须确保国家发展利益惠及广大民众，必须确保国家政权依据宪法平稳移交。

05

In terms of national development, a responsible government must strive to establish its national economic structure, in accordance with the natural and human endowments. It must establish the macro economic regulatory system to ensure the relative stable growth of the national economy. Experts say the worst scenario for any government is the frequent and excessive fluctuation of its national economy.
在国家发展方面，一个负责任的政府必须建立符合本国自然和人力资源禀赋的经济结构。政府需要建立宏观经济调控体系，确保国民经济相对稳定增长。专家说，一个政府面临的最坏境况莫过于国民经济频繁、大幅度波动。

06

In the field of social service, visionary national leaders should promote sustainable economic growth and social progress, which would help their people to effectively benefit from available jobs, disposable income and social services, etc.
在社会服务领域，具有真知灼见的国家领导人应推动可持续的经济增长和社会进步，促进国民在就业机会、可支配收入、社会服务等领域实实在在地受益。

07

It's true that democracies in many countries have become hostages of the

party politics and established interest groups. General elections are dominated by the candidates backed up by the financial tycoons and social elites. Ordinary people are only sought after during the campaigns and on the voting day.
事实表明，如今许多国家的民主政体受制于政党政治和既得利益集团。大选则被金融大亨和社会精英支持的候选人所把持。普通民众只是在竞选期间和投票日受到追捧。

08

In some countries, once the political parties or leaders win the national power, their utmost efforts would be to consolidate the power base and prepare for re-election, while the party in opposition or candidates would try in every way to defeat the ruling party or the leader in office.
在一些国家，政党或领导人一旦赢得国家权力，就会全力以赴巩固政权并争取连任。与之相对应，反对党或候选人则会竭尽全力击败执政党或领导人。

09

Equally important, no democracy is sustainable unless the government joins hand with its people, in order to advance economic growth and social progress. To be specific, there would be no real democracy when a country is still underdeveloped, or when the social wealth is increasingly flowing into the hands of business tycoons and social elites.
同样重要的是，除非政府携手本国民众，促进经济增长和社会进步，否则任何民主制度都不可能持续。具体而言，一个国家如果长期得不到发展，或者社会财富日益流入商业大亨和社会精英的手中，就无法实现真正的民主。

10

COVID-19, which happened at the end of 2019, fully exposed the soft spots of many quasi-democracies around the world. Many governments failed to implement policies to bring the deadly virus under control, and allowed their nations to slide into the double quagmire of pandemic and economic recession.

2019年底发生的COVID-19疫情，充分暴露了世界上许多假民主国家的软肋。许多国家政府未能制定政策有效控制这种致命的病毒，导致本国深深陷入疫情蔓延和经济衰退“双陷阱”。

11

It's a lesson for many developing countries that critical mass of capital is a must for realizing or maintaining tangible economic growth. National governments have to effectively address this issue, either through continuous economic development, or through sustainable expansion of foreign trade.

要想实现或保持可持续的经济增长，必须积累并拥有一定规模的民族资本，这对许多发展中国家来说都是教训。各国政府必须实现持续的经济发展或持续扩大对外贸易，方可有效解决这一问题。

12

It's also a lesson that international production chains and supply chains are both blessings and curses for the developing countries. On the one hand, those global chains are the necessary platforms for them to take part in international division of labor, and to expedite their economic growth. On the other hand, most developing countries have literally become the dumping grounds for the products and services by the transnational corporations. Worse still, they may become the victims of the depletion of natural resources and environment degradation.

还有一个教训：对发展中国家来说，国际生产链和供应链是福也是祸。

一方面，这些全球链条是发展中国家企业参与国际分工、加快经济增长的必要平台。另一方面，大多数发展中国家实际上已经成为跨国公司工业产品的倾销地。更为糟糕的是，这些国家可能成为自然资源枯竭和环境退化的受害者。

13

In sustainable nation building, there are many lessons for the developing countries to learn. First and foremost, governments have to avoid over ambitious projects which would suck off the already scarce capital used to create something tangible for the people. It’s a common phenomenon that many countries in the South would build grand stadiums, government office buildings and parliament buildings at the tax payers’ money.

关于可持续的国家建设，发展中国家必须吸取教训。首先，政府必须避免野心勃勃的项目，因为这些项目会吸走原本可望用来为人民创造实实在在利益的稀缺资源。一个普遍的现象是，南方许多国家将纳税人的钱用于修建超级体育场馆、政府办公大楼和国会大厦。

14

Meanwhile, governments have to select appropriate industries to place their national capital and the FDI. However, many governments have opened up too many economic sectors and launched too many projects that are beyond the stages of their development. Worse still, many projects failed to realize their initial goals, many others died halfway through the construction, which in turn worsened the national debt.

与此同时，政府必须选择合适的产业来投放国家资本和外国直接投资。然而，很多国家政府开放了太多的经济部门，启动了太多的合作项目，超出了其发展阶段需求。更糟糕的是，很多项目不能实现预期目标，还有很多项目在建设过程中成为烂尾工程，因而加重了国家债务负担。

15

Green development is a new mode of economic growth and social development, which aims at efficiency, harmony and sustainability. Since the 21st century, it has become an important trend of the global economy. Many countries take the green industry as an important measure to promote economic restructuring, highlighting the concept of green. Green development and sustainable development are in the same line of thought. It is not only the inheritance of sustainable development, but also the theoretical innovation of sustainable development in China. It is also a major theoretical contribution of China, in terms addressing the global ecological and environmental deterioration, which conforms to the evolution law of historical trend.

绿色发展是以效率、和谐、持续为目标的经济增长和社会发展方式。21世纪以来，绿色发展已成为全球经济发展的新趋势。许多国家把发展绿色产业作为推动经济结构调整的重要举措，突出绿色的理念。绿色发展与可持续发展在思想上是一脉相承的，既是对可持续发展的继承，也是可持续发展中国化的理论创新，还是中国应对全球生态环境恶化客观现实的重大理论贡献，符合历史潮流的演进规律。

16

In terms of FDI, many countries have wasted large amounts of foreign exchange, natural resources and human capital by constantly importing advanced technologies and production lines that are beyond their capabilities to master or absorb, which also resulted in the oversupply of products at the domestic markets. According to one report by the African Union, over the past 50 years or so, countries on the continent have spent billions of US dollars on the state-of-the-art technologies from outside, and received hundreds of technical assistances projects. Yet, few countries have realized their rapid industrialization and sustainable development.

在引进国际直接投资领域，许多国家不断引进超出本国产业吸收能力的先进技术和生产线，浪费了大量外汇、自然资源和人力资本，也造成国内市场产品供应过剩。根据非洲联盟的一份报告，在过去50年左右的时间里，非洲大陆的许多国家在国外的先进技术上花费了数十亿美元，并接受了数百个技术合作项目。然而，很少有国家实现了它们的快速工业化和可持续发展。

17

It’s true that the whole world is embracing the era of the dot.com economy. When the fourth industrial revolution is around the corner, countries around the world have to fasten their seat belts for both opportunities and challenges. Opportunity wise, they can take stock from the 5G and AI technologies to further modernize their industries and promote economic growth. Challenge wise, they have to constantly spend hard currency to develop or import new technologies and production lines, which would stretch thin their national capital, and drive some countries into sovereign debt traps.

毫无疑问，我们正在拥抱网络经济的时代。第四次工业革命即将到来，世界各国都必须系紧安全带，迎接机遇与挑战。从机遇方面讲，各国可以充分利用5G和人工智能技术进一步实现工业现代化，促进经济增长。从挑战方面讲，各国需要不断花费外汇研发或引进新技术和生产线，因而将给国家资本增添压力，并导致一些国家陷入债务陷阱。

18

Nowadays, political systems in the Western countries have been hijacked by the party politics and vested interest groups. National strategies and industrial policies have been fluctuating due to the constant changes of the national leaders or government in power, in line with the political cycles. General elections have become the critical links, by which political parties would compete with one another for the voters, either to win the national power or retain power. Whichever party is in power, it would spend more time on how

to retain power, rather than on the long-term interests of economic growth and social progress or overriding human and natural disasters.
如今，西方国家的政治制度已被政党政治和既得利益集团所掌握。国家领导人或当权政府时常更换，导致国家战略和产业政策波动日益加剧。大选已成为各有关政党赢得权力或保持权力而相互竞争选民的关键环节。无论哪个政党执政，都将更多的时间花费在如何保住权力上，而不是聚焦经济增长和社会进步等长远利益，或是应对人为或自然灾害上。

19

Many political systems around the world have demonstrated one fact that, in order to demonstrate the difference in governance, the new ruling party or national leader would always nullify the political agendas left by the previous ruling party or the former leader. Similarly, they would drastically readjust economic or social policies, and put on hold the agreements with the foreign countries. This would result in the periodical fluctuations of both domestic or foreign policies.
全球许多政治制度都表明了一个事实：为了显示其执政理念的不同，新执政党或国家领导人往往会取消前执政党或领导人留下的政治议程。同样，他们也会大幅度调整经济或社会政策，或终止与外国的协议。这些政策举措必将导致国内外政策呈现周期性波动。

20

Since the end of World War II, the US economy has long been the powerhouse of the global economy, and many countries used to take stock from its market, capital, technology and industrial chains for the economic growth. However, since the 21st century, the US economic engine has been losing steam as its annual growth has been slow, and the international credibility of the US dollar has been down sliding.
第二次世界大战结束以来，美国经济在很长时间里是全球经济的动力源，许多国家曾经从该国市场、资本、技术和产业链中获取经济增长的动力。但是，进入21世纪以来，由于经济年度增长放缓，美元国际信誉下滑，美国作为经济引擎正逐渐失去动力。

Part Two　Situational Dialogues

01

A: Well, I've been doing my dissertation entitled *Opportunities and Challenges for Developing Countries During the Post Era of Financial Crisis* for my MA Degree. I wonder if you could give me some advice in this regard. I know you are an expert in macroeconomics.

嗯，我正在撰写硕士学位论文，题目是《后金融危机时期发展中国家的机遇和挑战》。我想请您在这方面给我一些建议。我知道您是宏观经济学专家。

B: First of all, let me congratulate you on your endeavor. Of course, it's my pleasure to help you out to my level of the best. According to what I know, these are the things you need to look into. First, rapid process of industrialization has elevated the capacity of many countries to produce more commodities and services for both domestic consumption and for exports. Second, more and more manufacturing industries have generated more jobs which have allowed the growth of middle-class contingents. These two factors have provided the steam for many developing countries to maintain the momentum of economic growth even during the 2008 international financial crisis. Third, many developing countries are still in the middle of endowment exploitation and expansion, during which some countries could still maintain the momentum of economic growth for some time. Fourth, e-commerce would increase the knowledge "spill-over" benefits from the developed countries to the developing countries, which would exert significant impacts on innovation and productivity for the developing countries. Last but not least, the primary industries in many developing countries would not require much R&D expenditures on the technology renovation.

首先，祝贺你的努力。当然，我很高兴能尽力帮助你。据我所知，下列这些是你需要聚焦的。第一，快速工业化提高了许多国家为国内消费和出口生产更多商品和服务的能力。第二，越来越多的制造业创造了更多的就业机会，进而使得中产阶级队伍得以发展壮大。这两个因素使得许多发展中国家即使在2008年国际金融危机中仍能够保持经济增长势头。第三，许多发展中国家仍处于资源禀赋开发和扩张的阶段。一些国家还可以保持一段时间的发展势头。第四，电子商务增加了发达国家向发展中国家的知识利益溢出，对发展中国家的创新和生产力可望产生重大影响。最后，许多发展中国家的第一产业并不需要投入太多的资金进行技术革新。

A: Thank you very much for your advice, but what about the challenges?

非常感谢您的建议，那么，关于挑战方面呢？

B: Let me see, I will give you three points for reference. First, many developing countries have been implementing the regulatory and legal systems, which are not conducive to their economic growth. Second, as many transnational corporations have been withdrawing their capital from the host countries over the recent years, relevant destination countries are faced with less and less financial options. Third, mobile payment system, along with other online payment systems, have played a significant role in the growth of e-commerce around the world. However, this new trend is just too far beyond the reach of the people in developing countries.

让我想想，我给你三点建议供参考。首先，许多发展中国家一直在实行不利于经济增长的监管和法律制度。第二，由于近年来许多跨国公司从东道国撤出资金，相关国家可加利用的财政收入选择越来越少。第三，移动支付系统和其他在线支付系统在全球电子商务的发展中发挥了重要作用。然而，这一新趋势是许多发展中国家的国民无法企及的。

02

A: Some developing countries have managed to maintain the trend of economic growth and realize industrialization, while many others are still bogged down in the scenario of “middle-income trap”. What’s your take, Professor Edwin?

一些发展中国家一方面保持了相对快速的经济增长趋势并实现了工业化，但另外许多国家则仍挣扎于“中等收入陷阱”之中。这个问题您怎么看，埃德温教授?

B: Well, let me give you a short answer to your question. Generally speaking, many developing countries are still struggling in the middle-income traps in three areas. The first is the development modality trap, which is clearly demonstrated in the traditional land system, tax and revenue system, economic system, financial system and the social system, etc. The second is the development system trap, which is relating to the ever-widening gap between the urban and rural areas, between the rich and poor, among different social groups, which have become the stumbling blocks for many governments to push for the sustainable strategies and policies. The third is the technology trap. Due to the lack of financial capability as well as human capital, the key industries of many developing countries are dominated by transnational corporations, while the national companies have to spend the meager annual income to repeatedly import the technologies, critical component parts and operational systems.

让我简短地回答你的问题。总体而言，许多发展中国家仍在三个中等收入陷阱中挣扎。一是发展模式陷阱，主要表现在传统的土地制度、税收制度、经济制度、财政制度和社会制度等。二是发展体制陷阱，城乡差距、贫富差距、社会群体差距的不断扩大，已成为许多国家政府推动可持续战略和政策的绊脚石。三是技术陷阱。由于缺乏财政能力和人力资本，许多国家的关键产业被跨国公司所掌控，本国公司不得不定期花费微薄的国民收入重复进口先进技术、关键部件和操作系统。

03

A: Currently, your country has been moving forward in full steam in realizing the two centennial goals, but it's also faced with mounting challenges, especially in terms of the security with your neighbors. What's your take?
目前，贵国正在全速实现两个百年目标，但贵国也面临着越来越多的挑战，特别是在与周边国家的安全问题上。这个问题您怎么看？

B: Thank you for the question, and please allow me to take this opportunity to share with you what I have in mind. China is fully aware that the critical issue of peace and security are the two preconditions for the realization of the two centennial goals. Currently, China is faced with the following security issues. First, it's the strategic threat by some major countries headed by the United States, which has listed China as their primary competitor. Second, it's the legacy of the on-going competition over the sovereign rights over the islets and the territorial waters in the South China Sea between China and the claimant countries. When the US chooses to stir up the troubled water, the disputes are becoming more complicated. The third is the risk relating to the Korean Peninsula, which you all know for sure. The fourth is that the cross-strait relations are still the tough issues in terms of China's dream to realize national rejuvenation. The fifth is the instability in some neighboring countries, where domestic political, economic and social turmoil would produce ripple effects on China's security environment. Last but not least, it's the on-going non-traditional security issues that warrant closer cooperation between China and all the stakeholders, in order to promote common development, and maintain the regional peaceful environment.

谢谢你的提问，我想借此机会谈谈我的一些想法。中国充分认识到，和平与安全是关键问题，这是中国实现两个百年规划的两个先决条件。当前，中国正面临以下安全问题。一是以美国为首的一些主要国家的战略威胁，它们将中国列为主要竞争对手。二是中国与声索国之间在南海岛屿和领海主权的遗留问题上的矛盾。美国刻意挑起事端，致使地区和平稳定变得更加复杂。三是朝鲜半岛问题的风险，这个问题你们都很清楚。四是两岸关系依旧是中国实现民族伟大复兴的关键问题。五是周边一些国家政局不稳，国内政治、经济、社会动荡，对中国安全环境可能产生“蝴蝶效应”。最后，当前非传统安全问题持续存在，中国需要与有关各国加强合作，促进共同发展，维护地区和平环境。

04

A: Well, the Belt and Road Initiative has been in progress for years now. Could you kindly share with us what are the areas of cooperation that your government has been promoting?

“一带一路”倡议已经推进很多年了。您能否介绍一下贵国政府正在哪些方面推进合作？

B: That's a good question. As far as I know, Chinese government has launched bilateral and regional cooperation programs with the partner countries in the following areas. First, it's the joint construction of infrastructure, which would allow partner countries to unify their national markets for the future development. Second, it's the two-way trade, which would help partner countries to increase their domestic and foreign trade. Third, it's the two-way investment. When more and more

Chinese capital, in conjunction with the international capital, flows into the partner countries, they would be able to renovate their manufacturing and processing industries, taking stock from the Chinese market, capital, technology transfers as well as the Chinese corporate managerial know-how. Fourth, it's the cooperation in mature industrial technologies, which would help the partner countries elevate their manufacturing capacities, and up-lift their national productivity and competitiveness. I could go on with the list, but these are the major areas, where the BRI is increasingly known by the international community.

这个问题提得好。据我了解，中国政府与伙伴国在以下方面开展了双边和区域合作。首先是在基础设施领域进行合作，旨在促使伙伴国家整合本国市场，以利于未来的发展。二是双向贸易，这将有助于伙伴国家增加他们的国内外贸易。三是双向投资。随着越来越多的中国资本投向伙伴国家，后者可从中国市场、资本、技术转移以及中国企业管理知识等方面获得外部动力。第四，成熟的工业技术合作有助于提升伙伴国家的制造能力，帮助后者提高本国生产力和竞争力。我还可以列举更多的例子，但这些是影响“一带一路”在国际上提高知名度的主要因素。

Part Three　Common Expressions

- How much did the private sector contribute to your annual GDP last year?
  去年你们国家的私营部门对GDP的贡献额是多少？

- In general, the government of a sovereign country would select the leading industrial sector as the focus of national strategy, according to its resource endowments, capital, technical strength, which would provide steam for the development of other sectors. Therefore, the industrial policy roughly plays the following role.

  总而言之，主权国家的政府会根据其资源禀赋、资本、技术实力来选择主导产业部门，引导国民经济其他部门的发展。因此，产业政策大致发挥下列作用。
- The first is to regulate economic structure. Through the national development guidelines, the governments are to adjust their industrial structure nationwide, and facilitate conditions for the various industries, enterprises and regions to gain fair access to the factors of production, optimize economic scale, and promote the internal and external economic balance.

  一是调整经济结构。依据国家发展方针，政府会调整产业结构和全国布局，为各行业、企业和地区公平获取生产要素提供条件，优化经济规模，促进国内外经济平衡。
- The second is to promote the long-term economic development. By adjusting the industrial structure, governments are to optimize the allocation of resources, promote the steady growth of the national economy, balance the economic development between urban and rural areas, and realize the harmonious development of economy, society, people’s livelihood and ecology.

  二是促进经济长期发展。通过产业结构调整，政府优化资源配置，促进国民经济稳定增长，平衡城乡经济发展，实现经济、社会、民生与生态和谐发展。
- The third is to regulate the consumption behavior of government institutions, companies and citizens alike. Based on the adjustment of the market mechanism, they have to influence the immediate and long-term

consumption behaviors of the companies and citizens alike via commercial interest rate, taxation, local currency exchange rate, fiscal transfer and the construction of large-scale civil projects, which would ensure the benefits of economic development would be shared by the people at large, and promote economic growth from the consumption side.
三是调控政府机关、企业和国民的消费行为。以市场机制的调节为依据，通过商业利率、税收、本币汇率、财政转移和大型民生工程建设，来影响公司和国民的即期和长远消费行为，保障经济发展利益惠及广大民众，从消费端促进经济增长。

- The fourth is to influence the market supply. The governments are to promote or restrict the development of certain industries according to their domestic human and natural endowment, reform their industrial structure, adjust the relationship between various industries, in an effort to achieve the balance in supply and demand, domestic trade and foreign trade, and promote the sustainable development of national economy.
四是影响市场供给。依据本国人力和自然禀赋，促进或限制某些产业的发展，改造产业结构，调整各产业之间的相互关系，以努力实现供给和需求的总量平衡、内外贸平衡，促进国民经济可持续发展。
- Looking back at China's domestic politics in 2020, these are the outstanding achievements we could take pride on. First, the government succeeded in bringing COVID-19 under control in a matter of three months, and became the only major economy in the world to achieve positive economic growth. Second, China managed to achieve the goal of building a moderately prosperous society in all respects, and fully completed the goals of the 13th Five-Year Guideline. Third, China managed to achieve the strategic goal of poverty alleviation national wide. Fourth, China's per capita GDP exceeded US $10000, allowing China to join the rank of middle-and-high-income countries. Fifth, China successfully signed the regional free trade area agreement RCEP, and the

Bilateral Investment Agreement with the EU. Sixth, China managed to retain its position as the largest trading nation. Seventh, China managed to complete the 5G network construction covering most of the prefecture-level cities. Eighth, China accelerated the pace to become a scientific and technological power. For example, the global navigation network, Beidou, was completed and open to pubilc service, and Shenwu successfully collected lunar soil and returned to the Earth.

回顾2020年中国国内政治，有下列重大事宜值得关注。其一，中国政府与各族人民共克时艰，战胜新冠肺炎疫情，并成为全球范围唯一实现经济正增长的主要经济体。其二，中国宣告实现了全面建成小康社会的目标，全面完成了“十三五”的规划目标。其三，中国实现了全民脱贫的战略目标。其四，人均国民收入超过10000美元，进入中高收入国家行列。其五，中国成功推动商签RCEP自贸区协定并与欧盟签署双边投资协定。其六，中国成功保住了最大贸易国家的地位。其七，5G网络成功覆盖绝大部分地级城市。其八，中国加快成为科技强国的步伐，北斗全球导航网络建成并投入运营，神五成功采集月壤并返回地球。

第二十九章

国际经济

*

在全球化推动下，世界正日益成为一个“地球村”。跨国公司正在把生产链、价值链和供应链延伸到任何有生产要素可供利用的地方，或任何可寻求和维持市场份额的地方。同样，商品和服务在线上和线下都可以获得。信息可以通过互联网在任何地方获得。与此同时，拥有知识、天赋、技能以及工作语言的人比以往任何时候都拥有更好的职业前景。然而，你准备好了吗？

Chapter Twenty-nine

International Economy

*

Propelled by the globalization, the world is becoming a "global village". Transnational corporations have been extending their production chains, value chains and supply chains to any countries where the factors of production are available or any places where, they can seek or maintain market shares. Likewise, goods and services are available both on line and off line. Information could be available anywhere via the Internet. And, people with knowledge, talents, skills as well as the working language would have better careers than any time before. Nevertheless, are you prepared?

Part One　Things to Know

01

In general, the global economy today comprises several characteristics. The first is that globalization has become the primary force for the growth via the global networks of trade, investment, technologies, information, and transportation. Consequently, national economies have become more cohesive via global production chains, value chains and supply chains, as well as the regional economic integration.

总的来说，当今的全球经济有几个特点。一是全球化通过全球贸易、投资、技术、信息和交通网络成为推动全球经济增长的主要动力。因此，各国经济在全球生产链、价值链、供应链和区域经济一体化作用下，联系更加紧密。

02

The second is international trade, which has become an important component part of globalization. From the micro perspective, international trade provides partner countries with more business and employment opportunities, enables consumers to enjoy more goods and services, and helps the partner countries in raising the living standards of the people. From the macro perspective, it helps the partner countries to specialize in goods and service production, in accordance with their absolute or comparative advantages, in order to enlarge

their economic scales, improve productivity, increase competitiveness, etc.
二是国际贸易。国际贸易已成为全球化的重要组成部分。从微观层面考察，国际贸易能给伙伴国家带来更多商业和就业机会，有助于各国消费者获得更多的商品和服务，帮助伙伴国家提升人民生活水平。从宏观角度考察，国际贸易有助于伙伴国家发挥各自的绝对优势或比较优势，来生产和提供产品和服务，以扩大其经济规模，提高生产力，提升竞争力，等等。

03

The third is international finance, which is an important vehicle for companies to carry out business operation beyond their borders. When the local markets become fully competitive, some companies would extend their production and service networks into the international market via production chains and supply chains, which requires large scale financial input. With international financing, when companies produce products in the destination countries, they could benefit from the cost advantage or skilled labor supply. Furthermore, when companies outsource their production and processing links to the destination countries, they could concentrate their efforts in R&D and high-end production and marketing. Finally, companies could establish production lines in different countries and produce different products, which would benefit from diversified production.
三是国际金融。国际金融是公司在境外开展业务的重要载体。在面对本地市场的竞争激烈时，一些公司会通过生产链和供应链将其生产和服务网络扩展到国际市场，这就需要更多的资金投入。借助国际融资，公司在目的地国家生产和销售产品，可降低生产成本获得充足或熟练劳动力供应。此外，这些企业可选择将生产和加工环节外包给目的地国家，以便集中精力进行新产品研发、高端制造和营销活动。最后，企业还可以在不同的国家建立生产线，生产不同的产品，从多元化生产中获益。

04

The fourth is the global investment. Like international trade, international investment is critical for companies to expand their networks of production and services, enlarge their economic scales and elevate their competitiveness. In addition to exporting business, corporations can access new customers in the foreign markets, and become multinationals during the process. Generally speaking, cross boundary investment mainly takes the form of direct investment, which is aiming at controlling ownership of a business in another country. Many Chinese companies have been venturing out into the destination countries via direct investment along the Belt and Road.

四是全球投资。同国际贸易一样，国际投资对公司扩大生产和服务网络、扩大经济规模和提高竞争力至关重要。除了出口，企业还可以在国外市场获得新的客户，并在上述过程中成为跨国公司。一般而言，跨境投资主要通过直接投资形式进行，以期在东道国的目标企业中拥有控制权。中国的许多公司正通过直接投资进入“一带一路”沿线国家的市场。

05

Generally speaking, foreign direct investment flows to the economies, which would offer competitive workforce and above-average growth prospects for the investors. On the other hand, the FDI often brings in more than just the capital investment. It may include the transfer of technologies, overseas market access and business managerial know-how.

一般说来，外国直接投资通常流向能够提供有竞争力的劳动力和高于平均水平增长前景的经济体。另一方面，外国直接投资往往不仅仅是资本投资。它还可以包括技术、海外市场机会和商业管理知识的转让。

06

In general, the FDI appears in three forms: Horizontal, vertical and mixed. Horizontal FDI refers to the establishment of the same type of business by the transnational corporations in another country, while vertical FDI is to establish a related but different type of business in another country. Mixed FDI is to establish an unrelated business venture in the destination country. Apple’s investment in China is a typical example.

一般来说，外国直接投资主要有三种类型：横向型、垂直型和混合型。横向型投资是指跨国公司在另一个国家建立相同类型的企业，而垂直型投资是在另一个国家建立相关但不同类型的企业。混合型投资是指与东道国伙伴企业建立不同的企业。苹果公司在中国的投资就是一个典型例证。

07

From the perspective of market entry, FDI investors would venture into destination countries via the following channels. Firstly, they would incorporate a wholly-owned subsidiary or company in any country where they spot the potentials for profit. Secondly, they would acquire shares in an associated enterprise, which is easy to gain access to the market in the destination. Thirdly, they would gain control of an unrelated enterprise via merger or acquisition. Fourthly, they would participate in an equity joint venture with another investor or enterprise in the host country.

从市场进入的角度来看，外国直接投资的投资者通过以下几个渠道进入东道国市场。第一，他们会在有盈利潜力的地方成立一个全资子公司或分公司。第二，他们会收购联营企业的股份，以期轻松地进入外国市场。第三，他们会通过合并或收购的方式获得非相关企业的控制权。第四，它们将与另一投资者或企业在东道国组建一个合资企业。

08

Looking back into the history of national economic development, foreign direct investment is critical for the developing countries. Their companies need foreign funding and expertise to expand the production and marketing

scales. Meanwhile, the governments need foreign investment to boost manufacturing and processing industries, in order to create more jobs, modernize their economies, and elevate their productivity, etc.
回顾国家经济发展历史可发现，外国直接投资对发展中国家至关重要。它们的公司需要吸纳跨国资金和专业知识来扩大生产和市场规模。与此同时，这些国家的政府需要吸引外资发展制造业和加工业，以期创造更多的就业机会，促进经济现代化，并提高生产力等。

09

As a matter of fact, developed economies also need FDI, but their companies compete for it for different reasons. Most of these investments move across the borders through mergers and acquisitions between mature companies. Investment from these transnational corporations is either for restructuring or refocusing on core businesses, for the sake of market share, extension of life expectancy of technologies, products and production lines, etc.
事实上，发达经济体也需要外国直接投资，但它们的企业需要投资的原因各不相同。大多投资通过成熟公司之间的合并和收购进行。这些跨国公司投资旨在重组或重新聚焦核心业务，获得市场份额，延长技术、产品和生产线的预期寿命等。

10

Science knows no borders, and innovation has no limits. During the post 2008 international financial crisis era, it’s more important for the international community to move forward hand in hand, in order to address the challenges side by side, to promote common development, and to carry out technical cooperation via joint research and development, which are dedicating to the advancement of the global scientific and technological innovation, national economic growth, and the formulation of the community of shared future for economic development.

科学没有国界，创新没有极限。2008年后金融危机时代，国际社会更加需要携手前进，肩并肩应对挑战，以期促进共同发展，通过联合研发实现科技合作，致力于全球科技创新发展、国家经济增长和经济发展命运共同体的构建。

11

Since the 21st century, the global economy has been changing significantly in the way that is organized and governed. These changes would not only affect the flow of goods and services among countries around the world, but also the migration of people. Generally speaking, people choose to move into other countries, in order to improve their economic situation, or to escape from civil strife, persecution, and environmental disasters. However, globalization has introduced a third set of motivations called “network” factors, which includes the free flow of companies, production lines, and human capital, etc.
21世纪以来，全球经济组织管理方式上发生了重大变化。这些变化不仅影响到世界各国之间货物和服务的流动，而且也影响到人员的迁移。一般来说，人们选择移居他国，是为了改善经济状况，或是为了逃避内乱、迫害和环境灾难。然而，全球化引入了第三种动机，称为“网络”因素，其中包括公司、生产线和人力资本的自由流动等。

12

Based on China’s experience in attracting FDI, developing countries should design and implement long-term strategies, in line with their national situations. From the positive side, foreign direct investment would help diversify sources of capital. It would help seek stable and long-term capital input. It would provide critical capital to economic sectors in need of renovation and expansion. And, it would also provide technology as well as the managerial know-how, in order to expedite their national economic development.

依据中国吸引外资的经验，发展中国家应根据本国国情制定和实施长期战略。从积极的方面来看，外国直接投资有助于实现资本来源多样化，有助于寻求稳定和长期的资本投入，并为需要革新和扩大的经济部门提供资金。此外，外国直接投资还将提供技术和管理知识，加快东道国经济发展。

13

However, the developing countries must be fully aware of the following negative impacts. The first is that FDI is not suitable for strategically important industries. The second is that FDI owners may have less moral attachment. The third is that FDI enterprises may enter and occupy the markets of the destination countries at the expense of the domestic counterparts. Last but not least, FDI enterprises may end up dominating the life lines of the key industries of the host countries.

然而，各发展中国家必须充分认识到吸引外资可能产生的消极影响。第一，具有重要战略意义的行业不应吸纳太多的外国直接投资。第二，外国直接投资所有者可能不会遵循那么多的道德标准。第三，外国直接投资企业可能会以牺牲本国同行的利益为代价进入并占领东道国市场。最后，外国直接投资企业最终可能垄断东道国关键产业的生命线。

14

There has been a new scenario that more and more national governments are increasingly dependent on monetary tools to promote economic growth or maintain the momentum of economic development. However, over-reliance on monetary policy have led to the contraction of productivity growth. It is because banks would be less interested in lending to businesses in the real economic sector, favoring firms that are not credit-constrained. Since the 21st century, this trend is clearly demonstrated in the major developed economies such as the United States.

现在出现了一种新的局面，越来越多的国家愈发依靠货币工具来促进经济增长或保持经济发展。然而，过度依赖货币政策会降低生产力增长。因为银行对实体经济企业放贷的兴趣会减弱，转而青睐那些不受信贷约束的企业。21世纪以来，这种态势在美国等发达经济体表现得尤其明显。

15

From the postmortem perspective, over the past decades, developed economies have been applying quantitative easing (QE) policies, whereby central banks keep purchasing the government bonds or other financial assets, in order to inject more real money into the economy, in an effort to boost economic activities. However, the bulk of the liquidity would not go to the enterprises in the real economy but to the investment banks, future markets and investors at the stock market, as well as the mortgage and stock markets of the emerging economies, blowing up the bubbles there.

从事后分析的角度来看，在过去几十年里，发达经济体市场实施量化宽松政策，中央银行持续购买政府债券或其他金融资产，向本国经济注入更多资金，以期刺激经济活动。然而，大部分流动性并未流向实体经济企业，而是流向了投资银行、期货市场和股票市场的投资者，以及新兴经济体的抵押贷款和股票市场，从而加重了经济泡沫现象。

16

Currently, advanced and emerging markets have been embracing the fourth industrial revolution, during which the balance between technology integration, human capital investments and the innovative ecosystem will be critical for them to grasp the opportunity of the first-mover advantage. With the right skills and training, workers can become the major factors of production for national development. Therefore, governments investment in human capital is no longer a dispensable matter, but the bedrocks of the future growth.

当前，发达国家和新兴市场正在拥抱第四次工业革命。其间，在技术整合、人力资本投资和创新生态系统之间找到平衡至关重要，旨在未来实现国家先发优势。经过培训和具有技能的各界工人可以成为国家发展的重要因素。因此，人力资本投资不再是可有可无的选项，而是确保未来经济增长的基石。

17

Against the backdrop of globalization, economic scale, productivity and competitiveness are still the keys for the government to promote national development, and elevate people's living standards. Meanwhile, policymakers also have to look at the speed, direction and quality of economic growth at the dawn of the fourth industrial revolution. More importantly, sustainable economic growth remains a critical way out for all the developing countries to fight against poverty, promote social progress and protect environment, which are the preconditions for the international community to build the shared prosperity and manage the transition to the green economy.

在全球化的背景下，经济规模、生产力和竞争力仍然是政府推动国家发展和提高人民生活水平的关键。与此同时，在第四次工业革命之际，政策制定者仍需关注经济增长速度、方向和质量。更重要的是，可持续经济增长是各发展中国家消除贫困、促进社会进步和保护环境的重要出路，也是国际社会实现共同繁荣、绿色经济转型的前提条件。

18

When it comes to climate change, the traditional mainstream view has been that equality or sustainability must be at the expense of economic growth. Nevertheless, the lack of shared prosperity and environmental sustainability would be detrimental to productivity growth. Moreover, countries around the world should focus not just at the speed of economic growth, but also at its direction, which is geared to the environment sustainability and the shared prosperity.

在气候变化问题上，传统主流观点认为，平等或可持续发展必须以经济增长为代价。然而，缺乏共享繁荣和环境可持续性将不利于生产力的提高。此外，世界各国不仅应注重经济增长的速度，而且还应注重经济增长的方向，旨在促进环境的可持续性和共同繁荣。

19

During the fourth industrial revolution and the pending green economy, national leaders and governments must have the visions to place all the economic development on a win-win trajectory. They should discard the mindset to trade off between the economic growth and environment protection, and switch to a long-term approach to the balance of the two. The severe global warming and worsening natural disasters are just the wake-up calls.

在第四次工业革命和即将到来的绿色经济中，国家领导人和中央政府必须有远见，把所有的经济发展置于双赢的轨道上。他们应该摒弃在经济增长和环境保护之间权衡的思维方式，而是采取长期的策略促进两者平衡发展。严重的全球气候变暖和不断恶化的自然灾害已经敲响警钟。

20

Due to various reasons, countries at different development stages are implementing different strategies and policies in terms of economic growth and environment protection. However, some developed economies have refused to take the initiatives in cutting down on harmful emissions, and provide technological assistance to the least developed countries. Worse still, the Trump administration simply walked away from *the Paris Accord*. The Biden administration has promised to return to the Accord, but it still remains to be seen whether the US would really shoulder its responsibility as the main stakeholder.

由于各种原因，处于不同发展阶段的国家在经济增长和环境保护方面正在实施不同的战略和政策。然而，一些发达经济体拒绝主动减排，拒绝向最不发达国家提供技术援助。更糟糕的是，特朗普政府直接退出了《巴黎协定》。拜登政府已承诺回归该协定，但美国是否会真正承担起作为主要利益相关者的责任，仍有待观察。

Part Two Situational Dialogues

01

A: Talking about the globalization, the developed countries have been losing steam in leading the growth and expansion of the world economy, since the 2008 international financial crisis. I wonder if you could share with us what are the reasons behind, Mr. Howard?

说到全球化，自2008年国际金融危机以来，发达国家在引领世界经济增长和扩张方面已经失去了动力。霍华德先生，请跟我们分享一下背后的原因，好吗?

B: Well, from my humble perspective, these are the main reasons behind the scenario. From the perspective of international trade, the developed economies used to be the driving force. They used to be the major markets. They used to enjoy the super consumption capacity due to their ever-growing middle class. They used to enjoy the technology advantage and provide new products and services. Nevertheless, since the international financial crisis in 2008, their economies have been mostly sluggish, which has resulted in the contraction of their capacities to import things from around the world, and the flattening of the consumption power of the middle classess. In addition, developed countries have been implementing policies to encourage exports and restrict imports via discriminating tariff walls or trade wars, which have become the stumbling blocks for the developing countries to tap into their market.

嗯，据我的观察，这背后有很多原因。从国际贸易领域考察，发达经济体曾是主导动力。它们曾经是主要的市场。由于中产阶级的不断壮大，它们曾经享有主要的消费能力。它们曾经享受制造和提供新产品和服务的技术。然而，自2008年金融危机以来，这些国家的经济大多疲软，导致其从世界各地进口产品的能力减弱，导致中产阶级消费能力的萎缩。此外，发达国家一直在实施鼓励出口政策，并通过歧视性关税政策或贸易战限制进口，这已成为发展中国家进入其市场的绊脚石。

A: I see. What has happened to their investment capacities, then?

我明白了。那么，它们的投资能力发生了什么变化呢？

B: Well, we could trace the scenario back to the 1970's when transnational corporations from the developed countries competed with one another to outsource their production lines, processing and service activities to the developing countries around the world. Of course, these activities did provide the steam for the latter to expand foreign trade and expedite their industrial development. However, since the 2008 financial crisis, the developed countries suddenly discovered that their real economies had been hollowed out, and the virtual economies had been too sick to be rehabilitated. As the last resort, many governments tried to rejuvenate the middle and high-end manufacturing sectors and “force” their national companies to redirect their capital investment back to their home countries, which immediately caused the reversed flows of international capital.

这个原因可以追溯到20世纪70年代，发达国家的跨国公司竞相将生产线、加工和服务活动外包到世界各地的发展中国家。当然，这种趋势确实为发展中国家提供了经济动力，助力其扩大对外贸易，发展工业。然而，自2008年国际金融危机以来，发达国家突然发现其本国实体经济已被掏空，且虚拟经济已病入膏肓，难以恢复。作为最后手段，许多政府试图振兴中高端制造业，“迫使”本国企业将资本投入到本国市场，这种政策立即导致国际资本倒流。

02

A: Since the turn of the 21st century, the international community has been bogged down by the scenario of “soft global governance”, especially in the economic field. What’s your take?

进入21世纪以来，国际社会普遍陷入“软全球治理”的困境，特别是在经济领域。请问您如何看待？

B: To my research findings, several reasons may have contributed to this scenario. First, the Breton Woods System which is represented by the World Bank, the IMF and the WTO, has been losing its credibility as the governance institutions, and it has lost in touch with the new trends of the world economy. Second, the above international institutions have been losing their political will as well as their capacity to act in accordance with the ever-changing nature of the world economy, due to the changing policy of some major members. Third, the major players of the Breton Wood institutions have been losing political wills to shoulder their historical responsibilities, in terms of financial contribution and managerial know-how. Fourth, the Breton Wood institutions have been losing their capalities in terms of early warning to any crisis, as well as the capability to organize effective crisis management or provide effective means for economic recovery and growth. Last but not least, the redundant institutions are in want of reforms and renovations, in order to be at par with the “new normal” of the world economy in the 21st century, but the developed members have been reluctant in this regard, driven by their vested interests.

根据我的研究发现，可能有几个原因导致了这种现象。第一，以世界银行、国际货币基金组织和世界贸易组织为代表的布雷顿森林体系的管理机构可信度不断下降，它们的全球管理能力与世界经济新趋势脱节。第二，由于一些主要成员国的政策立场不断变化，上述国际机构正在失去依据世界经济不断变化的性质采取行动的政治意愿和能力。第三，在财政贡献和管理经验方面，布雷顿森林体系的主要参与者正在丧失承担其历史责任的政治意愿。第四，上述体系正在丧失对危机的预警能力、组织有效危机管理的能力，或为经济复苏和增长提供有效手段的能力。最后，为了适应世界经济21世纪“新常态”，上述过时的机构亟待改革和创新，但是发达成员方为保护既得利益，不愿改革。

03

A: Before the international community is fully aware, the fourth industrial revolution is at our doorsteps. I wonder if you could share with us about the benefits we could receive from this in-coming revolution, since you’re an economist.

国际社会尚待意识到，第四次工业革命已经近在咫尺。请问，您作为经济学家，能否与我们分享一下在这场即将到来的革命中我们能在哪些方面获益。

B: Well, the full scale and impacts are yet to be felt by the countries, companies and peoples alike, but we can say for sure that the in-coming industrial revolution will bring in the following benefits to all the stakeholders. The first is that new industries, new theories and technologies would assist countries and companies in elevating their productivity and competitiveness. Second, it’s the new business models and activities. When 5G and AI technologies join hands with the Internet of things, the fourth industrial revolution will further emancipate people from the traditional harsh manual labor, and transform many people into knowledge workers. Whether in office or at the production lines, knowledge will become an integral part of total planning and management by corporate leaders. As we know, during the previous industrial revolution, the main asset and primary driver of the industrial development were the machines and capital. People were necessary but replaceable, and machines could be bought. However, during the fourth industrial revolution, companies must learn to motivate their workers to release their full potentials. They must renovate or develop technologies. And, they have to form the new ways to compete at the domestic and international market. In short, the fourth industrial revolution will shape our future through its impact on government affairs, business operations, social communication as well as our living conditions.

是的，第四次工业革命对每个国家、公司和普通民众的影响尚未充分显现，但可以肯定的是，即将到来的工业革命可能给所有利益相关者带来以下好处。一是新产业、新理论和新技术将帮助国家和企业提高生产力和竞争力。二是将孕育新的商业模式和商业活动。在5G技术和人工智能技术与物联网携手的情况下，第四次工业革命将进一步把人们从传统的繁重体力劳动中解放出来，将许多人转变为知识工作者。无论是在办公室还是在生产线上，知识将成为企业整体规划、管理的一个组成部分。我们知道，在以前的工业革命中，工业发展的主要资产和首要驱动力是机器和资本。人力要素是必要的，但也是可以替代的；机械设备可以外购。然而，在第四次工业革命中，企业必须学会激励员工释放他们的潜能，必须革新或研发它们的专有技术，必须形成新的方式在国内和国际市场上参与竞争。简而言之，第四次工业革命将对政府工作、商业活动、社会交往，以及我们的生活条件均产生巨大影响。

04

A: Researches show there have been periods of drastic climatic changes, and since the mid-20th century, the rate of human impact on the climate and eco-systems have been unprecedented. Therefore, the international community should draw the lessons and redouble its efforts to jointly address this deadly scenario before it's too late.

研究表明，气候变化有剧烈时期，自20世纪中叶以来，人类活动对气候与生态系统的影响速度是前所未有的。因此，在为时不晚的情况下，国际社会应吸取教训，加倍努力，携手应对这一致命局面。

B: I couldn't agree more. Let me also say that managing climate change requires global action. First, all the UN members have to sign *the Paris Accord*, which would form the foundation for the international community to bring the climate change under control. Second, they should voluntarily make commitments to *the Paris Accord* and implement national strategies and policies friendly to the natural environment. Third, large economies, especially the developed economies must shoulder their historical responsibilities to take lead in environment protection. They should jointly research and develop clean technologies, in order to promote green production, transportation and consumption. Fourth, they should provide technical and financial assistance to the least developed countries which would help the latter catch up with the global campaign to combat climate change. Fifth, the international community should fortify the existing oversight institutions, in order to carry out more effective functions such as early warning, crisis control and disaster rescues, etc. Last but not least, the international community should establish an effective oversight system, which has the full mandate to reward the law-abiding countries and penalize the countries in question.

我完全同意。我还想指出，应对气候变化需要全球集体行动。第一，所有联合国成员国必须签署《巴黎协定》，这将为国际社会控制气候变化奠定基础。第二，各国政府需要自愿对《巴黎协定》做出承诺，落实国家对自然环境友好的战略和政策。第三，主要经济体，特别是发达经济体必须承担起历史责任，带头保护环境。他们应携手研发清洁技术，促进绿色生产、绿色运输、绿色消费。第四，他们要向最不发达国家提供技术和资金援助，帮助后者跟上全球应对气候变化的步伐。第五，国际社会应加强现有的监督机构，以便更有效地履行预警、危机控制、灾害救援等职能。最后，国际社会应该建立有效的监督制度，具有充分的授权奖励守法国家和惩罚问题国家。

Part Three　Common Expressions

- We managed to have the joint venture completed in just 14 months from the blueprint to the production line in full operation. Meanwhile, we managed to outsource the assembling and service activities to the partner countries in Africa so that we could concentrate our critical recourse in the R&D and the marketing.
  从计划蓝图到生产线投产，我们只用了14个月就完成了合资项目建设。与此同时，我们设法将组装和服务活动外包给非洲大陆的合作伙伴，以便集中优势资源进行技术研发和市场营销。
- With the joint efforts by both sides, we managed to recover the investment in three years. Meanwhile, over the past two years, we have been providing economic steam for the local community in terms of labor, service and small projects.

在双方努力之下，我们在三年内成功收回投资。同时，在过去的两年里，我们一直在劳动力、服务和小型项目等方面为当地社区提供经济动力。

- You need to find out the possible risks in the destination countries before you should sit down and draft your plan to invest in any foreign market. I also want you to know any reckless decisions would cost you dearly.
  在你坐下来起草投资外国市场的规划之前，你需要研究该国可能存在的风险。我还想跟你说，任何鲁莽的决定都将使你付出沉重的代价。
- *The 2030 Agenda for the Sustainable Development* was adopted by all the UN Member States in 2015, which provides a shared blueprint for peace and prosperity for the people and the planet, now and into the future. At its heart are the 17 Sustainable Development Goals (SDGs), which are an urgent call for action by all member countries, developed and developing alike, in a global partnership. They all agree that ending poverty and other deprivations must go hand-in-hand with strategies which would help to improve health and education, reduce inequality and promote economic growth. Meanwhile, they should also tackle the worsening climate change, and preserve our oceans and forests.
  2015年，联合国所有会员国通过了《2030年可持续发展议程》，为人类和地球现在以及未来的和平与繁荣描绘了共同的蓝图。它的核心是17个可持续发展目标(SDGs)，紧急呼吁包括发达国家和发展中国家在内的所有国家构建全球伙伴关系，采取联合行动。他们认识到，在消除贫困和其他制约因素、改善健康和教育、减少不平等和促进经济增长等领域，所有的国家必须携手同行，制定和实施共同的战略。与此同时，所有的国家还必须应对气候变化问题，努力保护我们的海洋和森林。
- Roughly, the key elements of the SDGs cover the following aspects. First, it’s to end poverty in all its forms. Second, it’s to end hunger, achieve food security and improve nutrition and promote sustainable agriculture.

Third, it's to ensure healthy lives and promote wellbeing for people at all ages. Fourth, it's to ensure inclusive and equitable quality education and promote lifelong learning opportunities for all. Fifth, it's to achieve gender equality and empower all women and girls. Sixth, it's to ensure availability and sustainable management of water and sanitation for all. Seventh, it's to ensure access to affordable, reliable, sustainable and modern energy for all. Eighth, it's to promote inclusive and sustainable economic growth, full and productive employment and decent work for all. Ninth, it's to build resilient infrastructure, promote inclusive and sustainable industrialization and foster innovation. Tenth, it's to reduce inequality within and among countries.
可持续发展目标的主要内容大致包括以下几个方面。第一，消除各种形式的贫困。第二，消除饥饿，实现粮食安全和改善营养，促进可持续农业。第三，确保健康的生活和促进所有年龄段的人的幸福感。第四，确保包容公平的优质教育，为所有人提供终身学习机会。第五，实现性别平等，赋予所有妇女和女童权利。第六，确保所有人都能获得并可持续地管理水和卫生设施。第七，确保所有人都能获得负担得起的、可靠的、可持续的现代能源。第八，促进包容和可持续的经济增长，促进充分和生产性就业，促进人人享有体面的工作。第九，建设有韧性的基础设施，促进包容并可持续的工业化，促进创新。第十，减少国家内部和国家之间的不平等。

- In addition, the SDGs also calls for the international community to realize the following goals: Make cities and human settlements inclusive, safe, resilient and sustainable; ensure sustainable consumption and production patterns; take urgent actions to combat climate change and its impacts; conserve and sustainably use oceans; protect, restore and promote sustainable use of terrestrial ecosystems; effective manage forests; combat desertification; halt and reverse land degradation and biodiversity loss; realize peaceful and inclusive societies for sustainable development, promote justice for all; build effective, accountable and inclusive institutions at all levels; strengthen the means of implementation, and revitalize the global partnership for sustainable development.

此外，可持续发展目标还呼吁国际社会实现以下目标：使城市和人类居住区具有包容性、安全性、复原力及可持续性;确保可持续的消费和生产模式;采取紧急行动应对气候变化及其影响;保护并可持续地利用海洋;保护、恢复和促进陆地生态系统的可持续利用，可持续地管理森林，防治荒漠化，制止和扭转土地退化和生物多样性丧失；为可持续发展实现和平和包容的社会，为所有人提供诉诸司法的机会，在各级政府机构建立有效、可靠和包容的机构;加强执行手段，重振可持续发展的全球伙伴关系。

- *The Paris Accord* is an agreement within the United Nations Framework Convention on Climate Change, on climate change mitigation, adaptation, and finance, which was signed in 2016. The goal of the Agreement is to limit global warming to well below 2 degrees Celsius, preferably to 1.5 degrees Celsius. To achieve this long-term temperature goal, countries should aim at reaching global peaking of greenhouse gas emissions as soon as possible to achieve a climate neutral world by mid-century. *The Paris Accord* is a landmark in the multilateral climate change process, because, for the first time, this binding agreement brings all nations into a common cause, which is to undertake ambitious efforts to combat climate change and adapt to its effects.

  《巴黎协定》是2016年签署的《联合国气候变化框架公约》关于减缓、适应和融资的协议。该协议的目标是将全球变暖控制在远低于2摄氏度的范围内，最好是低于1.5摄氏度。为实现这一长期气温目标，各国应尽快实现温室气体排放的全球峰值，到本世纪中叶实现碳中和。《巴黎协定》是多边气候变化进程中的一个里程碑，首次携手所有国家共同积极努力应对气候变化，并适应其影响。

- Under the framework of the Belt and Road Initiative, partner countries, relevant companies and individuals enjoy many opportunities in terms of infrastructure, trade, investment, technologies and management. All these areas would help the partner countries effectively promote development, fight against poverty, improve people's living standards, and realize the SDGs.

在“一带一路”框架下，合作伙伴国家、相关企业和个人在基础设施、贸易、投资、技术和管理等方面都可望获得更多的机会。这些均有助于伙伴国家有效促进发展、消除贫困、提高人民生活水平、实现可持续发展目标。

- The international financial crisis in 2008 has taught the developed countries a lesson that traditional economic theories are no longer fully applicable to the modern economies. Market economy is no longer the panacea for all the countries in term of sustainable economic growth. Even the United States, the most mature market economy, would become the source of global economic and financial crisis when the virtual economy is growing wild.

  2008年的国际金融危机给了发达国家一个教训，那就是传统的经济理论已不再完全适用于现代经济。市场经济不再是各国经济可持续增长的灵丹妙药。即使是市场经济最成熟的美国，在虚拟经济快速发展的情况下，也会成为全球经济和金融危机的源头。

- As the joint construction of the Belt and Road moves forward in full steam, more and more companies and enterprises have been extending their production chains, value chains and supply chains across the parter countries. During the above process, they could benefit from the financial services from the relevant banks or institutions. Furthermore, when more and more companies and enterprises are evolved in the joint construction, partner countries could take stock from the easy transactions in goods and service, technology transfers, the IPR cooperation, and managerial know-how, which would automatically generate new steam for their economic growth and social progress.

随着共建“一带一路”的全面推进，越来越多的公司和企业在“一带一路”沿线国家延伸产业链、价值链和供应链。在上述过程中，上述公司可以受益于相关银行或机构的金融服务。进而言之，随着越来越多的公司和企业参与“一带一路”合作共建进程，伙伴国家可以在商品和服务、技术转让、知识产权合作、管理经验等方面获得外部动力，助力各自经济增长和社会进步。

第三十章

国际政治

*

有一种流行的说法，当今世界，任何事离政治都不会很远。在全球化影响下，今日之世界正日益成为一个“地球村”，事情变化之快超出了人们的想象。因此，我们必须学习尽可能多的新知识，以尽可能多的新观念和新技能武装自己，特别是在国际政治领域。经验表明，那些不关心政治的人，很难在各自领域取得成功。

Chapter Thirty

International Politics

*

There has been a popular saying that nothing is too far away from politics in the contemporary world. Under the impact of the globalization, today's world is increasingly becoming a "global village", where things have been changing faster than we can ever imagine. As a result, we've got to learn as many new things as possible, and equip ourselves with as many new concepts and skills as we can, especially in the field of international politics. Those who fail to stay in touch with politics would find it difficult to succeed in whatever they do.

Part One　Things to Know

01

The most outstanding issue in international politics in 2020 was COVID-19 which caused the reshuffle of the balance of power among major economies and the global economic downturn. It took pains for the international community to realize the coronavirus would coexist with human beings for a long time in the future. Therefore, countries around the world have to put aside their political differences, and join hands in the fight against the deadly virus under the guidance of the WHO.

2020年国际政治中最突出的问题是新冠肺炎，它使主要经济体力量格局发生调整，全球经济下行。国际社会痛苦地认识到，冠状病毒将在很长一段时间内与人类共存。因此，世界各国必须抛开政治分歧，在世界卫生组织指导下携手抗击这一致命病毒。

02

From the post-mortem perspective, COVID-19 fully exposed the soft spot of the international community in term of public crisis management. Almost all the major countries initially turned the deaf ears to the early warnings by China and the appeals by the WHO, refused to join hands in the fight against the pandemic, and refused to kick alive their national crisis prevention mechanisms. Therefore, the deadly public health crisis soon drove many

countries into economic, political and social crisis.
事后来看，新冠肺炎疫情充分暴露了国际社会在公共危机管理方面的软肋。几乎所有主要国家最初都对中国发出的预警和世界卫生组织的呼吁置若罔闻，拒绝携手抗疫，拒绝启动公共危机预防机制。结果，这场致命的公共健康危机很快使许多国家陷入经济、政治和社会危机。

03

From the very beginning, many countries regarded COVID-19 as an incident health crisis, which would be like a large spill of the flu. Even experts in some developed countries said the virus would die out in a natural cause when the summer season came. Therefore, many governments simply chose to close their borders. Many governments did too little and too late, when they found their countries were also becoming the epiccenters. The pandemic soon became global. Worse still, the United States walked out of the WTO at the critical moment, and left the international campaign versus the deadly virus in disunity.
一开始，许多国家以为新冠肺炎疫情是一场类似流感暴发的健康危机。甚至一些发达国家的专家表示，当夏季到来时，这种病毒会自然死亡。因此，许多政府干脆选择关闭边境。当许多政府发现自己的国家也成为疫情暴发点时，才发现自己做得太少，也太晚了。这场疫情很快在全球范围流行。更糟糕的是，美国在关键时期退出了世界卫生组织，致使国际抗疫运动陷入分裂状态。

04

As many countries failed to bring the pandemic under control, vaccines became the last resort to save the relevant nations from the total break-downs of both economic and public health systems. According to the statistics by the WHO, more than 100 companies raced against the time to research and develop vaccines, which was the only hopeful remedial measures to save the

lives by the millions.
由于许多国家未能有效控制住疫情，疫苗成为拯救这些国家免于经济和卫生系统全面崩溃的最后手段。根据世界卫生组织的统计数字，100多家公司争分夺秒地研发疫苗，这是拯救数百万人生命的唯一可行的补救措施。

05

To the surprise of the international community, the coronavirus has been mutating fast, in order to adapt to the geographical and weather conditions, and are increasingly becoming drug resistant. Therefore, countries around the world are faced with a collective mandate to jointly research, and develop effective medicines and the new medicines, in order to effectively contain the pandemic.
出乎国际社会预料的是，这种致命病毒一直在变异，以适应不同地理和天气条件，耐药性不断增强。世界各国面临共同的使命，携手研发有效药物和新的药物，以便有效控制疫情。

06

According to the statistics from the World Bank and the IMF, due to the double impacts of COVID-19 and the global economic recession, the world economy in 2021 would continue to down slide before turning to the positive growth. This would drive millions of people back to poverty, and further lead to the breakdown of many national economies around the world.
根据世界银行和国际货币基金组织的统计，受新冠肺炎疫情和全球经济周期的双重影响，2021年世界经济将继续下滑，然后转为正增长。这将使数以百万计的人返贫，并导致许多国家经济崩溃。

07

At the end of 2020, the World Bank announced the prediction that among

all the major economies around the world, China would be the only country that realized positive growth, and served as the only engine for the world economy, not only in terms of trade, but also in the form of FDI.
据世界银行于2020年年底前发布的世界经济预测报告，在世界所有的主要经济体中，中国是唯一一个实现正增长的经济体，在国际贸易和直接投资领域均成为世界经济的唯一引擎。

08
It is not coincidental that contemporary Western political systems are now heavily fraud by the party politics, business tycoons, social elites, the divide between the rich and poor, the breakdown of national social cohesion, as well as the dis-function of the international relations.
政党政治、商业巨头、社会精英、贫富分化、国家社会凝聚力的瓦解以及国际关系的失调，使得当代西方政治体系严重舞弊，所有这些并非巧合。

09
The Cold War is long gone, but peace and development are still the scarce commodity, and wars and famines are still the two key issues confronting the international community. Worse still, the Cold War mentality is still lingering in the minds of some governments and national leaders, when they comes to foreign policy towards other countries.
冷战早已结束，但和平与发展仍未充分实现，战争与饥荒仍然是国际社会面临的两个关键问题。更糟糕的是，一些政府和国家领导人仍依据冷战思维制定对外政策。

10
Some sociologists believe that developed countries have both the moral and historical obligations to help the less developed countries to catch up with

industrialization and modernization. History will show the backwardness and detrimental living conditions among countries in the South will soon have the boomerang effect on those in the North.
有社会学家认为，发达国家在道义和历史上都有义务帮助欠发达国家赶上工业化和现代化的步伐。历史将告诉我们，南方国家的落后和不利的生活条件将很快对北方的发达国家产生回旋镖效应。

11

We all agree that one impact of poverty is the direct assault on human dignity or human rights. Therefore, the international community will never win the war against terrorism, unless countries around the world join hands to address the relevant global issues.
我们必须承认，贫困造成的政治影响是对人的尊严或人权的直接攻击。因此只有世界各国携手应对相关全球性问题，国际社会才能赢得反恐战争的胜利。

12

It's an open secret that, since the end of the Cold War, the war-torn or poverty-stricken countries have become the warm beds to breed terrorists. "9 · 11" has become a case in point. As one saying goes, poverty drives people to rebels.
众所周知，自冷战结束以来，饱受战争蹂躏或贫穷打击的国家正成为滋生恐怖分子的温床。"9·11"事件就是一个很好的例证。俗话说，穷者造反。

13

Experts have pointed out that the current North-South relations are the legacy of colonialism, industrialization and globalization, which have allowed the developed countries to "gracefully" or forcibly extract economic wealth from the developing countries via industrial chains, value chains and supply chains.

专家指出，当前的南北关系是殖民主义、工业化、全球化的后遗症，这种态势使得发达国家可以通过产业链、价值链、供应链巧取豪夺发展中国家的经济财富。

14

It's a sad fact that many developing countries are yet to realize the SDGs goals, which were set by the United Nations, and many countries have literally become the "failed states".

令人遗憾的是，许多发展中国家还没有实现联合国设定的可持续发展目标，许多国家事实上已成为“失败国家”。

15

The latest World Bank statistics show more than 100 countries are still under developed, and more than 3 billion people are still living under the poverty line by the UN standards. And, there are more than 2 billion illiterate adults across the world, and about half a billion school-age children simply can't afford to go to school.

世界银行最新统计显示，世界上还有100多个不发达国家，按照联合国标准，还有30多亿人生活在贫困线以下。此外，全世界有超过20亿的成年人依旧是文盲，大约5亿学龄儿童根本上不起学。

16

Economists say the international assistance can be a catalyst for the economic development and social progress in the recipient countries. Nevertheless, the important thing for the donor countries to do is to help the latter to develop their economies in their own capacity, and put them into the driving seats of economic development.

有经济学家说，国际援助可以成为受援国经济发展和社会进步的催化剂。然而，最重要的是，捐助国需要帮助受援国建立自主发展其经济的能力，并使得后者成为国家经济发展的主导。

17

There's no doubt that many donor countries have been attaching political conditions when they provide the financial or development assistance. For example, they would promote the Western political systems and values, which have been producing side effects on the traditional political, cultural and social foundations.

毫无疑问，许多援助国在提供资金援助或项目援助时都附加了政治条件。例如，许多捐助者趁机推销西方政治制度和价值观，严重破坏了传统政治、文化和社会基础。

18

Environment protection is the long-standing challenge to the North-South relations, which is an important precondition for the sustainable development of the world economy. It's a hard fact that developed countries are stepping back from their historical responsibility. They are reluctant to cut down on harmful emissions, in line with their commitment under *the Paris Accord*, and refusing to come forward with technical and financial assistance to the least developed countries in the campaign against the global warming.

环境保护是南北关系面临的长期挑战，是世界经济可持续发展的重要前提。发达国家正在逃避自己的历史责任，这是一个不争的事实。他们拒绝按照在《巴黎协定》中做出的承诺减少排放有害气体，拒绝在共同对抗全球变暖的行动中向最不发达国家提供技术和资金援助。

19

Since the turn of the 21st century, globalization is faced with many undercurrents as the United States has been pulling out from more and more multilateral institutions, and bending backward in protecting its vested

unilateral interests, based on its super military might, US dollar, science, technology and market.
进入21世纪以来，美国以其强大的军事、美元、科学技术和市场优势为基础，退出越来越多的多边机构，千方百计地保护既得利益，全球化进程面临诸多逆流。

20

Since the 2008 international financial crisis, the international relations have been undergoing drastic changes. To start with, economic globalization is facing headwinds. Global governance is slow in progress. The balance of power among major countries has been shifting dramatically. The center of the world economy is shifting from trans-Atlantic area to the Asia-Pacific area. The arm-twisting between the major powers has been intensifying. Climate and environmental problems are surging. Non-traditional security issues keep cropping up, etc. All these scenarios have jointly brought about the profound changes in the international political landscape unseen in a century.
2008年国际金融危机以来，国际关系发生了重大变化。首先，经济全球化遭遇逆风震荡；全球治理举步维艰；大国力量平衡发生巨变；世界经济中心正从大西洋两岸向亚太地区转移；主要大国的博弈日益加剧；气候与环境问题积重难返；非传统安全问题不断涌现。所有这些态势正引发国际政治局势百年未有之巨大变化。

Part Two　Situational Dialogues

01

A: Talking about the globalization, the developed countries have been losing steam in leading the growth and expansion of the world economy, since the 2008 international financial crisis. I wonder if you could share with us the reasons behind, Mr. Howard.

说到全球化，2008年国际金融危机以来，发达国家在引领世界经济增长和扩张方面逐渐失去动力。请问您能和我们分享其背景原因吗，霍华德先生。

B: Well, from my humble observation, these are the major reasons behind the scenarios. From the perspective of international trade, the developed countries used to be the dominating force for the economic growth. They used to be the major markets, and enjoyed the major consumption capacity due to the ever-growing middle class. Nevertheless, since the 2008 international financial crisis, their economies have been sluggish, and their capacity absorb the goods and service from the developing countries has been dwindling. As many developed economies have been under more and more pressure of sovereign debts, they have been cutting down budgetary and technical assistance to the developing countries. As the above economies have been implementing policies to revitalize their real economies, they have been competing with the developing countries for the FDI. Especially since the eruption of COVID-19, the developed economies have been struggling with their economic recovery and growth. I hope these reasons might be of some help to you.

好吧，依据我之拙见，以下这些都是主要原因。从国际贸易的角度来看，发达国家曾经是推动经济增长的主导力量。它们曾是主要国际市场。由于中产阶级的不断壮大，它们曾经是国际消费的主体。然而，自2008年国际金融危机以来，这些国家经济增长乏力，吸收发展中国家商品和服务的能力不断下降。许多发达经济体面临的主权债务压力越来越大，纷纷削减对发展中国家的预算和技术援助项目。上述经济体一直在执行振兴实体经济的政策，进而与发展中国家竞争外国直接投资。特别是新冠肺炎疫情暴发以来，发达经济体经济复苏和增长困难重重。我希望这些理由能对你有所帮助。

A: I see. Then, my next question is: How should the international community address this ever wider divide between the North and South, during the post era of the financial crisis?

我明白了。那么，我的下一个问题是：后金融危机时期，国际社会如何解决日益扩大的南北发展鸿沟问题呢？

B: Well, according to my understanding, the fundamental way to promote the North-South relationship is to establish a new international economic order. This is because the developed countries exploited and plundered developing countries mainly by the old international economic order. Countries in North and South should outreach to one another, reform the Breton Wood institutions, and establish the mechanisms to effectively oversight the economic activities by the transnational corporations. At the country level, developed countries have to open their markets, which would allow developing countries to really promote foreign trade. They should also provide adequate development assistance and technical support to the recipient countries to catch up with the industrialization and realize the 2030 Development Goals set forth by the United Nations.

根据我的理解，解决南北关系的根本途径是建立国际经济新秩序。这是因为发达国家主要通过旧的国际经济秩序剥削和掠夺发展中国家。北方和南方国家应相互协作，改革布雷顿森林机构，并建立有效的监督机制，监控跨国公司的经济活动。在国家层面，发达国家必须开放市场，使得发展中国家促进对外贸易。发达国家应该提供足够的发展援助和技术支持，助力受援国实现工业化进程，实现联合国2030年发展目标。

02

A: The fourth industrialization is around the corner, which is to bring huge impacts not only on the growth of the world economy, but also on the ways we live, work, travel and associate with one another. For one thing, it's going to further emancipate the productivity of the traditional industries via technological renovation. For the other, the industrial revolution is to usher in new industries, new technologies and new products, which would become the new engines for the economic growth of all the partner countries.

第四次工业化即将来临，它不仅将对世界经济增长产生巨大影响，而且将对我们的生活、工作、旅游、交往方式产生巨大影响。一方面，它将通过技术革新进一步解放传统产业的生产力。另一方面，工业革命将带来新的产业、新的技术和新的产品，这些产业将成为所有伙伴国家经济发展的新动力。

B: I couldn't agree more, but it's not a free ride for any country. From the macroeconomic perspective, countries in the North could take stock from their sound industrial foundations and strong capacity of technology domination, in order to realize the advantages of early growth opportunities. Meanwhile, countries in the South would not only have to catch up with the trend of the third industrial revolution, but also face the challenges resultant from the new revolution.

我完全同意，不过对任何国家来说都没有免费的午餐。从宏观经济角度看，发达国家可以充分利用其健全的工业基础和强大的技术主导地位实现经济增长先发优势。与此同时，南方国家既要努力追赶第三次工业革命的发展趋势，也要面对新工业革命带来的挑战。

A: You're right. From the micro economic perspective, companies from the North could fully utilize their existing and new technologies, in order to solidify their capacities to expand their market networks and their production chains. However, companies in the South would have to spend their meager capital to import new technologies and to compete with transnational corporations in new industries.

你说得对。从微观经济角度看，北方发达国家的公司可以充分利用它们现有的和新的技术巩固和扩大销售网络和生产链的能力。然而，南方发展中国家的公司将不得不花费有限的资金来引进新技术，并与跨国公司在新产业领域开展竞争。

B: You don't have to be that pessimistic, I'm afraid. As always, industrial revolution will bring in new technologies, which would help companies and enterprises in the developing countries to renovate their existing manufacturing and service sectors. And, the new revolution will also bring in new products and service, which will definitely help improve people's living standards.

恐怕你没必要那么悲观。如同以往发生的工业革命一样，新的工业革命将带来新技术，帮助发展中国家的公司和企业改造其现有制造业和服务业。与此同时，新的革命也会带来新的产品和服务，这肯定有助于提高人们的生活水平。

A: I know, but everything will come with a price, right?

我知道，但任何事情都是要付出代价的，对吧？

03

A: Mr. Lin Yang, President Xi Jinping recently put forward the statement that the world is undergoing profound changes unseen in a century. What's your take?

林洋先生，习近平主席最近提出了关于“世界百年未有之大变局”的论述。请问，对此您怎么看？

B: Let me see. Since 2018, President Xi Jinping has pointed out on many occasions that the world has been undergoing profound changes unseen in a century. These changes refer to the major trends of development, major changes, major adjustments, major turning points and the progress of the world, which have been profoundly affecting the direction and course of human history in a long time to come.

请让我想想。2018年以来，习近平主席在不同场合多次指出，当今世界正处于百年未有之大变局。所谓世界百年未有之大变局，是指在一个相对较长的历史时期内将深刻影响人类历史发展方向和进程的世界大发展、大变化、大调整、大转折、大进步。

A: Please allow me to prick your brain a bit further. Would you please explain a bit further the meaning of these great changes of the 21st century?

请允许我再考考您的智慧。您能给我们详细说说世纪大变局的具体内涵吗？

B: As far as I know, what President Xi Jinping has said about the major change unseen in a century mainly covers the following aspects. The first is the changing gravity center of the world economy. Right after World War II, the United States became the largest global creditor and exporter of capital. Simultaneously, the world economic center was shifting from the Eastern side of the Atlantic Ocean to the Western side. However, since the 21st century, the global economic center is shifting from the Atlantic to the Asia-Pacific, with the speed faster than ever before. The second is the changing world of political landscape. Since the beginning of the 21st century, non-Westernization and multi-polarization have been surging ahead hand in hand, and the arm-twisting and strategic competition among major powers order is facing challenges. The third is the changes in the process of globalization. To be specific, some major countries have lost the impetus to promote globalization, which is also unprecedented in history. Meanwhile, emerging economies have become new driving force, and the developed countries represented by Japan, Germany and France are still in favor of multilateralism and globalization, in line with their established interests. The fourth is the changes of domination of science and technology. Countries on both sides of the Atlantic used to play the leading role during the technological and industrial revolutions. However, in the new round, although the United States still retains the leading position, emerging countries such as China are also playing a prominent role. Meanwhile, artificial intelligence and biological genetic engineering have brought new challenges, which have made it difficult for the international community to build an effective regulatory system, etc. Last but not least, it’s the structural change in the global governance. On one hand, the objects of governance are becoming more and more complicated, which calls for the enhanced cooperation among all countries, especially the major countries. On the other hand, Western powers, which still clinch to the traditional mindset, are unwilling to assume historical responsibilities. Instead, they are stepping up competitions with developing countries, which has worsened the political environment for global governance.

据我所知，习近平主席所说的百年未有之大变局，主要包括以下几个方面。一是世界经济重心的巨变。第二次世界大战后，美国成为全球最大的资本债权国和输出国。与此同时，世界经济中心正从大西洋东岸向西岸转移。然而，全球经济中心正以前所未有的速度从大西洋向亚太地区转移。二是世界政治格局的巨变。进入21世纪以来，非西方化和多极化齐头并进，大国之间的高压态势和战略竞争加剧。国际政治秩序正面临挑战。三是全球化进程的巨变。具体来说，一些大国失去了推动全球化的动力，这在历史上也是前所未有的。与此同时，新兴经济体已成为发展的新动力，以日、德、法为代表的发达国家仍然从既得利益出发，支持多边主义和全球化。四是科学技术领域主导地位的巨变。在以往的技术和工业革命中，大西洋两岸的国家都发挥了主导作用。然而，在新一轮的谈判中，虽然美国仍然保持主导作用，但中国、印度等新兴国家也开始发挥重要作用。同时，人工智能和生物基因工程给国际社会带来了新的挑战，使国际社会难以建立有效的监管体系。最后是全球治理结构的巨变。一方面，治理的对象越来越复杂，需要世界各国，特别是主要国家加强合作。另一方面，西方大国仍固守传统治理规则，不愿承担历史责任。同时，它们加剧了与发展中国家的竞争，从而恶化了全球治理的政治环境。

04

A: When we recall the major international events for 2020, the biggest one must be COVID-19, which has so far claimed the victims of more than one hundred million around the world, and resulted in the death toll of more than three million. What would you say about this, my friend?

当我们回顾2020年的重大国际事件时，最大的肯定是新冠肺炎疫情。迄今，新冠肺炎已造成全球超过1亿人感染，导致300多万人死亡。我的朋友，关于这个现象你怎么看？

B: I couldn't agree more. The pandemic is set to become worse before the international community could come up with effective means to bring it under control. It's an irony that the countries in the North are suffering equally from the pandemic, despite the fact that they have built advanced systems and institutions in terms of public health, crisis prevention and management.

我完全赞同。在国际社会拿出有效的控制手段之前，新冠肺炎疫情蔓延将变得更糟。具有讽刺意味的是，尽管北方发达国家在公共卫生、危机预防和管理方面建立有先进的系统，拥有完善的医疗卫生服务机制，但它们也同样遭受疫情的冲击。

A: Worse yet, some developed countries have given up the national campaigns to fight against the pandemic, and wait for the vaccines to salvage the disaster. Consequently, more and more people have to suffer from infections and more people will die, before the vaccines would come into the market in large quantity.

更糟糕的是，一些发达国家放弃了抗击疫情的全国性运动，等待疫苗来挽救这场灾难。结果在疫苗大量投放市场之前，越来越多的人受到感染，越来越多的人死亡。

B: I want to add that COVID-19 has revealed the true nature of the Western democratic system. Taking the United States for example, when the pandemic was rampaging across the county, President Trump was still bending backward in restoring production and service.

我想补充的是，新冠肺炎暴露了西方民主制度的真实面目。以美国为例，当疫情在全国肆虐时，特朗普总统仍在努力恢复生产和服务。

Part Three　Common Expressions

- All countries, big or small, should be equal.
  国家不分大小，应该一律平等。
- Countries around the world have their rights to safeguard national independence and territorial integrity.

世界各国有权维护国家独立和领土完整。

- We are pleased to see that RCEP has come into reality when representatives from the 15 member states signed the agreement. This agreement will transform the 15 nations into the largest free trade area in the world, and facilitate conditions for the regional economy to realize sustainable growth.

  我们高兴地看到，《区域全面经济伙伴关系协定》已由15个成员国代表签署，成为现实。该协定将由15个国家组成世界上最大的自由贸易区，并促进区域经济可持续增长。

- Facts speak louder. Since World War II, there has been an international consensus that economic development, social progress and democracy are closely inter-related. No country can achieve real social progress without sustainable economic growth, governance of the national leaders as well as the transparency of the governments, in line with the laws and regulations.

  事实胜于雄辩。第二次世界大战以来，经济发展、社会进步和民主政治密切相关，这已成为国际共识。没有可持续的经济增长，没有国家领导人的治国理念，没有政府的透明，没有法律法规，任何国家都不可能真正实现社会进步。

- At the 75th anniversary of the United Nations, this largest international political institution is still faced with three major challenges. The first is how to uphold the equality of sovereign states, and oppose hegemonism. The second is how to readjust the direction of "international peace keeping", and oppose big countries from taking advantage of it. The third is how to promote international cooperation, in order to effectively resolve the global political, economic and social problems. The key is how to work together, in terms of promoting international peace, development and cooperation against the backdrop of the rapidly changing international situation.

  在联合国成立75周年之际，这个最大的国际政治机构正面临三大挑战。其一是如何坚持主权国家平等、携手反对霸权主义。其二是如何调整“维和”方向，反对大国从中渔利。其三是如何推动国际合作，解决全球性政治、经济及社会问题。关键是在快速变化的国际形势下，如何携手促进国际和平、发展与合作。

- The Bretton Woods institutions consist of the World Bank and the International Monetary Fund (IMF). They were set up at a meeting among 43 countries in Bretton Woods, New Hampshire, USA in July 1944. Their aims were to help rebuild the shattered postwar economy, and promote international economic recovery and growth.

  布雷顿森林机构由世界银行和国际货币基金组织构成。这个机构于1944年7月在美国新罕布什尔州布雷顿森林召开的43个国家会议上成立，旨在帮助重建战后破碎的经济，促进国际经济复苏和增长。

- In general, the Bretton Woods system established the rules for commercial and financial relations among member states under the 1944 *Bretton Woods Agreement*. The system was the first example of a fully negotiated monetary order, which was intended to govern monetary relations among independent states. The chief feature of the system was the obligation for each member country to adopt the monetary policy that maintained the fluctuation of its external exchange rates within 1 percent by tying its currency to gold, and the ability of the International Monetary Fund to bridge the temporary imbalances of payments. Also, there was the need to promote cooperation among member states to prevent competitive devaluation of the currencies.

  总的来说，布雷顿森林体系依据1944年《布雷顿森林协定》确立了成员国之间的商业和金融关系规制。这一体系是基于完全协商基础之上的首个国际货币秩序，旨在管理独立国家之间的货币关系。该体系的主要特点是，每个国家都有义务采取货币政策，则将本国货币与黄金挂钩，将本国货币汇率的波动控制在1%以内。同时，国际货币基金组织则为成员国弥补暂时的国际收支不平衡。此外，该体系还旨在促进会员国之间的合作，防止货币竞争性贬值。

- Since the 21st century, the Bretton Woods institutions are now in trouble, because of the profound disagreements among the large powers over the ownership structure, the direction of reform, and the way forward. To be specific, the World Bank and the IMF are now paralyzed by their incapacity to adapt to the rapidly changing world, and are slow in progress in terms of the structural reform.

  自21世纪以来，布雷顿森林体系已陷入困境，因为大国之间在所有权结构、改革方向和前进道路上存在分歧。具体而言，世界银行和国际货币基金组织无法适应快速变化的世界，结构改革进展缓慢。

- The World Trade Organization is an intergovernmental organization that regulates and facilitates international trade between or among member nations. It officially commenced operations on 1 January in 1995, pursuant to the 1994 *Marrakesh Agreement*, replacing *the General Agreement on Tariffs and Trade*, which was established in 1948. The WTO is the world's largest international economic organization, with 164 members representing 96% of global trade and global GDP.

  世界贸易组织是一个政府间组织，规范和促进成员方之间的国际贸易。根据1994年《马拉喀什协定》，世贸组织于1995年1月1日正式开始运作，取代1948年建立的《关税和贸易总协定》。世贸组织是世界上最大的国际经济组织，有164个成员，成员方占全球贸易和全球GDP的96%。

- There's no doubt that the WTO has been providing greater disciplines over the $5 trillion plus in the annual global trade in goods and services. However, the changing international economic environment has created series of significant challenges for the organization. The most obvious challenge is that the Doha Round, which is yet to reach the agreement to achieve the expected goals to further liberalize trade and reform the WTO.

长期以来，世贸组织为每年超过50000亿美元的全球商品和服务贸易提供了更严格的交易规制。然而，不断变化的国际经济环境给该组织带来了一系列重大挑战。最明显的挑战是多哈发展回合，在进一步实现贸易自由化和世贸组织改革等问题上，尚待达成一致。